CHALLENGING HISTORY

EUROPE
1500–1600

J.A.P. JONES

Nelson

Thomas Nelson and Sons Ltd
Nelson House
Mayfield Road
Walton-on-Thames
Surrey KT12 5PL
United Kingdom

© J.A.P. Jones 1997

First published by Thomas Nelson and Sons Ltd 1997

I⊕P® Thomas Nelson is an International Thomson Publishing Company
I⊕P® is used under licence

ISBN 0-17-435064-3
NPN 9 8 7 6 5 4 3 2

Typeset in 10/12pt ITC Garamond by Multiplex Techniques Ltd
Printed in China

Publication team:
Acquisitions: Roda Morrison, Steve Berry
Administration: Jenny Goode
Editorial Management: Simon Tanner-Tremaine
Freelance Editorial: Nick Brock
Marketing: Jane Lewis
Production: Liam Reardon
Picture Research: Image Select International Ltd
Design: Multiplex Techniques Ltd

Contents

Acknowledgements

Many generations of advanced level students have contributed much to the writing of this book. Their perceptive insights, challenging questions and lively opinions have made the teaching of advanced level History such a pleasure over the years. From Jeremy Cooper and Philip Hull in the class of '69 to Jennifer Lowis and Clare Gibbs in the class of '95, many individual students have helped to write this book.

In addition, many colleagues, not least in the History department of Poynton County High School, have generously shared their ideas on subject matter and methodology. Vince Crinnion contributed more than he could know: his untimely death deprived us all of a wonderfully inventive History teacher who was always able to capture the imagination and stimulate the mind of his students. Michael Jones, Cheshire's excellent English Adviser, has always been a great support to the whole series: his incisive comments, together with his generosity of spirit, have made him a good friend who has directly improved our work in the classroom.

Linda Stevenson has always been a perfect secretary.

In the summer of 1994, a School Master's Fellowship at Downing College, Cambridge allowed me to research and write a large section of this book. I wish to express my thanks to the staff at the college for their help during this period.

To all these people I offer my heartfelt thanks. Without their ideas and support this book could not have been written.

J.A.P. Jones
Cheshire 1997

To Huw

Credits

The author and publishers wish to thank the following for kind permission to reproduce photographs:

AKG: pages 7 top & bottom, 9, 12, 22, 25 top & bottom, 26 top & bottom, 27, 32 middle, 37, 55 top, 74, 80 top & bottom, 81 bottom, 133, 181, 189, 229, 240, 243, 245 top & bottom, 271; Ann Ronan Collection: pages 3, 32 top, 34, 44, 49, 65, 98, 99, 105, 130, 223, 242, 267, 316, 318 top & bottom, 329, 335 top & bottom; Art Resource: pages 2, 15, 16, 29 right, 148, 201, 227; Bibliothéque Publique et Universitaire, Geneva: page 109; Bridgeman Art Library: pages 30 top & bottom, 32 bottom, 35, 55 bottom, 56, 81 top, 124, 126, 131, 164, 180, 211, 251, 286, 287, 293, 299; Corbis/National Gallery, London: page 23; Edimedia: page 244; ET Archive: cover insert; Fotomas Index: pages 8, 28, 36, 51, 58 left & right, 68 top & bottom, 69 left & right, 87, 97, 135, 144 left & right, 196, 202, 206 top & bottom, 209, 222, 235, 249, 256 top, 306, 315, 321; Hulton Getty Collection: pages 153, 154; Image Select/Exley: page 317; Index: pages 132, 140, 178, 307; Mansell Collection: cover; Mary Evans Picture Library: pages 43, 71, 94, 208, 221, 225, 262, 263, 270; MAS: page 325; Pascal Lebrun/Gamma: page 169; Reunion des Musees: page 163; Roger-Viollet: pages 165, 256 bottom, 274, 275, 277; Spectrum: page 183; Trip/Bambridge: page 29 left

The author and publishers wish to thank the following for kind permission to reproduce copyright material:

Addison Wesley Longman Ltd for extracts from *Europe in the Sixteenth Century* by Koenigsberger, Mosse and Bowler (1989), *The Emperor Charles V* by M. Rady (1988), *Spain* 1469–1714 by H. Kamen (1983), *The Dutch Revolt* 1559–1648 by Limm and Richardson (1989); Professor James Atkinson for extracts from his book *Martin Luther and the Birth of Protestantism* (1968); Professor Philip Benedict for extracts from his book *Rouen during the Wars of Religion* (1981); Blandford Press, an imprint of Cassell plc, for extracts from *Renaissance, Reformation and the Outer World* by M.L. Bush (1965); Burns and Oates Ltd for extracts from *Catholicism Between Luther and Voltaire* by J. Delumeau (1977); E.J. Brill for extracts from *The Conquest of Poverty* by H. Heller (1986); Editions Gallimard, Paris for extracts from *L'Assassinat d'Henry IV* by Roland Mousnier (1964), translated by Joan Spencer and published in Great Britain by Faber & Faber; Edward Arnold/Hodder & Stoughton Educational for extracts from *Years of Renewal* by J. Lotherington (1988), *Imperial Spain* by J.H. Elliott (1963), *From Revolt to Independence* by M. Rady (1989), *The Catholic and the Counter Reformations* by K. Randell (1990); Professor Elizabeth Eisenstein for extracts from her book *The Printing Press as an Agent of Change* (1979); Greene & Heaton Ltd for extracts from *Philip II* by Geoffrey Parker, published by Cardinal (1979); The Hambledon Press for extracts from *Princes, Politics and Liberty* by N.M. Sutherland (1984), *Popular Culture and Popular Movements in Reformation Germany* by R.W. Scribner (1987); HarperCollins Publishers for extracts from *Six Essays on the Renaissance* by Wallace Ferguson (1953), *The Protestant Reformation* by L.W. Spitz (1969), *Reformation Europe* by G.R. Elton (1965), *War and Society in Renaissance Europe* by J.R. Hale (1985), *The Civilization of Europe in the Renaissance* by J.R. Hale (1994), *Renaissance Europe* by J.R.Hale (1971); Mr Richard Hay for an extract from *The Italian Renaissance* by Denys Hay (1961); Professor R.J. Knecht for extracts from his book Francis I (1982); Macmillan Press Ltd for extracts from *Thomas Muntzer* by T. Scott (1989); Oxford University Press for extracts from *Christianity in the West* by J. Bossy (1985), *The European Reformation* by E.W. Cameron (1991), *The Spanish Kingdoms,* vol.II, by J.N. Hillgarth (1978), *Early Habsburg Spain* by A.W. Lovett (1986), *International Calvinism* by Menna Prestwich (1985), *For the Sake of Simple Folk* by R.W. Scribner (1994); Routledge Ltd for extracts from *Henry IV* by D. Buissaret (1984), *Luther* by M. Mullett (1988), *Calvin* by M. Mullett (1988); Simon & Schuster for extracts from *The Catholic Reformation* by P. Janelle (1971); Thames and Hudson Ltd for extracts from *Charles V* by M. Alvarez (1975); Weidenfeld and Nicolson for extracts from *The Inquisition and Society in Spain* by H. Kamen (1985), Ferdinand and Isabella by F. Fernandez-Armesto (1975); Yale University Press for extracts from *The Huguenot Struggle for Recognition* by N.M. Sutherland (1980)

Every effort has been made to trace all the copyright holders, but if any have been inadvertently overlooked the publishers will be pleased to make the necessary arrangements at the first opportunity.

Editor's Preface

This book offers you the challenge of history. It encourages you to engage with the past in a creative and personal way; it also presents you with the many challenges which the past provides for present-day students. It demands a rigorous and scholarly approach. In return, we expect that you will increase your understanding, improve your skills, and develop a personal involvement in historical study.

The challenge is presented to you through the different components of each chapter:

Preview   Each chapter begins with a presentation which is designed to arouse your interest, and alert you to one or more of the major themes of the chapter.

Text   The text demands an active response from you. The book has been carefully written, designed and fully illustrated to develop your learning and understanding. Photographs, artwork, cartoons, statistical tables, maps, graphs are among the many visual images that reinforce the quality of the text.

Examining evidence   These sections present a wide variety of Historical sources, both primary and secondary. They encourage you to analyse the opinions of others, to assess the reliability of evidence, and to formulate and test your own personal views.

Focus   Focus sections zoom in on, and highlight, particular events, people and issues of the period. They are designed to enable you to see these more clearly and to find your way through the complexity of historical problems.

Talking Points   They are scattered widely throughout the book. By talking and listening, we can all learn about the major issues which translate the past into the present. In doing so, we question our own perceptions, test out our ideas and widen our range of interests.

Questions   Throughout the chapters, questions encourage you to consider what you see and read. They invite your personal response and encourage you to share it verbally with your fellow students, and in writing with your teachers.

Review   Each chapter contains an exercise, often a formal essay or question, which enables you to revise the learning and understanding of the whole chapter. You will find supporting ideas and structures to help you to formulate your answer.

This book offers you many experiences of History. It opens up to you the thoughts and feelings of contemporaries; it classifies the distinctive nature of your period; it places people, events and issues in the context of the flow of History. Just as important, it invites and encourages you to formulate your own personal insights and opinions in a living and developing debate. The challenge of History is essential to the vitality and well-being of the modern world.

J.A.P. Jones
General Editor

Introduction

One of the major challenges of the study of History is to think yourself into the past. In this case think yourself into 16th-century Europe. How did people feel and what did they think about in the local communities, towns and cities of 16th-century Europe? Is it possible for you to become familiar with their values and beliefs as well as their custom, their culture and their actions?

The following quotations from primary and secondary sources may help you, together with the pictures, to get a preliminary impression of life in the 16th century.

Indulgences were all important in a period when people were obsessed with the fear of death.

Koenigsberger, Mosse and Bowler, *Europe in the 16th Century*, 1989.

Not one in a million witches would be punished if the trial procedure were governed by ordinary laws. So, in the absence of a 'grave indicium' such as a pot full of human limbs, sacred objects, toads, etc. or a written pact with the devil (which must have been a rare collector's piece) circumstantial evidence was sufficient to mobilise the process. And the circumstantial evidence need not be very cogent: it was sufficient to discover a wart by which the familiar spirit was suckled; an insensitive spot which did not bleed when pricked; a capacity to float when thrown into water; or an incapacity to shed tears. Recourse could even be had to 'lighter indicia' such as a tendency to look down when accused, signs of fear, or the mere aspect of a witch, old, ugly or smelly. Any of these indicia might establish a prima facie case and justify the use of torture to produce the confession, which was proof, or the refusal to confess, which was even more cogent proof and justified even more ferocious torture and a nastier death.

H.R. Trevor-Roper, *The European Witch Craze of the 16th Century*, 1965.

'My belly is shoved up under my chin...
My beard faces skywards and the back of my neck is wedged into my spine...
My face is richly carpeted with the thick layer of paint from my brush...
I don't want to be here and I am no painter.'

Michelangelo in 1510 describes how he painted the ceiling of the Sistine Chapel in Rome.

What Happened in 16th-Century Europe?

The 16th century was a period of major change in Europe

- Ways of thinking were freed up after the sterile formulas of the Middle Ages. There were new inventions, new forms of creativity, new discoveries in Science and Art.
- Economic advancement produced a larger population, inflation, new industries and trade and advanced technologies.
- A stronger and more centralised government was reflected in the increased political authority of kings. This was the case in Spain, France, England and the Holy Roman Empire.
- The clarification of frontiers and borders between states led to a sharper definition of territory and a clearer identity for states.
- There were clearer systems for international diplomacy.
- Development of newer forms of warfare meant larger scale wars, as well as more expensive and longer lasting wars.
- Europe faced outward beyond the Atlantic and Indian Oceans into new worlds.
- The Roman Church reinforced its hold on much of Europe and strengthened the spiritual life of its members. Elsewhere, other forms of church organisation and ritual were also developed as the Reformation progressed.
- Most people in Europe saw little beyond their own local community. However, Europe was witnessing the development of popular culture and beliefs which saw its churches involved increasingly in the popular rites of passage.
- Society was increasingly violent with public executions, massacres, plagues, the assassination of major figures, and hand-to-hand warfare.

Think yourself into the 16th century. This involves asking important questions, like the following:

- Was it possible not to be a Christian in the 16th century?
- Was it possible for a villager to know much of the world beyond his nearest town?

These and many other similar questions are the substance of this book. They are also the challenge of History.

1 The States of Italy, 1450–1520

The Sistine Chapel

THE SISTINE CHAPEL CEILING PAINTED BY MICHELANGELO.

"Thereupon, having arranged to do all the work by himself, Michelangelo carried it well on the way to completion. He worked with the greatest solicitude and study and he refused to let anyone see him in case he would have to show what he was painting. As a result every day people became more impatient. The Pope was always keen to see whatever Michelangelo was doing and so naturally he was more anxious than ever to see what was being hidden from him. So one day he resolved to go and see the work,

1 Why do you think the Pope wanted to see the work, even before it was finished?

2 Why do you think the Pope would pay so much money for it?

but he was not allowed in as Michelangelo would never have consented. Now, when a third of the work was completed (as I found out from Michelangelo himself, to clear up any uncertainty) during the winter when the north wind was blowing several spots of mould started to appear on the surface. The reason for this was Roman lime... When Michelangelo saw what was happening he despaired of the whole undertaking and was reluctant to go on. However, His Holiness sent Giulano di Sangalo to see him and explain the reasons for the blemishes. Sangalo explained how to remove the moulds and encouraged him to continue. Then when the work was half finished the Pope wanted it to be thrown open to the public. Being hasty and impatient by nature he simply could not bear to wait until it was perfect.

As soon as it was thrown open the whole of Rome flocked to see it. The Pope was the first, not having the patience to wait until the dust had settled after the dismantling of the scaffolding. Now the Pope recognised Michelangelo's genius more clearly every day and wanted him to carry on and finish the work. And so in twenty months Michelangelo brought the project to perfect completion, without the assistance even of someone to grind his colours. Michelangelo at times complained that because of the haste the Pope imposed on him he was unable to finish it in the way he would have liked...

For this work Michelangelo was paid by the Pope three thousand crowns in several instalments, of which he had to spend twenty-five on colours. He executed the frescoes in great discomfort, having to work with his face looking upwards, which impaired his sight so badly that he could not read or look at drawings. This lasted for several months afterwards. ...

There is no other work to compare with the painting on the ceiling of the Sistine Chapel for excellence, nor could there be. It's scarcely possible even to imitate what Michelangelo accomplished. The ceiling has proved a very simple beacon to our art, of an inestimable benefit to all other painters, restoring light to a wall that for centuries had been plunged into darkness."

Giorgio Vasari, *Lives of the Artists*, Penguin edn, 1965.

Michelangelo started work on the ceiling of the Sistine Chapel in 1508 and completed the project in 1512. It established Michelangelo as the greatest living artist. The art historian Kenneth Clark has described the work thus:

When on 31st October 1512 the frescoes were officially unveiled, artists and connoisseurs were prepared for something which would change the course of painting; and that, in fact, was what it did; not only painting but the whole mode of feeling. The freshness and wonder of the early renaissance, the delight in living things, birds, children, flowers – all this was crushed by the oppressive awareness of human destiny. And instead of a natural ease of arrangement in which flower was set beside flower and face beside face, there came into being a new unity of struggle, the unity of Hercules grappling with the lion. When

MICHELANGELO BUONAROTTI.

the ceiling was finally unveiled Michelangelo was thirty-seven. He lived to be eighty-nine. In this half century he executed some of his greatest works. The mood becomes graver: the confidence in physical beauty diminishes, and is at last rejected with a kind of horror, but fundamentally there is an unvarying aim: to use the human body as an instrument with which to reveal the ascent of the human soul.

Quoted in J.H. Plumb, *Pelican Book of the Renaissance*, 1964.

Michelangelo was a genius. In the city-states of Italy in the 14th and 15th centuries, genius was able to flourish. Why? Why were there so many talented artists in one geographical area in so short a time? And why did the states of Italy, states like Milan, Rome and Florence, encourage their genius? In order to understand this, we need first to have a clear understanding of 15th-century Italy.

Italy in the Fifteenth Century

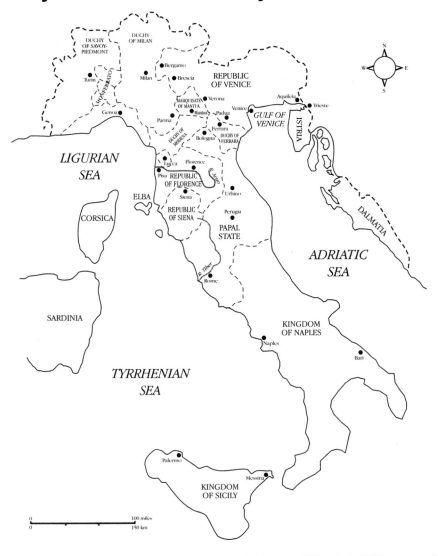

MAP OF ITALY AROUND 1500.

City-State	Population	Type of Government	Detail of Government
Venice	1.5 m	Republic with overseas Empire.	Controlled by a hierarchy of merchant families. Leading officers tended to become hereditary.
Milan	1.25 m	Duchy from 1454 ruled by Francesco Sforza.	Dictatorship which played an important role in Italian politics and warfare.
Florence	0.75 m	Republic led by wealthy Medici family.	System of Councils manned by 300 leading individual citizens. About 3000 citizens participated in elections to Councils.
Papal States	2 m	Elected Papal Monarchy.	Provincial vicars and City Governor were appointed and controlled by the Pope and his Captain General.
Naples	2 m	Hereditary Monarch.	King of Naples ruled large rural population. Alfonso of Aragon 1435–58 and his illegitimate son Ferrante were strong and determined rulers, in spite of opposition from the Pope in Rome.

THE ITALIAN PENINSULA IN THE 15TH CENTURY – THE FIVE MAJOR CITY-STATES

Most city-states in 15th-century Italy were ruled by a *Signory* of aristocrats. The great city-state of Milan was first ruled by the Visconti dukes and then by the Sforza family. Smaller states, like Urbino under Federigo da Montefeltro, were ruled by former mercenary captains, '*Condottieri*', who became civil dictators. These despots sought to enforce republican liberty and to protect the state against the other republics in the peninsula. The best example is that of Francesco Sforza in Milan, who took the republic by force in 1450, established himself as a dictator, and had his powers confirmed by the local Commune and the Emperor by 1454. He was a true master of the state, but his system was designed to rule in the people's interests.

The *Signory* also developed new mechanisms for government and administration and these subsequently spread north of the Alps in later centuries. A Privy Council and Chancellery to manage affairs of state and protect the rights of the subject was supported by a *Camera* (Chamber) which served as an Exchequer and local executive groups within the city itself. Each city would have its own *Podesta* (Mayor), and each district would be ruled by Captains of the Guard. Even local government systems under Vicars General and local commissioners were quite well developed.

Thus, while society north of the Alps was still organised on a rural and feudal basis, in Italy the city-state was already a significant civilising influence. Each city-state consisted of the city centre and the *Contado*, its supporting rural area. In Florence, for example, the important woollen industry depended upon woollen production in the Tuscan hills away from the city. Such involvement in the wealth of a city encouraged the development of republican feeling. In most Italian cities their town halls (*palazzo pubblico*) dominated the central city square. Perhaps most importantly, the major cities of Italy and the emerging cities north of the Alps were all centres of state government. One contemporary observer could note quite clearly 'it doth infinitely avail to the magnifying and making cities great the residency of the Prince therein. For where the Prince is resident there also the Parliaments are held and the supreme face of justice is there kept. All matters of importance have recourse to that face, all Princes and all persons of account, Ambassadors of Princes, and all agents of cities that are subject make their repair thither. All such as thirst after offices and honours rush thither. Thither are the revenues brought that pertain unto the state and there are they disposed of again.'

Undoubtedly, the 15th century was a violent age and, as one contemporary noted, 'violence worked like a yeast in the thought of men'. Yet the period between 1454 and 1494 in Italy was a period of peace. The five major Italian city-states had long had their conflicts, encouraged by uncertain boundaries between the states, shifting frontiers and traditional rivalries – Milan and Naples, Milan and Florence, Milan and Venice, Venice and the Papacy, and the Papacy and Naples. The Peace of Lodi in 1454 brought the five states together and they remained at peace until the French invasion of 1494.

This became therefore a period of political consolidation, economic wealth, and investment in culture. It was the period when the Arts in Italy truly began to flourish and spread their influence further north.

The Growth in Power of Florence

The wealth of Florence came largely from banking. In the 15th century, there were 80 banking houses in the city, chief among them being the House of Medici.

Giovanni de' Medici built up a bank from humble origins until there were major branches in 16 capital cities in Europe. Giovanni wisely avoided public life and spent his fortune on the construction of churches and works of art. He paid the architect Brunelleschi to build the famous Foundling Hospital. His only major contribution to public life won him great support from the poorer people of the city, when he persuaded the *Signory* to change the universal poll tax for a 1½% tax on capital. This penalised the rich but freed the poor entirely from the burden of taxation. His death in 1429 was much mourned by the vast majority of the Florentine population.

TALKING POINT
Creativity is a vital human activity. Which subjects in your school curriculum encourage it? What conditions in society encourage it and what conditions limit it?
What effects do climate and geography have on creativity?

TALKING POINT
What were the causes of violence in 15th-century Italy. Is there a relationship between violence and creativity?

COSIMO DE MEDICI.

Giovanni was succeeded by his eldest son, Cosimo, who continued his father's policy of retiring from public life and amassing a great fortune. He became the banker to the city and made loans and public expenses on his own account. He attracted and entertained great visitors to the city and used his banking influence to prevent wars. He also built many churches and became the patron of Brunelleschi, Donatello and Fra Angelico. Perhaps the high point of Cosimo's career came when Pope Nicholas V appointed the Medici to control the management of Papal finances in Rome.

His death in 1464 was followed by the short five-year reign of his ineffectual son, Piero, and then by the flourishing rule of his grandson Lorenzo. The nickname of Lorenzo de' Medici – the Magnificent – was appropriate. He was a shrewd politician, a wise statesman, a clever financier and banker, and the originator of the most refined Renaissance court in Italy. Where his grandfather had spent money lavishly on churches and works of art, Lorenzo preferred the more modest expenses of a court of philosophers led by Pico della Mirandola and Marsilio Ficino. Yet Lorenzo's city was still the home of great artists such as Michelangelo, Leonardo and Botticelli. Perhaps his most significant achievement was his victory over the Pazzi conspiracy and his defeat, more by diplomacy than war, of the hostile alliance of Naples and Pope Sixtus IV.

It wasn't until the last year of Lorenzo's reign, 1491, that the clouds began to gather. Critics began to comment publicly on the festivities with which Lorenzo entertained the people of Florence. A foreign monk from Ferrara called Savonarola preached a series of sermons in the church of San Marco, criticising Lorenzo for being a tyrant:

Tyrants rule because they are proud, because they love flattery, because they will not restore their ill-gotten gains. They allow bad officials to have their way; they yield to adulation; they neither heed the poor nor condemn the rich; they expect peasants and paupers to work for them free.

In 1494 a popular revolt broke out and the mob attacked the Medici Palace. Piero, Lorenzo's son, was driven into exile. The constitution was redesigned, with Florence now being governed by a Great Council, open to a quarter of adult males living in the city.

In 1498, Florence embarked on a damaging eleven-year war to capture Pisa. Only after this were the Medici family invited to return.

SAVONAROLA BEING BURNED AT THE STAKE FOR HERESY IN THE PIAZZA DELLA SIGNORIA IN 1498.

The Government and Economy of Florence

The government and economy of Florence was built around the twenty-one city guilds, particularly the seven major guilds. Chief among these were the *Arte della Lana* (the Guild of Wool Merchants) and the *Arte della Cambio* (the Guild of Bankers). The minor guilds served more humble artisans such as butchers, leatherworkers and stone masons, and beneath these was the vast majority of Florentines – cloth workers, labourers and boatmen.

All members of the guilds over thirty could be elected to public office in the city. Every two months, eight leather bags, called '*borse*', were taken from the church of Santa Croce and the names of citizens who were to serve on the councils were drawn out of the bags. Elected citizens were called '*priori*' and the government was called the '*Signory*'. Chief of these was the *Gonfaloniere* – the Standard Bearer of the city. In making major decisions, the *signory* had to consult a number of other elected councils, for example the Council of Ten who would advise on whether to make war or peace. In the event of a crisis the great bell in the Palace tower would sound its deep tone. As a result, it was known as the '*vacca*' or cow. On hearing the bell, all male citizens over the age of 14 were expected to march to the Piazza della Signoria to form a parliament. Whatever the crisis, an emergency committee would be set up and the people of Florence believed that this system guaranteed their freedom. Interestingly, of course, it was a system ideally suited to the manipulation of a powerful and wealthy family like the Medici.

TALKING POINT

Is dictatorship always a bad form of government? Why do we resist dictatorship in the modern world? How did politics in 15th-century Italy influence art?

A FLORENTINE BANKING HOUSE.

The economy in Florence under the Medici was extremely wealthy, being based primarily on the banking houses which Florentine citizens controlled in all the European countries. They loaned money at interest to many monarchs all over the world. This wealth came from the Florentine woollen industry, which exported dyed woollen cloth all over Europe. An important basis for the manufacture of cloth was the discovery of huge deposits of alum at Tolfa in the Papal states in the middle of the century. The Medici bank gained a concession on these deposits and the alum mined was used in the dying of cloth.

Indeed money was the most important commodity in Florence. The classic *Uomo Universale* Leon Alberti declared that 'no-one who was poor could find it easy to acquire honour and fame by means of his virtues'. Indeed, one of the international silk merchants in Florence observed that 'a Florentine who is not a merchant, who has not travelled throughout the world, seeing foreign nations and peoples and then returned to Florence with some wealth is a man who enjoys no esteem whatsoever'. The great and the good of Florence were distinguished by their fine palazzos, their country villas, their private chapels, their expensive and fashionable clothes, and their good marriages. The rapid growth of the city in the Medici years was described by Christopher Hibbert in his book *The Rise and Fall of the House of Medici*.

> The busiest parts of the city were the area around the stone bridge, the Ponte Vecchio, which spanned the River Arno at its narrowest point and was lined on both sides with butchers' shops and houses; the neighbourhood of the Orsanmichele, the communal granary, wherein some of the bankers set up their green cloth coloured tables in the street and the silk merchants had their counting houses; and the Mercatio Vecchio, the big square where once the old Roman forum had stood. Here the old market where the shops of the drapers and second

THE CITY OF FLORENCE AROUND 1500.

hand clothes dealers, the booths of fishmongers, bakers and the fruit and vegetable merchants, the houses of the feather merchants and the stationers and of candle makers. ...On open counters in the market, bales of silk and barrels of grain, corn and leather goods were exposed for sale, shielded by awnings from the burning sun. Here also, out in the open, barbers shaved beards and clipped hair, tailors stitched cloth in shaded doorways, servants and housewives gathered round the booths of the cooked food merchants, bakers pushed platters of dough into the communal oven, and furniture makers and goldsmiths displayed their wares. Town Criers marched about calling out the news of the day and broadcasting advertisements; ragged beggars held out their wooden bowls; children played dice on the flagstones and in winter patted the snow into the shape of lions, the heraldic emblem of the city. Animals roamed everywhere: dogs wearing silver collars; pigs and geese rooting about in doorways; occasionally even a deer would coming running down from the hills and clatter through the square.

In such a scene, dress was particularly important and there were rules against particular features of dress, not least for women. One official who was ordered to check up on the dress of the women in the city reported his failure to do so: 'in obedience to your orders I went out to look for forbidden ornaments on the women and was met with arguments such as not to be found in any book of laws. There was one woman with the edge of her hood fringed out in lace and twined round her head. My assistant said to her "What is your name? You have a hood with lace fringes". But the woman removed the lace fringe which was attached to the hood with a pin and said it was merely a wreath. Further along we met a woman with many buttons in front of her dress and my assistant said to her "You are not allowed to wear buttons". But she replied "These are not buttons. They are studs. Look they have no loops, and there are no buttonholes." Then my assistant, supposing he had caught a culprit at last, went to another woman and said to her "You are wearing ermine" and he took out his book to write down her name. "You cannot take down my name", the woman protested. "This is not ermine, it is the fur of a suckling." "What do you mean suckling?" "A kind of animal."'

TALKING POINT

Why is it not easy to legislate for social convention?

FOCUS

1.1 The Pazzi Conspiracy, 1478

Lorenzo de' Medici succeeded his father, Piero, as the influential leader of Florence in 1469. In later years he wrote this of his accession: 'Although I was only in my 21st year, the principal men of the city came to our house to offer their condolences and to encourage me to take on myself the care of the state as my father and grandfather had done.'

Yet every political leader arouses opposition. This is the story of the Pazzi conspiracy – an attempt by the aristocratic Pazzi family to settle some old scores.

1
Wealthy and proud, the Pazzi had been denied public office and the honours to which they were entitled, and they bore discrimination and abuse bitterly. The most sensitive of the family, Francesco, unable to suffer any longer, fled to Rome, where he fell in with a nephew of one of the most grasping and turbulent of the Popes, and between them they hatched a plot for their mutual benefit. As ambitious as he was low-born, Pope Sixtus IV was burdened with six nephews, three of whom he placed profitably in the Church and a fourth in Imola, one of the poorest and smallest of the papal fiefs. When Francesco proposed to create a vacancy in Florence, Sixtus fell in with the scheme and consented to second the Pazzi in ousting the Medici. Thus encouraged, Francesco returned to Florence to enlist his family. Jacopo de Pazzi, the head of the house, hesitated until he was convinced that the scheme had the blessing and the backing of the Pope.

2
The scheme was senseless on the face of it. A foreign potentate aiming to add Florence to the papal domain and impose a papal curb on a fiercely freedom-loving people, and relying on a Florentine family ambitious to fill the vacancy themselves. The plot was a patchwork of cross-purposes perfectly calculated to fail. Yet it nearly succeeded.

3
The Pope opened hostilities by cancelling the concession of the Medici bank in Rome and transferring it to the Pazzi; then he lent a helping hand to the plot by appointing as Archbishop of Pisa a member of another family hostile to the Medici, the Salviati. Notwithstanding these unfriendly acts, Lorenzo seems to have suspected nothing, although he refused Salviati admission to his see. In April 1478 the conspirators assembled in Florence and were hospitably entertained in Lorenzo's villa at Fiesole, where they planned to kill him during a banquet. However, his brother Guiliano was absent, and since the murder of both was essential to success, they postponed the blow until the following morning, during the celebration of High Mass in the Duomo (Cathedral), where both were bound to appear for the celebration of Easter Sunday.

4
The change created an unforeseen difficulty; the hired assassin suffered an attack of conscientious scruples and shrank from committing sacrilege as well as murder in the Cathedral; Francesco de'Pazzi, a priest, and an accomplice assumed his duties, but still another hitch developed. Giuliano was missing when the service began, and they were forced to fetch him to the slaughter, coaxing him out of bed, where he was nursing a bad knee. They braced him between them, embracing him fondly and feeling his body to make sure that he was unarmed, and brought the laggard limping to the altar; then, having finally united the victims, they struck. The church was crowded; the signal for attack was the solemn moment when the Cardinal who was officiating raised the Host and hundreds of heads bowed devoutly. Giuliano bent obediently, the priest behind his back struck the first blow, and Francesco finished him off with eighteen more – so furiously that he hacked himself in the leg and in the confusion was mistaken for one of the victims. Lorenzo defended himself, escaped with a gash in the neck, and ran into the sacristy, where his friends bolted the doors and waited for help.

5
In the meanwhile Archbishop Salviati, entrusted with the most difficult part of the undertaking, entered the palace to seize the Government. His confederates waited below in the chancery, where they locked themselves by mistake, while he mounted to the upper floor to parley with the Signory, but his agitation betrayed him and aroused their suspicion, and before he could summon assistance the gonfaloniere hanged him, stammering, from the window. The city was now in an uproar. Francesco de'Pazzi, weak from loss of blood, took to his bed and begged his uncle to rally the people to their cause. Sallying forth with a hundred armed men, Jacopo de'Pazzi roamed the streets raising the cry of Liberty! without arousing response, abandoned the attempt and fled. Lorenzo, escorted by his friends, returned home.

6

The mob avenged him loyally. Francisco de'Pazzi, dragged from his bed, was hanged beside the body of the Archbishop, dangling limply with a cluster of comrades overhead. A furious man-hunt followed: everyone even remotely connected with the conspiracy or suspected of sympathizing with it was brought to justice or mobbed; seventy perished in the first four days and two hundred more before the tumult subsided.

Jacopo de'Pazzi, caught and killed, was not allowed to rest in his grave: a horde of scavenging boys unearthed his body, dragged it through the streets, and flung it naked into the Arno. Of his ten sons and nephews, two were beheaded; one was saved by Lorenzo, who was his brother-in-law; the survivors were sentenced to imprisonment or exile, and even the name Pazzi was wiped out by proscription.

LORENZO DE MEDICI.

7

Infuriated by the failure of the plot, the Pope demanded that Lorenzo surrender and that the Florentine government answer before an ecclesiastical court for the crime of sacrilege committed on the person of the Archbishop. Lorenzo protested that his only crime was that he had not

allowed himself to be murdered; the Signory seconded him, circulated the confession of one of the conspirators exposing the complicity of the Pope, and appealed to the sovereigns of Europe for support.

8

The sovereigns of Europe sided with the Medici; the Pope excommunicated the Florentine state; the Florentine clergy outlawed him in turn; the Pope declared war. Brandishing both his spiritual and temporal arms, he forbade the faithful to trade with the rebellious republic, broke their previous alliances, prohibited any state from forming new ones or any soldier from taking service with them, and summoned to his assistance the Sienese republic and his feudal ally the

King of Naples; and their troops invaded Tuscany. The fortunes of war ran against the Florentines, and Lorenzo, unwilling to tax the loyalty of his people, volunteered to surrender himself, but the issue had long since outgrown a personal sacrifice and the Signory refused to abandon him. He insisted, however, slipped off to Pisa, and sailed for Naples to treat with King Ferrante.

9

Ferrante was a notoriously treacherous monarch, but, impressed by Lorenzo's daring, he detained him less as a prisoner than as a guest, listened to his arguments, and

consented to abandon the Pope. The Pope fumed, but an incursion of the Turks in Calabria compelled him, like Ferrante, to make peace.

10

The Pazzi conspiracy, formidable in its folly, failed; but it created a crisis and marked a turning point in Lorenzo's political career. To prevent its recurrence, he surrounded himself with an armed guard and adopted those precautions which his enemies denounced as a tyranny. He tightened his grip on the government, subordinated the Signory and the councils to a self-perpetuating privy council responsible to himself alone, and converted the controlling

influence created by Cosimo into absolute personal rule. Before the Pazzi conspiracy, he was the most fortunate of the Medici; after it, the most masterful; and 'I, Lorenzo' now assumed its full meaning for Florence. But the crisis had a further effect: it stimulated his powers as a statesman, and he devoted them diligently to preserving the balance of power and keeping the peace in Italy.

Text adapted from R. Roeder in J.H. Plumb,
The Pelican Book of the Renaissance,
Pelican, 1982.

---

1 Who were the Pazzi conspirators and what were their motives?

2 Why did the plot fail?

3 What does the plot tell you about the way Florence was governed in 1478?

4 In your own words, tell the story of the Pazzi conspiracy to a group of 13 year olds. Use no more than 200 words. Alternatively, tell the story in a storyboard cartoon of 10 frames to a group of 13 year olds.

Focus

1.2 The Nature of Politics and Government in 15th-Century Florence

Wallace Ferguson (in *Six Essays on the Renaissance,* Harper & Row, 1953), describes politics and government in Renaissance Florence.

" The political history of Florence is much more complicated, partly because her economy was more complex and still in process of evolution in the thirteenth and fourteenth centuries, but partly also because the Florentine citizens seem to have combined with their unusual intellectual and aesthetic interests a passion for politics. At times, indeed, they demonstrated an ingenuity in the construction of involved political institutions that fell just short of lunacy.

Florence was a commercial city, but it was not a seaport, and its great economic expansion in the late thirteenth and early fourteenth centuries resulted from a combination of commerce with banking and large export industries, of which the woollen cloth industry was by far the most important and employed about a third of the city's ninety thousand population. This adventurous and many-sided capitalist economy afforded unusual opportunities for the creation of new fortunes, and as a result the composition of the class of wealthy merchant bankers and industrialists who generally succeeded in dominating the city's politics was constantly changing. New families rose to wealth, while old families went bankrupt or invested their inherited wealth in land and rents, or simply frittered it away. In the last years of the thirteenth century the new rich combined with the middle class of guildsmen to disenfranchise the old aristocracy and set up a government controlled by the merchant guilds, with a minor share allotted to the lesser guilds of shopkeepers and artisans. The great mass of proletarian workers in the woollen industry, who were not permitted to organize in guilds, were excluded entirely from active citizenship. One of the chief reasons by the merchant employers in the great wool guilds felt it necessary to control the government was to keep these restless workers in subjection. The middle class of small guildsmen also feared the violence of the woolworkers who crowded the slums of the city, and so they generally followed the lead of the merchant industrialists. For a time in the middle of the fourteenth century, when the merchant class was weakened by depression and a series of bank failures, the lesser guilds gained a larger share in the government, but even then its policy was generally dictated by the merchant oligarchy.

The fact that executive power in the republican government was vested in a committee of priors, elected afresh every two months, made it almost inevitable that some extra-constitutional group should direct policy and give it some continuity. As a result, the vicissitudes of Florentine politics were caused more by changes in the composition of the ruling clique than in the republican constitution itself. When in 1434 a group of new families headed by the banker Cosimo de Medici took control from a clique of older families led by the Albizzi, there was no revolutionary change in the constitution. To quote Schevill, 'the new government was the old government operated by a different set of beneficiaries.' Under four generations of Medici leadership, the republic retained a semblance of democracy, although the sham became increasingly apparent, while the Medici directed affairs without holding actual public office, much after the manner of a modern municipal boss. It was in foreign policy especially, where continuity was absolutely essential, that the Medici made themselves indispensable. They were not Signori in the ordinary sense of the word, but they took their place as equals among the Princes of Italy. "

1 What does this extract tell you about the government of Florence in Lorenzo's time?
2 Does it support or oppose the impression gained in the earlier extracts?

The Papal States and the Power of Rome

By the 15th century the bishop of Rome, the pope, or 'Papa', was the ruler of three different territories. As the successor of St Peter, he was the head of the Roman Catholic church throughout the world. In addition, he was the ruler of the city of Rome and also the lord of the Papal states – extensive territories in central Italy.

Yet at the beginning of the 15th century, the power and authority of the pope was severely limited. From 1378 to 1429, there were in fact two popes and the more widely recognised was resident in Avignon in southern France – in 1409 there were in fact *three* candidates for the Papal throne. It was not until the reign of Pope Martin V (1417–31) that a single pope was recognised and permanently resident on the throne of St Peter in Rome. This confusion made it impossible for the Papacy to control powerful Roman families like the Orsini and the Colonna. In addition, it was impossible to rule the *Condottieri* captains, tough mercenary soldiers who robbed and plundered in the Romagna and other Papal states. Finally, it was extremely difficult for any one Pope to extend his authority over the wider church in Europe.

In order to re-establish their authority, popes like Martin V, Nicholas V (1447–55), Sixtus IV (1464–92), Alexander VI (1492–1503) and Julius II (1503–15), had to be worldly men who could assume power. They were hard-headed and ambitious and determined to control their territories.

Pope Martin V was a Roman and a member of the Colonna family. He ensured peace in the city itself and had such a powerful personality that he controlled the crime in the city and encouraged trade. He brought the Papal Court back to Rome and with it came pilgrims, merchants and Papal taxes.

Nicholas V was the son of a surgeon and delighted in books. He created the wonderful Vatican Library and ensured that manuscripts and scholars were brought to Rome. The classical scholar and translator Lorenzo Valla lived in Rome during this pontificate, and many teachers of Latin and Greek were welcomed to the city. Nicholas also began the process of rebuilding Rome. He began the plan for a new Roman city, to be dominated by St Peter's the new Papal Palace, and protected by the Castel Sant' Angelo. He used Florentine architects like Alberti to begin the building of churches, monasteries, palaces, theatres, gardens and town fortifications, at immense cost. His successors completed the destruction of ancient Rome, removing 2300 wagon loads of marble from the Colosseum in a single year and completed the planning of Nicholas's dream city.

Nicholas' successor, Sixtus IV was a brilliant administrator and generous patron of the arts. J.H. Plumb outlines his achievement:

> he widened streets, constructed bridges, built hospitals, erected churches, gave land to all who would build houses and palaces. He encouraged his Cardinals to foster the splendour of Rome: the market was expelled from the Piazza Navonna and the building of its churches and palaces begun. There was scarcely a ward of the city that Sixtus did not improve or adorn, but his greatest glory is the Chapel and the Vatican that bears his name. Utterly simple in design it served merely as a frame for his adornment and for this purpose

TALKING POINT

There is obviously a tension between the pope as a moral individual and the pope as an officeholder, with both sacred and secular responsibilities. In the 15th century, was it possible for one person to fulfil both functions? Is it possible today?

Sixtus brought the best artists in Italy to Rome – Signorelli, Botticelli, Perugino, Pinturicchio, Ghirlandaio and Rosselli.

It was in the following reign, of *Alexander VI* (1492–1503), that the pope's control over his territories in central Italy was emphasised. Pope Alexander's devotion to his son, Cesare Borgia, ensured that Cesare carved out a great central Italian kingdom. In spectacular victories, Cesare captured many powerful fortresses as well as great cities like Urbino. Indeed, Machiavelli so admired Cesare's achievement that he wrote his book *The Prince* to celebrate them. Unfortunately for the Borgia family, Pope Alexander died in 1503 and Cesare was struck down with a sudden illness. His kingdom collapsed as quickly as it had been set up. J.H. Plumb's summary of his reign is revealing:

> the depth and ferocity of the Pope's passion for his children have made him an ogre of history, making men forget his astonishing dignity, his overwhelming physical charm and the immense presence, as well as the animal vitality which made him as unwearying at work as at pleasure. His pontificate was far from disastrous for the Papacy. He brought its temporal possessions more firmly under its control and even though his intention to transfer these temporalities to his own family would, if realised, have ruined the church, yet the possibility that this could be achieved was so remote that the success of Cesare merely redounded into the advantage of the Papacy.

John Burchard, the Pope's Master of Ceremonies, described the elaborate protocol required of any ambassadorial visit to Rome. The pope always wore his triple crown as the emblem of the supreme monarch of Christendom. Visitors were always required to kiss his feet, as were cardinals and other members of the church. They approached the pope bareheaded, knelt before him and were then ceremoniously raised from their knees. The pope marked the forehead of any visitor with the kiss of peace and the sign of the cross. It was clear from this ceremonial that visitors and churchmen were welcome in Rome. But it was also equally clear that the pope was the Lord of the Church and the city. By 1500 the great city of Rome, with its wonderful palaces and churches, was the centre of their world and to the faithful this mattered much more than the possible venality of the Pope.

Examining the evidence

Rodrigo Borgia, Pope Alexander VI (1492–1503)

POPE ALEXANDER VI.

Pope Alexander VI was born in 1431, the son of a Spanish nobleman of the House of Borja. In 1456, at the age of only twenty-five, he was made a Cardinal of the Catholic church and the following year he became its Vice-Chancellor in Rome. Throughout his career the protection and patronage of his family was one of his major priorities. He had four children by unknown mistresses, including his first son, Pedro Luis, who became the Duke of Gandia in Spain. He had four children by Vanozza Catanei – Cesare and Lucrezia being the two best known. Vanozza herself was a respectable Roman woman from a high family who married several times. When he became pope, his mistress was Giulia Farnese by whom he had two children – Giovanni and Rodrigo.

In the years following his appointment as vice-chancellor, Rodrigo exercised great influence in Rome. During his ten years as pope, eight members of his family were made cardinals, which enabled him to exercise complete control in Rome and the Papal states. His son Cesare, a military captain of real ability and much malice, was his greatest ally. Geoffrey Parker in his edition of John Burchard's *At the Court of the Borgia* sums up the pontificate of Alexander VI like this: 'Borgian Rome was not so manifestly unlike the Rome of the rest of the Renaissance, nor was Alexander VI so different from other Popes, but for all opponents alike – the personal enemies of the family, the critics of official corruption in the church, and those who more basically attack the whole system of the Renaissance Papacy – the pontificate of Alexander VI came to symbolise all that was morally evil and abandoned.'

There are many primary sources which tell us about Alexander VI as a pope.

Source A
John Burchard's diary.
John Burchard was a German from Strasbourg who journeyed to Rome as a young man and in 1483 became Master of Ceremonies at the Papal Court. As such, he was involved in planning most of the major functions and ceremonial occasions in the court. He did this job until he died in 1506. From 1494, his diary is thorough and detailed, not only about Papal Ceremonial, but also about political matters in Italy and beyond. As such, it is a very intimate and detailed source of information about Alexander's reign.

> On the same day, Don Giovanni Sforza betrothed and took as his lawful wife, Donna Lucrezia Borgia, the Pope's daughter and still only a girl of thirteen. In the Palace, the Sala Reale and all the apartments were prepared with the most elaborate decorations of velvet coverings and tapestries.
>
> Don Juan Borgia, the Duke of Gandia, the Pope's son, was commanded by his Holiness to escort Lucrezia into the wedding. He brought her in as far as the last room, a negro girl carrying her train. Donna Julia Farnese, the Pope's concubine, and many other Roman ladies, numbering in all about one hundred and fifty, followed Lucrezia. On learning of their arrival the Pope entered and sat on his throne officially to greet the ladies. They passed in turn before him. His

Holiness dressed in a crimson hood was accompanied by ten Cardinals who took their seats by his throne. Then the Duke of Gandia approached with his sister the bride, to kiss the Pope's foot and they were followed by all the ladies; Don Juan and Donna Lucrezia and a few of the more prominent ladies remained kneeling by the Pope whilst the rest moved back to stand at his right. On his left, by the wall, stood Don Cesare Borgia, the Bishop elect of Valencia and another son of his Holiness, with many notables and ecclesiastics. ...

Shortly afterwards the Pope joined Donna Lucrezia and Don Giovanni in the Sala Reale. When he was seated on his throne they all enjoyed a series of entertainments. Four gentlemen recited some verses about love, after which two gentlemen, dressed up in fashionable clothes with a number of their friends, performed a comedy with such eloquence that everyone loudly applauded them. An assortment of all kinds of sweets, marzipans and drinks of wine in about a hundred basins and cups were brought in and carried round by chamberlains and grooms.

In the evening, the Pope gave a dinner for the bride and bridegroom and the guests included many ladies and four of the Cardinals.

In 1501 Lucrezia was married again.

On Saturday September 4th news came of the marriage concluded between Don Alfonzo, the eldest son of the Duke of Ferrara, and Donna Lucrezia Borgia. As a result of this news there was a continual cannonade from the Castel St Angelo from the hour onwards into the night. Next day, after dinner, Lucrezia rode from her residence to the church of Santa Maria Del Poppolo. She was dressed in a robe of brocaded gold with the veil drawn back and was escorted by three hundred horsemen. Four Bishops rode in front of her and she was followed by her footmen and servants. On the same evening the great Capitoline bell was tolled and many bonfires were lit throughout the city.

On Sunday evening, Don Cesare Borgia gave a supper in his apartment in the Apostolic Palace with fifty prostitutes in attendance, who after the meal danced with the servants and others there, first fully dressed and then naked. Following the supper lampstands holding lighted candles were placed on the floor and chestnuts strewn about, which the prostitutes naked and on their hands and knees, had to pick up as they crawled in and out amongst the lampstands. The Pope, Don Cesare and Donna Lucrezia were all present to watch.

On Tuesday 27th December the Pope donned his vestments and said in my presence that he had obtained the advice of some learned doctors at Law at the marriage contracted at Ferrara between Don Alfonso and Donna Lucrezia should be celebrated again in Rome, despite Cardinal Piccolomini's insistence that matrimony was a sacrament and therefore could not be repeated.

TALKING POINT

The celibacy of priests was an important issue in the 15th century, and it still is today. What are the advantages and disadvantages of clerical celibacy?

1 Comment on John Burchard's value as a primary source of the reign of Alexander VI.

2 Comment on Guicciardini's value as a primary source.

3 What does the reign of Alexander VI tell us about 'Renaissance Papacy'?

4 Geoffrey Parker sums up his view of John Burchard's diary as follows: 'With all the deficiencies that it possesses, the diary remains a valid witness to aid the understanding of a decade which was at once fascinating in its events and ideas, in the texture of its social life and in its characters, amongst whom Pope Alexander VI was pre-eminent.'
Do you agree with this opinion?

Source B

Guicciardini, *The History of Italy.*

Guicciardini was a Florentine and hence an enemy of Rome. He wrote his *History of Italy* in the mid-16th century and it was first published in 1561. He too wrote about the marriage of Lucrezia to the Duke of Ferrara.

> Now the Pope once again married off his daughter Lucrezia: this time to Alfonzo, eldest son of the Duke of Ferrara, with a dowry of one hundred thousand ducats in cash and many other gifts of greatest value. This marriage was arranged despite the fact the Lucrezia already had three husbands and was at that time a widow as a result of the death of one. Although this marriage was most unworthy of the House of Ferrara, and all the more unworthy because Lucrezia was illegitimate and stained with great infamy, the Duke of Ferrara consented because the French King, desiring to satisfy to the Pope in all things, gave strong arguments for the union.

Guicciardini also has a clear point of view about the morality of Alexander VI's Pontificate.

> Little by little Popes forgot about the salvation of souls and turned all their thoughts to worldly greatness. They began to appear more like secular princes than Popes. Their concern began to be no longer the sanctity of life or the propagation of religion, no longer zeal and charity towards their neighbours, but armies and wars against Christians, managing their sacrifices with bloody hands and thoughts. They began to accumulate treasures, to invest new cunning devices in order to gather money from every side. For this purpose they began to use their spiritual arms without respect, shamelessly to say sacred and profane things. The great wealth spreading amongst them and throughout their court was followed by pomp luxury, dishonest customs, lusts and abominable pleasures.

Review

Essay

'Why did 15th-century Italy become the centre of political and cultural activity in Europe?'

Every essay needs to be carefully considered and planned.

There are six stages in the planning and writing of an essay.

Stage 1: Audience and Information

Who will read the essay? This will dictate length, language and style.

How long should it be?

What are the KEY WORDS in the question? In this case, it is a Why? question, demanding a list of factors or reasons in its answer.

Stage 2: Planning

This essay demands an initial list of FACTORS which caused Italy to become the centre.

The factors are:

- Political.
- Diplomatic.
- Economic.
- Social.
- Military.
- Cultural.

These can become the basis for your main paragraphs. Omit the introduction and conclusion for now.

It is a good idea to frame these factors into a mind map and build up each factor.

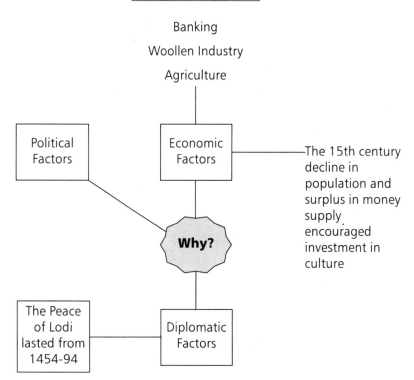

Stage 3: Research

Now read as many sources as you can and add detail to your mind map.

Always keep references for your sources.

Your mind map can be made more detailed (see J.H. Plumb, *Pelican Book of the Renaissance*, pp. 119–22).

Chapters 2 and 9 of this book will provide additional information.

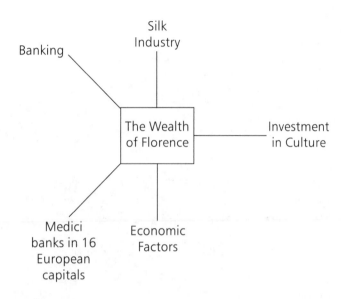

Stage 4: Reflection and Improvement

- Review your mind map against the essay question – have I answered it? – and against your initial information and audience – is the paragraph framework adequate? Is the language level good?

- You will also need to consider your first and last paragraphs. What is the purpose of an introduction? What is the use of a conclusion? Draft out some ideas for these two paragraphs: do they fulfil your purposes?

Stage 5: Draft

Write your initial draft, then conduct a further brief review, perhaps by consulting your sources again and adding any further pieces of information. It is helpful to write on alternate lines at this stage, to enable you to incorporate improvements.

It is certainly helpful to use a word processor. Then you can improve the essay as you write it.

Stage 6: Final script

2 The Italian Renaissance

PREVIEW

The Origins of the Renaissance

All art reflects the society which produces it. In the Middle Ages in Europe the hearts and minds of most people were focused upon God, Heaven and Hell. Life on Earth was a brief journey which prepared the soul for the afterlife. Medieval art was for the most part concerned with God and not man; as a result, most painting was two dimensional. This can clearly be seen on the ceiling of the 12th-century Baptistery in Florence. Medieval painters found it impossible to depict God, but it was easier to devise the figures of angels, saints and the all-powerful, dominating figure of Jesus Christ. The horrors of Hell were also a common theme in medieval art.

'CHRISTUS PANTOKRATOR' FROM THE 12TH-CENTURY BAPTISTERY IN FLORENCE.

In the 13th and 14th centuries, society began very slowly to take a different view: artists became more concerned with life on this earth, with the dignity of man, and with his creative potential. Although the religious basis of art remained, very slowly new approaches began to be used. These can clearly be seen in the paintings of early masters such as Cimabue and his pupil Giotto.

In poetry too, the 14th century witnessed the beginning of a new age. *The Decameron* of Giovanni Boccaccio was followed by what some believed to be the greatest poem ever written, *The Divine Comedy* of Dante. Perhaps the spirit of the age was best expressed in the writing of Petrarch, an admirer of ancient Greek and Roman forms: 'Maybe if – and this is my earnest hope – your life goes on long after mine, better times await you. This sleep of death will not afflict all your years. When the darkness breaks, the generations to come may manage to find their way back to the clear splendour of the ancient past.'

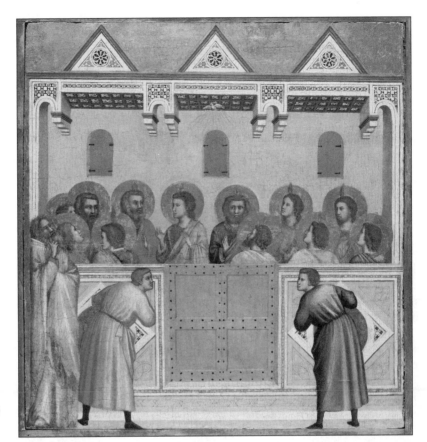

GIOTTO, *THE PENTECOST*.

THE TWO MEN IN THE FOREGROUND, EXCHANGING CONFIDENCES, GIVE A THREE-DIMENSIONAL ASPECT TO THE PICTURE AND A SENSE OF IMMEDIACY TO THE REPRESENTATION.

The Main Themes of Renaissance Thought

In the *quattrocento*, the 15th century, in Italy, men developed a new way of thinking about their world. Although the prime concern was still with God, Heaven, Hell and the afterlife, there was now an increased respect for the dignity of man and his considerable creative capacity on Earth. In addition, an increasing understanding of the laws which govern the universe and natural beauty and a respect for, and a revival of, the principles on which Greek and Roman civilisations had been based.

These main themes are wonderfully illustrated in a letter from Niccolo Machiavelli to a friend.

> When evening comes I return home from work and go into my study. On the threshold I strip off my muddy, sweaty and workaday clothes, and put on the robes of court and palace, and in this graver dress I enter the antique courts of the ancients and am welcomed by them. There I taste the food that alone is mine. There I make bold to speak to them and ask them motives of their actions and they, in all their humanity, reply to me. And for the space of four hours I forget this world, remember no vexation, fear poverty no more, tremble no more at debt: I pass indeed into the world of the ancients.

The themes can also be illustrated from the commentaries of Pope Pius II.

> All the hills about Siena were smiling in their vesture of foliage and flowers, and the crops were growing up in the fields. The Sienese countryside immediately around the city is indescribably lovely with its gently sloping hills planted with cultivated trees and vines or ploughed for grain overlooking delightful valleys green with pasture land and watered by never failing streams. There are also thick forests planted by nature or man, where birds sing most sweetly.

The Visual Arts

The towns and cities of 15th century Italy were exciting places, receptive to new ideas. Civic pride was at stake. Town councils were commissioning artists to produce sculptures, new buildings and great paintings, largely in the form of frescoes. These were works of art painted directly onto the walls of churches. Competitions were announced and the winners received financial rewards and a display of their work. New churches contained altars and side chapels, dedicated to families and guilds, and altarpieces, pulpits, and particularly family tombs were the order of the day. Patrons understood the work that artists were producing and gave them time, space and financial reward. As a result, innovative thinking was received by a welcoming audience and humanist ideas began to change peoples' perceptions of the world.

A discussion of one of the most important competitions – for the baptistry doors in Florence – is given later in this chapter.

In the visual arts, the consequences were very clear. Experiments in perspective and anatomy, and the depiction of emotional expressions on the faces of people were common. Colour, light and shade, were experimented with and oils began to be used. Landscapes were being drawn, flowers depicted, and even children took their place in paintings and sculptures. One of the most dramatic developments in painting and sculpture at this time was the acceptance of the nude – the human form in all its greatness and beauty was a particularly valued subject. Styles of painting were broad and spacious and at their heart was the ennoblement of the human figure, whether in an architectural or landscape setting.

Much of this was work the result of contracts drawn up between patrons and humanists. Money was advanced for the stain of marble or the purchase of colours. Artists, formerly regarded as craftsmen, were increasingly seen as intellectuals and a much higher value was placed on their skill. Interestingly, they would often include self-portraits or portraits of their patrons in their paintings and frescoes.

THE *ADORATION OF THE MAGI* BY FABRIANNO IS A WONDERFUL EXAMPLE OF EARLY 15TH CENTURY PAINTING, PRODUCED FOR THE COMMISSION OF A WEALTHY MERCHANT. THE SENSE OF PERSPECTIVE IS REAL AND HUMAN AND ANIMAL FORMS ARE GIVEN INCREASING CLARITY – EVEN THE SURROUNDING COUNTRYSIDE IS PRIZED.

FURTHER DEVELOPMENT WAS MADE BY MASACCIO – PARTICULARLY IN HIS FRESCOES FOR THE BRANCACCI CHAPEL IN STA MARIA DELLA CARMINE. IN THIS SECTION, *THE TRIBUTE MONEY*, THE DRAMA OF THE SCENE IS CLEAR AND THE REPRESENTATION OF INDIVIDUAL APOSTLES IS INCREASINGLY LIFELIKE.

IT IS WITH A DRAMATIC IMPACT FROM TWO GREAT PAINTINGS BY SANDRO BOTTICELLI, *THE BIRTH OF VENUS* AND *LA PRIMAVERA*, THAT THE LATE 15TH-CENTURY WORLD OF PAINTING MOVES ON. BOTTICELLI SET UP HIS WORKSHOP IN FLORENCE IN 1470 AND WAS PART OF THE PLATONIC SCHOOL OF FICINO, PICO DELLA MIRANDOLA AND OTHERS AROUND THE MEDICI PALACE. HIS PATRON WAS LORENZO AND HIS WORK WAS REMARKABLE. LOOK CLOSELY AT THESE TWO PAINTINGS AND DISCUSS WHAT YOU SEE.

The visual arts celebrated the naked body. It is interesting that we use words like 'nakedness' and 'nudity' differently. Why did Renaissance sculptors work on nude forms?

In sculpture, similar developments occurred and these reflected the same themes. One great master was Lorenzo Ghiberti, whose lifework were the bronze doors at the baptistry of Florence. He was followed by his pupil Donatello and superseded by the brilliance of Michelangelo's David which celebrated the male human form and the potential greatness of man.

DONATELLO, *DAVID WITH GOLIATH'S HEAD*.

Ghiberti's pupil Brunelleschi supervised the construction of the dome of the cathedral or *duomo* in Florence. He also designed the Foundling Hospital for Cosimo di Medici and many other wonderful buildings. It was, however, in Rome that architectural skill was developed to its highest degree, not least with the building of St Peter's and the Sistine Chapel, completed by Michelangelo under the commission of Pope Julius II. Perhaps the most interesting of architects was Francesco Giorgio. In a memo to one of his builders, he recorded: 'I should like the width of the nave to be nine paces, which is the square of three, the first and divine number. The length of the nave, which will be twenty-seven, will have a triple proportion. And this mysterious harmony is such that when God wished to instruct Moses concerning the form and proportion of the Tabernacle He gave him as a model the fabric of the world.'

What influences on the author can you detect in this quotation?

Other Major Developments in the Sciences and Literature

George Sarton, in an article on 'Science in the Renaissance', published in 1953, wrote that

> the Renaissance artists discovered the beauty of the human body, but that had never been completely forgotten. They discovered the beauties of ancient art, new accents in poetry, new rhythms in music; they discovered ancient books and were anxious to publish them. All that was very exhilarating.

In the field of Science and Mathematics, the novelties were gigantic, revolutionary. The Renaissance scientists introduced not a new look but a new being. The novelty of these discoveries was often so great that one could hardly speak of a rebirth. It was a *real* birth, a new beginning. The 15th century witnessed the beginning of trigonometry and algebra, not least in the use of operational symbols in the writing of equations. Perspective and proportion, the search for mathematical laws governing our world, were also essential features of 15th century Italy. Physics and biological science benefited from translations of ancient classical works, not least those of Aristotle and the medical scholars Galen and Hippocrates. Poggio Bracciolini discovered and translated the text of Lucretius' *De Rerum Naturae* and the whole wealth of Greek anatomy was uncovered for the west. The historian Eugene Garin emphasises the importance of the Renaissance in the development of science: 'the leap from quality to quantity, from finite to the infinite, from earth centred to sun centred universe and so on, was determined and made possible by a new attitude to reality, new horizons...'

Renaissance patrons also fostered an exciting expansion in literature. Machiavelli's *The Prince* and *The Discourses* are foremost amongst modern works of political theory while Guicciardini remains one of the founders of modern historical writing and his *History of Italy* tells us much about the developments in this period. Perhaps most importantly, the philosophers and theologians who gathered in the Platonic Academy of Lorenzo's Florence encouraged the writing of many philosophical tracts. The ancient Greek philosopher Plato was at the heart of much of the idealism and Marcilio Ficino, in his tract on the Christian religion, could indicate the mood of the times. 'Every religion has something good about it, so long as it is directed towards God, the Creator of all things. Divine providence does allow rites to differ. It is more important to the King of Kings to be truly honoured than to be honoured with any particular gesture. He prefers to be worshipped in any manner and however unfittingly so long as it be human.'

NICCOLO MACHIAVELLI.

TALKING POINT

Humanists knew that they would benefit from reading classical texts in their original languages.
What are the historical problems if we cannot read and understand texts in the original language?

TALKING POINT

It is interesting that great artists in the Renaissance were elitists, not socially but intellectually. In many ways, they were looking after their own interests, rather than contributing to the knowledge of humankind. Under what conditions does genius flourish?

The Bronze Doors of Lorenzo Ghiberti

What does this section tell you about life and work in 15th-century Florence?

In 1635 Richard Lassels, an Englishman, visited Florence and went to see its magnificent cathedral. 'Near to the Duomo stands the baptistery, or round church of St. John, where all the children of the town are baptised. The bronze doors of it, three in all, are admirable, especially that which looks towards the Great Church .... These doors are all of brass, historied into figures, containing the remarkable histories of both the Testaments.'

One hundred and fifty years earlier, Michelangelo had stood on the same spot and gazed in wonder at the East Door. He called it the 'Gates of Paradise'.

BAPTISTRY: NORTH DOOR.

EAST DOOR: THE GATES OF PARADISE.

Lorenzo Ghiberti (1378–1447)

The sculptor of both doors was Lorenzo Ghiberti. He was born in 1378, the son of Amona Fiore and Cione di Palago. His father died in 1406 and his mother married her probable lover Bartoluccio di Michele. Bartoluccio became Lorenzo's teacher in goldsmithing and later adopted him as his son.

In 1400 a serious plague affected the city of Florence – it was said that as many as 11,000 died in the hot summer months. Ghiberti fled to safety in Pesaro and received commissions from the Malatesta Duke to work on frescoes for the cathedral walls. However, while he was away a competition was announced in Florence which was to change his life. With the blessing of his patron, he hurriedly returned home. Apart from occasional visits to Siena, Rome and Venice for commissions or to escape the plague, he remained in Florence for the rest of his life, working on just two bronze doors.

BRUNELLESCHI,
THE SACRIFICE OF ISAAC.

GHIBERTI,
THE SACRIFICE OF ISAAC.

The Competition for the East Door, 1400–3

The wardens of the cathedral announced a competition. They wished to have a new bronze door on the Eastern side of the Baptistery of St John, across from the new main door of the newly established cathedral. They decided to devote a year to the competition and invited seven sculptors to take part: two, Ghiberti and Filippo Brunelleschi, later the builder of the cathedral's magnificent dome, were local men, the others were from Tuscany. All competitors were to work on a plaque on the same subject – the sacrifice of Isaac. There were 34 judges and the two best entries were agreed to be those of Ghiberti and Brunelleschi.

The voting of the thirty-four judges appears to have been very close; indeed some commentators suggest that the vote was probably tied. Ghiberti himself was in no doubt in his autobiography, written in 1445.

> This trial demanded considerable knowledge of the sculptor's art. Without a single dissenting voice the experts, as well as my fellow competitors, honoured me by the presentation of the victor's palm... Thirty-four judges, all agreed in testifying to my victory.

Ghiberti's account seems unlikely to be true. It is more probable that he and Brunelleschi were asked to undertake the work together, but that the temperamental Brunelleschi refused and went off to Rome to study architecture.

In 1403, Ghiberti was given the contract. The door he produced, however, eventually became the North door, and in 1406 he was given a second contract to produce an East Door of ten Old Testament plates.

The East Door: The Gates of Paradise

In his autobiography, Ghiberti describes his work on the East Door.

> So I began measuring out the panels which were to illustrate, with a multitude of figures, stories from the Old Testament. I took great pains to observe all the rules of proportion, and, as far as lay in my power, to imitate nature in just relationships and contours. In some stories I introduced nigh a hundred figures, in some less, in others more. Truly I worked with the greatest diligence and love.
>
> There were ten stories altogether and all the architectural settings introduced were in perspective and so true to life that they looked like sculpture in the round... They are carried out in very low relief, and the figures visible on the nearer planes are bigger than those on the distant ones just as they appear in real life.

Indeed, Ghiberti, the perfectionist, devoted the rest of his life to the ten panels. Bronze casts were thrown away, and new casts produced, until the effect was as near perfect as he could manage.

Study some of the panels in detail and read what Ghiberti himself wrote:

In the fourth panel the three angels appear to Abraham...Also in the scene in which he has unrobed Isaac and is about to sacrifice him but for the angel, who, pointing at the ram, stays the hand that holds the knife.

In the Sixth, how Joseph is thrown into the well by his brothers, is sold into bondage and brought before Pharaoh. How he interprets Pharaoh's dream as a prophecy of great famine...Joseph is held in high honour by the Pharaoh. Then there is the scene in which Jacob sends his sons and Joseph, recognising his brothers, informs them that unless they return with their brother Benjamin, they will not receive any grain... Benjamin is brought before Joseph who makes himself known to his brothers.

In the ninth panel David kills Goliath...

Two Opinions about the East Door

The entire work in detail is a striking example of what may be accomplished by the skill and energy of the sculptor-artist in dealing with figures, some in relief, some in half relief, some in bas-relief, in invention and the composition of figures and in the striking attitudes of the women and men, the variety of the buildings and perspectives... Indeed the doors may be said to be perfect in every particular, the finest masterpiece in the world.

From Vasari's *Life of Ghiberti*, written about a hundred years later.

Ghiberti was a very slow worker. It took him years to produce a piece of jewellery or a slab for a tomb... It took him his whole life to produce two doors.

We have not the same patience or the same faith in the value of beautiful things; we cannot wait so long for a single work. We know how short life is and we do not quite believe that art is long. Thus our works spring up as quickly as weeds.

L. Goldscheider, *Ghiberti*, 1949.

1 Do you agree with Vasari's conclusions about the East Door?
2 What does the evidence above suggest about Ghiberti?
3 What does the evidence tell you about life and art in early 15th-century Florence?

A Modern View of Lorenzo Ghiberti

Until about 1412 Ghiberti was the leading artist in Florence... Others became his competitors only after 1412 – Donatello, Masaccio, Nanni and Brunelleschi. Of course, each of these masters had his own answers to the newly posed questions – the nude, the draped figure, movement, space, expressiveness, the encounter with antiquity.

Ghiberti's solutions are as fully Renaissance as anybody's. But he obviously fused both the new tasks and the heritage of classical antiquity with that constant personal note – grace and elegance, balance and moderation, perfection in both technique and detail.

R. Krautheimer, *Lorenzo Ghiberti*, 1970.

Does the evidence in th focus section bear out Branofsky's judgement?

2.1 An 'Uomo Universale', Leonardo da Vinci, 1452–1519

Leonardo was one of the first men in whom the Renaissance expressed itself in a new way, not as a recovery but as a discovery... Leonardo's most profound gifts make him seem modern to us today, five hundred years after he lived.

J. Branofsky in J.H. Plumb, *Pelican Book of the Renaissance*, 1982.

Biographical Sketch

Leonardo was born near Florence in 1452, the illegitimate son of a lawyer, who recognised his talent and apprenticed him at the age of fourteen to Verrocchio, one of Florence's foremost artists. The young Leonardo soon surpassed his master in his eye for perspective and detail. He developed a lifelong fascination with mathematics and mechanics which led to thousands of detailed sketches of the natural and scientific world. Around the age of 30, he left Florence for Milan and the court of Lodovico Sforza. Here he developed his interests and skills still further although the invasion of Milan by the French in 1499 left him wandering from city to city. He spent the last years of his life as the guest of King Francis I in Amboise in France, where he died in 1519.

Leonardo the Civil Engineer

In addition to his plans for bridges, canals and drainage schemes, Leonardo submitted to Lodovico Sforza schemes for improved town planning. Towns, he says in a memo to Lodovico, 'will make beauty and its name inseparable companions. It will be useful to you and the furtherance of your glory'. Leonardo's towns were to contain ten thousand houses each and be built away from the congested areas by the sea or by rivers. He devised schemes for public latrines and sewage removal and by means of a special device in chimneys he thought he would be able to eliminate smoke in the towns. The designs for the towns themselves were astonishingly bold. He imagined two layers, one above the other, with the other level for noble people and a lower town for the common town who worked to serve the nobility above.

Leonardo the Scientist and Inventor

It was in Milan, for Lodovico Sforza, that Leonardo did much of his best and most inventive work. Here he drew maps, made automata for dramatic productions, proposed irrigation schemes and installed central heating.

He invented a rudimentary helicoper and parachute, a lifejacket, an excavator, a swing-bridge and an instrument for measuring wind speed.

Many of his inventions were for military purposes including a cannon, catapult, machine gun and tank. He also recognised the value of an understanding of hydraulics and planned ambitious projects to drain the Pontine Marshes for Pope Leo X in Rome, and to build sophisticated systems of canals with pumps, locks and tunnels to link Florence to the sea. His careful observations are perhaps the feature that has attracted most interest is his desire to understand the mechanics of flight. This led to his precise drawings for the wings of bats and his several flying machines were based also on a careful observation of the flight of birds. His scientific inventions also had an impact on his painting. His careful observation of the penetration through mist of red but not blue, light, led to a greater development of the practical rules governing perspective in painting.

LEONARDO'S DESIGN FOR A GIANT CATAPULT.

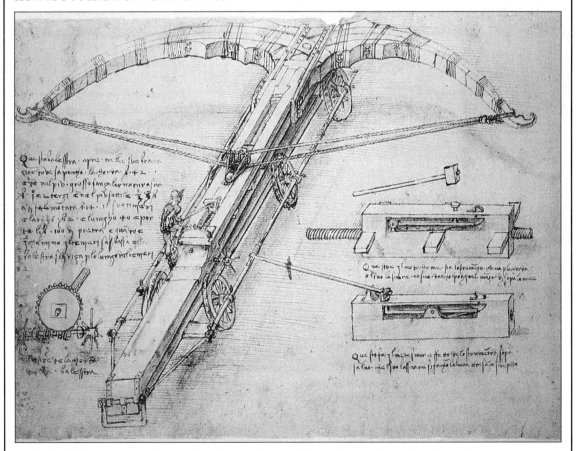

Leonardo the Anatomist

Leonardo was working at an important time in the history of medicine. The vague theories of medieval Europeans were being challenged by the writings of Arab doctors and scientists. Yet still most doctors in Italy believed that the four humours governed all physical and mental functions. In this context Leonardo's desire for accuracy led him to dissect many corpses. Most challenging was his innovative method of ensuring accurate sections through the brain. In using the methods for metal casting he filled the ventricles or cavities of the brain with wax in order to preserve precisely their size and shape after the wax had cooled and hardened.

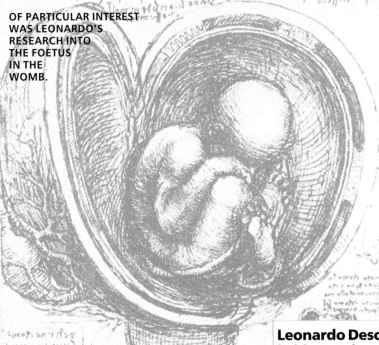

OF PARTICULAR INTEREST WAS LEONARDO'S RESEARCH INTO THE FOETUS IN THE WOMB.

Leonardo was also a botanist. His drawings of the veins of a leaf showed his fascination of the processes needed for life and unlike many of his contemporaries, his paintings emphasised external beauty and form. Leonardo's idea of the perfect body came from an understanding of how muscles in the skeleton were joined to create an inner form. For Leonardo, art and science were clearly essential partners. He used his artistic skills to serve anatomy.

Leonardo Describes his Skill in his Notebooks

The painter who has a knowledge of the nature of the sinews, muscles and tendons will know very well in the movement of a limb how many and which of the sinews are the cause of it, and which muscle by swelling is the cause of the contraction of that sinew; and which sinews expanded into the most delicate cartilage surround and support the said muscle.

Leonardo Describes Dissection in his Notebooks

I have dissected more than ten human bodies, destroying all the various members, and removing even the very smallest particles of the flesh which surrounded these veins without causing any effusion of blood other than the imperceptible bleeding of the capillary veins. And as one single body did not suffice for so long a time, it was necessary to proceed by stages with so many bodies as would render my knowledge complete; and this I repeated twice over in order to discover the differences.

Does the evidence in this focus section bear out Branofsky's judgement?

1 In what ways did Leonardo pursue new ideas and discover new things?

2 What do you learn about Leonardo the man from this evidence?

3 Vasari describes Leonardo on his death bed 'and he protested that he had offended God and mankind by not working at his art as he should have done'. Why then has the twentieth century so admired Leonardo?

4 What is the difference between the 'Uomo Universale' and being a 'Jack of all trades'?

5 Leonardo saw the Renaissance 'not as a recovery but as a discovery'. Write your own summary of Leonardo's importance to the Renaissance.

Vasari in his biography of Leonardo describes *The Last Supper*

Leonardo brilliantly succeeded in envisaging and reproducing the tormented anxiety of the Apostles to know who had betrayed their Master. So in their faces one can read the emotions of love, dismay and anger, or rather sorrow, at their failure to grasp the meaning of Christ. And this excites no less admiration than the contrasted spectacle of the obstinacy, hatred and treachery in the face of Judas, or indeed, in the incredible diligence with which every detail of the work was executed.

Leonardo the Painter

It is regrettable that Leonardo's most famous painting, the *Mona Lisa*, has overshadowed much of his other work. One of his most significant frescoes, now damaged by age and damp, is on the wall of the refectory in the Convent of Sta Maria della Grazia in Milan. *The Last Supper* depicts one of the most significant moments in Christ's life. Leonardo's painting is not simply a recreation of an event. It also reveals depths and layers of meaning through its grouping of the twelve apostles in four threes, around the central serene figure of Christ, already moving beyond the temporal to the spiritual. Here we can see the way that all four humours – choler, phlegm, sanguine and melancholy are represented and at the same time the four interpretations of scripture – literal, allegorical, moral and mystical – can be recognised. Christ's announcement of His betrayal and the interweaving of the institution of the Eucharist provide a challenging scene. The gestures and expressions of the men are those of real people and this is especially so of Judas who is not isolated on the opposite side of the table but is shocked and paralysed at his betrayal. Thus, Leonardo has captured the eternity of a moment in time for those thirteen people.

The Causes and Main Features of the Italian Renaissance

The *quattrocento* in Italy was a period of dramatic and unprecedented cultural change. Painters, sculptors, architects, philosophers, writers and scientists were all developing new ways of examining their world and of depicting the life of man. By the end of the century great artists were respected, even revered, by kings so that early in the following century Leonardo da Vinci could die in the arms of King Francis I of France and the Holy Roman Emperor Charles V could stop to pick up the paintbrush of the Venetian Titian. Michelangelo, after many hours on the scaffold under the ceiling of the Sistine Chapel and irritated by the pope's impatience for the work to be completed, could raise his voice to Pope Julius himself.

The causes of such rapid and dramatic change are always difficult to understand and explain. Certainly the history of the peninsula had something to do with it. The Roman Empire had created a city life which barbarian invasions could not remove. Medieval feudal society, strongly established in the rural and agricultural communities north of the Alps, was never as strong in Italy. Throughout the Middle Ages, while crusading armies passed back and forth, Italian cities were always involved in trade s trade with the east and trade north of the alps. Traders became bankers and financiers and Italian merchants opened branches of their banks in the major cities of Europe. At the cross-roads of Europe, new ideas flourished: artistic ideas from Flanders were swapped for the medical, scientific and mathematical knowledge of the Arabs. In addition, the original writings of Latin and Greek authors were discovered and the writings of Aristotle became well known in the thirteenth century. The late Medieval Ages was also a period of violence: *Condottieri* captains, often hired to protect a city, eventually took it under their wing and established their rule. Their tyranny was often beneficial and the cultural patronage of tyrannical dukes like the Montefeltro in the city of Urbino, the Gonzaga in Mantua, and the Sforza in Milan provided a clear lead for the rivalry of other cities in the *quattrocento*.

Perhaps it was the rediscovery of, and respect for, classical scholarship that most highlighted the dramatic changes of the 15th century. Early enthusiasts like Petrarch saw themselves overturning centuries of error in badly translated texts, and returning to pure, original and elegant Latin. Classical literature was seen as the basis of a civilised life. Very significant was the rediscovery of Greek. Aristotle's philosophy and Euclid's mathematics had never really been lost and the fall of Constantinople in 1453 probably stimulated the learning of Greek through the arrival in Italy of a number of Greek scholars. This prompted work on the translation of the philosophical and political works of Plato, the fifth century BC Athenian scholar who made the greatest contribution to Greek thinking. Plato's idealistic emphasis on the idea of the good prompted the development of symbolism in 15th-century Italian culture. This is perhaps most clearly seen in the great paintings by Botticelli but also in the poetry of another member of the Platonic Academy, Poliziano. He celebrated Platonic love, not as is often thought today merely a love without sexual expression, but rather a vision of love transcending the physical to attain a pure and spiritual union. The writings of Plato also made a significant contri-

Plato saw reality in ideal forms. This 'idealist' philosophy has influenced thinkers for over two thousand years.

bution to the development of Italian theology. Pico della Mirandola was remarkable in his expression of the idea of the soul as 'the immortal essence of man'. The gift of God was the gift of freedom for man spiritually to ascend or descend according to his choices and judgements.

This search for truths led to an increasing interest in manuscripts, libraries and bookshops. The dramatic discovery of ancient manuscripts in medieval monasteries like Bobbio and St Gall in Switzerland were of considerable value. New Roman and Greek authors were discovered and translated. The Medici sent ambassadors like John Lascaris to the east who brought back over 200 manuscripts for their library. And patrons in Rome, like Pope Nicholas V, 'addicted to books', saw an increase in Greek books, for example the 33 per cent increase in Nicholas V's Vatican library in 1455. The parallel revival of Hebrew, also at the Court of Pope Nicholas V, and through the interests of Pico della Mirandola in Florence, resulted in more advanced biblical scholarship and led to the early 16th-century translations of The Bible into the vernacular.

All of these developments were of course aided by the technological advances in printing. By the year 1500, there were 73 printing presses in Italy and the press of Aldus Minutius in Venice had published most of the major Greek classics by this date. One scholar in Florence could write in a letter to a friend:

> going lately into one of the public offices in the city, I found a number of young clerks neglecting their business and lost in the study of a book which had been distributed to them in sheets. When I asked what new book had appeared, they answered *Politian's Miscellanies*. I mounted their desks, sat down among them and began to read with equal eagerness. Then I sent at once to the booksellers stall for a copy of the work.

Perhaps the greatest creative force came from the alliance of humanist artists and aristocratic patrons. The growth of the Renaissance court became the most formative influence on cultural development and was quickly copied north of the Alps. Patron and artists shared a common language and could discuss the main themes of the movement such as the dignity of man and his creative potential.

In Florence, it has been cogently argued that humanists identified with the Republic and this resulted in a significant increase in the social status of the artist and also in his willingness to paint, design and build in order to glorify the Republic. Alfred von Martin wrote in his book *The Sociology of the Renaissance* that, 'the centre of gravity of medieval society was the land, was the soil. With the Renaissance, the economic and thus the social emphasis moves into the town; from the conservative to the liberal, for the town is a changeable and changing element'.

In the 1490s, the centre of attention moved from Medici patronage in Florence to the patronage of the Borgia popes in Rome. Alexander VI furthered the work on several Roman churches and constructed the Borgia apartments at the Vatican. His successor, Julius II, began the building of the new Basilica of St Peter and, of course, Michelangelo was commissioned to paint the ceiling of the Sistine Chapel. Perhaps it was the rebuilding of Rome as the great centre of Christendom that was the greatest achievement of the Renaissance popes.

The *quattrocento* in Italy thus saw the emergence of a set of new values. If the Middle Ages had idealised poverty, the Renaissance idealised wealth and put it to creative use. If the Middle Ages had idealised the ancient lineage of nobility, the Italian Renaissance idealised an intellectual elite capable of demonstrating the perfectibility of man. If the Middle Ages had idealised religion, the quattrocento put high value on the pursuit of power and the use of power to benefit mankind. It is clear that the influence of 15th century Italy on the whole of 16th century Europe was immense.

REVIEW

The Main Masters of the Italian Renaissance

From this chapter and your own reading, complete the following box for the most important Renaissance masters.

Artist	Dates	Main Works	Themes

Now suggest which of the themes in the last column would be likely to influence 16th-century Europe.

3 Christian Humanism and the Northern Renaissance

The Nature of Renaissance Europe

No slice of historical time is self contained. But what has usefully come to be referred to as the 'long' 16th Century does have a coherence of its own. It was the first age in which the words 'Europe' and 'European' acquired a widely understood significance. It saw the emergence of a new and pervasive attitude to what were considered the most valued aspects of civilised life. It witnessed the most concentrated wave of intellectual and creative energy that had yet passed over the continent, with the culture of Renaissance Italy reaching its apogee and being absorbed or rebuffed by other vigorously developing national cultures. It was a period in which there were such dramatic changes of fortune for better or worse that more people than ever before saw their time as unique, referring to 'this new age', 'the present age', 'our age; to one observer it was 'a blessed age', to another 'the worst age in history'.

J.R. Hale, *The Civilisation of Europe in the Renaissance*, 1993.

TALKING POINT

Do all people see their own age as unique? Does this give a special meaning to the work of the Historian in that he or she can relate the experience of the past to the present?

1 What is the argument expressed in the above paragraph?
2 What, according to Hale, gives the 16th century its coherence?

1 Identify the trends in this passage.
2 What would be the likely consequences of these trends?

The medieval view of European society had been that it constituted a stratified Christian cooperative. According to its moral of the Three Estates, the masses of the Third laboured for the Second Estate of warrior leaders who protected them, and for the clerical members of the First, who prayed on behalf of both. From the 14th Century this simple model had come under strain. Knights had become Estate Managers as well as warriors. Members of the Third Estate had become ever more widely differentiated in status and activity. From the mid 15th Century the pace of challenge to the model increased, the proportion of well off and socially inconspicuous commoners grew with commercial prosperity, the enhanced status of the legal and medical professions and the extending bureaucratic reach of central and municipal governments. The clerical Estate became less clearly defined, in perception if not in function, by the Reformation, by the suppression of monastic prayer houses and the loss of the clergy's quasi-monopoly of learning. The image of the Second Estate became further blurred by marriages between blood and wealth, reliance on court service and a form of education akin to that of the non-noble. In the 16th century there were complaints about the English knights who could not ride, Spanish Hidalgos who could not shoot, Italian Conti whose swords only left their scabbards in personal quarrels. It was not that aristocrats felt less conscious of their birth, or that commoners withheld deference from their rank, but that the estate to which they belonged had lost something of its separate clarity.

J.R. Hale, *The Civilisation of Europe in the Renaissance*, 1993.

The Roman Catholic Church and Christendom in the late 15th Century

In the late Middle Ages, the Roman Catholic church reached every corner of Europe and touched the life of every man and woman. Its organisation was powerful, from the pope down to the most humble parish priest. Its personnel formed a coherent group through the Ceremony of Ordination and the laying on of hands on priests. The law of the church operated everywhere and its landed wealth, acquired through centuries of gifts, was legendary.

The Renaissance popes regarded themselves as the successors of St Peter, but, more importantly, they were also secular Italian princes. Popes like Alexander VI and his son Cesare Borgia were primarily concerned to enlarge and enrich Papal land holding in central Italy.

Bishops too were more feudal overlords than church leaders. Chosen from the upper nobility, often for political reasons, they formed some of the most significant power blocks in Europe. Similarly, ordinary parish priests suffered the same problems of ignorance, political irregularity, and often immorality.

The extent of the priestly population at this time was quite striking. The German city of Cologne had a population of 40,000, of whom more than 6000 were priests. Similarly, Hamburg had a population of 12,000 and 450 were priests.

The major concern of the Roman church at the end of the 15th century was money. And the evils of simony, nepotism, pluralism and absenteeism all involved cash. For example, a newly appointed bishop had to surrender his first year's income to the pope – a procedure known as the 'Payment of Annates'. If there was a vacancy for a new bishop, and this continued for some time, the income from the bishopric also reverted to the pope. Large sums of money were involved: from Liege in Belgium for example, 7200 gulden were forthcoming, and from Salzburg in Austria 1000 gulden. In addition, a newly appointed archbishop paid the pope 10,000 gulden for his *pallium* – the piece of ermine fur which was placed as a cloak around his neck.

These were large sums of money and the burden usually fell on the ordinary people of the parish or see. As a consequence, the Roman church charged its members for all services – for marriages, baptisms, confessions and burials. The cost of a court case in a church court was excessive and appeals against legal decisions were passed all the way up to Rome, often at great expense. The worst abuse surrounded the sale of indulgences a this caused particular offence and financial difficulty in the Holy Roman Empire and the Low Countries. Sins were forgiven at a price, and the money ended up in Rome.

There is significant evidence that the ordinary people of the parish were deeply involved in religious life in the late 15th century. No longer did they support large monasteries or build great cathedrals. Instead, they gave their support to their local parish church or chantry priest or local brotherhood. In exchange for prayers, often for the souls of dead relatives, they gave what little they had. In every village in Europe, there were local indicators of piety – roadside altars, memorial windows, and statues of saints, as well as new hospitals, colleges and universities. Pilgrimages to new shrines were common and collections of holy relics were also widespread.

AT THE SAME TIME, LITERACY LEVELS AMONG THE LAITY WERE INCREASING. MANY NEW MUNICIPAL SCHOOLS WERE BEING FOUNDED AND PAID FOR, OFTEN BY CITY COUNCILS. NEW UNIVERSITIES WERE FOUNDED: BY 1500, THERE WERE 79 UNIVERSITIES IN EUROPE AND, FOR EXAMPLE, NEW COLLEGES WERE ADDED AT THE UNIVERSITIES OF OXFORD AND CAMBRIDGE. ALL OF THIS ACTIVITY ENCOURAGED A NEW MYSTICAL PIETY.

The Brethren of the Common Life, a monastic group based in Deventer in the Netherlands, were typical in in founding a school as well as focusing on the mystic faith of ordinary people. There was a new art form in Europe, the Pieta. This was a sculptured image of Christ taken from the Cross and held in the arms of His Mother Mary. It encouraged a new simplistic focus on the figure of Christ.

It was not surprising then that heresy and criticism of the church was widespread during the late Middle Ages. The Lollards in England, the Waldensians in southern France and northern Italy, the Hussites in Bohemia and the eastern part of the Empire, were typical of many who concerned themselves particularly with the weaknesses of Catholic priests.

Criticisms of popes were also widespread. Not only was their lifestyle largely secular, but more importantly they were seen as denying their original foundation. The legend continued that St Peter had travelled from Jerusalem to Rome after the Crucifixion of Christ. It was to Peter that Christ said 'you are Peter and upon this rock will I build my Church'. Legend persisted that Peter was buried in the catacombs of Rome and subsequent bishops of Rome claimed their right to be Peter's successors. These twin thrusts of the Petrine Commission and the Apostolic Succession gave the bishops of Rome much popular power. Throughout the Middle Ages, they augmented this power by claiming the rights to crown and enthrone Emperors, as the pope had done to Charlemagne in the splendid ceremony on Christmas Day in 800 in Rome. Yet this only increased the criticism of the Papacy following the Great Schism and the Avignon Schism. Now two rival popes – and sometimes three – competed for the Primacy, which much reduced their credibility. In addition, the strong thrust in the later Middle Ages for a Council of the Church further weakened Papal overlordship. Through the conciliar movement, many bishops argued that a Council of Bishops had more right to decide policy than one bishop of Rome. In the 14th and 15th centuries, Church Councils at Basle and Constance not only condemned heretics like John Huss, but also claimed to legislate for the church. This was a time when Papal leadership was in significant doubt.

JOHN HUSS.

The Context of Popular Religion

Historians have been struck in this period by a singular ferment within Christianity, the heightened religious sensibilities, the almost obsessive pre-occupation with death, salvation, and the future of man.

There were good reasons why this should have occurred. Times were bad, beyond anything which men could recall. Several factors built up a momentum which took on catastrophic proportions. The last decades of the 15th century were years of price fluctuation caused by bad harvests; the year 1500 saw a total crop failure in all of Germany. The peasants reacted with violence. In Alsace they founded a conspiratorial organisation to overthrow the existing order, but everywhere in the Empire looting and pillaging took on such proportions that by 1501 a paid police force became a necessity for the first time.

Rising prices and bad harvests were accompanied by the ravages of war. The wars of rival factions in Switzerland in 1499 affected not only this region but also Swabia and the Tyrol. Whole villages were depopulated and the bonds of the old and settled order were utterly destroyed. Through all this these scourges which descended upon man were less important than the inroads made by epidemics. The plague, and a new disease, syphilis, seemed to herald a coming change in the order of things, that great catastrophe which precedes the total reformation of man and society about which medieval prophecy had spoken so eloquently...

Such is the background to the heightened religious sensibility at the turn of the century which gripped all the diverse classes of the population. Men believed there must be some sense to this chaos and they found it by turning to various sources of inspiration in order to overcome the unpalatable present.

Koenigsburger, Mosse and Bowler, *Europe in the 16th Century*, 1989.

1 In what ways did the Roman church influence the lives of all men and women in Europe in 1500? Was it possible not to be a Christian?

2 List the criticisms which were made of the church.

The hopes and understanding of ordinary men and women were often simple. They looked to the church for blessings: Holy Water, exorcisms and charms could ward off fire, disease and death. They regularly petitioned the saints – a woman in labour, for example, would call on St Margaret for help. Local groups had their local saints and processions on the appropriate saint's day were an important feature of local community life. Baptisms, weddings and funerals were all religious ceremonies and important rites of passage. Feasting, dancing and singing were common.

Men and women also sought a better future. Prophecy and astrology could always be called upon to help. A typical written account was that of Lichtenberger in his prognostications in 1488. In the short term, he forecast wars, rebellions and plagues – this would be followed, he claimed, by a phase of universal peace. Men and women saw the early 16th century as a period of transition, but it was actually an age which had a clear coherence.

EXAMINING THE EVIDENCE

Renaissance Popes

The Historian acts like a detective working on a particularly difficult case. The witnesses are long since dead, the evidence is lost or concealed. The Historian, however, has the exciting task of piecing together the fragments of the story to make as complete a picture as he can.

The Historian will meet with evidence in three forms:
- Fact.
- Opinion.
- Speculation.

All of these will be acquired and assimilated to help him form:
- Judgement.

Thus, the Historian becomes a skilful and independent challenger of History.

Many questions immediately arise:

- Where will we find our facts? Do they come from primary sources or secondary sources? For example, do artists or cartoonists inevitably create drawings with a strong element of personal bias? How can we trust our facts? Are secondary sources inevitably less reliable than primary sources?
- As we consider the sources we begin to form our opinions. How can we remain objective as we do this? Should we retain some subjectivity if we are to be independent challengers of other peoples' history?
- Sometimes the evidence is very limited indeed. Often then we need to speculate or guess. 'There's no smoke without fire'. Alternatively, we 'wonder if ...'. Often we have almost nothing to go on and speculation is the only way forward.

Given all these forms of evidence, we must form a considered judgement of our own. The evidence will often be conflicting, sometimes heavily weighted in one direction or another. Yet our own conclusions are the stuff of History and enable us to challenge the conclusions of others.

Read carefully through the evidence below on the Renaissance Papacy and then test yourself on your skill as a detective or a Historian.

1 List several facts of which you can be certain and at the side of each briefly explain why the fact can be trusted.

   Fact   **Reason for Accepting it as True**

2 Take each extract in turn and identify the opinion of the author about a pope or popes. What do all these opinions have in common which means that they cannot be regarded as facts?

3 The two questions above will have led you to begin to think and wonder what is and isn't true, what to accept and what to reject. You will also be wondering about the evidence for particular opinions. 'There's no smoke without fire'. For example, in source F below, we read of Pope Alexander VI's Reform Bull of 1497. Cardinals were 'not to employ boys or young men as body servants'. We may speculate about why this was included.

   Now find at least two other examples of where we may reasonably speculate about the lifestyle of the Renaissance popes and quote the source of your speculation.

4 Now we must form a reasoned and sensible judgement about Renaissance popes. What makes it difficult for us to do this? What would your judgement be?

Source A

In general, and leaving aside accusations of personal immorality, none of which – once they had assumed office – can be proved, Popes were criticised for excessive pomp, political militancy, manipulation of the college of cardinals, the sale of offices, and nepotism. The triple nature of the Papacy (its spiritual leadership, its sovereign role as a political entity, the states of the Church, and its governorship of a financial empire) were thrown into high relief by the almost constant threat of diplomatic pressure or actual war.

J.R. Hale, *Renaissance Europe*, 1971.

Source B

At last a sincere and well meaning man, Pius III, was raised to the Papal throne; but his untimely death frustrated his plans.

P. Janelle, *The Catholic Reformation*, 1971.

Source C

The Popes of this period were worldly men, unattractively self indulgent, and harmful to the reputation of the church... Alexander VI kept a mistress for whom he found a convenient cuckold for the sake of appearances, countenanced murder for his own ends and patronised sexual orgies at the Curia. Julius II lost all sense of justice and humanity when it came to the reconquest of the Papal temporalities.

P. Laven, *Renaissance Italy*, 1966.

Source D

The Lateran Council first met on 2 May 1512... In his sermon at the opening of the first session, Giles of Viterbo advised the Church to give up the use of material weapons and to confine herself to that of spiritual weapons, piety and prayer, the cuvass of faith and the sword of light... On 17 May, Thomas Cajetan further stressed the necessity of Papal authority and the submission of members to their Head, the Vicar of Christ... No voice among the assembled fathers was raised to assail his views.

P. Janelle, *The Catholic Reformation*, 1971.

Source E

These Popes in fact carried out a great deal of work of consequence. Bulls of Sixtus IV and Alexander VI defined the spheres of influence of the new colonial powers, Portugal and Castile... Julius II assembled and Leo X continued the Fifth Lateran Council... A Bull against simony was published by Julius II in 1505... And one particular achievement stands out: their success in establishing the primacy of the Papacy over rival aspirants to power within the framework of the Roman Church.

P. Laven, *Renaissance Italy*, 1966.

Source F

They needed money to raise armies and play the diplomatic game from a position of strength. They needed loyal lieutenants and Popes found it harder to secure them than did other Princes. They needed to behave like other territorial rulers and their growing ability to do so, threw the secular aspect of their papal role into higher relief. Even so the multiple role was familiar to influential visitors, diplomats and churchmen, from the similar roles played by leading clerics in their own countries. Popes were criticised for particular policies, seldom for acting as politicians. Hearing of the death of Alexander VI in 1503, a Florentine merchant passed on the news to an associate abroad with no reference to Alexander's moral or spiritual qualities. He simply prayed that 'with the help of God' a Pope would be elected capable of keeping order in Central Italy, for 'business in all regions in this section is in such a state that it must be stimulated'.

Frequently appointed young, and coming from Palace rather than Parish, it's possible that a majority of cardinals had never heard a confession or addressed a congregation. Some flavour of their manner of life was given by an abortive Reform Bull of Alexander VI in 1497.

Cardinals were not to take part in tournaments or carnivals, or go to secular plays, their households were not to number more than eighty of whom at least twelve should be in Holy Orders, they were not to keep more than thirty horses and they were not to employ boys or young men as body servants.

J.R. Hale, *Renaissance Europe 1480–1520*, 1971.

Examining the Evidence

The Importance of Printing

We should note the force, effect, and consequences of inventions which are nowhere more conspicuous than in those three which were unknown to the ancients, namely, printing, gunpowder, and the compass. For these three have changed the appearance and state of the whole world.

Francis Bacon.

How important was the invention of movable type printing by Gutenberg in Mainz in 1453? Did printing facilitate the dramatic spread of new and challenging ideas at the turn of the century? What sort of books were published and how many people were able to read them? Where were the printing presses situated and who controlled the production?

These are controversial questions which indicate clearly that it is not as simple as Francis Bacon made out.

JOHANN GUTENBERG READING PROOFS WHILE HIS ASSISTANT WORKS THE PRINTING PRESS.

Source A

In 1483 the Ripoli Press in Florence charged three florins per quinterno for setting up and printing Ficino's translation of Plato's dialogues. A scribe might have charged one florin per quinterno for duplicating the same work. The Ripoli Press produced one thousand and twenty five copies; the scribe would have turned out one.

E. Eisenstein, *The Printing Press as an Agent of Change*, 1979.

Source B

Contemporary evidence must be handled with caution, for it often yields false clues to the numbers of books involved. Since it was customary to register many texts bound within one set of covers as one book the actual number of texts in a given manuscript collection is not easily ascertained. The objects counted as one book often contained a varying combination of many.

E. Eisenstein, *The Printing Press as an Agent of Change*, 1979.

Source C

The invention of printing included a number of innovations: movable metal type, oil based ink, wooden hand presses. In addition footnotes, tables of contents, cross-referencing and other devices all made printing more complex. Initially hand-copied work and printed work seemed very similar as these two extracts from the printing of the Bible in Mainz showed.

DEFINING THE INITIAL SHIFT

The visual image has always had a more powerful impact than the written word. Why would this be particularly so in early 16th century Europe? Can you find examples of where it is so today?

Source D
The printer's workshop.

Source E

The printed book could be said to have 'arrived' between 1500 and 1510. Little by little, it displaced the manuscript in library collections, relegating it to second place, and by 1550 the latter was hardly used, except by scholars for special purposes.

A revolution like this is explicable only if we recall the high, and constantly mounting, output of the first presses. As we have seen, the 30,000–35,000 different editions printed before 1500 that have survived represent 15–20 million copies. But there were still more in the 16th century. It is sufficient for our purposes to recall some figures we have previously encountered. In Paris more than 25,000 editions were published in the 16th century; in Lyons, probably 13,000; in Germany about 45,000; in Venice 15,000; in the Low Countries more than 4,200 in the first half of the century; in England, 26,000 in English alone before 1640, of which about 10,000 were of the 16th century. We can deduce from these figures that some 150,000–200,000 different editions could be shown to have been printed between 1500 and 1600. If we assume, for convenience, 1,000 as an average edition, then between 150–200 million copies were published in the 16th century. This is a conservative estimate and probably well below the actual figure. Of course, it does not compare with today's output, when in France alone about 15,000 different editions are legally deposited each year, each generally in an edition of between 5,000 and 10,000 copies, not counting pamphlets and periodicals, some of which are printed in editions of 500,000.

L. Febvre, *The Book as a Force For Change*, 1984.

TALKING POINT
Why would the spread of printed material be viewed with concern by authorities such as governments and churches?

Source F

Who were the reading public?

F.1   First some information about the reading public. It is not surprising if a number of those wanting to start their own private libraries grew in the course of the 16th century and if the number of books in these private libraries also rose steadily. Of 377 private libraries in the late 15th and 16th centuries, of which we have catalogues, 105 belonged to churchmen, and a rather larger number (126) were owned by lawyers.

Certainly in the 16th century members of the legal profession were an important group among booksellers' customers but they, together with a few merchants or artisans, were not the only people who bought books. There was always the trade in popular literature. Calendars, lives of the saints, almanacs and Books of Hours sold in larger numbers to a much wider public.

F.2   Printed propaganda was addressed to the entire German people, but few of them were able to read it, for the Reformation emerged in a society with limited literacy. It is not possible to measure literacy in early 16th century Germany with any accuracy but it was certainly restricted both geographically and socially. It was more concentrated in towns and in the more culturally advanced south west. The presence of schools is only a crude indicator but in Wurttemberg there were as many as 89 schools by the 1520's and at least half of the towns boasted a school. By contrast there were no more than a handful of schools in Saxony by the late 1520's, all of them urban.

R.W. Scribner, *For the Sake of Simple Folk*, 1994.

TALKING POINT
The early 16th century was a dramatic age of invention and discovery. Many of these challenged peoples' assumptions.
The late 20th century has also been an age of rapid change. Compile a list of similarities *and* differences between the two periods.

Source G

What sort of books were printed?

More than 50 per cent of all books printed in Strasbourg in the 15th century were religious while fewer than 10 per cent were by classical authors. From 1500 to 1520, 33 per cent were either Latin or Greek texts or works by contemporary humanists and only 27 per cent were connected with religion. The following table shows an analogous evolution in Paris, although one slower to take effect:

Year	Total Production	Religious Works	Latin, Greek & Humanist authors
1501	88	53	25
1515	198	105	57
1525	116	56	37
1528	269	93	134
1549	332	56	204

Source H

Even though block print and letter press may have originated as separate innovations and were initially used for diverse purposes (so that playing cards and saints' images for example were being stamped from blocks at the same time that hand illumination continued to decorate many early printed books), the two techniques soon became intertwined. The use of typography for texts led to that of xylography for illustration, sealing the fate of illuminator along with that of scribe. When considering how technical literature was affected by the shift from script to print it seems reasonable to adopt the strategy of envisaging a 'double invention: typography for the text, engraving for the images'. The fact that letter, numbers and pictures were all alike subject to repeatability by the end of the 15th century needs more emphasis. That the printed book made possible new forms of interplay between these diverse elements is perhaps even more significant than the change undergone by picture, number or letter alone.

E. Eisenstein, *The Printing Press as an Agent of Change*, 1979.

Source I

There was a danger of being beguiled by the very skill of Reformation propaganda into accepting its own claims at face value. The role played by printing is undeniable, but overconcentration on the printed word may seriously distort our understanding of how Reformation ideas spread among the population at large.

Even for those who could read, the popular broadsheet made propaganda more persuasive and entertaining. We have an excellent example of the process described in a 1524 pamphlet 'a dialogue between a Christian and a Jew'. A Jew and Evangelical Christian fell into conversation at an Inn and the Jew produces a woodcut he has picked up on this travels. The Christian uses the woodcut to explain to the Jew the main points of Evangelical belief as the woodcut depicts them. When they part the inn servant, who has listened to them with interest, promises to set their conversation down in print along with the woodcut. The case shows the ideal balance of oral, visual and printed means of communication as it is found during the Reformation.

Whether the discussion is fictitious or not is of little relevance; more importantly, the author of the 1524 pamphlet wished to show the Reformation ideas were spread effectively by the spoken word, aided by the use of pictures.

R.W. Scribner, *For the Sake of Simple Folk*, 1994.

Source J

> But the point is that by the 16th century the printed book had been produced in sufficient quantities to make it accessible to anyone who could read. It played a central role in the diffusion of a knowledge of classical literature at the beginning of the century and later in the propagation of Reformation doctrines; it helped to fix the vernacular languages, and encouraged the development of national literatures.
>
> L. Febvre, *The Book as a Force For Change*, 1984.

Source K

> The third way in which ideas and attitudes came from Italy was in print: I say in print because I wish to include engraved pictures whose influence on northern artists was obviously great – though I believe we do not yet know enough about it properly to evaluate it. As for the printed book, this was Germany's contribution to the Renaissance.
>
> Printing as such is, however, beside the point: the books printed were in the north what the north had long read – the old romances, the Bible, the Service and the school books. But granted a public for the new Italian values these could spread quickly by the new media. This is very clearly seen in the field of learned works where the Italian printers early established their leadership: Aldus Manutius of Venice is the great example of this. It was Aldus who first used italic type in 1501, thus giving wide diffusion to the humanist hand, examples of which were of course to be found entering northern Europe as soon as it was used in books and dispatches... The Italians had theorists at work who were particularly adapted to instruct the northern world in the Renaissance attitude to politics... The book I am thinking of is Castiglione's *The Courtier* drafted in 1508 and printed in 1528.
>
> D. Hay, *The Italian Renaissance*, 1977.

1 Which extract suggests that the printing press was a revolutionary agent of change? Which extracts have reservations?
2 What are the arguments expressed in sources I and J?
3 Use all the evidence to compile a report on the contribution of printing to the spread of Renaissance ideas.
4 In many revolutions in History, new technology has played a major part. Consider the importance of printing as you read about the major changes in 16th-century Europe.

The Main Features of Northern Humanism

Painting

From around 1400 men and women acquire a three-dimensionality of body and an instantly decipherable play of facial expression that makes them appear different in kind from their flatter, more passive medieval forbears. They stand in groups as though they can move in a moment into a different relationship with one another...

J.R. Hale, *The Civilisation of Europe in the Renaissance*, 1993.

VAN EYCK'S PAINTING *THE BETROTHAL OF THE ARNOLFINI* (1434) IS A 15TH-CENTURY MASTERPIECE, NOW IN THE NATIONAL GALLERY IN LONDON. THE PICTURE SHOWS A YOUNG ITALIAN BUSINESSMAN IN BRUGES PLEDGING HIS FUTURE TO HIS WIFE-TO-BE. THE WONDER OF THE PICTURE IS PARTLY CONTAINED IN THE MIRROR ON THE BACK WALL WHICH REFLECTS OTHER PERSONALITIES WHO WERE IN THE ROOM. EVEN THE SMALLEST DETAILS ARE CAREFULLY DEPICTED – LIKE THE APPLES ON THE CHEST.

ALBRECHT DURER, *PORTRAIT OF THE ARTIST'S FATHER*.

THE DOYEN OF NORTHERN PAINTERS WAS ALBRECHT DURER (1471–1528). HE, TOGETHER WITH HIS FOLLOWER LUCAS CRANACH, WAS THE LEADER OF A GERMAN SCHOOL OF PAINTING THAT FLOURISHED IN THE 1520S AND 1530S AND THEN FADED AWAY. DURER'S WOODCUTS, ETCHINGS, WATERCOLOURS AND OIL PAINTINGS WERE A MAJOR FORCE IN THE SPREAD OF LUTHERAN IDEAS IN GERMANY. HE VISITED VENICE AND THE NETHERLANDS IN THE EARLY PART OF THE 16TH CENTURY AND ABSORBED MANY ITALIAN AND DUTCH IDEAS. BECAUSE OF HIS LUTHERAN FAITH, HE FOCUSED HIS PAINTING ON RELIGIOUS SUBJECTS SUCH AS APOSTLES AND THE PASSION OF CHRIST.

Christ's lash spotted body has the yellowish green of decay. Though the mouth gapes in an exhaustion beyond recovery, the fingers twist upwards from the sagging crossbar to which His hands are nailed and blood glistens at the tips of His clubbed and clawlike feet. And the pointing finger of the Baptist, himself resurrected by the artist from his execution by Herod, consults the book of the future and from it declares in the inscription beside him 'He must increase'. Neither in colour nor in its treatment of historical time any more than in its scale could such a work have occurred to an Italian.

J.R. Hale, *The Civilisation of Europe in the Renaissance*, 1993.

IN GERMANY IT WAS ALMOST A CENTURY LATER THAT MATHIS NITHARDT PAINTED THE ISENHEIM ALTARPIECE, YET ITS POIGNANT AND DRAMATIC DEVELOPMENT OF THE AGONY OF CHRIST ON THE CROSS WAS A PAINTING BEYOND INFLUENCE.

Music

Like painting, northern music had its origins in the Netherlands. At the very end of the 15th century, two composers, Jean D'Okegem and Jacob Obrecht, were beginning to develop new musical ideas. Polyphony and the use of the voice in music were carried forward by Adrian Willaert. This Flemish musician directed the choir at St Mark's Cathedral in Venice, showing the way in which artistic ideas could travel from north to south as well as from south to north.

However, perhaps it was the religious reformers of the early 16th century who did most to bring music to the people. Martin Luther himself used music in his services. His first hymnal was published in 1524, composing many of his own hymns – such as 'A mighty fortress is our God'. John Calvin also gave prominence to the use of music in religious services. While Luther used German folk tunes for his hymns, Calvin adapted French 'chansons' to his metric psalms.

Christian Humanist Theology

The father of German humanists was Rudolf Agricola (1443–85). Agricola was educated in Groningen in the Netherlands by the Brethren of the Common Life. He studied in the Rhineland and then spent ten years in Italy, devoting himself to the study of the classics. He concerned himself with humanist education, writing a famous textbook on logic and urging the importance of grammar and rhetoric in public life. He wrote a compendium of ancient history and was learning Hebrew when he died.

Another pupil of the Brethren of the Common Life was Conrad Mutianus (1471–1526). Mutianus also travelled widely in Italy and, on his return to the Netherlands, studied Plato and St Paul's Epistles.

Perhaps the best known of the German Reformers was Ulrich von Hutten (1488–1523). Hutten was concerned with the reform of Christianity and the improvement of priests. He supported educational reform and emphasised the importance of Greek and Hebrew studies. He also took an interest in the major debates of the day and in 1515 he joined the debate between liberals and reactionaries over humanist reform.

The most significant French contemporary of Ulrich von Hutten was Lefevre D'Etaples (1455–1536). Lefevre was in Italy from 1492 to 1507, and returned to become librarian of the monastery in St Germain-des-Pres. Like his German contemporaries, he pursued the rebirth of Christianity through his study of scripture and his interest in the classics and philosophy. He encouraged the examination of manuscripts and historical scholarship. In 1512, he translated the Epistles of St Paul and urged scholars to translate the Bible from the original Greek and Hebrew.

For a discussion of the Catholic and Lutheran cycles of salvation, see Chapter 4.

Indeed it was Lefevre who anticipated Luther's writings on justification by faith when he redefined the Greek word 'metanoeite'. This he translated as 'repent' instead of 'do penance' – a change of definition which had major implications for the Roman Catholic cycle of salvation. Lefevre was condemned as a heretic by the Sorbonne, the University of Paris, and he withdrew to Meaux where he and his followers remained under the protection of the king's sister.

Education

The humanists of northern Europe enthusiastically sponsored educational development. Their reform programme espoused universal compulsory education, teaching as a divine vocation, and the importance of the humanist curriculum. Throughout Europe, schools and colleges were sponsored, many of them taking as their example the Brethren of the Common Life in the Netherlands. Perhaps most notably, in England John Colet founded St Paul's School in the late 15th century and Humphrey, Duke of Gloucester, was the patron of the Bodleian Library and a number of Oxford colleges.

TALKING POINT
should education be compulsory? Is education an entitlement of all people? Was a different kind of education more appropriate in the 16th century? Is there an absolute ideal for education?

Classical scholarship was at the heart of all this work and the study of Greek and Hebrew enabled scholars to research and translate the Bible without recourse to the copying errors of the Latin Vulgate. Only in the original could scholars really study classical philosophy and literature and historians were keen to question and challenge their texts.

Learning was beginning to take on a new meaning and the educational programme of the Northern reformers began to break the arid rigidity of the medieval scholastics.

Erasmus and his Influence on Europe

DESIDERIUS ERASMUS (1466–1536).

Erasmus' Life and Career	
c1466–9	Brethren of Common Life at Deventer in Holland.
1486	Entered Augustinian Monastery at Steyn after both his parents died of plague.
1492	Ordained as a priest.
1495	Student at Paris. Montague College (where Calvin and Loyola also studied in later years).
1500	Publication of 'Adages', a collection of proverbs in Greek and Latin.
1500	Study in Paris and then England.
1504	Publication of the 'Handbook of the Christian Soldier' or 'Enchiridion' – 'an inward religion of the heart'.
1506	'In Praise of Folly', a satire on the stupidity of Men and Women.
1509–15	Study in Cambridge, Professor of Greek and Theology.
1516	Publication of Greek version of New Testament. Erasmus in Brussels, released by pope from all obligations towards his religious orders.
1518	'Julius Exclusus'.
1521–7	Lived at the house of the publisher Froben in Basle. Edited writings of Early Church Fathers.

Erasmus was the greatest literary figure of his age. He was the personal friend of most Northern humanists, travelling widely from one European university to another and studied extensively in Paris, Cambridge, Louvain and Basle. Much of his influence came from the clarity and beauty of his style: 'We kiss the shoes of the saints and their dirty handkerchieves, yet we leave their bodies, their most holy and efficacious relics, neglected.'

Erasmus was the intimate of great publishers and lived for much of his later life in the household of the Froben family in Basle. He was the friend of Thomas More, John Colet and other humanists.

Erasmus exercised his influence through his own personal example, through his friendships and through the literary quality of his writing. He was a master of Latin and Greek, but he always believed that his writing should open up knowledge to those who only read in the vernacular. The dialectic of the medieval schoolmen held no appeal for him – he severely lampooned them in 'The Praise of Folly' – rather he valued Hebrew and Greek in an attempt to uncover the genuine meaning of early church texts. In the 'Handbook', he several times stresses the great importance of reading the early church fathers in order to uncover the truth about St Paul, and he himself spent many years translating and editing the works of Jerome, Augustine and others. In breaking the church's control, he highlighted its abuses and its follies, and he then replaced them with his own interpretation of early Christian values: simplicity, piety and faith.

Perhaps most important of all, Erasmus was an enthusiastic letter-writer. In the 1520s he entered, rather reluctantly, into debate with Martin Luther and his supporters. Their subject was: how best to reform the church. Erasmus' view was clear, as he wrote in a letter to Philip Melanchthon in 1524:

> The Pope's advocates have been the Pope's worst friends, and the extravagant Lutherans have most hurt Luther. I would have held aloof if it had been possible. I am no judge of other men's beliefs. There are actors enough on the stage, and none can say how it will all end... True, Christendom is corrupt and needs the rod, but it would be better, in my opinion, if we could have the Pope and the princes on our side.

3.1 The Writings of Erasmus

Some Themes and Characteristics in Erasmus' Writings

The following themes and characteristics appear regularly in Erasmus' writings.
Study the writings that follow and identify examples of themes and characteristics.

- Anti-clericalism – criticism of Catholic priests, monks and nuns.
- Anti-Papalism – criticism of popes.
- Belief in education to overcome ignorance and enable people to read the Bible.
- Anti-Ritual – criticism of rituals of Catholic church and a belief in simplicity of prayer and worship.
- Belief in Scriptures.
- Emphasis on Latin and Greek and Hebrew – to study the Bible in its earliest forms.
- Humour and satire.
- Ability to paint pictures and characters in words.

Extracts from Erasmus' Writings

Source A

Nothing is more agreeable than peace, nothing is more frightful than war... The fields are
rich with harvests, the meadows with cattle, the sea with fish. Why does this not suffice us?
Tears start as one views the calamities of our time. Harvests are burned, villages are given to the flames.
Some labourers are killed, some captured, some become fugitives, women are abused, virgins violated,
wives abducted, no read is safe from this tiger or violence.

'Oration on Peace and Discord', c.1490.

Source B

I would like to point out two weapons that we should use to combat sin. These weapons are prayer and
knowledge. St Paul... commands us to pray without ceasing. Pure prayer, directed to Heaven, is able to
subdue passion. Knowledge or learning fortifies the mind with salutary precepts and keeps virtue ever
before us... There is really no attack from the enemy, no temptation so violent, that a sincere resort to Holy
Writ will not easily get rid of it. There is no misfortune so sad that a reading of the Scripture does not render bearable...

I am going to lay down a fourth rule: Make Christ the only goal of your life. Dedicate to Him all your
effort, and don't look upon Him as a mere word, an empty expression, but rather as Charity, Simplicity,
Patience, and Purity – in short, in terms of everything He has taught us.

'Handbook of the Christian Soldier', 1504.

Source C

To whom shall we pray? To God. But how shall a miserable little creature like man come before Him in
whose present angels tremble? Shall I lift myself up and talk with Him who inhabits eternity? Yet the publican cried unto Him and was heard...

How shall we pray? Not interminably. If you are going through a round of prayers, you might as well be
rolling rocks like Sisyphus. Don't bellow like a soldier, or croon like a singer...

Prayers should not be tedious. Pray that rulers should be given wisdom not victory in war. Pray not for
one king, but for all. Pray for the Turks, that they be given mercy not destruction.

'Treatise on Prayer', c.1519.

Source D

Marriage is the most appropriate of all unions because it is based on nature, law and religion. It should be for life – any marriage which is capable of being dissolved, never was marriage at all...

Because marriage is for life, it should not be entered into lightly, but soberly. Marriage should be with the consent of parents, but they should not force the unwilling. Never let your daughter marry a leper or a syphilitic, nor give her to a dissolute knight, better a solid farmer...

'Treatise on Marriage', c.1521.

Source E

Dame Folly applauds inadequate bishops: 'They are satraps caring nothing for religion, its blessings and its ceremonies, and holding it cowardly and shameful for a bishop to die otherwise than in battle their clergy valiantly follow their example and fight the warriors for their tithes.'

'In Praise of Folly', 1506.

Erasmus' Achievement

More than any writer, he created an atmosphere within which the church had to wither or else be reformed.

A.G. Dickens, *The Age of Humanism and Reformation*, 1977.

His vocation – to reform society and the Church through education.

R.H. Bainton, *Erasmus of Christendom*, 1988.

He envisioned the restoration of that Golden Age of those first centuries of Christendom, when, as he imagined, Christianity and classical antiquity were in harmony

L.W. Spitz, *The Protestant Reformation*, 1971.

For Erasmus, religion tended to become intellectualized. Learning and piety were fused. The pious Christian must have a clear conscience, and make his peace with God; a clear conscience meant a mind open to the pleasures of learning, study and the writing of good literature.

Erasmus' popularity was not only that of a Reformer, but increasingly that of a critic of contemporary society.

Koenigsberger, Mosse and Bowler, *Europe in the 16th Century*, 1989.

1 What explains Erasmus' popularity and influence in early 16th-century Europe?

2 Were Erasmus' attempts to reform the church through peaceful evolutionary means like education possible?

3 Bainton said of Luther and Erasmus: 'The one slugs, the other reasons... One may bludgeon, the other pierce, one may denounce, the other reason.'
In what ways did later reformers need Erasmus?

4 In what senses was Erasmus a 'man for all seasons'?

Review

The Causes of 16th-Century Change

In any major change or revolution, a number of causal factors are likely to be present. These include:

- The role of dynamic individuals who lead, encourage, set a vision etc.
- The place of technology in facilitating or leading the change.
- Good communications.
- A market for new goods, or a home for new ideas.
- Dissatisfaction with the existing order.

How important was printing and technological innovations in furthering the new ideas of 16th-century Europe? What contribution was made by oral communication in a largely illiterate age? What were the 'markets' for the new ideas? Which dynamic individuals played a major role and how?

It is often helpful to explore a Historical problem by using a mind map or patterned note. Thus:

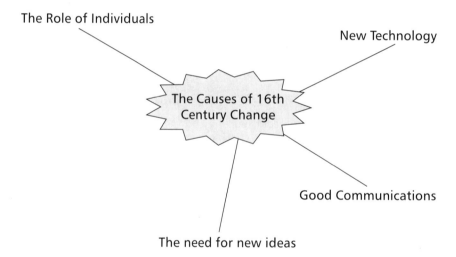

See if you can add further to this mind map.
Now re-read this chapter and build up the different sections of the map. Place each in its own pattern, thus

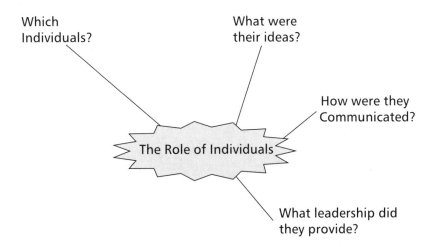

Which Individuals?

What were their ideas?

How were they Communicated?

The Role of Individuals

What leadership did they provide?

You can explore this even further:

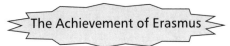

The Achievement of Erasmus

REVIEW

Christian Humanism and Italian Humanism

Essay

'What were the main differences between Christian Humanism in Northern Europe and the Italian Humanism of the Renaissance? In what ways did Italian Humanism influence the North?'

Like all essays, this one must be tackled in six stages.

> Consider the amount of time you should allocate to each of the stages below so that you can plan your time effectively.

Stage 1

Examine closely the wording of the questions. There are two separate but connected questions here.

The first one requires you to investigate the differences between Christian Humanism in the North and the main themes of the Italian Renaissance. You can read about these in Chapter 2.
The second question, which will form the second half of your essay, requires you to examine the ways in which Italian influences penetrated Northern Europe.

You should also consider who will read your essay and an appropriate length for it.

Stage 2

The initial plan.

On a clean sheet of paper, write the first question on the top line and the second question half way down. Then under the first question make a list of dot points which will be differences between the North and Italy. Alternatively, use a patterned note or mind map.

Then do the same for the second question, to identify Italian influences on the North.

Stage 3

Research.

Now read as many sources as you can gather about these two questions. Add information to your dot points and also add references to appropriate sources for quotations or particularly valuable pieces of information. In your research, separate opinions from facts.

Stage 4

Drafting.

It is usually wise to use a word processor for this as it saves time in improving the draft.

Using what will now be your detailed plan, draft out your paragraphs in order, omitting at this stage the introduction and conclusion. Try to draft appropriate signposts in the first sentence of each paragraph.

Stage 5

Review of the draft.

Now read through your draft and check it against your reading and your notes. Challenge yourself with the following:

- Are the points in my paragraphs relevant to the two questions?
- Have I started a new paragraph for each new important point?
- Is the first sentence of each paragraph a useful signpost to its content and argument?
- Have I comprehensively provided an answer to each question?
- Have I written in sufficient detail to support my arguments?

Stage 6

Final writing.

Firstly draft out an appropriate introduction and conclusion. Think carefully about the purpose you wish these two paragraphs to serve. What is an interesting way to lead into this question and an effective way to end your argument?

Now write out the polished version of your essay.

4 Martin Luther and the German Reformation

Preview

'The Incombustible Luther'

AN ENGRAVING OF MARTIN LUTHER, FROM A PAINTING BY LUCAS CRANACH.

Even during his own lifetime Martin Luther was thought to have special powers. Stories circulated that his portrait would not burn when it was cast into flames along with his banned books. Increasingly, his followers viewed him as 'incombustible'.

At Luther's funeral in 1546, his supporter John Bugenhagen preached the sermon, proclaiming that: 'You may burn a goose, but in a hundred years will come a swan you will not be able to burn.' In 1415, the Catholics in Bohemia had burnt John Huss at the stake, so it became an important piece of symbolism that Luther would not burn. In the early 16th century burning at the stake was the common fate of those condemned as heretics by the Catholic church. In 1519 Luther's books were burnt in many Catholic centres in Germany. In addition, in the same year, his effigy was burnt in Rome and there was a great fear that his personal appearance at the Imperial Diet of Worms in 1521 would result in his own death at the stake. However, it was not to be, and Luther's symbolic invincibility had a major influence on the rest of the 16th century.

R.W. Scribner, in his *Popular Culture and Popular Movements in Reformation Germany* (Hambledon Press, 1987), has clarified the position: 'Most of the tales of incombustibility, and of the miraculous in general, produced after Luther's death were recorded by Lutheran Pastors... Whether this occurred out of piety, curiosity or incredulity, the result was the same: Church leaders effectively created a cult of Saint Luther, which they popularised well into the 19th century.'

As you read this chapter, try to identify the many personal contributions which Martin Luther made to the German Reformation.

The Immediate Impact of Martin Luther

Luther's fame spread rapidly throughout Germany following the posting of the 95 theses at Wittenberg in November 1517. The Papal messenger, Aleander, said at the Diet of Worms in 1521:

> The people kiss these pictures of Luther. Such a quantity have been sold that I was not able to obtain one. A cartoon has appeared showing Luther with a book in his hand, accompanied by Hutten in armour with a sword, under the caption 'champions of Christian liberty'. Another sheet portrays Luther and Hutten. Erasmus is playing the harp as David did, in the background is John Huss. In another picture the Pope and the Cardinals are being bound by soldiers. I cannot go out into the streets but the Germans put their hands on their swords and gnash their teeth at me.

Similarly, one of Luther's friends, a printer from Switzerland, wrote to him in 1519:

> Valseus Almonius, a printer of Leipzig, gave me some of your books which he had bought at the last fair in Frankfurt. I immediately reprinted them. We have sent six hundred copies to France and Spain. They are being sold in Paris and even read and approved by the Brother Doctors of the Sorbonne as certain of our friends have assured us. Some of the learned say that they have hitherto missed among those who study the scriptures the same freedom that you show. A book seller of Pavia also has taken a good part of your books to Italy to distribute them among all the cities. Nor does he do so much for gain as to encourage study. He has promised to send verses written in your honour by all the learned men in Italy. We have sold out all your books except ten copies and never remembered to have sold any more quickly.

Indeed, one contemporary made even more sweeping claims: 'Luther's New Testament in German had been so widely spread by the book printers that even tailors and shoemakers, and indeed women and simple idiots, who had accepted this new Lutheran Gospel – though they could read only a little German – read it eagerly as if it were a fountain of all truth. Some learnt it by heart.'

Discuss the meaning of the
following important words:
What do they mean to you?
Church
Theology
Reformation

TALKING POINT

Martin Luther clearly had a vital influence on the movement known as the German Reformation. The Roman Catholic church in Germany was attacked and criticised by a number of reformers, and Luther was foremost among them. Between 1517 and his death in 1546 Luther challenged Catholic theology and produced his own theological statements. He set up a new church in German states like Saxony with its own church services and its own ministers. He thus brought about a radical change in the lives of German peasants, town and city dwellers, and noblemen and churchmen. This reforming statement is known as the German Lutheran Reformation.

In this chapter, we shall look at the reasons why this occurred and the contribution made to it by Martin Luther himself and various other groups of people in Germany. In Chapter 8, you will read about the political changes which occurred in the Holy Roman Empire of Charles V as a result of this Reformation.

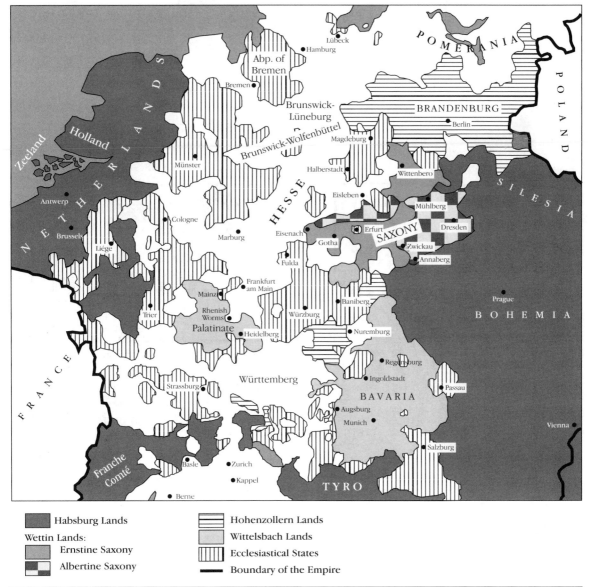

▨ Habsburg Lands	▤ Hohenzollern Lands
Wettin Lands:	▦ Wittelsbach Lands
▨ Ernstine Saxony	▥ Ecclesiastical States
▨ Albertine Saxony	━ Boundary of the Empire

The Roman Catholic Church on the Eve of the Reformation

What do these pictures tell us about the state of the church at the start of the 16th century. What impression would these images convey to people who could not read or write?

ROMA CAPVT MVNDI

CHRISTVS.

Ihesus fatigatus ex itinere sedebat sic supra fontem. Iohannis. iiij.
Si quis vult venire post me; abneget semetipsum, tollat crucem suã, & sequatur me. Matthei. xvi.
Et baiulans sibi crucem, exiuit in eum qui dicitur Caluarie locus, Iohã. xix.

ANTICHRISTVS.

Capitulũ. Si quis suadente diabolo & similia satis superq; probant quam libenter Papa crucem aduersitatis toleret, qui omnes quicunq; manus in sacerdotes injiciunt, maledicit, & diabolo tradit. Si etiam fert crucem Papa, vt baptisati Christiani cogãtur eum humeris suis portare.
B iij

Throughout the 16th century, politics bedevilled the Church hierarchy. As was outlined in Chapter 1, the so-called 'Renaissance popes' were really Italian secular princes concerned with their lands in central Italy. Many archbishops and bishops were equally concerned with landed wealth and the Archbishops of Metz, Trier and Cologne were three of the seven electors of the Holy Roman Empire.

The Roman Catholic church survived throughout the Middle Ages because it provided the only route for the individual soul to achieve salvation in Heaven. As E.W. Cameron states in his book *The European Reformation* (Oxford University Press, 1991):

> late medieval religion was at least officially about saving souls. Individual souls were saved, not in a once for all act of redemption, but by a life long course through a cycle of sin, absolution and penance. This cycle was determined by the two great facts of religious life: human sin, that is repeated breaking of the moral law of God, and the forgiveness of sins, offered through the Church by the Sacrament of Penance.

The Background

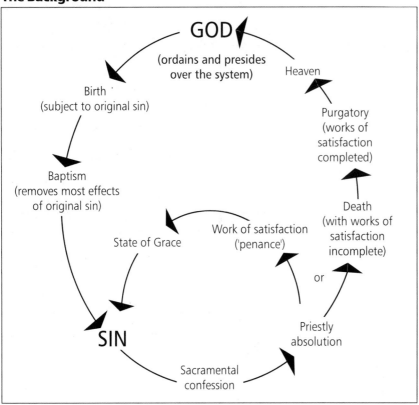

THIS FIGURE SHOWS THE CYCLE OF SALVATION FOR A CHRISTIAN BELIEVER. FOR MOST OF HIS LIFE, A BELIEVER PASSED AROUND THE LOWER PART OF THE CYCLE. BY THE CONFESSION OF SIN AND THE PERFORMANCE OF PENANCE, THE CHRISTIAN WAS ABSOLVED AND A STATE OF GRACE WAS RESTORED. SHOULD ANY PENALTY REMAIN UNEXPIATED AT DEATH, IT WAS ATONED FOR IN PURGATORY.

Regular confession and penance was clearly a heavy burden on the individual believer. However, there were ways of softening the burden. Most laymen made their confession no more than once a year and it was possible to bypass a heavy penance by the purchase of an indulgence. These were writs given in return for money which excused the purchaser from any penance or suffering in purgatory on the assumption that he repented and confessed his sins. Too often it became easy to buy an indulgence from a local chantry priest. One German witticism which went back to the 12th century told of the priest who read the lesson for the day 'here beginneth the Holy Gospel according to the Mark'. By the year 1500, indulgences were becoming inflated. Plenary indulgences abolished all penalties and were offered by Papal indulgence sellers like John Tetzel, a Dominican monk who toured many parts of Germany in the early years of the 16th century. Purchasers were allowed to choose their own confessor and could be absolved of all their sins, even those so severe that normally the pope alone could forgive them.

This popular theology was underpinned by the thinking of the medieval 'Schoolmen', the university scholars in Theology. All agreed that man needed God's Grace to be saved. But it was difficult to understand the relationship between Grace and man's goodness. Could man be saved simply by confession and penance, and at what point was God's Grace involved? The Catholic church argued that priests alone had received the power to transmit God's Grace. To love God was to be worthy of His Grace and that Grace could be imposed through the Church. Thus the authority of the Church was supreme. 'Tradition' was the handing down of beliefs and practices through the centuries, and it confirmed that supremacy. The Communion of Saints was an indicator of the Church's links with Heaven. Perhaps the most powerful indicator of the Church's position was the role of the priest in the Mass. Through the process of transubstantiation, the priest blessed the bread and it became the Body of Christ. Thus the member of the congregation received Christ's Body and God's Grace through the mediating role of the priest and the Church.

THIS CONTEMPORARY SATIRE SHOWS THE POPE ON HIGH AND JESUS IN THE STABLE.

However, the church in 1500 also had many critics. Anti-clericals opposed the powerful position of the priests and opposed their absenteeism, ignorance, and the fact that they often purchased their positions. Bishops often held more than one see and clearly were unable to do an effective job. In addition, indulgence sellers were heavily paraded in processions and carnivals: in Germany in particular people felt robbed of money that was going to Rome. Some critics became heretics: those who refused to accept the dogma and tradition of the church. They were often burnt at the stake.

Luther's Life and Work, 1483–1546

Luther's Life to 1517

1483	Luther was born in Thuringia, the son of Hans and Margaretta Luther. The family were peasant miners from a very conservative religious background. Luther was very strictly brought up.
1501	Luther studied at the University of Erfurt.
1505	Luther became an Augustinian monk at Erfurt. The story goes that he became a monk as a result of a promise he made to St Anne who protected him after he was struck by a thunderbolt during a storm.
1507	Luther was ordained as a priest.
1511	Luther was appointed to lecture on Biblical Theology at Wittenberg University in Electoral Saxony.
1515	Luther lectured on St Paul's 'Epistle to the Romans' and emphasized his crucial ideas on 'Justification by Faith Alone as a route to Salvation'.

The Lutheran Revolt 1517–21

September 1517	Luther published his 'Disputation Against Scholastic Theology'. This showed that he had completely broken with the Catholic theology in which he had been trained.
October 1517	Luther may have pinned his 95 Theses on the door of the University Church at Wittenberg.
October 1518	Cardinal Cajetan, the representative of Pope Leo X, summoned Luther to Augsburg to answer for his sins.
July 1519	Johann Eck, the Papal representative, openly debated with Luther at Leipzig. The audience consisted of a panel of theologians and local dignitaries.
1520	Luther writes and publishes 24 books. The three most famous were 'The Address to the German Nobility', 'Of the Liberty of the Christian Man', and 'On the Babylonian Captivity of the Christian Church'. Printing presses circulated these all over Europe.
June 1520	The pope published his Bull 'Exsurge, Domine' condemning Luther. It was read in every parish church. Luther publicly burned the Bull.
April 1521	The Diet of Worms. Luther was given a safe conduct to appear before the Emperor Charles V and all the princes at the Imperial Diet. Luther refused to change his beliefs. The Edict of Worms banned Luther and his works.

The Mature Luther

1521   Luther was captured by the soldiers of the Saxon Elector, Frederick the Wise, and secretly hidden, for his own protection, in the castle of the Wartburg. The Elector's support during the next four years was crucial.

1522   Luther returned to Wittenberg.

1525   Marriage to Catherine von Bora and the beginning of his family life.

1526   Luther published 'The German Mass', a Lutheran Eucharist Service for use throughout Saxony. He also wrote many hymns and urged princes to set up schools with funds from confiscated monastic lands.

1529   Luther published the 'Great Catechism' and the 'Small Catechism', a full statement of beliefs and Church services for adults and children.

1546   Luther died. His last years were spent in improving his translation of the Bible into German.

The Spread of Lutheranism in Germany

1521–2 The Lutheran Reformation in Wittenberg was led by Andreas Carlstadt in Luther's absence.

1524–5 The Peasants' Revolt was finally brutally crushed by nobles. Luther did not support the revolt and published 'Against the Thieving Hordes of Peasants'.

1525   Albrecht of Hohenzollern, Grand Master of the Teutonic Knights and Duke of Prussia, became a Lutheran and his territory was reformed.

1526   Philip, Duke of Hesse, did likewise. He became one of the political leaders of Lutheranism.

1527   John, Frederick the Wise's successor as Elector of Saxony, converted. Others followed.

1530   Diet of Augsburg. The Emperor Charles V invited both Catholics and Lutherans to an Imperial Diet to see if a solution to their differences could be found. Charles wanted a united Empire to fight against the Turks. The moderate Lutheran Philip Melanchthon produced a compromise, 'The Marburg Colloquy', but it was not accepted by extremists on both sides.

1531   The Lutheran princes and cities formed the Schmalkaldic League.

1534   The large Duchy of Wurttemberg joined the Schmalkaldic League.

1541   Diet of Regensberg. Charles V made one last attempt to unite the two sides, but failed.

1547   Battle of Muhlberg. Charles V's armies defeated those of the Schmalkaldic League, but Charles underestimated the strength of Lutheranism, and was outmanoeuvred by Lutheran politics.

1555   Charles V abdicated and agreed to the Peace of Augsburg. The principle 'Cuius Regio, eius Religio' allowed Lutheran princes to establish the Lutheran reform in their territories.

4.1 Luther and his Protestant Family

Luther's wife Catherine von Bora

Catherine was born in 1499 and placed in a convent at the age of ten when her father remarried. She took vows at sixteen, but, along with a number of other sisters, she became dissatisfied with her life in a nunnery. Luther helped them to make the arrangements for their escape, concealed in a herring barrel, and she then lived for two years in a house in Wittenburg where she learned how to manage household accounts. She was admired and courted, and at the age of twenty-six was clearly an attractive young woman. However, despite several offers of marriage, she was still unattached in 1525.

The Marriage of Luther and Catherine in 1525

Luther described his reasons for marrying thus: it would 'please his father, anger the Pope, make the angels laugh and the devils weep and would seal his testimony'. He married as an example to his followers and to show his belief in the importance of family life. At the beginning of their relationship he wrote to a friend 'I am not madly in love but I cherish my wife'. A year later, he could afford to say 'my wife is affable beyond anything I dared to hope, I would not change my poverty for the riches of Croesus'.

Catherine was clearly a remarkable woman, making a significant contribution to Luther's life. Her home was perhaps the first Protestant 'Parsonage' and the atmosphere there of warmth, affectionate duty and tender devotion, coupled with unsentimental and down-to-earth hard work, was a model for the Lutheran family way of life. Luther himself could write 'nothing is more sweet than harmony in marriage. It offers the greatest sphere for good works because it rests on love.'

The match clearly benefited Luther. He had slept in an unmade bed until Catherine took him in hand. Indeed, he declared himself amazed to find her pigtails on his pillow when he woke in the morning.

Catherine as a Household Manager

Catherine was an extremely capable organiser and manager of a huge household. The Elector of Saxony gave the couple the Augustinian Cloister, where Luther had lived as a monk. It had forty rooms on the first floor and individual bedrooms on the second floor. A regular stream of visitors meant that, on many occasions, all the rooms were occupied. The Luthers had six children, as well as aunts, uncles, nephews and nieces. Foreigners visited them from abroad and refugees would often arrive unannounced. Catherine herself herded, milked and slaughtered cattle, made butter and cheese, brewed, planted and reaped, and generally ensured the effectiveness of the establishment. She installed a bath and a brew-house, developed the kitchen garden, and acquired a brook for fresh fish.

Luther the Father

Luther's children were evidently a great source of delight to him and he learned a great deal from them about the development of human nature and how the home can provide and nurture a love of godliness. He and Catherine had six children:

- Hans, born June 1526.
- Elizabeth, born December 1527.
- Magdalen, born December 1529.
- Martin, born November 1531.
- Paul, born January 1533.
- Marguerita, born December 1534.

Elizabeth died within six months of her birth.

Luther was far from sentimental about his family and is recorded as saying to one of his children 'Child, what have you done that I should love you so? What with your befowling the corners and bawling through the whole house?'

In 1538 he is recorded as saying, 'Christ said we must become as little children to enter the kingdom of heaven. Dear God, this is too much. Have we got to become such idiots?'

Luther appears to have been a stern father who tempered his discipline with considerable concern for his children's spiritual welfare. It was perhaps the death of Magdalen, at the age of fourteen, that most clearly illustrates Luther as a father. As she lay on her death bed Luther prayed 'Oh God I love her so, but Thy will be done.' When she died in his arms he said 'You will rise and shine like the stars and the sun. How strange it is to know that she is at peace and all is well and yet to be so sorrowful.'

The German Reformation and the Family

In recent years, Historians have shown much interest in the history of family life. The American Historian Steven Ozment has recently published *When Fathers Ruled*, an extremely stimulating study of the effect of the Reformation on family life in Europe.

During the Middle Ages, marriage was seen as a lowly ideal. Only celibacy was the perfect state for men and women, and celibacy within an enclosed Order was preferred. The Lutheran Reformers, following Luther's own personal example, set the family ideal above the celibate ideal. Erasmus described the vows of celibacy as 'superstition' which came from an inadequate understanding of human nature. The Reformers indeed saw marriage and the family as the freeing of men, women and children from the slavery of religion. Marriage was now seen as the essence of God's plan for human beings, rather than a status of secondary importance. Priests could and should marry and this was a means of salvation from their struggle with their inhuman vows.

The marriage services published in Wittenberg in 1524 and Nuremberg in 1526 stressed the joint nature of the couple. The husband was the toiler, and the wife was the bearer of the pain of childbirth. The home was not a private world but an open example to all, the place to shape the virtues, character and values of the people. Through the family came education, help with the Church, neighbourliness, friendship and protection for the poor and those in need. R.H. Bainton has written in his book *Here I Stand* (1994), 'The home and marriage in a sense displaced the monastery as the route to Heaven and the source of training in Godliness.' In marriage the husband was to provide for the welfare of his wife and family, protect them and rule them. He was to be firm but fair. The wife was not to be the servant of her husband but the "hausmutter" and to command great respect. There are several written warnings to men not to beat their wives for 'the two are one flesh and no man but a frantic furious wretch will beat himself'. Marriages were thought to work best where the woman was perhaps twenty to twenty-four years old and the man perhaps five years her senior. And also where both share the same religious beliefs, a similar economic and social background, and where there was support for the marriage from both families.

The Reformers clearly accepted that where a marriage had broken down it could be dissolved. Martin Bucer in Strassburg argued for divorce if 'true love and all pleasure has left the union'. Johannis Brenz and Johannis Bugenhagen both wrote pamphlets on divorce. Indeed, Brenz writes rather in the style of a modern marriage counsellor...

> Because people who marry remain different and some totally lack the will to agree and cooperate, in time obstinacy and hatred overwhelms some marriages. For this reason, and in order to protect such couples from greater harm and unhappiness, Moses in the Old Testament favoured their divorce, reasoning that while it did not accomplish anything positive it at least prevented further and greater evil.

The family was the home for rearing and educating children. Reformers castigated the parents of their day for their laxity. In Nuremberg, Veit Dietric criticised negligent parents. 'Today you find few parents who once mention study or work to their children. They let them creep about idly, eating and drinking whenever they please, casually dressed in ragged pants and jackets. Through bad example and lax discipline children learn to curse and swear, lie and steal.'

Otto Brunfels, in contrast, describes a typical day in the life of a properly reared child.

Sleep neither too little nor too much. Begin each day by blessing it in God's name and saying the Lord's Prayer. Thank God for keeping you through the night and ask His help for the new day. Greet your parents. Comb your hair and wash your face and hands. Before departing for school ask Christ to send His Spirit without whom there is no true understanding. Remember also however that the Spirit only helps those who help themselves. Do not greet the Saints or ask them for enlightenment...

Read incessantly; make your heart a library of Christ. Read something specific from the scriptures every day. Do not go to sleep until you have memorised a few new verses. Punish yourself when you have neglected your reading...

Brunfels also makes great play of table manners.

Make sure your nails are cut and your hands washed. Sit up straight, comply with the requests of those around you, do not drink too much wine and be mindful of what is fitting for one of your age. Serve yourself only after others have been served. If seconds are placed on the table, politely refuse.

Discipline within the family was very important. Discipline based solely on praise was regarded with suspicion and a very harsh parent was preferred to one who was lenient and indulgent. Corporal punishment was favoured when needed and was to be administered by the father coolly and with calm exclamation and justification. However, corporal punishment should always be administered within a framework of a loving family. Luther himself revealed in 1537 in a table talk that his entry into a monastery had been partly a cowardly response to his parents' harsh discipline.

There were clear expectations of children within family life. Johann Agricola wrote 'One Hundred and Fifty-Six Common Questions' in 1528, in which he tried to provide answers for children to the major questions of life. The Strassburg Catechism of 1534 included the following dialogue between father and child.

Father: What does it mean to have God for one's father?

Child: Two things. As I have been created by God and re-created to eternal life I love God totally... and I shall never forget that He is my Father and that out of His Fatherly love He will give and do more for me than any earthly parent ever could....

The Reformation changed family life in Europe dramatically. The values and attitudes of the Reformers were inculcated into their children in the family home, which was a significant way of ensuring that the roots of the Reformation were deep and firmly held.

Luther's Theology

Martin Luther broke the stranglehold of the Roman Catholic church over the lives of the people of Europe. He did this by showing them a new way to heaven, a new route to salvation. For Luther, Heaven could be achieved without all the church's paraphernalia of confession, penance, sacraments and indulgences.

For Luther and the other reformers God was all-powerful. Only through God's Grace could man achieve the forgiveness of his sins and salvation. Faith was therefore at the heart of Luther's message:

> a sure and constant trust in God's good will towards us... Nothing else than trust in the divine mercy promised in Christ... This trust in the goodwill or mercy of God first calms our hearts and then inflames us to give thanks to God.

Faith was not a good work which man could achieve. Rather, it was a gift, an unearned blessing from God.

'The sun which illuminates God's Holy Church' was Luther's belief in Justification by Faith Alone. 'Man cannot be saved or justified by his good works, but only by his complete faith in God.' It was in 1515, when Luther was lecturing on St Paul's Epistle to the Romans at Wittenburg, that he stumbled upon the truth. In this passage written just before he died he referred back to his conflict in 1515.

> I greatly longed to understand Paul's Epistle to the Romans and nothing stood in the way except that one expression 'the justice of God' because I took it to mean that justice whereby God is just and deals justly in punishing sinners.
>
> My situation was that, although an impeccable monk, I stood before God as a sinner troubled in conscience and I had no confidence that my merits, my good works, would assuage him. Therefore I did not love a just and angry God but rather hated and murmured against Him. Yet I clung to the dear Paul and had a great yearning to know what he meant.
>
> Night and day I pondered until I saw the connection between 'the justice of God' and the statement that 'the just shall live by his faith'. Then I grasped that the justice of God is that righteousness by which, through Grace, God justifies us through our faith.

Thus the Roman Catholic penitentiary cycle is replaced by a new Lutheran one.

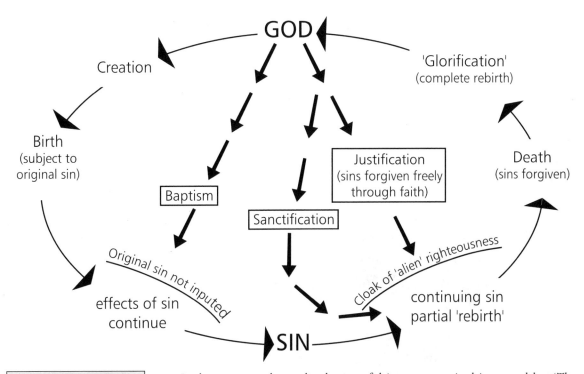

GOD

Creation

'Glorification'
(complete rebirth)

Birth
(subject to
original sin)

Justification
(sins forgiven freely
through faith)

Death
(sins forgiven)

Baptism

Sanctification

Original sin not inputed

Cloak of 'alien' righteousness

effects of sin
continue

continuing sin
partial 'rebirth'

SIN

Discuss the meaning of this
very important passage.
What is 'the law'?
Why is it unnecessary in
Luther's 'Ethical Society'?

Luther summed up the heart of his message in his pamphlet 'The Freedom of a Christian', published in 1519.

> The Christian has all that he needs in faith and needs no works to justify him; and if he has no need of works he has no need of the law; and if he has no need of the law surely he is free from the law that Christian liberty, our faith, does not induce us to live in idleness or wickedness but makes the law and works unnecessary for any man's righteousness and salvation.

Alongside his theology of salvation, Luther was forced to challenge the authority of the Roman Catholic church. When he opposed the selling of indulgences in Wittenberg, the pope brought the full weight of 'Roman Catholic tradition' to bear. One thousand years of Papal arguments were difficult to resist. But Luther found an authority even more powerful – that of the Word of God as revealed in scripture: 'The Pope, Luther, Augustine, Paul, or even an Angel from Heaven – these should not be masters, judges or arbiters, but only witnesses, disciples and confessors of scripture.' Thus, all beliefs had to be tested by the Word of God; they would be rejected if support were not found in scripture. Clearly, Luther's emphasis on scripture gave added power to his belief in the priesthood of all believers and his reluctance to accept a mediating role for priests. Now that the Bible was translated into German, men and women could learn to read for themselves in order to understand its message.

TALKING POINT
The Roman Catholic church was organised as a hierarchy; the Lutheran church allowed the people to be more involved. What are the benefits and difficulties of these two different ways of running an organisation like a church?

Luther also had to deal with the seven Sacraments of the Roman Catholic church. These were 'the most solemn of the rituals whereby the medieval church claimed to mediate divine Grace reliably and predictably to the believer' (E. Cameron).

The Roman Catholic church accepted seven such rituals or Sacraments: Baptism, the Eucharist or Mass, Marriage, Penance, Confirmation, Ordination, and the Last Sacrament. In all of these rituals, the mediating role of the priest was paramount.

Luther and other Reformers needed to define Sacraments anew. What was a Sacrament and what benefits did it bring to the recipient? Immediately, five of the seven Catholic Sacraments were rejected and downgraded to mere rituals of the church, because they had no precedence in scripture. Only Baptism and the Eucharist were allowed as Sacraments by the Reformers. In Baptism and in the Last Supper God made a clear promise to men. Luther argued that 'where there is a divine promise, there faith is required'.

THE TITLE PAGE FROM THE FIRST EDITION OF LUTHER'S GERMAN TRANSLATION OF THE BIBLE.

AN ILLUSTRATION OF THE LUTHERAN SACRAMENTS OF BAPTISM AND COMMUNION.

Luther also abolished the Sacrament of the Mass and replaced it with a ritual of Holy Communion, which had strong Biblical origins and was a natural way of worshipping God. Luther clearly rejected the Catholic idea of the Mass as 'a good work and a sacrifice which conferred merit on the recipient'. In addition, offering the Sacrament of the Bread alone to the congregation while the priest received both the Bread and the Wine, was anathema to Luther. Luther simplified the meaning of the Communion: 'as if Christ was saying "I promise you the forgiveness of all your sins and life everlasting. And that you may be absolutely certain of this irrevocable promise of mine, I shall give my body and pour out my blood, confirming this promise by my very death, and leaving you my body and blood as a sign and memorial of this same promise"'. Luther also took issue with the Catholic concept of transubstantiation: the idea that the priest, by laying on his hands on the Bread, changed its essence from Bread to the Body of Christ, and from Wine to the Blood of Christ. In 1520, Luther concluded that 'real Bread and real Wine remained on the Altar, in which Christ's real Flesh and real Blood are present.' For Luther there were two realities in the Bread and the Wine. The 'substance' of Bread and Wine were together mingled with the reality of the Body and Blood of Christ. 'Let us not dabble in too much philosophy. Christ desired to keep us in a simple faith, sufficient to believe that His Blood was in the cup'.

In order to deliver this theology, Luther rejected the whole structure of the Roman Catholic church. In its place he suggested a 'community of the faithful' in which all believers were priests. There was no need for consecrated priests to mediate between man and God. Men and women could themselves pray directly to their Lord and worship Him. Preaching ministers who conducted services and preached sermons replaced mediating priests.

THESE TWO PICTURES EMPHASISE THE CENTRALITY OF THE WORD IN LUTHERAN SERVICES.

In 1520 he wrote: 'Baptism, Gospel, and faith alone make a spiritual and a Christian people. The Pope can never make a man into a Christian or into a spiritual man by ritual. We are all consecrated priests through Baptism. Whoever comes out of the water of Baptism can boast that he is already a consecrated priest, Bishop and Pope.'

The Reformation in the German Cities

It was in the cities that the Reformation made sensational progress during its first two decades.

L.W. Spitz, *The Protestant Reformation*, 1969.

In the years immediately after the Diet of Worms in 1521, the Reformation spread to many German cities. The social structure of the cities favoured reform. The bishops and clergy were now less involved in city government and artisans formed the majority of the population. Guilds were influential and welcomed reform because the reformed religion encouraged their continued participation. In addition, wealthy patrician merchants served on city councils and, although they did not often initiate reform, they were happy to support it. Finally, peasants living in the hinterland of cities were interested in the preaching of reformers.

A new ethic developed and Luther's beliefs encouraged it. This was the concern for the good of all, illustrated by the emphasis on the quality of priests and the salvation of all people. Johann Eberlin, in his pamphlet 'The Fifteen Confederates', published in 1519, stressed the drive towards a new social and religious Utopia. The Reformation clearly promised a profoundly better, more ethical society.

Evangelical preachers flocked to the new cities. The spoken word was powerful in an illiterate age. Cartoons and images, as well as plays, processions and carnivals encouraged popular understanding. The appeal of the message was strong and was typified in Luther's sermon on penance in 1519.

You should not be debating whether or not your contrition is sufficient. Rather you should be assured that, after all your efforts, your contrition is not sufficient. That is why you must cast yourself upon the grace of God and never doubt that you have come to faith.

This message appealed to negative feelings about the Catholic church. Anti-clerical feelings, opposition to church taxes, church courts and particularly the indulgence sellers, was rife. Evangelical simplicity and the simplicity of the New Testament story was valued. Lazarus Spendler, in a pamphlet published in Nuremburg in 1519, accused Roman Catholic priests of changing the mild yoke of the Gospels into a terrible burden. Monks and nuns were also censured. Johann Eberlin's 'Fifteen Confederates' was highly critical of them. He urged parents: 'Send not your daughter into a convent until you have read this little book'.

In addition, Luther very directly encouraged reform in the cities. His large volume of correspondence was increasingly addressed to them.

Many city councils received encouragement from him. For example, in 1523 he wrote to the city council of Leisnig suggesting an order of worship. Circular letters also encouraged the councils. In 1524 he wrote 'to the council men of all cities that they establish and maintain Christian schools'. His particular fervour was shown in a letter of 1525 'the imperial cities are now already consulting together to be able to remain on the side of the Gospel in spite of the great threats made against them by furious sovereigns'.

L.W. Spitz argues, in his book *The Protestant Reformation*, that the process of reform in German cities was 'nearly everywhere the same'. This consisted of some of the following stages:

- The patrician class of wealthy merchants were unlikely to be involved early on.
- Wandering preachers arrived in the city and were joined by local priests.
- Artisans were receptive. They enjoyed the anti-clerical messages and the positive messages of faith and salvation.
- Artisans put pressure on city magistrates and the major guilds to accept reform.
- In many cities, the role of a heroic individual leader was evident.

This process is clearly illustrated by Spitz's description of the Reformation in the city of Hamburg.

The Reformation in Hamburg

The story of the Reformation in Hamburg is beautifully documented and conforms to the classic pattern. This old Hanse city with 13,000 to 15,000 inhabitants was slightly smaller than Lubeck at that time. The city was heavily churched with a strong Cathedral Chapter and several monasteries. The tax-paying citizens were resentful of the ecclesiastical exactions and the tax exemptions given the Canons and Orders when the Council raised taxes to strengthen the municipal fortifications and built a canal. There were sixteen to twenty-three Canons, a hundred priests at the four parish churches, plus two hundred clerics saying Masses and other services. The leading intellectual on the eve of the Reformation was Dr Albert Krantz, a noted historian, who read Luther's Ninety-five Theses with approval just before his death on December 7, 1517. A mandate from the city council in 1521 warned against the efforts of Luther. But soon evangelical preachers were active in the city. Students went to study at Wittenberg and Rostock, famous for their humanist curricula. On the Leipzig and Zurich pattern, disputations were held which led to some Protestant gains. In St Catherine's Church, Stephan Kempe, a Franciscan, emerged as a Bible-preaching reformer. Johann Widenbrugge, a Premonstratensian, came to the city from a nearby monastery to instruct the people in the Scriptures. Soon demonstrations involving 500 to 2,000 people developed, but the movement gained new converts.

In 1524 St Nicholas Church called Johannes Bugenhagen, City Pastor in Wittenberg, but the city council would not approve the call. Not until 1528 did the Council, with new members, yield to the pressure and allow Bugenhagen to come to Hamburg. He preached, lectured, colloquized, counselled, persuaded, and organized. Before he left he prepared a Church Order that was accepted by the Council and the citizens and celebrated in a Service of Thanksgiving on May 23, 1529. Bugenhagen's Church Order was put into effect by Dr Johannes Hoeck, called Aepinus (d.1553), Hamburg's first Superintendent over the course of the next two decades. His work was embodied in a second great Church Order, the Aepinian Order of 1556.

The Reformation had triumphed thoroughly against the determined opposition of Canons, Nuns, Monks, Papal Emissaries, and a conservative patrician Council. Hamburg followed the classic social pattern, but the Reformation was in a very real way the work of heroic and dedicated individual men.

L. W. Spitz, *The Protestant Reformation*, 1969.

TALKING POINT
Are revolutionary movements always led by 'heroic and dedicated' individuals?

The Reformation, Popular Religion and Popular Culture

The Reformation was clearly more than a change in the religious beliefs of certain individuals. It permeated many cities and influenced the lives of artisans and rural peasants. Indeed, Lutheran religious beliefs became part of the popular religion and popular culture of 16th century Germany.

During the 15th century, all classes of society – the nobles, the educated, people of the church, city dwellers, and peasants – experienced the same religious excitement and piety. There were good reasons for this excitement. Times were bad, even catastrophic. Price rises caused by bad harvests, dramatic crop failures and the ravages of local wars resulted in peasant violence. In 1501, pillaging was so bad that paid police forces were provided in various parts of the Empire.

Epidemic, plague and a new disease, syphilis, added to the confusion. To many they seemed an act of God, an act of revenge for the evils of mankind. Between 1499 and 1502 in the Holy Roman Empire, many regions were decimated by the Black Death. In addition, the ravages of syphilis were painful and often ugly: indeed in 1500 preachers loudly called for special pilgrimages in order to stem its attack.

Popular piety was aroused in order to try to appease the wrath of God. Holy water, exorcisms and charms were only part of the response. The ringing of consecrated church bells, the use of priestly curses, and the petitioning of various saints were other approaches.

One of the most common methods was the use of carnival, a procession of Holy men and women in an attempt to communicate with God. The earliest Lutheran carnival took place in Wittenberg on 10 December 1520. R.W. Scribner tells the story:

TALKING POINT
'The first Protestant groups did not succeed by violent political revolt but by winning established political support. Luther spoke for every Reformer when he praised the politically non-revolutionary character of the Reformation.'

S.C. Ozment, *The Reformation in the Cities*, 1975.

Does the evidence in this chapter support Ozment's view?

In this case, it is suggested
that the carnivals fuelled
concerns about the state of
the Catholic church. In
different circumstances,
might public processions
and festivals be used as a
safety valve to relieve the
pressure for change?

That morning, in the presence of University officials, Luther had formally burnt the Papal bull condemning him. After lunch about one hundred students staged a carnival procession. They set up a float on which a giant Papal bull was erected on a mast like a sail. The float was filled with students, one clad as a charioteer. A trumpeter held a Papal bull affixed to his sword. The charioteer caused great amusement as the float was taken merrily through the town where it was greeted with much laughter. Accompanying students gathered firewood as they went, tossing it into the wagon along with books and images of Luther's opponents such as Eck. The float returned to the embers of the morning fire, the students rekindled it and threw into it the bulls and books. The procession was held around the fire with the students singing a requiem and popular songs. According to a report to the Bishop of Brandenburg, someone was dressed as the Pope and threw his tiara onto the flames.

There were many other anti-Catholic plays and processions. Scribner continues the story.

In Goslar on 17 February 1530 a carnival procession sang satirical songs against the clergy, expressing the sentiments that 'the Cathedral was a whore house.' In a mock palm procession the Emperor was placed on an ass and the Pope on a sow. The mass was formally interred on the market place and satirical songs were sung against the Emperor. In Munster the carnival procession was staged by students where clergy, monks and nuns were yolked to a plough which was then pulled through the streets. These figures were costume journeymen and as they went some of them sprayed the streets with Holy water and carried relics as the Cathedral canons were accustomed to doing in their processions.

Indeed, Scribner argues that the popular carnival was a form of collective behaviour in which the world of the Roman Catholic church was turned upside down. It enabled young people to express their concerns about the established order of previous generations. It illustrated a set of values which were bound up with the new Lutheran way of thought.

In the 16th century, ordinary people experienced religion in two basic ways. Firstly, it was the setting for the various 'rites of passage' which marked out the stages of each individual life cycle: birth, marriage, the baptism of a baby, and death. The other kind of experience was the annual cycle and ritual of the church year. This focused particularly on the church services at Christmas, Easter and Whitsuntide. The major mysteries of the Incarnation and birth of Jesus Christ and His death and Resurrection were celebrated over the twelve days of Christmas from 25 December to 6 January and the events of Holy Week from Palm Sunday to Easter Sunday. Martin Luther's reformed religion fitted in better with popular religion and popular culture than the previous Catholic ritual had done.

Lutheran reformers had a different view of salvation from Catholic priests. They were opposed to many Catholic ceremonies like processions, most of the Seven Sacraments, and a highly ritualised Latin procedure of the Mass.

Yet the change in the world of popular religion was not as dramatic as this evidence may suggest. Many Protestant clergy continued to believe in signs, prophecies and miracles, and many Catholic practices and rituals were continued.

The Spread of Reformation Ideas

It was remarkable how quickly the new religious ideas spread throughout Germany. This spread has long been attributed to the influence of the printing press. The views of Luther and other reformers became accessible to a mass reading public almost as soon as they were written.

However, other means of communication played an equally important part. As Scribner has commented: 'the German Reformation was the first great age of mass propaganda.' We have already seen how the use of images in woodcuts and paintings made an impact on peoples' aittitudes. Yet perhaps the most important form of communication, however, was popular preaching. Sermons, hymn singing and word of mouth transmission of ideas were all important. Towns interested in reform first invited a preacher to proclaim the Word of God. The sermons were not always held in the conventional way. Preachers would often invite debate from the congregation, or would preach outside the church. In Saxony in August 1522, a local schoolmaster, John Zymler, preached in the churchyard to a great crowd and in Ulm in 1530, the preacher, Conrad Sam, was interrupted during the sermon by a member of the congregation. As Sam later made his way home, he was interrupted again and a long and passionate debate occurred. The matter was reported to the town council as a potential cause of disturbance. Indeed, religion became a popular debating point. Whether it was in the reading of pamphlets or broadsheets or discussion of the Bible in someone's house, ordinary people became convinced of the new religion. In 1533 one man in the city of Speyer went to his neighbour, who was known to be a devoted reformer, and the two men read and discussed the Bible together. As a result, the first man was converted to Anabaptism as a result.

TALKING POINT
Are revolutionary movements always assisted by technology?

It is clear from all this evidence that the German Reformation had powerful popular roots. It dug deep into the life of the ordinary people, peasants and citizens of the Empire. Because its roots were so deep, it quickly established itself and became difficult to remove.

Other Reform Groups and the Peasants' Revolt of 1525

In addition to Lutheranism in its many guises, other reform groups spread throughout the Empire. Several of them emphasised the second coming of Christ and the millenarian ideal. Hans Romer seized the city of Erfurt at the end of 1527 and established a New Jerusalem before the last days in 1528. Similarly, Hans Hut argued for the end of the world in 1528 and Melchior Hoffman expected the new Jerusalem to appear in Strassburg.

Perhaps it was in the city of Munster that the rule of the saints before the Second Coming was fully practised. A prophet from the Netherlands called Jan Matthys abolished all institutions, even those of the family and monogamy, in the city. When he died, Jan Beukels took over. He was clearly unstable, practised polygamy and killed members of his own harem. Catholics and Lutherans joined together to besiege the city in 1535. Their final victory convinced many Germans that religious anarchy was now under way.

More pacific and moralistic Anabaptists were organised in the Netherlands and parts of north-east Germany. Menno Simons, from Friesland, influenced many areas with his Mennonite Anabaptism. David Joris, from Basle in Switzerland, similarly had much influence. Both stressed the inner light of the soul and the importance of human willpower. Such sects made the religious life of the Empire very complex. In Zwickau, the so-called 'Zwickau prophets' claimed to have a personal revelation from God and to have divine inspiration to interpret the Word of God. Indeed they were saying little more than Luther's statement that the ordinary man could read and understand the Bible as well as a priest.

The German Peasants' War of 1525

It was the greatest social upheaval in German history before the 20th century.

H.G. Koenigsberger,
Early Modern Europe, 1987.

The Main Events of the War, 1524–5

June 1524   First protest in Swabia – peaceful gathering of large numbers of peasants to present petitions to their Lord that he might dispense justice. The rising was disobedient but orderly.

August 1524   Rebel bands infected other areas throughout the Black Forest and Thuringia by the spring of 1525. Rebels lived off the land and pillaged nunneries, monasteries and castles. Initial successes came from the lack of the standing army amongst the Princes.

Summer 1525   State and Catholic authorities responded with brute force. The Protestant, Philip of Hesse, and the Catholic Duke George of Saxony, defeated the Thuringian peasants at the Battle of Frankenhausen in June. It has been estimated that 100,000 rebels died in the crushing of rebellions in various parts of Germany.

Causes of the Peasants' Wars: Religious, Economic, Social and Political

Before Luther was born, peasants had been forming Bundschuh leagues.

Indeed, there had been many outbreaks of rebellion by the peasants all over Germany before the Reformation – 1476, 1492, 1493, 1502, 1513, 1514. All had been quelled by brute force and all had concluded in failure.

A.G. Dickens, *Reformation and Society in Sixteenth-Century Europe,* 1966.

'Bundschuh' – the laced-up shoe of the peasant, in contrast with the buckled shoe of his overlord, indicated his servitude.

Outside the towns and cities, the majority of Germans lived in villages, on the land, tilling it with indefatigable labour and primitive technology. Many historians have tried to generalise about the conditions of the German peasant in the age of the Lutheran Reformation. Was the peasant well-off or starving? Was his standard of living getting better or worse? The answer is that few generalisations can be made. So many millions of Germans were peasants; the very term – Bauer – is so vague and covers so many sub-types; and conditions varied from region to region of the Reich.

M. Mullet, *Luther,* 1986.

Yet Mullet goes on to describe the four generalisations which can be made about the condition of the peasants in 15th and 16th century Germany. These four general conditions help us to understand part of the peasants' motivation to rebel:

- Though earlier generations of peasants had benefited from scarcity of numbers following the Black Death of the mid-fourteenth century, numbers were now going up again, holdings were being split, and lords could once again exploit the peasants' excess numbers to drive hard bargains with them and impose fresh burdens.

- Almost regardless of economic conditions, many peasants were still consigned to serfdom and felt the shame and inconvenience of this antiquated system which lowered their dignity and restricted their freedom – for instance, to marry how they chose.

- The peasants clearly felt that their own village community ways of upholding justice and law were being invaded by lords' courts, often using the 'new' Roman law.

- The peasants felt oppressed by a host of cash payments and dues, notably the tithe or 10 percent levy on produce paid to the Church.

There has been much discussion of the causes of discontent and unrest in the peasantry. Of much greater consequence than material poverty (which certainly existed in south-west Germany, where many plots of land had been subdivided almost to vanishing point) was the fact that the peasants were almost without rights. They had no freedom, for they were subject to lords who had control over land, over justice, and over the peasant's own person, and hardly anywhere did they have official representation... Their rights were even further diminished by unlimited compulsory service which heightened the tension.

F. Lau and E. Bizer, *A History of the Reformation in Germany to 1555,* 1969.

One of the most contentious issues has been the role of Luther in the Peasants' War. The German Historian P. Blickle has argued that social protest became justified by Luther's interpretations of the Gospel. Indeed, the role of evangelical preachers, most famously Muntzer and Carlstadt, undoubtedly contributed to the motivation of rebels in some areas. But to what extent did this religious influence actually provoke rebellion? And did this influence dramatically alter the character of the 1525 rebellion from that of previous uprisings?

The Peasant War represented an attempt to overcome the crisis of feudalism through a revolutionary reshaping of social and seign-eurial relations on the basis of 'the Gospel'.

P. Blickle in R. Scribner and G. Benecke (eds), *The German Peasant War of 1525: New Viewpoints,* 1979.

The evangelical message brought to this long tradition of peasant protest the sanction of a higher authority for their demands and grievances, the Word of God, a more concrete form of the 'divine law' to which they had sometimes appealed earlier. The Word of God as they understood it taught that serfdom was contrary to the freedom of Christians, that tithe was not justified in the Bible, and that any demands not founded on the Word of God should be held to be invalid.

R.W. Scribner, *The German Reformation,* 1986.

If Blickle is right, then there was a mass popular reception of evangelical ideas among the peasantry, and we can certainly speak of the German Peasants' War as an evangelical-social movement. However, it is also possible that many of the statements expressing radical biblicism were written into peasant manifestos by leaders from the educated urban elite.

R.W. Scribner, *The German Reformation,* 1986.

Muntzer came to Muhlhausen, and there he was responsible for fomenting a peasants' war. In front of the pulpit he unfurled a long, silk banner, emblazoned with a rainbow and the motto, 'The Word of the Lord Abideth Forever'. 'Now this is the time', he cried. 'If you be only three wholly committed unto God, you need not fear one hundred thousand. On! On! On! Spare not! Pity not the godless when they cry. Remember the command of God to Moses to destroy utterly and show no mercy. The whole countryside is in commotion. Strike! Clang! Clang! On! On!'

R. Bainton, *Here I Stand*, 1994.

What was the German Peasants' War, 1525?

You will note that Historians often use labels to describe things. The German Peasants' War is typical of the use of such labels.

> The last unintegrated wave of protest that swept over the whole of central Europe was primarily urban... Each wave of revolt was distinct in time, motivation, leadership and duration.
>
> H. Kamen, *European Society 1500–1700*, 1992.

What does Kamen suggest about the label 'German Peasants' War'?

Was it war?

Many issues surround the nature of the uprisings. Did peasant rebels seek a conservative return to the past or a radical approach to the future? Did evangelical preachers influence their cause? And who wrote their various complaints?

Was it German?

While most of the rebels were German speaking and inhabited the Holy Roman Empire the term German is misleading. The uprisings were confined to South and Central Germany and there was little participation in Bavaria. North Germany was hardly touched.

Were they peasants?

It is clear that the uprisings were carried out by peasants, miners, citizens of towns, and the poorer disenfranchised citizens of cities.

The Twelve Articles of Memmingen

The Twelve Articles (below) constitute one of the more moderate peasant manifestos, yet even these famous demands were not representative of the Peasants' War as a whole.

In addition, it is quite possible that such manifestos were drawn up by educated, middle-class leaders, and therefore differed slightly from the true sentiments of the ordinary rebels themselves.

The twelve articles were:

Note the influence of Lutheran beliefs such as the priesthood of all believers and the authority of Scripture on these articles. Luther's complex theological ideas were often misunderstood and transferred from a religious to a social context.

1. The right to elect their own pastor.
2. Freedom from the small tithe (but agreement to pay the grain tithe). ·
3. The abolition of bond-service since all men were redeemed by the love of Christ. They promised however to obey their lawful elected rulers in all things reasonable.
4. Freedom to hunt and fish.
5. A share in the forests for domestic fuel.
6. Restriction of compulsory service.
7. Payment for labour over and above the contract. (Payment for overtime, as we should now say.)
8. Reduction of rents.
9. Cessation of arbitrary punishments.
10. Restoration of the pastures and fields which had been taken from the communes.
11. Abolition of the right of heriot, by which widows and orphans were deprived of their inheritance. (Heriot meant originally restoration of weapons to the lord on decease of tenant.)
12. All these demands to be tested by scripture and if not in agreement therewith, to be withdrawn.

What was the Role of Luther in the German Peasants' War?

Luther's political convictions remained somewhat typical of the middle and upper social orders. God may have stricken our princes with madness; they may be 'the greatest fools or the worst rogues on earth', yet Mr Everyman is manifestly unfitted to correct their faults. It was not during the Peasants' Revolt but four years earlier in 'Christian Nobility' that Luther declared, 'I will always side with him, however unjust, who suffers rebellion, and against him who rebels, however unjustly'.

A.G. Dickens, *The German Nation and Martin Luther*, 1974.

In your secular government all you do is fleece and tax to maintain your own pride and splendour, until the poor common man can no longer sustain the burden. The sword is at your neck.

Luther's 'Exhortation to the Peace', 1525.

Luther... stood on such firm principles that from the very outset he wages total war against spiritualistic and anarchic radicalism, a war wherein he would use but one weapon and that was words. It was only at the eleventh hour when the peasantry were already engaged on brutal offensive action, and when Luther had already failed in his mission of reconciliation, that he counselled war to the death against persistent lawless devilry as the only effective course then open to bring the rebellion to an immediate end... What Luther saw at stage was the Gospel. Had it been identified with civil war and rebellion it might have been crushed, in Germany at least. The violence of his language is the measure of the issue that was at stake.

J. Atkinson, *Martin Luther and the Birth of Protestantism*, 1968.

If the peasant is in open rebellion, then he is outside the law of God, for rebellion is not simply murder, but it is like a great fire which attacks and lays waste a whole land. Thus, rebellion brings with it a land full of murders and bloodshed, makes widows and orphans, and turns everything upside down like a great disaster. Therefore, let everyone who can, smite, slay and stab, secretly or openly, remembering that nothing can be more poisonous, hurtful or devilish than a rebel. It is just as when one must kill a mad dog; if you don't strike him, he will strike you, and the whole land with you...

...if the ruler is a Christian and tolerates the Gospel, so that the peasants have no appearance of a case against him, he should proceed with fear. First he must take the matter to God, confessing that we have deserved these things, and remembering that God may, perhaps, have thus aroused the devil as a punishment upon all Germany. Then he should humbly pray for help against the devil... Then... offer the mad peasants an opportunity to come to terms, even though they are not worthy of it. Finally, if that does not help, then swiftly grasp the sword.

Luther, 'Against the Murderous and Thieving Hordes of Peasants' from E.G. Rupp and B. Drewery, *Luther: Documents of Modern History*, 1970.

Note the difference in tone between the first and second paragraphs. Though the second paragraph is more representative of Luther's initial response to the peasants' actions, it is the first paragraph for which 'Against the Murderous and Thieving Hordes of Peasants' is notorious. Do you think Luther's apparent change in attitude was unreasonable or incomprehensible?

What an outcry I have caused with my little pamphlet against the peasants! Everything God has done for the world through me is forgotten. Now lords, priests and peasants are all against me and threaten me with death.

Luther, in a letter to friends, announcing his marriage, quoted in H.J. Hillerbrand, *The Reformation in its own Words,* 1966.

... that one sentence of Luther's, 'smite, slay, and stab', brought him obloquy never to be forgotten. He was reproached by the peasants as a traitor to their cause, though he never ceased to be held responsible by the Catholic princes for the entire conflagration. The peasants in consequence tended to find their religious home in Anabaptism, though this point must not be overdone... [In fact] to the end of his life Luther's congregation consisted largely of the farmers around Wittenberg. Nevertheless, Luther's stand was contributory to the alienation of the peasants.

R. Bainton, *Here I Stand,* 1994.

The effect of this apparent betrayal on German perceptions of Martin Luther can only be a matter of conjecture... Did Luther's 'safe' attitudes in 1525 make his Reformation acceptable to German princes and other rulers? In the years after 1525, large areas of Germany accepted the Lutheran Reformation in a formal and constitutional way.

M. Mullet, *Luther,* 1986.

...the Catholic princes held Luther responsible for the whole outbreak, and colour was lent to the charge by the participation on the peasants' side of hundreds of Lutheran ministers... The rulers in Catholic lands thereafter use the utmost diligence to exclude evangelical preachers, and the persistent Catholicism of Bavaria and Austria dates not so much from the Counter Reformation as from the Peasants' War.

R. Bainton, *Here I Stand*, 1994.

The Defeat of the Peasants' War

The peasants' cause was just, their demands most moderate and fair. The tragic mistake they made was in identifying the religious cause of Luther with their own social and economic cause.

J. Atkinson, *Martin Luther and the Birth of Protestantism*, 1968.

The main reason for the peasants' defeat was that they fought in 'groups' ... and had leaders... but no coherent direction, many programmes – both utopian and realistic – but no actual policy. Division amongst the peasants themselves – some advocating a return to the 'old justice' by restoring lost liberties, and others seeking a 'divine justice' in the shape of a new ordering of society – positively encouraged their opponents to play one off against the other.

F. Lau and E. Bizer, *A History of the Reformation in Germany to 1555*, 1969.

A chronicler described the fate of the peasants and Thomas Muntzer in the crucial battle at Frankenhausen:

Then they advanced towards the peasants and began to fire. The poor people just stood there and sang, 'Now we pray the Holy Spirit', as if they were insane. They neither resisted nor fled. Many comforted themselves in Thomas' great promise that God would send help from heaven, since Thomas had said he would catch all bullets in his coat sleeves...

Otto H. Brandt, 'Die Historie Thomas Muntzer', in H.J. Hillerbrand, *The Reformation in its Own Words*, 1966.

1 What was the role of individuals in causing and perpetuating the uprisings?

2 Is it meaningful to use labels like 'the German peasants' war'?

3 Is it fair to link the social and economic uprisings with the religious Reformation?

After the defeat of the Peasants' War, the desire for 'evangelical preaching' remained strong among Alsatian peasantry, but the determination of Catholic authorities not to concede it, and the caution of reformed authorities about being involved in renewed social upheaval led to a loss of religious fervour. By the 1540's the complaint was of peasant indifferent to reform, rather than enthusiasm for it. This echoes the view of many historians that there was rather less enthusiasm for evangelical ideas in rural areas after 1525. Perhaps such ideas had not struck very deep roots in the peasantry, or the peasants were moved to abandon their initial interest out of disillusionment with the failure of Luther and other prominent reformers to support their call for social justice on the basis of the Word of God.

R.W. Scribner, *The German Reformation*, 1986.

FOCUS

4.2 The Life and Work of Thomas Muntzer

Thomas Muntzer was, in many ways, a typical Reformation radical. Read the following section and identify what he contributed to the Reformation. Assess also why he remained on the periphery of the movement.

THOMAS MÜNZER,
STOLBERGENSIS, PASTOR ALSTED.

Muntzer was driven by a radical apocalyptic vision, believing that the end of the world was imminent.

He felt that this would rectify many of the glaring injustices suffered by Christians in the world. Initially, he demanded that the princes should step in to further reform, to hasten the rule of the Saints. Then he quickly went a stage further, threatening the princes that if they did not fulfil their Christian duty, they would suffer the wrath of God and that the task of rooting out the ungodly would be taken up by the Saints themselves.

History has remembered only the violent Muntzer wielding the sword and heaping salvos of abuse upon his enemies. It has forgotten the more gentle Muntzer, the theologian steeped in mystical resignation, that pastor ministering to his flock, the first liturgist of Protestantism. The legend of Muntzer, constructed by the Wittenberg orthodoxy of Luther and Melanchthon, seized deliberately upon the image of the fanatical insurrectionary in the peasants' war, and belittled or ignored his theological erudition, his intellectual creativity and above all his earnest humanity.

Tom Scott, *Thomas Muntzer*, 1989.

The Main Events of Muntzer's Life

1489?	Born at Stolberg
1512–20	Early career as student, assistant teacher and chantry priest.
1520	Preacher at St Mary's Church in Zwickau.
1521	Visit to Prague and publishes Prague Manifesto.
1523	Pastor of St John's Church Allstedt and marriage to former nun Ottilie von Gersen. Publishes German Church Service, including the German Evangelical Mass and forms first Allstedt League of thirty members.
1524	Interrogated by Allstedt councillors for his views and flees the city. First visit to Muhlhausen.
1525	Returns to Muhlhausen and becomes rector of St Mary's Church. Musters the Muhlhausen militia and forms the Eternal League of God. Introduces reformation to Muhlhausen and joins peasant rebellion in Thuringia.
May 1525	Leads Muhlhausen contingent at Battle of Frankenhausen. Muntzer captured and tortured. Muhlhausen captured by the princes and Muntzer executed.

Leipzig Debate, 1519

He probably travelled to Leipzig in June 1519 to attend a public disputation between the Wittenberg Reformers and their Catholic opponents. Muntzer was no more than a silent spectator at the rounds of theological jousting, but he cannot fail to have digested the essential messages of the reforming party: that the Church as it stood, Roman and Pontifical, constituted a grave historical deformation of early Christianity.

It can be no coincidence that Muntzer straight away set about furiously buying books on the history of the early Church. From a Leipzig bookseller, he ordered *Eusebius's Chronicle* in two volumes, *Josephus's Jewish War*, *The Complete Jerome*, and *The Letters and Sermons of Augustine*. He must also have bought the ten volumes of *Eusebius's History of the Church*.

Tom Scott, *Thomas Muntzer*, 1989.

You breathe nothing but slaughter and blood.

Johann Agricola, 1521.

This accusation followed a sermon on Muntzer in 1520 at Zwickau against a local Catholic priest. As a result of the sermon, an angry congregation pelted the priest with dung and stones in the churchyard, and he only escaped with his life by fleeing the town.

The Prague Manifesto

But St Paul writes to the Corinthians in the third chapter of the second Epistle that the hearts of men are the paper or parchment on which God's finger inscribes His unchangeable will and His Eternal wisdom. A writing which any man can read provided his mind has been opened to it... God has done this for His elect from the very beginning so that the testimony they are given is not uncertain but an invincible one from the Holy Spirit.

Thomas Muntzer, 'The Prague Manifesto'.

The German Church Service Published in Allstedt

This was a prayer book for all the offices of the church year and was the first prayer book in the German language. The key features were:

- It simplified and reduced the Catholic services.
- It contained a German evangelical Mass.
- Transubstantiation was replaced by 'the mystery of God entering man's soul and filling it with His Spirit'.
- It advocated the joyful singing of psalms and hymns to familiar tunes.
- It included prayers and responses by the congregation.
- It stressed baptism and the Eucharist as sacraments.

Muntzer's Letter to the People of Allstedt, 27 April 1525

The pure fear of God be with you, brothers. What are you still sleeping for, why have you not recognized the will of God – do you think He has abandoned you, is that it? Ah, how often have I told you that God can only reveal Himself in this way, in your apparent abandonment. If not, the offering of your broken and contrite hearts must be in vain. And you must then come into another kind of suffering. I tell you again, if you won't suffer for God, then you will be devil's martyrs. So take care,cheer up, do your duty, and stop pandering to those fantastic perverts, those knaves. Get going, and fight the battle for the Lord! It is high time, keep the brethren together so that they do not mock the divine witness, or they will be all destroyed. The whole of Germany, France and the Roman lands are awake – the Master will start his game, and the knaves are for it! At Fulda in Easter week four collegiate churches were destroyed, the peasants in Klettgau and Hegau are up, three thousand strong, and the longer it goes on the more they are. So now On! On! On! – it is time to hunt the knaves down like dogs – On! On! On! – have no mercy even though Esau gives you good words – Genesis XXXIII. Do not look at the misery of the godless. They will beg you, will whine and cry like children. But you are to have no mercy, as God commanded through Moses – Deuteronomy VII – and has also revealed to us. Get going in the villages and town, and especially with the miners and the other good fellows. We must sleep no more... And see, as I write, here is a piece of news which has just come in – from Salza – how the good people there have taken Duke George's officer from his castle... the peasants of Eichsfeld have turned enemies to their lords and in brief will have none of their favour. Here's an example for you! On! On! On! Time's up! Balthasar and Bartel Kruimp, Valtin and Bischoff, you lead the dance out on to the floor! ... On! On! On! Let not your sword grow cold, let it not be blunted. Smite, cling, clang, on the anvil of Nimrod, and cast the tower to the ground ... On! On! On! while it is still day – God goes ahead of you, follow, follow, follow – be not fearful, for God is with you, and you shall not be put off by the numbers against you, for it is not your battle but the Lord's. So go to it through God who will strengthen you in the right faith, without any fear of man...

Thomas Muntzer, 'A servant of God against the godless', from
G. Franz, *Muntzer, Schriften v Briefe*.

REVIEW

1 What does Scribner mean by the last sentence?
2 Is it fair to publish articles which simply suggest possibilities rather than argue for complete theses?
3 Scribner argues that the traditional view 'no longer fits the facts'. What are the 'facts'? Is there such a thing as a fact in History? There are no action replays – and even the camera can lie!
4 Is the Historian's job to awaken in us new ways of making sense of the past? What does this mean? And how can Historians best try to do it? Or is the Historian's job to convince us that there is no sense to be made of the past, because, like the present, it is incomplete and mutable?

A SATIRICAL CARTOON SHOWING MANY ASPECTS OF LUTHER'S WORK. WHAT DIFFERENT FEATURES CAN YOU SEE IN THE PICTURE?

R.W. Scribner, in his introduction to *Popular Culture and Popular Movements in Reformation Germany*, refers to 'the conviction of pious Protestant historians that the Reformation was unified and directed by Lutheran theology.'

He then goes on to argue that:

> it is clear that this traditional view no longer fits the facts... but there is no attempt here to suggest a full-blown alternative. The 'Social History' of the Reformation is too recent to do so, and the articles presented here are mostly of a preliminary nature. There is no need to apologise for this incompleteness. It represents the obligation of the historian to regard his or her task as incomplete, to try continually to ask further questions, and to realise that writing history partakes of the very incompleteness and mutability of life itself.

5 John Calvin and the Second Wave of the Reformation

PREVIEW

The Human Dimension

In the Spring of 1541 John Calvin was invited by the Genevan Small Council to return to their city.

The son of a French notary from Noyon, educated in Paris, Orleans and Bourges, he had probably converted from Catholicism in the late 1520s. Geneva had already broken with Rome and now the Small Council wanted a religious leader to establish the Reformed Religion in the city.

Between 1541 and his death in 1564, Calvin worked ceaselessly to provide the lead they required. He struggled to overcome opposition, to gain support, to change men's attitudes and beliefs. He was a foreigner, never a member of any council, and he accepted

IOH. CALVINUS THEOLOGUS
NATUS NOVIODUNI X. IUL. MDIX.
DENATUS GENEVÆ. XXVII MAIJ MDLXIIII.
Gallia me recipit doctore & Scotia Christum:
Pastorem sepelit culta Geneva suum.

JOHN CALVIN (1509–64).

Genevan citizenship only in 1559. He suffered long periods of illness and exhaustion, yet he never ceased his labours.

This chapter tells the story of a remarkable achievement. It is a story of enormous human commitment in two senses: Calvin's own total commitment to his – and his God's – cause, and also his ability to gain a similar commitment from others, sometimes in the face of stern opposition.

In his summary of John Calvin's career, Michael Mullet wrote:

> Perhaps, had Calvin lived to see the agony of his beloved France through decades of religious warfare, he would have moderated the uncompromisingly adversarial tone that he used. With the wars of religion well under way, Calvin, in his mid 50's, looked and was old, bowed down by a lifetime's overwork and a settled anxiety state, in constant unappeased pain. His acute terminal illness brought out more sharply than ever the human miracle of John Calvin.
>
> M. Mullet, *John Calvin*, 1988.

The Genevan Reformation Before Calvin

Professor Geoffrey Elton has provided the following description of the city of Geneva in the early 16th century.

> The City of Geneva, French speaking but not of France, was in some ways particularly well suited to become the seat of Calvin's true Church. Subject to its Bishop, it had experienced the usual difficulties of medieval towns with ecclesiastical overlords in obtaining freedom and self-government. A third party in the conflict were the Dukes of Savoy, who by the fifteenth century had secured a permanent hold on that particular episcopal mitre. From 1511 onwards, Bishop and Duke tried to restore their ascendancy by reducing the city's hard-won liberties, but their successes were cut short in 1525–26 when Geneva obtained the friendship and support of Bern and Fribourg. The Bishop fled the city in 1527 and concerted military action with Savoy, so that the elected syndics of Geneva declared the seat vacant in 1534. The town's armed resistance triumphed early in 1536 when Bernese troops dispersed the Bishop's somewhat casual investment and went on to attack Savoy. Bern had hopes of establishing suzerainty over Geneva, but the citizens' desire for independence was greater than their fear of a Savoyard revival, and the aggressive neighbour city had to be content with an alliance. A town which had won its freedom in a battle with an episcopal Lord was manifestly ready for the Reformation, and from 1533 evangelical preachers had been active there with much encouragement from the magistrates.

In addition, Geneva was in economic decline. It had been an important mart town in the later middle ages, commanding a crossing of the Alpine road with the route down the Rhone into France.

But in the later fifteenth century France and Savoy had begun to boycott its prosperous fairs, partly for political reasons and partly in order to promote the rising prosperity of Lyons. At the same time, Bern was overtaking the Rhone city as a centre for trade passing through Switzerland. Thus the Geneva of the Reformation was struggling against decay, its poor, often unemployed, and its richer merchants nothing so splendid as they had been. It would seem that declining prosperity expressed itself in a growing recklessness; sober trading gave way to speculative gambling, and the general uncertainty led to a somewhat feverish public and private life.

It is essential to stress that the Protestant Reformation occurred in Geneva before John Calvin arrived. After the defeat of Savoy in 1536, the City Council forbade all priests from celebrating Mass. On 21st May citizens gathered in the Church of St. Pierre and swore they would 'live according to the Word of God'. They agreed to reject all Catholic ceremonies and send all their children to a new school. Farel presented a plan to organize the new Church and in November he was joined by Calvin. They were charged to take the Reformation on into a second wave.

G.R. Elton, *Reformation Europe*, 1985.

John Calvin's Life and Career: Main Events

1509	Birth in Noyon, Northern France, the fourth son of a local lawyer and church official.
1521	Received a church office to finance his education.
1523	College de la Marche in Paris. Friendship with humanists such as Olivetan and scholars such as Bude.
1528	Studied law at Orleans.
1532	Published a Latin commentary on Seneca's *De Clementia*. Humanist features revealed.
1533	Fled from Paris after a lecture in favour of Lutheranism by his friend Nicholas Cop.
1528–34	Experienced religious conversion. Precise date not known.
1534	'Day of the Placards' in France. Calvin's brother executed as heretic. Calvin fled to Basle.
1535	Published first edition of *Institutes of the Christian Religion* in Basle – a clear and powerful statement of his theology.
1536	Arrived in Geneva after intervention of Farel. Presented to the Council a proposal called 'Articles concerning the Organization of the Church and of Worship in Geneva'.
1538	Forced to leave Geneva for exile in Strasburg, after opposition to his reforms.
1541	Returned to Geneva. Great public welcome. Published *Ecclesiastical Ordinances*, a detailed survey of how church and state should be governed.
1555	Calvin's main opponents defeated. His main rival, Ami Perrin, the leader of the Libertine group fled. Calvin's influence unchallenged for next nine years.
1564	Death in Geneva.

John Calvin's Early Life and Career

Extracts from a Biography by Theodore Beza, 1564
This biography was published within a few weeks of Calvin's death and written by the man who succeeded him as Minister of the Church of Geneva.

1 Beza claimed to be a 'Spectator of Calvin's conduct for sixteen years'. What are his conclusions about Calvin's conduct? Does he have appropriate evidence for them?

2 Apply possible dates to the five extracts quoted here.

3 What impression do you gain of French politics at this time?

4 What picture does Beza present of Calvin? Why did a young man aged 24 commit himself so powerfully to a cause?

5 Beza's biography was written in Latin. Can you guess roughly when this translation into English was made?

Having set out for Orleans to study law, Calvin, in a short time, made such astonishing progress, that he very often officiated for the professors, and was considered rather a teacher than a pupil...

Some persons, still alive, who were then on familiar terms with him, say that, at that period, his custom was, after supping very frugally, to continue his studies until midnight, and on getting up in the morning, to spend some time meditating, and digesting what he had read in bed. While so engaged he was very unwilling to be interrupted. By these prolonged vigils, he acquired solid learning and an excellent memory: but it is probable he also contracted that weakness of stomach, which afterwards brought on various diseases, and ultimately led to his untimely death.

About this time, Calvin renouncing all other studies, devoted himself to God, to the great delight of all the pious who were then holding secret meetings in Paris.

It was not long before an occasion occurred for strenuous exertion... [Nicholas Cop preached a sermon in Paris and was ordered to appear before the Sorbonne]. He accordingly set out, but being warned on the way to beware of his enemies, turned back, and afterwards quitting the country, retired to Basle. Search was made at the College of Fortret where Calvin was residing. He happened not to be at home, but his papers were seized, and among them numerous letters from his friends...

The rage of the infatuated monarch Francis was so inflamed, on account of certain squibs against the mass which had been circulated all over the city... that he appointed a public fast, during which he went to church with his three children, with his head uncovered and carrying a blazing torch as a kind of expiation. He ordered 32 Martyrs to be burned alive (eight at each of the four most public places in the city) and declared with solemn oath that he would not spare even his own children if they were infected with those dire heresies.

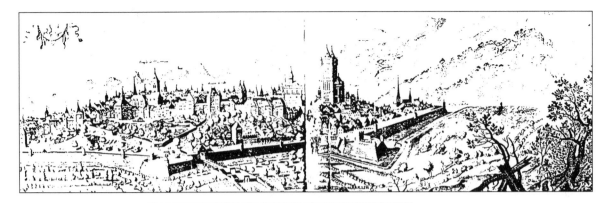

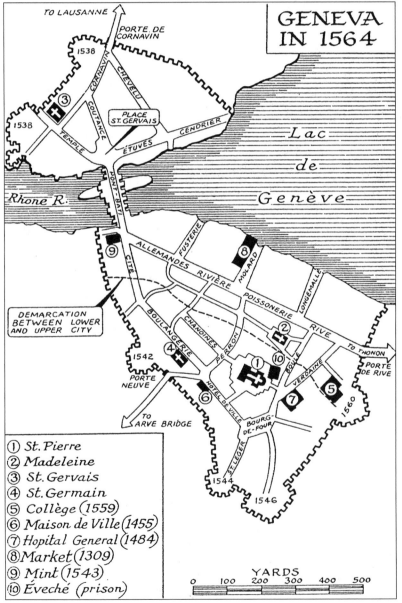

GENEVA IN 1564

TO LAUSANNE
PORTE DE CORNAVIN
1538
CHEVELU
NAVIGATION
COUTANCE
PLACE ST. GERVAIS
TEMPLE
ÉTUVES
CENDRIER
1538
③
Rhône R.
Lac de Genève
PONT-BATI
CITÉ
⑨
ALLEMANDES
FUSTERIE
RIVIÈRE
MOLARD
POISSONERIE
⑧
LONGEMALLE
RIVE

DEMARCATION BETWEEN LOWER AND UPPER CITY

BOULANGERIE
CHANOINES
PERRON
②
⑩
TO THONON
PORTE DE RIVE
1542
④
PORTE NEUVE
①
HÔTEL DE VILLE
BOULE
VERDAIRE
⑤
1560
⑥
⑦
TO ARVE BRIDGE
BOURG-DE-FOUR
ST. LÉGER
1544
1546

① St. Pierre
② Madeleine
③ St. Gervais
④ St. Germain
⑤ Collège (1559)
⑥ Maison de Ville (1455)
⑦ Hôpital General (1484)
⑧ Market (1309)
⑨ Mint (1543)
⑩ Évéché (prison)

YARDS
0   100   200   300   400   500

TALKING POINT

In what ways do the picture and plan of the city corroborate Elton's description? Was it 'well suited to become the seat of Calvin's true Church'?

Calvin's Personal Life in Geneva, 1541–64

Calvin occupied a large house in the heart of the city. He lived with his wife, Idelette, and her daughters, his brother Antoine and Antoine's wife and children, and their family servants. Calvin lived in a most humble manner. His house and its furniture belonged to the Council: 'I am still using someone else's furniture. Neither the table at which we eat, nor the bed on which we sleep, is my own.'

Calvin's wife did not enjoy good health. She was ill for most of 1545, 1547 and 1548, and died in March 1549. 'Truly mine is no common grief. I have been bereaved of the best friend of my life... During her life she was the faithful helper of my ministry.' Calvin and Idelette had one son who died soon after his premature birth. Calvin's brother Antoine was less fortunate in his marriage: in 1557 his wife was taken in adultery with Calvin's servant, the hunchback Daguet. Calvin's step-daughter Judith was also caught in adultery, and both these events caused Calvin much shame.

Calvin's daily life was long and arduous. One of his neighbours, the lawyer Germain Colladon, wrote a biography soon after Calvin's death.

> As to his ordinary life, everyone will bear witness that he was very abstemious, without any excess or meanness, but a praiseworthy moderation. It is true that for his stomach's sake he abstained from some common foods that he was fond of, but this was without being fastidious or troublesome in company.
>
> One fault he had was that in his abstinence he took little regard to his health, mostly being content for many years with a single meal a day and never taking anything between two meals... His reasons were the weakness of his stomach and his migraine, which he said he had proved by experiment could be remedied only by a continual diet. Sometimes I have known him go without any food into the second day.
>
> Being so frail he also slept very little; but for all the lassitude that ensued from this he never failed to be ready for his work and the exercises of his office. When it was not his turn to preach, he had books brought to him in bed at five or six o'clock, so that he might compose, having someone to write for him. If it was his week, he was always ready at the hour to go into the pulpit; then afterwards at home he lay down on the bed fully clothed and pursued his labours on some book... This is how in the mornings he dictated the most of his books, when he could give his genius full flow.
>
> I do not believe there can be found his like. For who could recount his ordinary and extraordinary labours. I doubt if any man in our time has had more to listen to, to reply to, to write, or things of greater importance. The multitude and the quality alone of his writings is enough to astonish everyone who looks at them, and even more those who read them... He never ceased working, day and night, in the service of the Lord, and heard most unwillingly the prayers and exhortations that his friends addressed to him every day to give himself some rest...

In all his work, Calvin was surrounded in the Rue des Chanoins by old and trusted friends. His next-door neighbour, Nicholas Cop, had fled Paris before Calvin in 1533. Round the corner lived Francois Bude, son of the influential French humanist Guillaume. Other neighbours included Laurent de Normandie, a lawyer from Noyon and now a great publisher, and Robert Estienne, another Frenchman, who moved to Geneva in 1550 and became its foremost printer.

Many of his neighbours were also members of the Venerable Company of Pastors, and the vast majority were fellow refugees from France. In fact, most of the city's doctors, lawyers and ministers were immigrants. It was not until 1573 that a man born in the city became a member of the Venerable Company of Pastors.

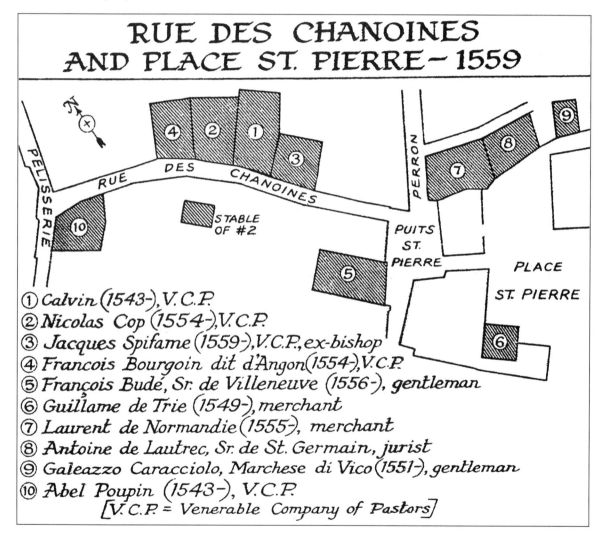

RUE DES CHANOINES AND PLACE ST. PIERRE – 1559

① Calvin (1543-), V.C.P.
② Nicolas Cop (1554-), V.C.P.
③ Jacques Spifame (1559-), V.C.P., ex-bishop
④ Francois Bourgoin dit d'Angon (1554-), V.C.P.
⑤ François Budé, Sr. de Villeneuve (1556-), gentleman
⑥ Guillame de Trie (1549-), merchant
⑦ Laurent de Normandie (1555-), merchant
⑧ Antoine de Lautrec, Sr. de St. Germain, jurist
⑨ Galeazzo Caracciolo, Marchese di Vico (1551-), gentleman
⑩ Abel Poupin (1543-), V.C.P.
[V.C.P. = Venerable Company of Pastors]

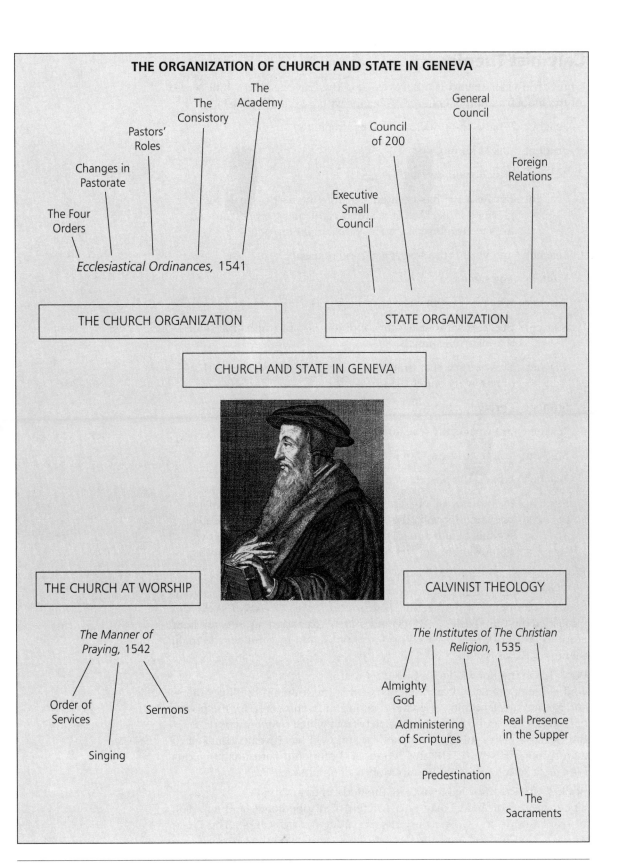

THE ORGANIZATION OF CHURCH AND STATE IN GENEVA

The Academy

The Consistory

Pastors' Roles

Changes in Pastorate

The Four Orders

General Council

Council of 200

Executive Small Council

Foreign Relations

Ecclesiastical Ordinances, 1541

THE CHURCH ORGANIZATION

STATE ORGANIZATION

CHURCH AND STATE IN GENEVA

THE CHURCH AT WORSHIP

CALVINIST THEOLOGY

The Manner of Praying, 1542

Order of Services

Sermons

Singing

The Institutes of The Christian Religion, 1535

Almighty God

Administering of Scriptures

Predestination

Real Presence in the Supper

The Sacraments

Calvinist Theology

John Calvin's Christianity is best revealed in the Catechism which he wrote for the indoctrination of children. It begins with essential beliefs:

Teacher: What is the principal end of human life?

Student: It is to know God.

Teacher: Why do you say that?

Student: Because He has created us and put us on earth to be glorified in us. And it is surely right that we dedicate our lives to His glory, since He is the beginning of it.

Teacher: And what is the sovereign good of men?

Student: The same.

Teacher: Why do you call it the sovereign good?

Student: Because without it our condition is more unhappy than that of brute animals.

Teacher: Thus we see that there is no unhappiness so great as that of not living under God.

Student: Certainly.

Teacher: But what is the true and correct knowledge of God?

Student: When we know Him in order to honour Him.

Teacher: What is the proper way to honour Him?

Student: By putting all our trust in Him; that we serve Him by obeying His will; that we go to Him in all our needs, seeking health and all good things from Him; and that we acknowledge, in our hearts as well as with our mouths, that all good comes from Him alone.

Calvin's Catechism, first printed in 1545, was able to build on his great classic statement of faith, the *Institutes of the Christian Religion*, published first in Basle in 1535 and much expanded in several later editions. The *Institutes* is based on four books, and they reflect the main themes of Calvin's faith:

Book 1: 'On the Knowledge of God the Creator'
God is omniponent and omniscient: 'God is the fountain of all goodness and we must seek nothing elsewhere but in Him... This sense for the power of God teaches us the full meaing of piety from which religion is born.'
But because man's mind is confused by sin, God has revealed himself to man through His Word: 'By this Word, God rendered faith unambiguous for ever, a faith that should be superior to all opinion.'

Book 2: 'On the Knowledge of God, the Redeemer in Christ'
Since the Fall of Adam, man is convicted of disobedience and sin. The Word of God in the Gospels reveals the atonement of Christ, The Elect, who trust in Christ, receive the benefit of his sacrifice on the Cross.

Book 3: 'On the Manner of Receiving the Grace of Christ'

The Holy Spirit brings faith to the believer's heart. God has chosen those who are sacred for Eternal Life, and condemned the others to damnation.

Book 4: 'On the Outward Means by which God invites us into the Fellowship of Christ'

This book describes the role of the Church and the Sacrament. The Church is invisible, made up of more chosen to be saved and only God 'knows them that are His'.

In another sense, the Church is visible in the world: wherever men confess a belief in Christ and worship the true God. The Songs of the True Church are the preaching of the Word of God, and the proper administration of the two Sacraments: Baptism and the Lord's Supper. 'When we speak of Sacraments, two things are to be considered, the sign and the thing itself. In Baptism the sign is water, but the thing is the washing of the Soul by the blood of Christ.'

In the Lord's Supper, Calvin joined other reformers in rejecting transubstantiation. Calvin agreed that Christ was bodily in Heaven, yet he was also really and spiritually present in the bread and wine. 'From the physical things set forth in the Sacrament, we are led to spiritual things by a kind of analogy. Thus, when bread is given as a symbol of Christ's body, we must at once grasp this compassion: as bread nourishes and keeps the life of our body, so Christ's body is the only food to invigorate and enliven our soul.'

> How would you challenge Calvin's theological ideas? What questions would you ask of them?

The most difficult element in Calvin's theology is his great emphasis on the doctrine of predestination. Salvation can only come from God, and God has predestined those who are saved. People cannot do anything to further their cause. God has total power and He cannot be questioned. 'As scripture clearly shows, we say that God established by His eternal and unchangeable plan those whom He long before determined once for all to receive into salvation.'

'The decree, I admit, is a fearful one. And yet it is impossible to deny that God foreknew what the end of man was to be before He created him.'

The Genevan Congregation at Worship

'La Manyere de Faire Prieres' ('Book of Services') (1542)

The manner of praying in the French Churches, both before the preaching and after, together with French Psalms sung in the said Churches. Followed by the order and form of administering the Sacraments of Baptism and the Holy Supper of our Lord Jesus Christ, of Espousal and Confirmng the Marriage before the Congregation of the Faithful... The whole according to the Word of our Lord.

Teach and admonish one another in Psalms, in praises and in spiritual songs with Grace.

Sing to the Lord a new song. Let his praise be heard in the Congregation of the Faithful.

Let all who have breath praise the Lord.

The Order of a Sunday Morning Service

Minister: The Confession: 'Let us confess our sins to Almighty God...'

Minister: The Absolution: 'To all those who in this way repent and seek Jesus Christ for their salvation, I pronounce absolution in the name of the Father, and of the Son, and of the Holy Spirit. Amen.'

Congregation: Singing the first four Commandments

Minister: Prayer: that these laws be 'Written in our hearts so that we may seek only to serve and obey Thee.'

Congregation: Singing: Remaining six Commandments (as Minister enters pulpit).

Minister: Prayer, followed by Lord's Prayer.

Congregation: Singing a Psalm.

Minister: Sermon.

Minister: Bidding Prayer: 'Now let us fall down before the Majesty of our good God, praying to him that he will give his grace not only to us, but also to all peoples and nations of the earth.'

Minister: Prayers (for rulers, pastors, the Church, the salvation of all men etc.) followed by explanation of the Lord's Prayer.

Congregation: Singing a Psalm.

Minister: Blessing.

Congregational Singing

Among other things which recreate men and give him pleasure, music is either the first or one of the main; and we should reckon it a gift of God intended for this use... We experience that it has a great secret and almost incredible virtue to move hearts in one way or another... Singing incites us to pray to, and to praise, God, to meditate on his works that we may love, fear, honour and glorify Him... When we sing the Psalms, we are certain that God is putting words in our mouth and they are singing in us to exalt His glory.

Calvin, 'Epistle to the Reader'.

The Sermon

The Sermon was at the heart of the Genevan service, and Calvin was a brilliant preacher. He spoke from the heart, with a passionate, lively, direct and clear delivery. He preached without notes, but had a superb memory for the details of biblical meaning, having written commentaries on most Biblical passages. Moreover, he always meticulously prepared his thinking:

If I should enter the pulpit without deigning to glance at a book and frivolously think to myself, 'Oh well, when I preach, God will give me enough to say'... and do not carefully consider how I must apply Holy Scripture to the edification of the people, then I should be an arrogant upstart.

The main themes of Calvin's sermons were very clear. He stressed God's promises of eternal life and God's goodness and mercy; he urged the congregation to obedience and self-sacrifice. The people found the sermons difficult, but they struggled to understand because the sermon explained the Word of God, 'the Word that God Himself speaks'. Sermons explained the scriptures and the congregation was keen to understand.

TALKING POINT

What does the term 'indoctrination' mean? Is it fair to apply this word to Calvinism?

A CALVINIST TEMPLE.

Calvin preached almost every day and often twice on Sundays at the Church of St. Pierre. From 1549 we have a remarkable record of each sermon he preached, because a Frenchman, Denis Rageunier, took notes in shorthand. The sermons were then copied up and bound in sets. We know, therefore, the details of the 189 sermons on the Book of Acts preached on Sundays between 1549 and 1554, and also the text of his weekday sermons (174 on Ezekiel, 159 on Job, 200 on Deuteronomy, and many more). It was a remarkable series of expositions, and it was no surprise that his listeners became well trained in Christian theology to an intense degree.

Yet, while his main purpose was to expound the Word of God, his sermons were also very relevant to his congregation. One sermon, 'Ephesians', included this statement:

> Women have been allowed for a long time to become increasingly audacious. And besides, speech apart, they wear such provocative clothes... Ribald songs too are part of their behaviour... It is hard to discern whether they are women or men.

Another sermon, on 'Jeremiah', contained the following passage:

> This is similar to the invasion, the Turks today. For, you might ask the Kings of France and their Councillors, 'whose fault is it that the Turks come to us so easily?' It is because you have prepared the way for them by sea, because you have bribed them, and because your ports are open to them. And yet they have exercised the greatest cruelty towards your subjects.

And the reaction of several members of his congregation to this sermon can easily be gauged. 'When the Lord afflicts a country by wars, the rich make great gains'.

What would be the likely discussion at the church doors following these sermons?

5.1 John Calvin's influence over Geneva, 1541 – 64

Not for a moment should Geneva be dismissed as a brain washing tyranny. The system sought – and generally obtained – a willing and enthusiastic response from the individual.
A.G. Dickens, *The Age of Humanism*, 1977.

Pierre Ameaux, a manufacturer of playing card, 1546, called Calvin an evil man, a preacher of false doctrine. Arrested, tried by Small council, fined 60 crowns and public apology. Appealed, appeal heard by Council of 200. Sentence reduced to private apology to Calvin. Calvin objected and said he would preach no more. Riots in city. Council of 200 gave way. Ameaux parades through Geneva in his shirt, begging God's pardon.

1. Which of these three opinions receives strongest support from the information given?

2. Write, in one or two paragraphs, a statement of your own opinion of Calvin's influence over Geneva.

1547 letter found by Calvin in pulpit of St. Pierre. 'Big pot-belly, you and your fellows would be wise to shut up. If you drive us too far, you will curse the day you stripped your monastery... Beware of what I say'.
A Libertine, *Jacques Gruet*, was arrested and his house searched. Incriminating letters were found, critical of Calvin and of his religion. 'Do not be ruled by the voice or will or one man.' After prolonged torture, Gruet confessed that all laws made by man, that he had been in contact with a foreign power, that he had tried to subvert Church ordinances etc. Gruet sentenced by Consistory Court and hanged. 1550 workmen found gross obscenities under the floor of his house

Calvin faced no local opposition of any stature whatsoever. There were very few educated men who might have opposed him in Geneva.
W. Monter, *Calvin's Geneva*, 1967.

About 1545 and 1546 the uncoordinated opposition began to coalesce into a party. The name of Libertine describes them well. Their motive was political in that they were attempting to overturn Genevan law relating to Church Order.
T.H.L. Parker, *John Calvin*, 1975.

Laws against Taverns and Drunkenness, 1546
Closed taverns and opened 5 'Abbayes' – non-profit making religious houses. Grace before eating and drinking. Psalms sung, no dancing, nor swearing. Popular pressure removed the 'Abbayes' and restored the taverns.

A letter found in the house of Jacques Gruet
Men have many and diverse opinions in them. Each individual would wish to be ruled as he liked... Everyone who deliberately injures another deserves to be punished. But suppose I am a man who wants to eat his meals as he pleases, what affair is that to others? Or if I want to dance, or have a good time, what is that to do with the law? Nothing!

The Libertine Party did not like consistent discipline. It consisted of several inter-related families: Favres, Vandels, Bertheliers,. Septs. Many were members of Councils or Syndics. 'Les Enfants de Geneve'.

Ami Perrin was the leader of the Libertines, a syndic and Captain General of the Genevan army. In 1546 his wife as accused, with other notables, of dancing at a popular party. The Consistory Court imposed punishment but the Perrins denied it. Calvin wrote to him, stating that he ought to devote himself to 'the primary virtue of obeying God and maintaining good order in the Community'. In 1547 Perrin returned to Geneva and his wife was arrested and made to apologise. Perrin took the sentence as an insult and objected; he was promptly arrested and imprisoned. He was also accused of plotting with the French army. Rioting resulted in the release of Perrin and his restoration to the Council. In 1552, the Libertines won a majority of Council seats and Perrin was made First Syndic and Captain General. Conflict again broke out between Consistory and Council. Calvin admitted defeat and offered to resign.

Geneva had no police force. Men were encouraged to report their neighbours. Admonishment was the most common punishment.

The Organisation of the Genevan Church

When Calvin settled in Geneva for the second time in 1541, The Council wished to provide a detailed statement for the good ordering of the church. These *Ecclesiastical Ordinances* were drafted by a committee of Ministers and Councillors in two weeks. They were then revised by the Council of 200 before being made law in November 1541.

THE ECCLESIASTICAL ORDINANCES, 1541				
ORDER	PASTORS 'VENERABLE COMPANY'	ELDERS	DOCTORS OR TEACHERS	DEACONS
MAIN FUNCTION	PREACH AND ADMINISTER SACRAMENTS	PROVIDE DISCIPLINE	TEACH THE FAITHFUL AND REMOVE DOCTRINAL ERRORS	CARE FOR SICK & NEEDY
APPOINTMENT	ELECTED BY PASTORS CONFIRMED BY COUNCIL	12 LAYMEN CHOSEN FROM COUNCILS SERVE FOR ONE YEAR OR MORE	CHOSEN BY PASTORS CONFIRMED BY COUNCIL	ELECTED BY COUNCILS
DUTIES	DAILY & SUNDAY SERVICES WEEKLY MEETING TO STUDY BIBLE WEEKLY CHILDREN'S CATECHISM CLASS	DISCIPLINE OF CHURCH	PROFESSORS OF NEW & OLD TESTAMENTS SCHOOLMASTERS FOR BOYS' & GIRLS' SCHOOLS – PRIMARY SCHOOL IN EACH PARISH	CHARITY COMMISSIONERS DISPENSE RELIEF TO NEEDY & TO HOSPITAL SICK

Consistory Court met each Thursday. Responsible for discipline.

Church Court, but lay majority (6 pastors, 12 elders). Listened to offenders – dismiss those who see reason. Punish others – warnings, then deprivation of Lord's Supper and Reporting to Council.

Calvin's Church of Geneva... was an ideal construct. Formal distinctions between spiritual and temporal authority were, however, often buried in practice.
    W. Monter, *Calvin's Geneva*, 1967.

'The Church could not hold together unless a settled Government were agreed on, such as is prescribed to us in the Word of God and as was in use in the Early Church'. The tasks of the church were clearly defined: to preach the Gospel and administer the Sacraments, to teach the Faith and to care for the sick and needy, and finally to provide discipline.

THE GOVERNMENT OF THE STATE IN GENEVA

EXECUTIVE POWER   **SMALL COUNCIL**

'Messiers de Geneve'

25 Men Led by 4 Syndics

Included Treasurer and 2 Secretaries

Met Three Times Each Week

Conducted Foreign Affairs

Ran Finances And The Mint

Supervised City Regulations

Supervised Death Sentences

Dispensed Justice in Civil & Criminal Cases

Legislative Body

Council of 200

Met Once a Month

Passed Laws

Granted Pardons

Elected 25 Members of the Small Council

Legislative Body

General Council

All Male Citizens

Met Twice A Year

November: Fix Wine

Prices & Elect

Judges

January: Elect 4 Syndics

N.B. All Magistrates Were Native-Born Genevans.
Mostly they came from City Merchant Families.

To accomplish this task, four orders were needed, and they were supported by an Ecclesiastical Consistory Court. Study the chart on page 112. What strengths can you identify in the Genevan Church? What difficulties may have arisen in implementing the Ordinances? On what issues would greater clarification be required?

Calvin clearly saw the need to have a coherent group of pastors in The Venerable Company. Four new French pastors were appointed in 1543 and another four by 1545. Previous occupants of the posts were relegated to rural parishes. In addition, Calvin removed Sebastian Castellio, the principal of the College or Upper School, formerly a friend, but now a bitter opponent. Further, by 1546, Geneva gained clear control from Berne, over twelve rural parishes and new French pastors were appointed to these too.

The pastors were at the heart of Genevan society. Calvin himself set an astonishing example for taking services: as an illustration, he personally celebrated 270 weddings and 50 baptisms in the decade 1550–9. The pastors visited the sick and needy. Each Saturday after dinner they visited the prison. Each Thursday, they joined the twelve elders in the weekly meeting of the Consistory Court, 'to keep watch over every man's life.' This body was not a court for trial and punishment, rather was it to hear moral offences and admonish offenders. Penalties for not attending church, or for deliberate coughing during sermons, were common. The Court admonished the widow, who said 'Requiescat in pace' over her husband's grave: Latin Calvinist rituals were to be removed. It also warned five elderly men, who in the late 1550s could still not recite their Catechism.

Most important to Calvin's Geneva and its church was the founding of the Academy in 1559. Under the Headship of Theodore Beza and the staff of the school at Lausanne, who had recently resigned in protest to their overlords and migrated en bloc to Geneva, the college became famous for its scholarship throughout Europe. As Calvin had written in the *Ecclesiastical Ordinances*, 'a College should be instituted for instructing children, to prepare them for the Ministry as well as for civil government'. By 1564, there were over 1300 students at the school.

The Crisis, 1553–5

During 1552, the Libertine party were increasing their influence. In the elections of February 1553, they gained a narrow majority on the Small Council, Perrin was made First Syndic and his post as Captain General was revived. His brother-in-law, Pierre Tissot, was made Treasurer. The intermarriage of the three families – Vandels, Septs and Favres – now enabled Perrin to exert complete control.

Towards the end of 1552, three of these men – Balthazar Sept, Philibert Bonna, and Philibert Berthelier – followed a minister, Raymond Chaviset, a friend of Calvin and a member of the Company of Pastors, as he walked to the church of St. Pierre. They called repeatedly after him and shouted insults. As a result, the Consistory Court excommunicated the three men.

Who was now in control in Geneva? The *Ecclesiastical Ordinances* of 1541 gave the Consistory the right to excommunicate. But it said nothing of the offender's right of appeal or about who could remove excommunication.

After three months of debate, Balthazar Sept requested that he be allowed to take Communion and that his child be baptised. The Consistory said that this could not be permitted because he had been excommunicated. The Small Council, in support of Sept, summoned the pastors and asked them to justify all their excommunications. The pastors refused and threatened resignation. Calvin was distraught. In July, he offered the Council his resignation, but Perrin and his supporters turned it down. They did not want Calvin attacking them from a stronghold like Basle or Bern.

At this point, the city was overtaken by the public trial and execution of the declared heretic, Michael Servetus. Servetus's blatant criticisms of Calvin aggravated the problem, for his trial was conducted by the Small Council, and Perrin was keen to humiliate Calvin further. However, Servetus's guilt was confirmed and agreed by all, including other Swiss cities. Perrin still refused to accept the verdict and tried unsuccessfully to get the case transferred to the Council of 200. Servetus was sentenced to death and he was burned on 27 October 1553. 'His was the only case, but at the same time an extremely significant case, of a man put to death for his religious opinions in Calvin's Geneva' (W. Monter, *Calvin's Geneva*, 1967). The affair restored some of Calvin's purpose and revived his commitment.

He needed it, because early in 1554, Philibert Berthelier revived the issue of excommunication. This time there was a debate in the Council of 200 and the following decision was announced: 'As for the Lord's Supper, the Consistory has not the power to forbid anyone without the command of the Small Council. But if there is someone that the Consistory feels should not receive the Supper, it will be told to the Council who will discuss this and will decide whether he should be forbidden or not.' Calvin, of course, could not accept this verdict. He asked for a further debate in the General Council and this was granted.

Berthelier was again refused Communion in the summer of 1554 and the Small Council set up a commission to review the situation. Their Recommendation, in January 1555, was 'to respect the edicts passed by the General Assembly in 1541'. This implied that the Consistory had the power to excommunicate. More crucial, however, was the result of the elections to the Small Council in February.

The Calvinists were aided, as one eye-witness reports, 'by the votes of those angered by a Government for relatives'. Younger men now won control: the four Syndics were all Calvinists and the Small Council and the Council of 200 were purged of Perrin's supporters. Civic rights were granted to many French immigrants.

On 16 May, Perrin, now facing defeat, hosted a dinner for his supporters. Several took to the streets, and Perrin, in a spirit of bravado, took the symbolic baton of office from the new First Syndic, as he stood guard over a house in which immigrants were living. At midnight, the Small Council met in emergency session. They dispersed the crowd. Over the next two days, they interviewed many witnesses including Calvin. He depicted Perrin as inciting the crowd to riot and Perrin and others were indicted for sedition. One contemporary source tells how a friend of Perrin left the Council meeting at this point, by feigning a call of nature, to tell the deposed Captain General. Perrin and his allies fled the city in secret, and their flight seemed proof of their guilt. They were tried and condemned to death in their absence. Concerted opposition to Calvin's policies was ended.

Examining the Evidence

The Genevan Budget

Examine the following sources, and use them to comment on the statements at the end.

Source A

The Genevan Budget, 1544.

Receipts:

Public seals used at Town Hall and Civil Court	fl. 490
Farm of Halles (customs duties)	fl. 1,003
Farm of gabelle on wine	fl. 1,886
Farm of gabelle on meat	fl. 1,653
Farm of gabelle on salt	fl. 629
Tolls on Rhone (80 fl.) and Arve (230 fl.) bridges	fl. 310
Taxes on weighing and exporting wheat	fl. 313
Tax on fishermen (550 fl.) plus Wednesday fishermen	fl. 615
Farm of five public squares, plus rent of meadow near walls	fl. 90
Rents of butchers' benches at two market places	fl. 300
Charities owed to Convent at Rive	fl. 100
Rent for the large powder mill and hemp works	fl. 95
Rent from the 'large inn called the Lyon d'or'	fl. 156
Rent from eight different houses	fl. 143
Rent from homes of two Artichauds (Monathon, Chapeau-rouge)	fl. 29
Rent from various meadow and pastures	fl. 30
Fines to reclaim houses and church of St. Germain	fl. 94
Quitrents on twenty-three other houses	fl. 346
Quitrents on mills	fl. 20
Tithes from four parishes, two rural	fl. 425
Creation of ten new bourgeois	fl. 315
Six fines, nearly all on reinstated Artichauds	fl. 3,211
Sales of public properties (a horse, a house for 878 three rural tithes for appx. 1,500 fl.)	fl. 3,383
Received from other tithes and capitations	fl. 463
Profit made from loans	fl. 288
Farm of revenues of mandement of Peney-Satigny	fl. 3,260
Revenues of three rural parishes (Bourdigny, Peissy, Dardagny)	fl. 29

Glossary: The Artichauds were a defeated rebel group whose property was confiscated in 1540. They were pardoned and allowed to return in 1544.

Revenues of parish of Armoy and priory of Draillant (Chablais)	fl.	878
Revenues of mandement of Jussy	fl.	1,610
Revenues of St.-Victor (formerly held by Cluniac monks)	fl.	3,129
Revenues of twelve rural parishes (Malval, Russin, Celigny, Moens, Cartigny, Bossey, Laconex, Lully, Valleiry, Chancy, Neydens, plus 'Membre d'Erchan' and various back debts) formerly held by cathedral canons	fl.	2,444
Lods (property-transfer tax) on 21 estates	fl.	1,177
TOTAL	fl.	29,437

Expenditures:

Purchases for public domain (a house near Town Hall: 467; parish tithes of Troinex: 1,890; a small tithe, 210 fl.)	fl.	2,706
Quitrents and interest paid (93% at Basel)	fl.	6,213
Wages for Petit Conseil and for Council of Two Hundred	fl.	1,180
Cash given to public almshouse	fl.	1,477
Wages of Syndics (312fi fl.) Secy. (125) & Treasurer (250)	fl.	687
Wages of Artillery-master, Fortress and Building Supervisors	fl.	251
Wages of Sautier (Council valet) and liveried guests	fl.	401
Wages of hospitalier (100 fl.) heralds, surgeon	fl.	182
Wages of guydons, chasseurs, belliers, coquins	fl.	131
Wages of four regents at public school	fl.	541
Wages of clock supervisors (three men)	fl.	177
Wages of clock supervisors at St.Gervais (two men)	fl.	128
Wages of eleven night-watchmen and gatekeepers	fl.	289
Wages of chatelans at Peney and Celigny	fl.	137
Wages of seventeen ministers of the Word of God	fl.	3,995
Wages for sessions of the Consistory	fl.	78
Wages for inspections of rural parishes by Council & clergy	fl.	54
Wages and expenses of judicial executions	fl.	63
Pensions of Bonivard, Meigret, & six former priests	fl.	1,543
Expenses for recovering certain tithes & privileges	fl.	397
Expenses of Chambre des Comptes & building supervisors	fl.	193
Expenses of chatelans and artillery-master	fl.	189
Expenses of farmers of Armoy-Draillant pastor's salaries	fl.	295
Various civic expenses, include. public arquebus contest	fl.	374
Public works done by smiths and gilders	fl.	133
Works by painters, glassmakers, locksmiths, saddlers etc.	fl.	35
Works by carpenters (929 man-days)	fl.	471
Work by masons and grain-carriers on fortifications	fl.	324
Expenses for metal, labour and ammunition	fl.	395
Expenses for public livery and purchase of oak trees	fl.	311
Additional wood purchased, including kindling	fl.	633
Gifts made by government	fl.	169
Extraordinary and unlisted expenses	fl.	296
Embassies and messengers (chiefly in France)	fl.	3,698
Banquets, incl. imports of wine and game (chiefly for Bernese)	fl.	920
TOTAL	fl.	29,453

Source B

Customs duties and Gabelle on meat.

TABLE 1 FARM OF HALLES (CUSTOMS DUTIES).
The best guide to the volume of Genevan commerce, this tax was often farmed annually instead of triennially, and the farmers always paid promptly, which shows that it was relatively easy to collect.

1536	608 fl.	1546–8	950 fl./yr
1538	680 fl.	1549	1,792 fl.
1539	1,085 fl.	1550	1,802 fl.
1540	846 fl.	1551	1,840 fl.
1541	1,112 fl.	1552–3	2,645 fl./yr
1542–4	1,150 fl./yr	1554	2,526 fl.
1545	1,116 fl.	1555	3,154 fl.

TABLE 2 GABELLE ON MEAT.
Similarly farmed annually, provides an index of population.

1536	1,450 fl.	1548	2,100 fl.
1538	1,570 fl.	1550	2,620 fl.
1541	1,716 fl.	1551	3,130 fl.
1544	1,650 fl.	1552	3,445 fl.
1545	2,125 fl.	1553	3,400 fl.
1547	2,052 fl.	1554	3,590 fl.
		1555	3,640 fl.

Source C

Genevan master printers.
Among the master printers in Geneva from 1550 to 1564, only one of the 35 who signed a book was a native Genevan; When the magistrates officially regulated the size of this industry in 1563, they permitted 24 master printers to operate 34 presses. Apart from two Italian printers, they were all immigrants from France. The only large publishers in Geneva, each with four presses in 1563, were the house of Estienne and Jean Crespin, the martyrologist. Nearly all Genevan printers handled devotional literature; nearly all printed some works by Calvin, who saw 160 editions of his books come off Geneva's presses between 1550 and 1564. The annual production of book titles in Geneva rose steadily in the 1550s and reached a peak early in the 1560s.

If we move from the master printer, not necessarily an entrepreneur, to the financiers of Geneva's printing industry, we again discover French refugees. The kingpins of this publishing industry, the men who could promote the really large ventures, were two immigrant *libraires*: Laurent de Normandie and Antoine Vincent. The latter, a wealthy publisher from Lyon who emigrated to Geneva in December 1559, was involved in numerous speculations. By far the most important among them was his leadership of the consortium which printed a massive quantity of Hugenot Psalms, with lyrics by Beza and Clement Marot, in 1561 and 1562. This enterprise has been described as the largest single printing venture to be launched in the 16th century. If has left traces of 19 separate editions in Geneva, seven editions in Paris and three editions in Lyon.

TALKING POINT

Geneva contained many refugees. Is there a link between economic success and high levels of immigration? Was Geneva a 'melting pot' of ideas and cultures?

1 The following opinions come from William Monter, *Calvin's Geneva*, 1967. In the light of the extracts, comment, in detail, on each statement in turn:
1.1 'Balancing the Genevan budget was a difficult task each year';
1.2 'The Reformation was profitable in Geneva';
1.3 'Geneva was not an especially rich city';
1.4 'Geneva's emphasis on her printing industry, which had become her first and only export trade';
1.5 'The precise phases of Geneva's economic evolution are still mysterious'.
2 What clues appear in the extract which the Historian could pursue to try to clarify Geneva's economic development?
3 Is it possible to establish a relationship between Geneva's religion and her economy?

Geneva alone printed at least 27,400 copies of these musical Psalms by 1562, and about a third of the city's presses were being used for this project alone. Copies of these psalms were sold in cities as distant as Antwerp – in fact, wherever there were French Protestants. Antoine Vincent appears as the chief, if not the sole financier of this entire venture. He bought mountains of paper for it, including the total output of a Genevan magistrate who was obliged to work day and night to fill Vincent's orders, thereby annoying his neighbours and incurring a large fine. Vincent had to hire two extra typecasters who did nothing but prepare the fonts used for these psalms. Before he died in 1568, Vincent had engaged in many other enterprises, which his biographer describes as important but difficult to identify with certainty.

Our knowledge of Vincent's business activities centres around his most important editorial enterprise; while our knowledge of his chief rival, Laurent de Normandie, is based primarily on his post-mortem inventory of 1570. A boyhood friend of Calvin and once Mayor of Noyon, he had fled to Geneva soon after the visit of an Inquisitor in 1547. He renounced his legal career soon after arriving in Geneva, and by 1554 he entered the printing industry in partnership with another refugee. De Normandie worked on a large scale, financing several of Geneva's poorer master printers and selling his books through a network of *colporteurs*, brave peddlars who distributed these forbidden books throughout the Kingdom of France. At least twenty of the *colporteurs* who worked for him ended as Huguenot martyrs. Few of the editions that De Normandie sold were bound; most were small, designed to be slipped hurriedly into one's pocket.

The overall size of his operations is quite impressive. His inventory of 1570 lists over 200 accounts due, some of them very large, and a stock of almost 35,000 books on hand. Over 10,000 volumes of his stock represented titles by Calvin, and more than 12,000 volumes were Bibles or parts of Bibles (including 2,800 of Vincent's *Psalms* of 1561). His total stock was worth nearly 20,000 livres tournois, a very respectable sum for any European merchant, though not large enough to put him in the topmost rank among 16th-century entrepreneurs. De Normandie may have been Geneva's largest publisher, but it is next to impossible to determine how his business volume and total assets compare with those of other Genevan merchants.

REVIEW

John Calvin in the Hot Seat

Just before he died in 1564, John Calvin met the members of the City Council in Geneva to explain his work over the previous twenty-three years. Effectively, they put him in the hot seat and asked him questions. What questions would you have asked him? Compile your own list of the following:

- Questions of fact.
- Questions for interpretation: 'What did you mean by...?'
- Questions of causation: 'Why did you (do or say) ...?'

Now compile an obituary of Calvin, perhaps as Beza, his friend and successor, may have written it. Then perhaps as a critic such as Ami Perrin may have written it.

In his pamphlet 'Apology to the Nicodemites' (1544), Calvin wrote, 'There are some people who reckon that I am too harsh, and complain because I treat them too brutally. If you ask them the reason for their dissatisfaction, it is because they cannot bear to be hurt'.

In a letter to Mrs Anne Locke, in Geneva in 1556, John Knox described Geneva as 'The most perfect school of Christ that was in the earth since the days of the Apostles.'

6 The Spain of Ferdinand and Isabella, 1469–1515

PREVIEW

Spain in 1469

A dry and impoverished land; 10% of it solid bare rock; 35% poor and unproductive; 45% moderately fertile; 10% rich. A peninsula separated from the continent of Europe by the mountain barrier of the Pyrenees – isolated and remote. A country divided within itself, broken by a high central table land that stretches from the Pyrenees to the southern coast. No natural centre, no easy routes. Fragmented, disparate, complex of different races, languages and civilizations – this was, and is, Spain.

... Yet for a few fabulous decades Spain was to be the greatest power on earth.

J.H. Elliott, *Imperial Spain*, 1963.

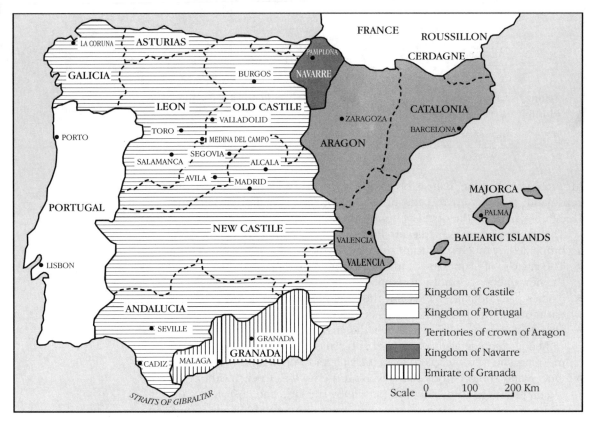

SPAIN IN 1469.

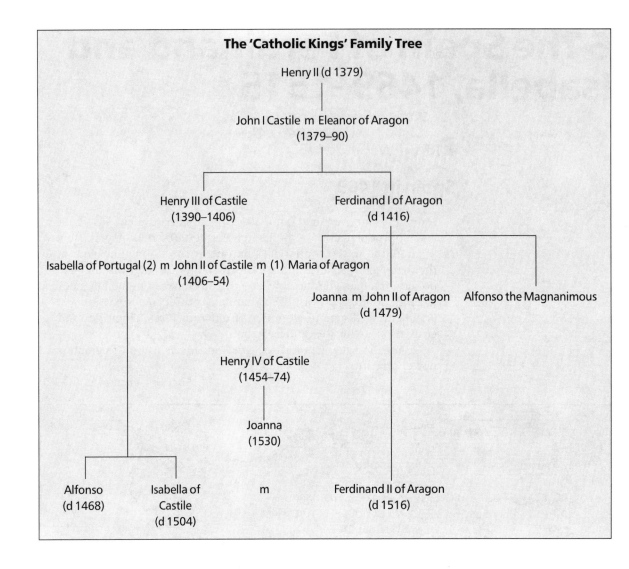

The 'Catholic Kings' Family Tree

Henry II (d 1379)

John I Castile m Eleanor of Aragon
(1379–90)

Henry III of Castile
(1390–1406)

Ferdinand I of Aragon
(d 1416)

Isabella of Portugal (2) m John II of Castile m (1) Maria of Aragon
(1406–54)

Joanna m John II of Aragon
(d 1479)

Alfonso the Magnanimous

Henry IV of Castile
(1454–74)

Joanna
(1530)

Alfonso
(d 1468)

Isabella of
Castile
(d 1504)

m

Ferdinand II of Aragon
(d 1516)

In 1469 Isabella, the half-sister of King Henry IV of Castile, married Ferdinand, the heir to the throne of Aragon. In 1474 Isabella became Queen of Castile on the death of her brother.

The accession of medieval kings and queens in Castile was accompanied by much significant ritual and symbol:

- The citizens of major cities gathered in the market place and welcomed the new queen with noisy acclaim.
- Nobles paid homage by kissing the new queen's hand and taking an oath to be faithful to her.
- On attaining womanhood, the new queen spent one night alone in the cathedral, keeping vigil over sword and armour at the main altar. In the morning, she took the sword from the altar and wore it around her waist.
- Queen and subjects took oaths to bind themselves to each other. The queen promised to protect her people by the laws and customs of the realm, to recover lands formerly held, and to be a good queen – pious, articulate and fearless.

- The queen also mounted the Royal Horse, a horse subsequently to be ridden by no-one else.
- The standards of ways of Castile were raised to a cry of acclamation. This was a particularly important ceremony and Isabella always claimed that the Castilian standards were raised for her but not for the rival candidate to her throne, Joanna.

The Civil War 1474–9 and the Accession of Ferdinand and Isabella to Castile and Aragon

In 1474, King Henry IV of Castile died. Castile was already an economically rich state and Seville was one of the biggest and richest cities in Europe. The inheritance was worth waiting for. There were two major candidates for the throne. One was Joanna, Henry's 12-year-old daughter from his marriage with Joanna of Portugal. Joanna had no husband but was supported by a number of very powerful noblemen, including the Marquis of Villena. The other candidate was Henry IV's half-sister, the 23-year-old Isabella, who five years previously had married Ferdinand, the heir to the throne of Aragon.

Both candidates had hereditary claims to the throne, but heredity was only one factor in the accession. As outlined above, the traditions of popular acclamation and court ritual were also important. Within twenty-four hours of the death of Henry IV, Isabella had herself proclaimed in Segovia as 'our Queen and Lady' – even before Ferdinand could join her. There was support for both candidates in the Royal Council, with Villena and the Archbishop of Toledo providing particularly powerful support for Joanna. Isabella's main strength was that in 1468 she had been publicly recognised as heiress by the late king, and by February 1475 she had the support of most of the cities of Castile.

But in 1475 the situation swung dramatically Joanna's way when her uncle, King Afonso V of Portugal, made an alliance with France and threatened to invade Castile from both the west and the north-east. The civil war that resulted was confused and often bloody. For Ferdinand and Isabella, it was also extremely expensive; their concessions to noble families like the Villena, and their grants of privileges to major cities like Burgos and Toledo, cost them considerable wealth. In May 1475, King Afonso of Portugal invaded and was betrothed to his young niece. The regions of Andalucia and Galicia were particularly supportive of the Portuguese. After much skirmishing, Ferdinand defeated Afonso at the Battle of Toro in 1476, the signal for Afonso and Joanna to flee to Portugal and most Castilian cities and nobles to declare their support for Ferdinand and Isabella. The civil war was effectively over.

Ferdinand and Isabella promptly pursued the pacification of Andalucia and Galicia: some nobles were executed, many castles were destroyed. In 1477, they made peace with France which lasted until 1494, and in the following year the birth of their son John ensured the future succession. With the death of John II of Aragon in 1479 and the peace treaty with Afonso of Portugal, Ferdinand and Isabella were finally confirmed as the undisputed successors of Henry IV. Subsequently, Joanna's betrothal to Afonso was nullified by the pope and she entered a convent.

TALKING POINT

Ferdinand and Isabella ruled jointly. Can you identify some advantages and problems of joint rule?

Focus

6.1 Isabella, Queen of Castile

QUEEN
ISABELLA
AT PRAYER.

Using the material in the focus and the rest of the chapter, create a pen portrait of Queen Isabella. Confine yourself to no more than 250 words.

Some contemporary quotations:

- 'A mistress of dissimulation and simulation.'
- 'Take care not to mix cruelty with the execution of justice.'
- 'More remarkable than her remarkable husband.'
- 'Tallavera encouraged Ferdinand to "improve the treatment of your excellent and very worthy wife"'.
- 'Two mortal bodies animated by one spirit.'

Isabella the Woman

Were Castilian nobles correct to assume that Isabella would be easier to control than Ferdinand?

Why was she able to inspire so much loyalty and devotion in her supporters?

She possessed the qualities of an ideal queen: dignified, pure, pious, intelligent, determined and loyal. She was always very careful, even at the age of forty-four, to sleep surrounded by her children or servants. Thus, she allayed any criticism of sexual misconduct.

- She was never taught Latin but she decided to learn it later in life and had a Latin/Castilian dictionary produced.
- Her reading tastes can be discovered from the books in her library, medical books, spiritual works, Castilian not Latin books, written in a more popular style, some licentious reading. She was intelligent but unlearned and unintellectual – for example, her handwriting was poor.

Isabella the Patron of the Arts

She preferred the Flanders School of Painting to that of Spain. It was pure and pious, but optimistic and not over-rich. Did this accord with her own temperament?

She was the chief patron of Columbus. Did this allow her to have adventure at a distance? Why was she prepared to support him?

What expectations did women in 15th-century Spain have of marriage?

How did Ferdinand and Isabella rule together – was it a genuine Royal coalition? Did it enhance their marriage as well as their government?

Isabella the Wife

Isabella was always anxious to be known as an utterly faithful wife.

She feared for herself and her children if there was any suspicion of unfaithfulness. Compare the fate of Joanna, her half-sister.

Her first reaction to Ferdinand was a very positive and excited one.

She was constantly upset by Ferdinand's infidelities, but delicately able to remove his mistresses from court. For example, Beatrix of Bobadilla was sent to the Canary Islands with the minimum of fuss.

In spite of his infidelities, she was devoted and loyal to him.

Isabella the Mother

In 1475, she hastened to respond to the threat from Afonso V's invasion during the Civil War. She was 23 years old and pregnant at the time. As a result of her political response, she miscarried.

She felt immense responsibilities to secure the succession as well as to maintain her position as queen.

Prince John was spoiled with excesses of rose syrup as a child, but he lacked Isabella's loving presence.

She was keen to marry off her five-year-old daughter Isabel in order to secure Castile for the future. Her duty as queen often dominated her decisions as a mother.

Considerable grief at her childrens' sad fates, for example Isabel's first husband was killed in a hunting party to celebrate their wedding, and she herself then died in childbirth eight years later, a year after her brother John's death.

Isabella the Queen

On 13 December 1474, she declared herself queen before consulting Ferdinand. He suspected treachery. This was an inauspicious start to their reign.

Her duty to Castile was overpowering. For example, would she produce a male heir in the summer of 1475, or would she lead her forces in the Civil War?

The birth of Prince John on 30 June 1476 was one of the factors which ended the Civil War.

Isabella as a queen at court revealed a very determined personality of purity, chivalry and courtly love.

Dancing and music were very popular and women often danced together.

Isabella loved jousting and dressed lavishly for court occasions. In April 1475 in the midst of a civil war and pregnant with a child, she nonetheless attended a joust.

She gave no support for bullfighting which she found disgusting.

She usually segregated sexes at mealtimes, although allowing them occasionally to eat together.

The Establishment of Peace and Order in Castile and the Enforcement of Royal Authority

Ferdinand and Isabella were astute – and lucky – politicians, whose major achievement was to bring peace and order to a Spain torn by civil wars and to restore the royal authority of the crown over a wide variety of local rites and privileges.

The four major kingdoms of Spain – Castile, Aragon, Catalonia and Valencia – all had their separate *Cortes*, their own financial institutions, and their own laws. Most Spanish cities also had their own rites or *'fueros'*.

FERDINAND AND ISABELLA PRESENTING FENNEL FLOWERS.

The Catholic Kings were personal rulers who asserted royal authority through political control, and administrative and judicial reform. Like all medieval kings, their power lay in the monarchy in their personalities. Government existed wherever they happened to be. There was no capital city. This was particularly hard on Ferdinand's kingdom of Aragon, because he spent most of his time in Castile. Similarly for thirty years, Isabella and her advisers were constantly on the move throughout Castile, both in war and in peace.

Peace, order, and the enforcement of royal authority were accomplished through a number of political, administrative and judicial developments:

- The use of the Councils of State.
- The enforcement and development of royal justice.
- The clarification of local administration through the power of the *Hermandades* and *Corregidores*.
- The partnership between the crown and the aristocracy.
- The control of towns and cities.
- The control of the Military Orders.
- The clarification of their relationship with the *Cortes* of Castile.
- The enforcement of their authority in Aragon, Catalonia and Valencia.

The Councils of State

The government of Spain was organised under the Royal Council, or the Council of Castile. In theory, all nobles and bishops were entitled to attend its meetings, but in practice it was run by a small number of university-trained lawyers, called *Letrados*. In 1493, the Council consisted of eight or nine members, all of whom had to have at least ten years' study of law. The Royal Council was sub-divided into a number of major sub-committees which later became councils in their own right. They included sub-committees for Foreign Policy, Justice, Finance, Local Administration, and a sub-committee for each of Aragon, Catalonia and Valencia. In the course of their reign, additional councils were also developed. The Council for the Inquisition was formed in 1483, that for the military orders in 1489.

This system of councils allowed Ferdinand and Isabella to rule their kingdoms even during their absence. It also put in place a professional bureaucracy of *Letrados*, formerly members of the lower nobility, to whom powers could be delegated. This system became the basis for the central government of Spain throughout the 16th and 17th centuries.

The Enforcement and Development of Royal Justice

During the civil war, many local communities continued to be outside the king's justice. In order to bring peace to Spain, the Catholic Kings had to enforce their own jurisdiction. Their personal supervision of judicial proceedings was all important. At the start of their reign, the Royal Council met as a court twice a week. Gradually, however, it became apparent that it should meet in a fixed place rather than following the monarchs. Three courts, called *Audiencias*, were set up, the main one being at Valladolid. In addition, local courts were set up. Those officials who were given power to administer local justice in the countryside and in the towns set up their own courts and a right of appeal was allowed to the *Audiencias*.

The Catholic Kings also tried on several occasions to codify the many conflicting legal traditions in Castile. The Laws of Toro in 1505 were the last attempt, but they failed to resolve conflicting local interpretations. It was not until the reign of Philip II, late in the 16th century, that a further attempt was made.

Interestingly, none of these developments was new. All were rooted in the medieval past of Castile. Perhaps the only significant new development was the insistence on the use of the *Letrados*.

The Administration of Local Government

The crown brought peace and order to each local area in Spain by setting up the *Santa Hermandades*. These were local brotherhoods of law officers who could command small forces of horsemen or archers. They served as a police force, but also as a local law court. Their justice was often peremptory. As one contemporary put it: 'it was so severe that it appeared to be cruelty, but it was necessary because all the kingdoms needed peace. There was much butchery with the cutting off of feet, hands and heads'.

The initiative for the *Hermandades* came not from the crown, but from the towns. Indeed, it too was an initiative with its roots in the medieval past. In 1476 and 1477, Isabella established *Hermandades* throughout Spain with power in all rural areas outside walled cities. In 1484, the system was to prove its worth by creating a local army for the war with Granada. The assembly of towns, which co-ordinated the *Hermandades*, began to provide a standing army (initially of 3000 men) and to find money to finance it.

In the cities, Ferdinand and Isabella used the Institution of *Corregidores*. These were local judges who held local courts, and by 1494 54 towns and cities were governed by them. They were able to maintain royal jurisdiction against all parties. A decree of 1500 identified all the duties of the *Corregidores*: to watch over the city, to organise its food supply, to maintain public order, and to emphasise the power of the crown.

The Partnership of the Crown and the Aristocracy

As in all European states in the second half of the 15th century, the relationship between crown and aristocracy was crucial to the maintenance of peace and good government. Spanish Historians have traditionally taken the view that the aristocracy prospered during periods of civil war. They took over much local control, built castles, and reduced the authority of the crown. To such Historians, the reign of Ferdinand and Isabella saw the ending of this independence, as the aristocracy were crushed under the foot of the 'Catholic Kings'.

This opinion is no longer tenable. It is now clear that Ferdinand and Isabella pursued a compromise with the nobles in order to establish a mutually beneficial partnership. Certainly, there were episodes which suggested a concentration on the exercise of royal power. For example, in royal tours in 1476 and 1477 and in the *Cortes* of Toledo in 1480, local castles were destroyed. In addition, grants of revenue to members of the aristocracy were reduced and the lands they had been given after 1464 by the crown were taken away. The crown thus recovered thirty million *maravedis* a year.

However, there was much more to it than this. The crown made contracts with the important aristocratic families. The nobles had their grants and rights confirmed and often received financial reward. In return, they gave up their local castles and often their local governorships. Furthermore, after the *Cortes* of 1480 many nobles retained the right to collect local taxes, including the profitable *alcabala* – a sales tax. After the conquest of Granada in 1492, many noble houses gained newly acquired land and privileges.

One of Isabella's greatest political skills was her ability to marry off the members of feuding noble houses, thus bringing their feuding to an end. Even the most rebellious tended to be well looked after, so that in 1477 one local justice could complain that rebellious nobles were too well treated.

Thus, although the crown became the most potent political force in Spain, the nobles retained their legal, economic and social importance.

Towns and Cities

Ferdinand and Isabella were determined to rule with the help and support of important citizens who controlled the towns and cities. During the Middle Ages, many towns and cities had been given their own charters or *fueros*. They also had much land outside their walls and extended their power widely. At the *Cortes* of Toledo in 1480, the crown strengthened its control: all cities which did not already have a town hall were to build one within two years; records were to be kept of all laws and privileges; and *Corregidores* were to be appointed to all the main towns. On the other hand, it is clear that local citizens retained their power and influence. Through the *Cortes* and through the Junta of the *Hermandades*, local townsmen were consulted on a wide variety of issues. In addition, local townsmen collected the *alcabala* tax themselves and therefore felt in control.

The Control of the Military Orders

TALKING POINT
Were Ferdinand and Isabella new monarchs? In what senses did they continue medieval traditions?

In late medieval Spain, there were three military orders of Chivalry. Their many members were bound by religious vows, but they were also military bodies, attempting to recapture Spain from the Muslims. The orders possessed vast lands, together with castles and fortresses, and they played a significant role in the civil war which followed the death of Henry IV.

Isabella was determined to control them. Ferdinand was elected Grand Master of each of the Orders in turn: Calatrava in 1487; Alcantara in 1494; and Santiago in 1499.

The *Cortes*

The *Cortes* of Castile consisted of two representatives of all the major cities in the state. By the time of Ferdinand and Isabella, its power was severely limited. At the *Cortes* of Toledo in 1480, only 17 cities were represented – and in each case by only a minor noble, or lawyer. The duties of the *Cortes* were now merely advisory and it was the crown which passed legislation. From 1480 to 1498, the *Cortes* of Castile was not summoned and the crown used the *Hermandades* to raise money for the army instead. Later in the reign, it was summoned again, but only to provide subsidies for the crown.

In spite of this it is clear that Ferdinand and Isabella regularly consulted their people. The Junta of the *Hermandades* was an annual means of talking with representatives of the towns and cities. Ferdinand and Isabella were quite clearly keen to balance the political powers of all the major forces in their realm.

What Underpinned the Policies of Ferdinand and Isabella in Castile?

- A government geared to fighting wars.
- The civil wars 1469–74, the wars against Portugal 1474–9, the wars in Granada culminating in 1492, and the wars in Italy from 1495.
- The establishment of absolute rule and national unification.
- The setting up of a modern, bureaucratic and even mercantilist state.
- The establishment of 'new monarchy' or the continuation of medieval methods.
- The rule over 'an unwieldy conglomerate of men'.

Each of the above factors influenced the policies and actions of Ferdinand and Isabella. Can you find examples to support each factor? As you read the rest of this chapter, try to identify the importance of each factor in prompting Ferdinand and Isabella's actions.

Ferdinand – King of Aragon, Catalonia and Valencia

FERDINAND, KING OF ARAGON, CATALONIA AND VALENCIA.

The Crown of Aragon consisted of a number of territories in north-eastern Spain and southern Italy, along with the Balearic Islands and Sicily. Compared with a population of over five million in Castile, with all its obvious wealth and power, the crown of Aragon had a total population of probably less than one million. The only large city was Valencia with perhaps 75,000 people, and the largest city in Aragon itself was Barcelona, with a population of around 20,000.

The various territories of the crown of Aragon also lacked political and economic influence. Catalonia was regularly buffeted by plague. Valencia failed in 1483 to get permission to import Castilian wheat. And apart from Valencia, the territories of Aragon could contribute little towards the economic wealth of the monarchs.

Yet the most significant issue at this time was that Ferdinand preferred to spend his time in the government of Castile. In a reign of 37 years, he spent less than three years in Aragon, and about the same in Catalonia. He spent only six months in the kingdom of Valencia. However, he was well advised by a civil service of Aragonese and Catalan secretaries, and he spent many hours listening to their descriptions of the problems of Aragon and Catalonia.

Ferdinand therefore ruled the crown of Aragon by enabling the oligarchies of the major cities to run their own affairs. Yet, as in Castile, he was determined to exercise his influence. He developed a new system for the selection of office holders, which was widely adopted after 1487. In the 1480s, he introduced the Inquisition into the crown of Aragon and the *Hermandad* was revived in 1487. It was never easy to overcome the local feuds between various Aragonese nobles, yet the constant work of the *Hermandad* enabled Ferdinand at least to keep an eye on the situation.

Throughout this work, Ferdinand convened the *Cortes* of Aragon on only six occasions. The meetings produced subsidies but the towns were distrustful and suspicious of an absentee king. The *Cortes* always insisted on redress of grievances before the subsidy was given.

In Catalonia, Ferdinand defeated the rebellion of the peasant Remensas in 1486, largely by buying the support of nobles and leaders of the Church. He also developed a programme for economic recovery in Catalonia. For example, he regulated trade and industry in Barcelona, thus freeing trade to reach the British Isles, the Canaries and North Africa. One foreign visitor in the year 1502 could say of Barcelona: 'the city is full of manufacturers with infinite merchandise'.

The Roman Catholic Church and Relations with Jews and Muslims: The Ending of *Convivencia*

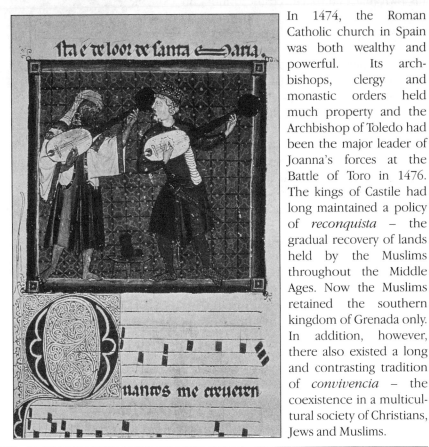

THE SPIRIT OF *CONVIVENCIA* IS CAPTURED IN THIS ILLUSTRATION OF A MOOR AND A CHRISTIAN PLAYING THE LUTE TOGETHER, TAKEN FROM A BOOK OF MUSIC PUBLISHED IN THE 13TH CENTURY.

In 1474, the Roman Catholic church in Spain was both wealthy and powerful. Its archbishops, clergy and monastic orders held much property and the Archbishop of Toledo had been the major leader of Joanna's forces at the Battle of Toro in 1476. The kings of Castile had long maintained a policy of *reconquista* – the gradual recovery of lands held by the Muslims throughout the Middle Ages. Now the Muslims retained the southern kingdom of Grenada only. In addition, however, there also existed a long and contrasting tradition of *convivencia* – the coexistence in a multicultural society of Christians, Jews and Muslims.

It was possible to identify a number of different religious groups in Spain in 1474:

- *Muslims*: those living in the independent kingdom of Granada.
- *Mudejares*: Muslims living elsewhere in Spain.
- *Moriscos*: Muslims who had been converted to Christianity.
- *Jews*.
- *Marranos*: Jews who had become Christians.
- *Mozarabes*: Christians who lived mostly in Granada under Muslim rule.
- *Catholic Spanish Christians*.

The Catholic church was wealthy and powerful and a source of possible dissent. From the beginning of their reign, Ferdinand and Isabella determined to control it and to unite church and state. In 1478, they held a Synod of Spanish bishops in the city of Seville. The Synod agreed the king's rights to appoint bishops and for bishops to reside in their sees. In addition, in 1501 and 1508 Papal Bulls gave them control of appointment of bishops in the New World.

CARDINAL CISNEROS, ARCHBISHOP OF TOLEDO.

The most significant figure in the leadership of the Catholic church was Isabella's former confessor Cardinal Cisneros. As Chancellor of Castile, and from 1495 Archbishop of Toledo, he was a great patron of learning who founded the University of Alcala from his own funds and financed the printing in 1517 of the multi-language Bible, the *Complutensian Polyglot*. He encouraged Hebrew and Jewish scholars and welcomed the works of Erasmus and other European humanists. In addition, he tightened up monastic discipline and held a Synod in 1497 to insist on the recording of Baptisms and regular attendance at Communion. He also encouraged the development of the Order of Jeronimites – there were 49 houses by 1516. However, in spite of his work there was a very limited reform movement in Spain. The genuine need for religious reform, so evident in other countries in Europe in the 16th century, was not allowed to touch the Spanish Church.

It was in the *reconquista*, and particularly the conquests of Granada, that Ferdinand and Isabella placed their main effort between 1482 and 1492. Certainly Ferdinand's military leadership was an essential factor in the final entry into the city of Granada in January 1492. One contemporary eye-witness called it 'the most distinguished and blessed day there has ever been in Spain'. Another said 'this kingdom, which for seven hundred and eighty years has been occupied by infidels, has been won to the Glory of God and the exultation of our Holy Catholic faith'. On 2 January 1492 Ferdinand and Isabella, headed by a huge silver cross, a gift from the pope, received the surrender of the city of Granada. In 1494 Pope Alexander VI bestowed upon Ferdinand and Isabella the title of the 'Catholic Kings'.

THIS WOOD RELIEF FROM THE CAPILLE REAL, GRANADA, SHOWS FERDINAND AND ISABELLA ENTERING THE CITY ON 2 JANUARY 1492.

Their credibility was much enhanced, as the result of a crusade with support from people from all over Europe. Yet the war had been extremely expensive and could only have been won with the support of Papal funds to the tune of 800 million *maravedis* between 1484 and 1492, grants from the *Hermandades*, and forced contributions from the Jews of approximately 58 million *maravedis*.

Initially the terms given to the Muslims in Granada enhanced the traditional policy on *convivencia*: they were promised freedom of worship, freedom to wear their own costumes, to conduct their own education and to hold their own law courts. Gradually in the 1490s, however, this policy was overtaken by Cardinal Cisneros. In 1499, with Isabella's support, he announced the policy of forcible re-conversion. An immediate but brief Moorish revolt was followed by the three-month revolt of the Alpujarras in 1500. This was the excuse Cisneros needed and in 1502 an Edict announced that all Muslims who refused Baptism were to be expelled from the whole of Castile. With this decree, Islam disappeared from Spain. This enabled Cisneros to revive a crusading movement and in 1509 he led an expedition to North Africa and captured Algiers and Tripoli.

The consequences of the loss of the Muslim population were dramatic. Perhaps half of the Muslims, some 200,000 people, sought refuge overseas. The agriculture and trade of Granada were damaged beyond repair, although many Andalucian peasants moved into Granada to try to continue its farming traditions. The traditional trade between Spain and North Africa was ended.

The treatment of Jews in Spain was similarly hostile and again the ending of the policy of *convivencia* was evident. The Inquisition was established in 1479 and extended to cover the whole of Spain. Ferdinand's initial intention was to deal with wavering new Christians, both *Conversos* and *Moriscos*. However, the Inquisitor General, the Archbishop Torquemada, took his responsibilities very seriously: he probably authorised the burning of over 2000 Jews, and in some areas it was a holocaust. Perhaps 700 Jews were burned in Seville in the 1480s, and another 5000 received other punishments. The Toledo *Cortes* in 1480 announced the end of *convivencia*. Jews were to wear badges and had to live inside their ghettoes. The notorious Edict of 1492 declared that all Jews were to be given four months to be baptised or to leave Castile. It was an edict with dramatic consequences. Following its introduction, it is likely that 150,000 Jews fled from Castile and 30,000 from Aragon.

Henry Kamen describes the consequences very graphically:

> the immense and tragic exodus of the people who had known no other home – both rich and poor, old and young, struggling abroad with meagre possessions allowed them, cheated and robbed at every stage of their journey – ended the long history of Jews in Spain.

The treatment of the Jews and Muslims had sharpened the debate about *convivencia*: would Spain continue as a pluralist and multicultural society, or would it develop as a singular Christian community with one faith and one law? There is much debate over the racist attitude of Ferdinand and Isabella and of that of the Spanish people. However, some were clearly racist, and one contemporary describes the abhorrence of Christians for Muslims who took regular baths. These caused 'weakness of body and too much delight, from which came idleness and from idleness evil and ugly pleasures... Therefore we believe that it pleased God's justice to punish them so that even the dogs of that city should not live'.

The Economy and Financial Reform

The reign of Ferdinand and Isabella witnessed no major social changes in Castile or Spain. Indeed, their reign largely confirmed the importance of rank and status. Those who made their wealth from trade or industry pursued the status of *hidalgos* with great enthusiasm, and the rank of nobility, with all the exemptions it brought, was much sought after.

The Castile of Ferdinand and Isabella consisted of perhaps five or six million people. Most of these lived in small rural communities, although there were 18 established towns, and the city of Seville was one of the largest in Europe. Otherwise the land was owned by the nobility or the church or the crown. Peasants worked on their lord's land in return for the use of their own allotments. Alternatively, they paid rent.

The economic life of the realm was clearly of great importance. J.H. Elliott in *Imperial Spain* has summarised it thus:

> During Isabella's twenty-nine year reign in Castile no less than one hundred and twenty-eight ordinances were made, embracing every aspect of Castile's economic life. The export of gold and silver was

What were the likely consequences of forcible conversion? Can this method of removing Jews from Spain be compared to the treatment of Jews in Nazi Germany?

forbidden; navigation laws were introduced to foster Spanish ship building; the gold system was tightened up and re-organized; sporadic attempts were made to protect Castile's textile industries by temporary import prohibitions on certain types of clothes, and Flemish and Italian Artisans were encouraged to settle in Spain, by a promise of ten years exemption from taxes.

It would be misleading to describe these ordinances as pieces of an economic programme, since this implies a coherent design which did not in fact exist. The economic legislation of the Catholic Kings is best seen as their response to certain immediate and pressing problems.

Agriculture remained extremely primitive, and the population of Castile was growing and increasingly difficult to feed. The soil was poor and not well irrigated or fertilised. In years of bad harvests, as from 1502 until 1509, the government was forced to allow the import of foreign corn. In 1502, they imposed a maximum price for corn. None of these measures encouraged corn production.

Indeed Ferdinand and Isabella's main concentration was on wool production and the privileges of the monopolistic *Mesta* – a guild of sheep owners. J. Klein, in his book on the *Mesta*, has made clear their approach. 'The policy of aggressively promoting wool exports became the key note of the commercial programme of those royal devotees of mercantilism... Every possible device of the new Government was turned to the task of concentrating the energies and resources of Castile to sheep farming'. In 1476 the crown reduced local sheep taxes and in 1480 the *Cortes* of Toledo ordered the destruction of enclosures allowed under Henry IV. In 1489 the sheep routes from north to south of Castile were enlarged and legislation in 1492 and 1511 codified the *Mesta's* powers. In 1500 the *Mesta* was to be led by a president, a senior member of the Royal Council, and the *Mesta* had thus become effectively a Department of State. The number of sheep rose from 2.7 million in 1477 to almost 3.5 million in 1526. The wool trade certainly brought Castile closer to both Navarre and Catalonia and the export of wool to England and Flanders paved the way for future political alliances.

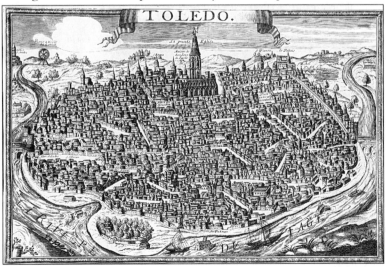

THE CITY OF TOLEDO
AROUND 1500.

Other industries suffered dramatically by comparison. There were many difficulties in the way of industrial development in Castile. Capital and skilled workmen were in short supply and communications were poor. Ferdinand and Isabella did try to improve the roads of Castile and several new routes were constructed to link the north with the kingdom of Granada. A postal system was also developed. The three major industries of Castile – silk in Granada, cloth manufacture and iron manufacture in the north – all made limited progress. The import of foreign cloth certainly weakened the cloth manufacture of Castile and the expulsion of Jews and Muslims had an adverse effect on all industrial development.

It was in the regulation of trade that the work of Ferdinand and Isabella was most notable. They reorganised the fairs of Medina del Campo in 1483 and merged and enlarged other fairs in Castile. They regulated the wool trade through a system of convoys and Burgos became the centre of the Castilian wool trade. The whole export system was clarified by the creation of the *Consulado* of Burgos in 1494. Wool was prepared throughout Castile, sold to merchants at local fairs, and then transported to Burgos which served as a centralising focus for all exports. Certainly wool trade increased and an additional navigation Edict of 1500 ensured that Castilian goods were exported in Castilian ships. In 1503, furthermore, the idea of monopoly was extended to the House of Trade in Seville. This focused all imports and exports to the new world and gave Seville a very powerful monopoly over future trading developments.

Other industries were also subject to government controls: arms manufacture, shipbuilding, even horse breeding, were controlled as an important element in the war effort.

Finally coinage was reformed during the reign. An Edict of 1497 established three major coins: a gold coin, or *ducat*, a silver coin, or *real*, and a copper coin called a *blanca*. Indeed the ducat became the chief coin throughout Spain.

Financial Administration

The financial programme of Ferdinand and Isabella was by no means new. Their expenditure was very significant.

- The cost of the regular army: 80 million *maravedis* in 1504, compared with 20 million in 1482.
- Grants and pensions: 112 million in 1504, compared with 52 million in 1483.
- Court expenses: 35 million in 1504, compared with eight million in 1480.
- Foreign wars: in 1504 a quarter of all income was used on the wars in Italy.
- Marriages of princesses: 50 to 60 million each.

In order to meet these very large expenses, Ferdinand and Isabella used both ordinary and extraordinary taxation.

The ordinary sources of income included the *alcabala*, profits from industry, taxes on the *Mesta*'s flocks and customs duties. The end of the Civil War enabled them to stabilise their income, and by 1504 their income from ordinary revenue had doubled to 315 million *maravedis*. Economic progress enabled this to rise still further.

The real need was to increase the income from extraordinary taxes. In 1500 the military orders contributed over 27 million *maravedis*. Papal grants, and grants from the *Cortes*, produced huge sums. Almost 300 million *maravedis* came from the *Cortes* alone between 1500 and 1504. The increase in extraordinary taxation of 66 per cent was the significant factor in the economic stability of Ferdinand and Isabella's reign.

Unfortunately for Castile, two major consequences of their financial policy were damaging. Firstly, after 1489, Ferdinand and Isabella began to pay off their debts at high rates of interest in the form of *Juros* (government bonds). By 1504 the annual interest was 112 million *maravedis* and it continued to rise. Secondly, the ability of the people of Castile to pay taxes was dramatically reduced. The clergy were made exempt from the *Alcabala*, the cities compounded by paying a lump sum, and the nobles were allowed to collect their own. Such political brinkmanship had obvious political advantages, but the financial consequences were severe.

EXAMINING THE EVIDENCE

Opinions of Historians about Ferdinand and Isabella

The sources which survive for the history of their times are so extensive that they could not fairly be managed by a single author, even after a lifetime's study...

Most of the existing books on Ferdinand and Isabella have failed to present them convincingly, because the subject overlaps with so many areas of polemics: whether the evils of the Inquisition outweigh its virtues; whether the expulsion of the Jews benefited or disadvantaged Spain...

F. Fernandez-Armesto, *Ferdinand & Isabella*, 1975.

Spanish Historians have always regarded the reign of the 'Catholic Kings' as having special significance: they were the last Spanish rulers of Spain and they travelled so widely that they were seen directly by most of their subjects.

Yet their reign has been the subject of great debate.

When we read a work of History, we must always ask THREE fundamental questions:

* WHAT IS THE CONTEXT IN WHICH IT WAS WRITTEN?
  When was it written? What were the influences on the author?
* WHAT WAS THE AUTHOR'S PURPOSE IN WRITING?
  Why was it written?
* WHAT OPINIONS IS THE AUTHOR EXPRESSING?

Let us consider the work of four groups of writers about Ferdinand and Isabella.

- 15th and 16th-century contemporary writers.
- The 19th-century American Historian W.H. Prescott.
- 20th-century Spanish Historians writing during General Franco's fascist control over Spain in the 1940s and 1950s.
- Recent Spanish, English and American writers.

Source A

15th and 16th-century contemporary writers.

In what context did they write?

The monarchs were still alive and widely praised.

The monarchs travelled widely throughout their realms and were seen by all.

Many people expected a Second Coming in the year 1500.

A Messiah was looked for.

Civil wars had been ended.

Most were Catholic writers.

Ferdinand and Isabella restored the old Castilian policy of one Catholic faith.

What was their purpose?

Can you suggest what it may have been?

What opinions did they express?

They were Kings of this realm alone, of our speech, born and bred among us... They knew everybody, always gave honours to those who merited them, travelled through their realms, were known by great and small alike.

The Admiral of Castile.

They crushed the Mohammedan sect and extinguished heretical perversion.

Obituary on their tomb in Granada.

Many men believed (that Isabella) was created miraculously, for the redemption of lost kingdoms…

Contemporary writer.

We owe everything to him.

Philip II (1559–99) of Ferdinand.

Source B

W.H. Prescott, *The History of the Reign of Ferdinand and Isabella*, 1841.
In what context did he write?

New England in the 19th century was still 'blisteringly anti-Spanish', founded on English 16th-century Elizabethan attitudes. In the mid-19th century, Americans were anti-Spanish – they supported Latin American independence movements around this time. Previous American Historians of Spain described Spain as barbaric and greedy.

What was his purpose in writing?

> His search for truth carried him triumphantly through a maze of prejudiced and conflicting evidence... He shed his heritage of prejudice and blazed a trail for a new assessment, an Independent American evaluation of Spain and her culture.
>
> C. H. Gardiner, Edition of Prescott, 1962.

What opinions did he express?

The Establishment of the Modern Inquisition

Notwithstanding the show of prosperity enjoyed by converted Jews, their situation at the accession of Ferdinand and Isabella was far from secure. The clergy, especially the Dominicans, were not slow in sounding the alarm; the superstitious populace, easily roused to acts of violence in the name of religion, began to exhibit the most tumultuous movements, and actually massacred the constable of Castile in an attempt to suppress them the year before Isabella's accession. After this period, the complaints against the Jewish heresy became still more clamorous, and the throne was repeatedly beset with petitions to devise an effectual means for its extirpation. It is easy to discern the secret envy entertained by the Castilians of the superior skill and industry of their Hebrew brethren, and of the superior riches which these qualities secured to them, and to suspect that the zeal of the most orthodox was considerably sharpened by worldly motives.

The cry against the Jewish abomination now became general. Among those most active in raising it were the Dominican Prior of the Monastery of St Paul in Seville. He loudly called for the introduction of the Holy Office. In this he was vigorously supported by others. Ferdinand listened with complacency to a scheme which promised an ample source of revenue in the confiscations it involved. But it was not so easy to vanquish Isabella's aversion to measures so repugnant to the natural benevolence and magnanimity of her character. Her scruples indeed were rather founded on sentiment than reason, and learned theologians seriously disputed whether it would be permitted to make peace with the infidel and even whether promises made to them were obligatory on Christians.

Isabella's serious temper, as well as early education, naturally disposed her religious influences. Notwithstanding the independence exhibited by her in all secular affairs, in her own spiritual concern, she uniformly testified that deepest humility, and deferred too implicitly to what she deemed the superior sagacity of her ghostly councillors.

Thomas de Torquemada had earnestly laboured to infuse into Isabella's young mind, to which his situation as her confessor gave him such ready access, the same spirit of fanaticism that glowed in his own. Fortunately, this was greatly counteracted by her sound understanding and natural kindness of heart. Torquemada urged her, or indeed as is stated by some, extorted a promise that 'should she ever come to the throne she would devote herself to the extirpation of heresy, for the glory of God and the exultation of the Catholic faith'. The time was now arrived when this fatal promise was to be discharged.

It was not until the Queen had endured the repeated importunities of the clergy, particularly of those reverent persons in whom she most confided, seconded by the arguments of Ferdinand, that she consented to solicit from the Pope a Bull for the introduction of the Holy office into Castile... The Queen however, still averse to violent measure, suspended the operation of the ordinance until a more lenient policy had been first tried.

What opinions does Prescott express about
  (a) Isabella's character?
  (b) The Jews?
  (c) The Catholic church in 15th-century Spain?

Comment on Prescott's literary style. How would you describe it?
  (a) List any powerful words which he uses to show his own feelings. Does such a use of language inhibit or enhance his ability to convey facts?

WHAT IMPRESSION IS CONVEYED BY THIS 19TH-CENTURY SPANISH PICTURE OF THE CONVERSION OF THE MUSLIMS?

Source C
20th-century Spanish Historians writing during the reign of the Fascist president, General Franco.
In what context did they write?

Civil War between Fascists (Franco) and Communists 1936–9.
General Franco's rule in Spain in the 1940s and 1950s
Crushing of 'Red' Communist opposition
Alliance between Fascists and Roman Catholic church in Spain.
Attempts in Spain to canonise Isabella.

What were their purposes in writing?

Can you suggest any?

What opinions did they express?

Acclamation of Ferdinand and Isabella's autocratic rule.
Ending of Civil Wars.
Crushing of nobility, towns, etc.
Crushing of minority groups.
Alliance with Catholic church.
Enforcement of Inquisition.

Source D
Recent Spanish, English and American writers.
In what context and under what influences are they writing?

Can you suggest any? Read the works of J. H. Elliott, H. Kamen, J. N. Hillgarth on, for example, the Spanish Inquisition, to formulate your thoughts.

What are their purposes?

Again suggest your own.

What opinions do they express?

Finally, the Catholic Kings encouraged the emergence of a society in which the pluralistic outlook of convivencia was explicitly rejected in favour of the majority culture of Old Christians. The Muslim and Jewish heritage was repudiated, at first only in religion, but later also in its other forms and cultural survivals, until the drive against semitism became a national obsession.

Ferdinand and Isabella cannot be blamed for this development, since they were in no sense racialist; nor can they even be credited with the passion for religious unity, since the Mudejars of Aragon continued to survive as Muslims for some twenty years after the death of Isabella. Nonetheless, their religious policy, which was undoubtedly popular, achieved a superficial consensus at the expense of nurturing beneath the surface tensions and divisions which created within a united Spain a society of conflict.

Henry Kamen, *Spain 1469–1714*, 1983.

What opinions does Kamen express about Ferdinand and Isabella's policies?

Summary Opinions of Modern Historians

The monarchs imposed on their realms an extraordinary degree of political and economic control, not out of a conscious desire to create an 'absolute' or 'modern' state, but because of the emergency conditions arising out of the circumstances in which they seized the crown, and contriving from the interminable strains imposed by war... (they governed) a state permanently organised for external war

F. Fernandez-Armesto, *Ferdinand & Isabella*, 1975.

The rulers of Castile... expressed their power in the crudest and ultimate manifestation of personal power: in personal acts of violence... Juan de Mariana, a Jesuit and a keen observer of 16th Century political life, put it best '...It was the custom of men to carry the title of Kingship in the point of their lances and in their weapons. The strongest is the one who captures the jewel (the crown). And he wins it from his opponent without regard for the laws which are silent in the face of the noise of arms, of trumpets or drums'.

...Alas! ...let us remember that Franco's only claim to legitimacy was to be the 'caudillo', the old medieval leader of hosts, by the grace of God, victorious in the field, against the Red Infidels of the 20th century.... Unfortunate Castile! Unfortunate Spain!

T.F. Ruiz, *The City and the Realm*, 1992.

Their religious policy, which was undoubtedly popular, achieved a superficial consensus at the expense of nurturing beneath the surface tensions and divisions which created within a united Spain a society of conflict

H. Kamen, *Spain 1469–1714*, 1983.

For the late 'doyen' of Spanish scholarship, Don Ramon Menendez Pidel, the reign of the Catholic monarchs was one 'which for all Spaniards represents a happy age'... This nostalgic view of the age has been shared by many non-Spanish historians. Nevertheless, it may be questioned.

One need not blame or praise the monarchs for the involvement in northern Europe which was ultimately to prove so disastrous to their Habsburg successors. Some of the less happy, long term, results of the reign – the confirmation of the growing dominance of the nobility and of the Mesta – may be attributed to them. The relative neglect of the Crown of Aragon was to sew a crop of dragon's teeth for later centuries.

But perhaps one regrets most deeply the decision taken by Ferdinand and Isabella to end the 'convivencia' of the peninsula, by expelling the Jews, persecuting the 'conversos' and forcing Spanish Muslims into nominal conversion... The inscription on the monarch's tomb in Granada, with its selection of only two of their achievements, the destruction of the Islamic 'sect' and the extinction of heresy present an 'Inquisitorial version of their reign'. It ended one epoch and began another.

J. N. Hillgarth, *The Spanish Kingdoms*, vol. 2, 1978.

Which of these four Historians best captures the achievement of Ferdinand and Isabella?

REVIEW

The Achievement of Ferdinand and Isabella

Influences and Legacies on their Reign

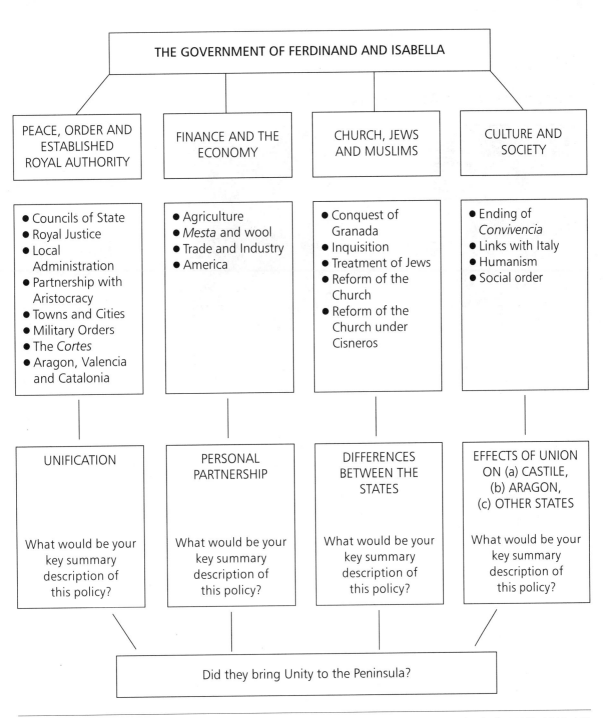

THE GOVERNMENT OF FERDINAND AND ISABELLA

PEACE, ORDER AND ESTABLISHED ROYAL AUTHORITY

- Councils of State
- Royal Justice
- Local Administration
- Partnership with Aristocracy
- Towns and Cities
- Military Orders
- The *Cortes*
- Aragon, Valencia and Catalonia

FINANCE AND THE ECONOMY

- Agriculture
- *Mesta* and wool
- Trade and Industry
- America

CHURCH, JEWS AND MUSLIMS

- Conquest of Granada
- Inquisition
- Treatment of Jews
- Reform of the Church
- Reform of the Church under Cisneros

CULTURE AND SOCIETY

- Ending of *Convivencia*
- Links with Italy
- Humanism
- Social order

UNIFICATION

What would be your key summary description of this policy?

PERSONAL PARTNERSHIP

What would be your key summary description of this policy?

DIFFERENCES BETWEEN THE STATES

What would be your key summary description of this policy?

EFFECTS OF UNION ON (a) CASTILE, (b) ARAGON, (c) OTHER STATES

What would be your key summary description of this policy?

Did they bring Unity to the Peninsula?

7 The Renaissance Monarchy of Francis I and Henry II of France

PREVIEW

The Renaissance Monarchs

FRANCIS I.

HENRY II.

A goodly prince, stately of countenance, merry of cheer, brown coloured, great eyes, high nosed... fair breasted and shouldered, small legs, long feet...

A contemporary description of Francis I by English chronicler Edward Hall.

Francis's love of violent sport made him particularly accident-prone... In hunting, as in war, Francis displayed great physical courage... A wild boar... battered its way up a staircase leading to a loggia where the King and his courtiers has assembled. Panic seized the spectators, but Francis, showing as much composure 'as if he had seen a damsel coming towards him' faced the boar and transfixed it with his sword.

R.J. Knecht, *Francis I*, 1982.

Awkward, taciturn, morose, unsociable, he seems an altogether different being from the bright, intelligent lad on the eve of his departure for Spain. The boy's spirit had been crushed by his dreary existence... So profound was the impression that his sufferings left upon him that in 1542 the Venetian Ambassador wrote that few pages at the Court could ever remember to have heard him laugh from the heart.

Noel Williams, *Henry II*, 1910.

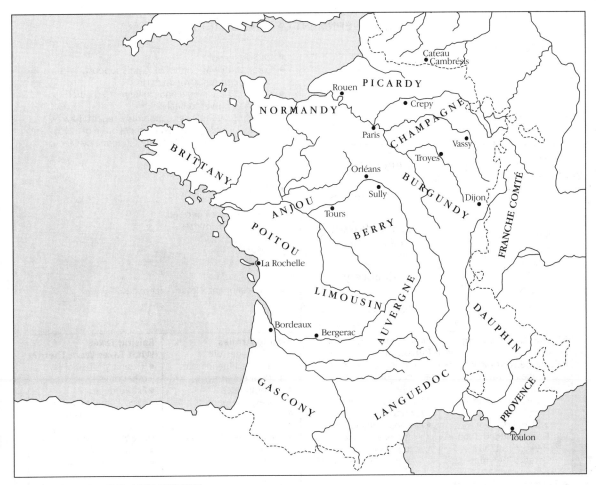

MAP OF FRANCE IN THE 16TH CENTURY.

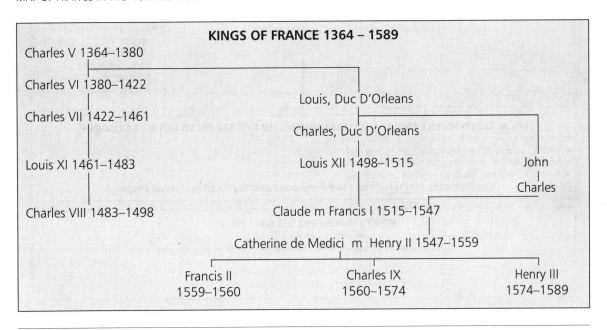

KINGS OF FRANCE 1364 – 1589

Charles V 1364–1380

Charles VI 1380–1422

Louis, Duc D'Orleans

Charles VII 1422–1461

Charles, Duc D'Orleans

Louis XI 1461–1483

Louis XII 1498–1515

John

Charles

Charles VIII 1483–1498

Claude m Francis I 1515–1547

Catherine de Medici m Henry II 1547–1559

Francis II
1559–1560

Charles IX
1560–1574

Henry III
1574–1589

THE GOVERNMENT OF FRANCE 1515

King

Francis I – 1515–1547

Henry II – 1547–1559

and his Court

- Hereditary right
- Coronation was symbol of God's support. God's Representative on Earth
- Anointing the King's body in Reims Cathedral. King had power to heal sick
- 'The King Never Dies' – appoints a regent if away. Francis I 1523 appointed mother Louise of Savoy. Henry II 1552 appointed wife Catherine de Medici.

King's Council

20 or so Nobles

Counseil Privé was Inner Council

- Followed King's person
- King in Council decided policy on any matter

Chancery

Turned Policy Into Laws

- Chancellor and Notaries (Lawyers)

Making Law & Giving Justice	Local Enforcement & Patronage	Raising Armies	Raising Taxes
• **Parlement of Paris** + Ratified Royal Edicts + Wished King to Observe Fundamental Laws + 5 Chambers, but Francis I added 3 more + Henry II 1547 v. Heretics 'Chambre Ardente' • **6 Provincial Parlements** + Regional Law Courts	11 Provincial Governors • Princes of Blood & High Nobles • King delegated Royal Authority to them • Patronage in regions + appointed 'gendarmes' to local armies + appointed household officers + filled vacancies in courts + advised King on bishops etc.	• 1445 Charles VIII established 'gendarmes' (permanent army) • 15 companies • Artillery companies • Mercenaries Royal army in 1559 was 50,000 = largest in Europe	**What Taxes Were There?** • 'Ordinary' - feudal & other dues • Extraordinary - *Taille* (land tax) - *Gabelle* (salt tax) - *Aides* (tax on goods) **How Were They Levied?** • 'Ordinary' - 4 'Trésoriers' • 'Extraordinary' - 4 'Généraux des Finances' Each given a 'Generalité' sub-divided into 'Elections' • Francis I reformed the system 1523 Tresorier de L'Epaine 1542 Generalité subdivided into 16 smaller districts.

LOCAL GOVERNMENT AND ADMINISTRATION AND JUSTICE 100 OR SO ROYAL 'BAILLIAGES'

- Each headed by a 'Bailli' & many other office holders
- Francis I sold 3,000 additional offices to levy money
- Bailli raised local army, his court heard appeals from lower courts
- He also published statutes and royal decrees

Local Estates Protected the Tax Exemptions and Rights of Provincial People

WHAT POWERS DID THE KING HAVE?

WAS HE AN ABSOLUTE KING?

Claude de Seyssel, *The Monarchy of France*, 1515

or

WAS HE A CONTRACTUAL KING?

Guillaume Budé, *The Institution of the Prince*, 1515

This chapter is a study of change, and the forces which produced it.

TALKING POINT

The Concept of Power

- Who, in your experience, has power? How does he or she use and exercise it?
- What is the difference between power and influence?
- Who has influence and how is it exercised?
- What is political power? Who has it? What's the difference between political power and political influence?
- What is leadership? In what different ways can it be exercised? When is it effective to use a 'tell' style of leadership? When is it effective to use a more 'sharing' style?
- What is absolute power? What can an absolute king do? How is an absolute king different from a dictator? And from a tyrant? What consequences does absolute monarchy have for its subjects?
- What is limited monarchy? How, wisely, might a king or president have his power limited? What are the consequences of limited monarchy for subjects?

The Renaissance Monarchy of Francis I and Henry II

During the reigns of Francis I and Henry II, French monarchy and government was at a watershed. It was still a medieval monarchy, which looked back to the feudal and contractual ways of the Middle Ages, yet it was increasingly powerful in an increasingly centralised kingdom. Thus it looked forward to the absolute monarchy of the *Ancien Regime* of Louis XIV, Louis XV and Louis XVI and the ending of that absolute monarchy in the French Revolution.

An American professor, J. Russell Major, has described the monarchy of Francis I and Henry II as 'popular and consultative': 'It had a feudal-dynastic structure, and its powers were severely limited by the powers of the various bodies in the Provinces. It had to depend on popular support'. The territories of the French kingdom were still newly acquired. The boundaries of France were not yet finally fixed. Only in 1532 was the Duchy of Brittany finally added to France, and it was not until 1552 that the north-east bishoprics of Metz, Toul and Verdun were added. Calais was captured from the English in 1558 and the Duchy of Savoy was occupied by a royal army between 1535 and 1559.

THE MARRIAGE OF HENRY II AND CATHERINE DE MEDICI AS PAINTED BY VASARI.

In addition, the France of the Renaissance monarchs was a long way from the centralised monarchy of Louis XIV. Many complicated local rights and privileges and exemptions still existed and local estates were always keen to defend their financial privileges. J.H. Shennon, in his book *Government and Society in France*, stresses the power of the monarchy: '...the monarchy is the focusing lens through which French government and society should be viewed; it gave impetus to political action and point to social aspirations'. Yet Shennon emphasises that kings were obliged to govern justly through the Coronation Oath, and uphold the fundamental laws of the kingdom. 'Another limitation upon the exercise of royal authority was the tradition that the King should seek advice before taking important decisions', this was a long- standing concept in France, and many bodies, like the Parlement, the estates, and other central and local institutions, reflected this.

The Authoritarian Rule of Francis I and Henry II

In his *The Making of French Absolutism*, David Parker observes that: 'Authoritarian by nature, Francis I had the means to rule more or less as he wished'. He clearly understands the personal power and influence which was at the heart of the reign of both Francis I and his son Henry II. When this power was threatened, their response was often angry and severe. Thus they came as personal sovereigns to control and dominate the many different groups in France.

- ## The Concordat of Bologna 1516 with the Catholic church

The king's power was always reflected in his relations with the pope and the Gallican Church. In 1438 the Pragmatic Sanctioning of Bourges had confirmed the king's right to nominate his own candidates to bishoprics, and rejected the pope's claim to annual payments from France.

In 1516 Francis I had just won the Battle of Marignano against the Spanish. He now wanted to pursue his conquests in Italy, but he needed Papal support for his attack further south. Pope Leo X was keen to make an agreement with Francis. The Concordat of Bologna restored, in theory, a number of Papal rights. Papal annates were to be allowed and the Pope could confirm royal nominations to bishoprics.

The Parlement of Paris and the Gallican Church were extremely angry at Francis's move. The king, however, brooked no resistance. When the Parlement refused to register the Concordat, Francis declared there would be only one king in France and not a Senate as in Venice. After a number of threats from the king, Parlement registered the Concordat, though claiming they were acting under duress.

- ## The regency of Louise of Savoy 1523–7

During the second of Francis's Italian wars he was defeated and captured at Pavia in 1525. Immediately the Parlement protested to his mother, the regent Louise of Savoy, about their role, and urged her to take vigorous action on a number of fronts. After the Treaty of Madrid, when Francis returned home, he immediately attacked the Parlement. In 1527 a *lit de justice* was presented. The king was carried aloft on his couch and lectured the Parlement that it should not meddle in affairs of state or attempt to modify royal legislation. In addition, every year the Parlement should ask the king to confirm its powers. Immediately after he had dropped this bombshell, Francis left the Parlement without giving its members an opportunity to reply.

- ## Assembly of Notables 1527

Neither Francis I nor Henry II ever called a meeting of the Estates General. However, in 1527, Francis needed exceptional taxation – two million gold crowns – to ransom his two sons left as hostages in Spain. He summoned an Assembly of Notables, with representatives from the church, the Parlement, as well as local baillis, and Provincial Governors. He appealed to them not to ratify the Treaty of Madrid and he asked them for extraordinary taxation. In a personal speech, however, he made it clear that he was simply honouring the delegates, not consulting them. The Assembly gave him everything he asked for.

- ## The Monarchy's relations with local Parlements

King Francis I was determined that the six local Parlements should be only law courts, with no right to question his edicts. A typical case in point is his treatment of the Parlement of Rouen in 1540. Members of the Parlement refused to register all the points in one of Francis's edicts. On 4 August, just as they were leaving for their summer recess, the members were told to remain in session. On 26 August, the king announced his impending arrival. Early in September, the Parlement were visited by the King's

Chancellor, who reprimanded them for four hours. On 10 September the king cancelled several of their recent decrees and closed them down until further notice. Only in January 1541 was the Parlement re-opened – and even then nine members were banished from its sessions.

What does this incident tell you about the nature of French monarchy?

- ● **The monarchy's relations with Provincial Estates**

The Provincial Estates could only be summoned by the king. He fixed the agenda and the point of the meeting and the place of the meeting, and he appointed the chairman. His representatives could forward his demands and listen to the requests of the Estates. This usually took place once a year. In 1538, in a particularly angry mood, Francis ordered his representatives at the Estates of Languedoc not to reply to their grievances until they had agreed his taxes. The Estates protested, but finally agreed.

- ● **The Provincial Governors**

In the early 16th century there were eleven Provincial Governors who had important power over the border regions of France. Initially they were set up to defend the realm, but Francis I also appointed additional governors in central areas. The Provincial Governors were important people: they were princes of the blood or members of the high nobility. They included Francis's sons, some of his brothers-in-law, and his favourite, and even the husbands of his two mistresses.

Provincial Governors were the King's Royal Commissioners and they were given the same honours as the king. Their powers were not clearly defined. They lived permanently at court and it was often their practice to exercise patronage in their district. In 1515 the Governor of Ghent was instructed 'generally to do in other things all that we would see and recognise as necessary to the good of ourselves and our affairs and useful to our country'. Governors appointed local household officials, members of the local gendarmerie and members of their own very large private households.

Although governors were appointed by, and removed by, the king, they were still potentially dangerous to him. As a source of factional power, they contained the seeds of future conflict during the second half of the 16th century.

From this section it will be clear that a French king in the 16th century had considerable power and authority. Was the government of Francis I very different from government today!?

Economic Trends and Social Structures

The economy of France during the reigns of Francis I and Henry II was, in Knecht's repeated phrase, 'in good shape'. Yet the social structure contained within itself the seeds of its own collapse in the second half of the century.

Between 1450 and 1550 France was economically fortunate. Harvests were good, population and trade were expanding, the great plague had ended and even wars were significantly reduced. There were signs of economic recovery after the Hundred Years War. Agriculture was improving, new towns were growing, new industries were being set up. As a result, in spite of increasingly heavy taxation, the reign of Francis and Henry saw a relative absence of popular unrest.

The wealth of France during the first half of the 16th century was undoubtedly increasing.

AGRICULTURAL IMPROVEMENTS

In the century after 1450 the cultivation of land increased after the ravages of the Hundred Years War. The lot of the average peasant improved as work became more plentiful with the need to feed an expanding population. Interestingly, there was little technological improvement in farming, so that the doubling of the population began to cause significant problems. It was no longer possible after 1540 to produce enough corn to feed the growing numbers. This increased grain prices and caused grain shortages, which in turn caused starvation. The peasant revolts of the second half of the century owe much to these problems.

URBAN GROWTH

Towns also increased in size and Paris, Lyon and Rouen were amongst the largest in Europe. Another forty French towns boasted more than 10,000 inhabitants. Interestingly, of the 15,101 patients admitted to the Hotel-Dieu in Lyon between 1520 and 1563, over 60 per cent came from outside the city. This demonstrates the movement into the expanding towns Even so, only a handful of towns could be classed as industrial, like Amiens, Toul and Lyon, since all three were centres of textiles industries.

FRANCE 1501–50

MINING, PRINTING AND OTHER INDUSTRIES

In many areas of France, there was already the basis for later industrial growth. Mining was encouraged in order to provide the weapons of war, and the new printing industry was growing rapidly. Paris saw the first printing press in 1470, and a second one was added in Lyon in 1473. By 1500, more than 30 towns had printing presses. Lyon quickly became the centre of the French printing industry.

THE GROWTH OF TRADE

By 1500, cities such as Rouen and Lyon had become regional centres for international trade. France had all the necessities for her own economy – corn, wine, salt, and a variety of textile industries.

POPULATION

In 1550, the population of France was perhaps 15 million. This may well be double the figure for 1450. The main reasons for this dramatic increase were the ending of plague and the reduction of war, but the absence of any significant grain famine also improved diet.

> This country, thanks to its size, has a great variety of soil and products. These are of such high quality and so abundant there are enough for France and even for foreign countries.
>
> Marino Cavili, Venetian Ambassador, 1546.

> The peasants were in complete subjection, more ill-treated and oppressed than dogs or slaves.
>
> The Earl of Surrey, September 1522.

> The seemingly contradictory comments of contemporary observers are not irreconcilable: from about 1520 France's prosperity was under attack; it did not collapse however until the second half of the century.
>
> R.J. Knecht, *Francis I*, 1982.

The Individual Contribution of Francis I to Economic Trends

Francis's control of trade

Unusually in the 16th century, Francis I began to see France as an economic entity. In this he anticipated the mercantilist developments of the 17th century.

- In 1517 he proposed a dramatic scheme for wholesale economic reform and presented it to an assembly representing 52 of the leading towns. Their replies were largely negative and parochial and Francis shelved the scheme.
- Customs Reform

Francis imposed many customs duties. For example, in 1517 a duty on the imports of cloth of gold or silver and goldsmiths' work and jewellery. In 1544 he set up the first *duan* or customs system, in Lyon, and in the same year he appointed a Controller General to supervise the customs system.

- Reform of the Coinage

Francis issued many edicts to regulate and improve the minting of coins. Coin clippers were punished and Francis fixed the values of gold and silver in order to prevent depreciation of the coinage.

- In a series of decrees between 1537 and 1541, Francis also regulated Bills of Exchange, so that foreign merchants could trade in France more easily.

One of Francis I's major contributions to the economy was the promotion of Lyon as the second city of France. In 1540 Francis decreed that spices could only be imported into France through Lyon, Marseilles and Rouen. In addition, he encouraged the printing and silk industries in the city. By 1554 Lyon's silk industry was employing 12,000 workers.

Similarly, Francis I encouraged the Mediterranean trade of the port of Marseilles. The yield from harbour taxes in 1500 was around 400 livres. By 1542, it was over 3,000 livres. The population doubled between 1520 and 1554. Because of Francis's links with the Ottoman Turks, trade developed between Marseille and the French trading posts in Beirut and Tripoli.

However, perhaps the most significant contribution made by Francis was the encouragement of the Atlantic Seaboard. Rouen, Nantes, La Rochelle and Bordeaux all flourished in his reign. Bordeaux's prosperity undoubtedly came from the revival of local vineyards.

In spite of the increasing economic wealth of the country during the first half of the 16th century, the winds of change were blowing and significant economic and social problems were emerging. The costs of warfare in Italy were extremely high. Inflation was affecting everyone for good or ill. The traditional aristocracy suffered while many merchants prospered. Urban investment in land dispossessed many peasantry and the food supply could not keep pace with population growth. Furthermore, the financial reforms of Francis I, furthered by his son, created a new bureaucracy of officeholders. This new class of professional bureaucrats was to have a significant impact on the future of France. With the collapse of feudalism the protection offered by feudal lords was reduced and replaced by a system of patronage and clients. The power of provincial governors is a reflection of this. All of this took place amidst the growth of religious dissent, which provided a cause for displaced social groups to cling on to.

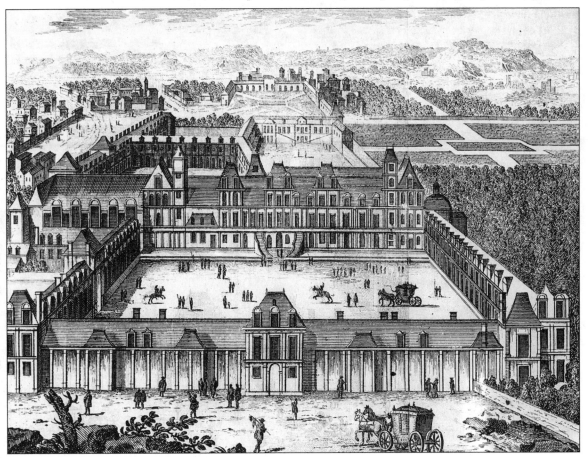

A SIGN OF POLITICAL AS WELL AS ECONOMIC STRENGTH, THE PALACE AT FONTAINEBLEAU WAS ONE OF SEVERAL PRESTIGIOUS PROJECTS PURSUED BY FRANCIS I.

The consequent social forces were well beyond the king's control. The independent nobility formed themselves into factions. In addition, a growing urban merchant class accompanied the development of an urban proletariat, urban poverty and vagabondage. Finally, peasants, weighed down by the demands of church, king and lords, began a process of popular revolt that spread well into the second half of the century and beyond.

Focus

7.1 The Conards and the Mardi Gras at Rouen in 1542

ROUEN IN THE 16TH CENTURY.

As they had for generations, the people of Rouen celebrated the end of winter of 1542 with a Mardi Gras Carnival. That year the organisers of the festival chose an extraordinary theme for the parade – the death of trade.

The immediate occasion for the mourning was the start of another Habsburg–Valois War. The town was cut off from its most important markets, its trade was crippled, its industry was halted amid widespread unemployment. Thousands of craftsmen were forced out of work and many merchants were brought to the point of ruin. Accordingly, the Mardi Gras parade was transformed into a mock funeral.

At the head of the courtege marched a cripple called 'Diligence. He was followed by the servants of the 'House of Trade' bearing placards labelled 'The Poor Commune'. There next appeared a cart bearing 'The Republic', preceded by thirty-six orphans carrying candles. Next came the funeral bier of trade drawn by two horses named 'Greed' and 'Misfortune. Then followed the King of the carnival, Aurus he was called, the Abbot of the 'Conards', with his retinue of Church Cardinals. There marched next the Chancellor of France, designated the 'unfortunate chancellor'. In honour of the plague there then appeared the grand patriarch of the pox with a retinue of servants sporting disfigured noses. Next there appeared sixteen figures called the 'shadows of Conardee', dressed from head to foot in light costume 'tincture of manure' with openings only for mouth and eyes. The attendants of these characters passed out verses to the crowd as they passed. These attacked the competence of the city fathers, the multiplication and sale of offices at the expense of the people, the misuse of public authority and the abuses of misconduct of the Church.

What questions would you wish to ask about this text, taken from Henry Hellas' book, *The Conquest of Poverty*, 1986?

The following day the Conards produced a play in the city. The three central characters – church, nobility and poverty – each settled down to do their washing. Poverty soon finds himself doing the dirty washing for all three and when he tries to protest, nobility thrashes him. Poverty then continues to wash and begins to work particularly on the linen of the Church. Again, he objects. This time nobility and the church together drive him off. The message of the play is clear. In the antagonism between nobles and commons, the church clearly takes sides. Indeed, its own wealth, demonstrated by the vestments of the clergy, is a source of much opposition.

The Conards was an abbey of youth, a confraternity similar to many others throughout France. As winter passed into spring, the season of Lent was preceded by a Mardi Gras carnival. It is particularly interesting that the Conards of Rouen were controlled by aristocratic families in the city who provided the money for the procession. The Abbey of Conards had approximately two thousand five hundred members. Each paid a small subscription. Most were the sons of members of the towns' notables and merchants, people who were members of the Parlement, the Bailliage and other local government organisations. They were also the sons of the great merchants who organised the production and export of cloth, hosiery, hats, hardware and other manufacturers in the city. Rouen was perhaps the third largest town in France at this time with a population of 78,000, and it was always closely linked to Paris.

Yet the grip of the wealthy on the Abbey of the Conards was limited. The procession and the play always represented the view of rank and file members. The floats of the procession often contained political protest against the rich and powerful.

In short, 'the carnival was a characteristically urban cultural form, a popular festival which reflected the mentality of the young and the plebeians, an outlet for the discontent of the populous'.

What does this incident tell us of the economic and social tensions which existed in a major French city like Rouen?

The Growth of Heresy, the Reformed Church and Persecution

The punishment of the Meaux Heretics became one of the most celebrated events in the martyrology of 16th century protestantism... What is interesting is the ritualised form in which this legalised killing was acted out. Mangin's house was demolished, the fourteen leaders marched from the chateau of Meaux past the Cathedral and across the river to the place of execution. Thousands came from Paris and the Brie countryside to attend the procession and to watch the burning. While thirty-six of the heretics were forced to watch, the fourteen were burned to death. A young boy, arrested with the others, was suspended over them and sang hymns while the flames consumed his comrades. The next day a great procession in honour of the Holy Sacrament took place. First came the students from children of the town, then some three thousand people carrying torches, followed by the clergy who escorted the Holy Sacrament. Afterwards there marched the defiled and remaining heretics, notables, the bourgeoisie... Then the crowd listened to a sermon from the Dominican Friar and then returned the Holy Sacrament to the Cathedral where the heretics were forced to perform still further acts of atonement. Such executions and processions had become common place in France since the 1520's, but the scale of ritual murder at Meaux surpassed anything witnessed to date. The procession following the burnings represented the reassertion of 'the rite ordering' of the social hierarchy.

H. Heller, *The Conquest of Poverty*, 1986.

The events in Meaux in 1546 were the culmination of three decades of growth in heresy in France. Luther's writings entered France, more particularly Paris, in 1517, and circulated until 1521 when the Sorbonne condemned them. The king was committed by his Coronation Oath to remove heresy from his realms, but his involvement in foreign wars diverted his attention. In any case, he was keen to encourage the learning of humanists and it wasn't easy to separate Lutherism from humanism in these early days. A reforming group, led by Lefevre D'Etaples and Farel, assembled at Meaux in 1521. They were searching for a purer spirituality and a number of their members were celebrated humanists. The Parlement of Paris was anxious to act to shut out this pernicious enemy. It issued an edict stating that no books be published in France without the consent of the Sorbonne. Lefevre was accused of heresy and the Parlement condemned his translations of both the Old and New Testaments. During the remainder of the 1520s, it was difficult for Francis to act, not least because of his long imprisonment and the Regency of Louise of Savoy. Only when the number of heretics became significant did Francis become involved.

On the night of 18 October 1534, Protestant broadsheets were published in several major towns. One of them was pinned on the door of the king's bedchamber at Amboise The king could not ignore the personal insult of this 'Affair of the Placards'. The broadsheets contained a direct attack on the Catholic Mass and the Eucharist was one issue which Francis sought personally to defend. From now on, repression was the order of the day. The Edict of Fontainebleau in 1540 gave overall control of heresy cases to the Parlements. In 1542, the Sorbonne provided the first index of forbidden books and the following years witnessed a number of heresy prosecutions by the Parlement of Paris.

The accession of the melancholy Henry II in 1547 immediately confirmed the drive for persecution. An Edict of 5 April confirmed the use of judicial torture and decreed public whipping and cutting off the tongue for the offence of blasphemy. In November, Henry confirmed the appointment of the Dominican Friar Mattheas Ory as Inquisitor for France. The following month another edict banned the publication of books on the Index. However, the most significant development was the creation of a new chamber, the *chambre ardente*, in the Parlement of Paris with the exclusive purpose of hearing heresy cases. In the six months before the inception of the new Chambre, 57 heresy cases were heard in Paris, with two victims being sentenced to death. Over the following 17 months, 215 cases were heard and 37 death sentences were passed. On the other hand, 39 victims were exonerated and the rest received varying sentences. Forty-one were publicly whipped. 'These figures', as F.J. Baumgartner has stated in his biography of Henry II, 'are perhaps somewhat less severe than one would be led to expect from a court with such a reputation for harshness' The severity of the sentence on three victims in 1548 cannot be doubted:

> The victims should be placed in a tumbrel in front of the hurdle and led to the Plas Maubert where four gibbets shall be erected, the first of which should be taller than the others by one foot. Onto this the principal author of the crime and offences should be lifted, and onto the other three should be lifted the others. And around each gibbet, and at the same time, a large fire should be lit and the prisoner should be burned alive and their bodies consumed and reduced to ashes.

In 1551 King Henry II codified the suppression of heresy in the all-embracing Edict of Chateaubriant. N.M. Sutherland has described it as 'a shift in emphasis away from a negative opposition towards a positive and pervasive persecution'. From now on heresy cases were to be tried in church courts. The detail of the Edict of Chateaubriant is reflected in the issue of censorship. The possession, production, sale and dissemination of religious books was banned. There was rigid control of printing and detailed inspection of bookshops. Informers were to receive one third of the confiscated property of the convicted. Magistrates were actively to seek out heretics and also to search houses for forbidden books. A further edict in 1557 developed the repression still further: all heretics were to be punished by death and there was to be no moderation in any case.

In the face of the severity of this persecution, what enabled the Calvinist church in France to grow? In her book *International Calvinism*, Menna Prestwich has clarified the main issues.

Why was Calvinism welcomed in some sections of society and not in others? How is its geographical dispersion to be explained? Why was Calvinism a religion of artisans rather than of peasants? How were Calvinist ideas disseminated and what is the relative importance of anti-clericalism, economic factors, and intellectual appeal in accounting for their impact?

Many questions are difficult to answer. Were the Calvinist meetings democratic in their structure, or was Calvinism an oligarchy which disciplined its members? It is very difficult to understand such issues in detail.

We can, however, understand many of the factors which helped the Calvinist church to grow in France in this period. Printing was a central factor and Calvinism was a religion of the book. Paris and Lyon quickly became main printing centres, and in spite of censorship Calvin's texts rolled off the presses. Music was also important. Calvin composed hymns himself and his metrical psalms were published in 1539. A further translation of 50 psalms by Marot appeared in 1543. The singing of Calvinist congregations became a feature of their churches and a unifying spiritual force. Martyrs on their way to the stake and demonstrators in Paris and Huguenot armies in the wars, all sang metrical psalms, such as 'Let God arise, let His enemies be scattered' (Psalm 68).

The smuggling of books and psalms from Geneva and Strasburg to the towns and cities of France was a regular occurrence, symbolised by the pack-man and his donkey, Calvinist tracts secreted among his bags. One selling his wares in Troyes unwisely tried to sell an anti-clerical pamphlet to a fervent Catholic, was informed upon, and went to his death singing psalms. Given the high levels of illiteracy, even among urban artisans, personal preaching, which could summon audiences of thousands, was again extremely important – as it had been for the works of Luther in Germany.

'By 1560', according to Menna Prestwich, 'the geographical contours of Calvinism were emerging clearly. There was a wide scattering of churches with a constellation in Normandy and a thick clustering south of the Loire forming a crescent which curved to the south of the high plateau of the Auvergne and had Lyon and La Rochelle as its tips. It had taken a remarkably short time to break through the crust of local habit and custom'.

Social and economic factors played a critically important part. Natalie Zemon Davis has shown how the journeymen printers of Lyon welcomed the Calvinist cause. It gave them a control of their own destiny at a time when they were working in groups of two or three in subjection to a master printer. It also gave them a focus for their social lives to replace the repetitive games which had hitherto dominated their humdrum evenings. If they were the quickest group in Lyon to attach themselves to the Calvinist cause, after the massacre of St. Bartholomew's Eve in 1572 in the French Wars of Religion, they were also the quickest to convert back to Catholicism.

TALKING POINT
Why is music such an important part of Calvinism? What role does it play?

Ladurie's book *The Peasants of Languedoc* also cites social and economic factors: plague, famine and the flight of the rural port to the towns caused insecurity and popular revolt. Brigandage and vagrancy added to the climate. Moreover, in the 1540s in the city of Tours, an industrial crisis took place. Silk manufacturing collapsed because of the Habsburg–Valois wars and unemployment was rife. Following this crisis, the silk industry was transferred to Lyon. Apprentices and journeymen, as well as master craftsmen, vented their anger through a major uprising in the city. In the same period, at Meaux, the Calvinist leaders were carders of wool. Pierre Le Clerc was the elected minister of the congregation and he and his fellow heretics were all mechanicals and artisans.

Whatever the urban support, however, it was perhaps the support of the court and the cities which gave Calvinism its greatest political leverage. Margaret d'Angouleme, the sister of King Francis I, married Henry, King of Navarre. She was a woman of great personal piety and appointed bishops in Languedoc and rectors of universities. Between 1558 and 1562, many members of the nobility became Calvinists, providing further impetus and support to the movement.

The Calvinist church in Paris (founded in 1555) had two noblemen as pastors – Morel and Chandieu. The church had been set up by a third given the nickname of Ferriere and when 130 Calvinists were arrested after the service in the Rue Saint Jacques in 1557, 30 of them were nobles.

In the regions, Calvinist churches were protected and supported by important noble families. Easily the most important were Antoine of Bourbon, the King of Navarre, and the leading members of the House of Montmorency. Francoise Andelot and Gaspar Coligny were important military figures in France and both were genuine converts to the Calvinist faith. Andelot, for example, went on an evangelising tour around the Loire Valley in 1558, founding 12 new churches and making many conversions among the nobility. The role of these men in the Religious Wars that followed was very significant.

Nobles in the towns, especially lawyers and councillors, members of the local Parlement, were also welcome converts. It was rumoured in 1562 that up to a third of the members of the Parlement of Paris were Calvinists.

Examining the Evidence

John Calvin and the growth of Calvinism in France

There are individuals – quite rare – who because they have such powers themselves become the historical force... Calvin's greatness arose from his sense of the historic moment, or to put it another way, the way he applied his genius to the times... The parallel made between a theoretical vision and organising genius of Calvin and Lenin is a suggestive one. Evaluating Lenin's contribution to the Russian Revolution, Trotsky spoke of him as the embodiment of all the revolutionary currents in Russia.

Source A

Calvin's letter to the faithful in France, 24 July 1547.

> I entreat you my dear brethren to hold steady upon your course and let no fear upset you, even though the dangers are more evident now than ever before. May the trust which God commands us to have in His grace and in His strength always be an impregnable fortress for you.

Source B

Calvin's letter to Bullinger about the Edict of Chateaubriant, 15 October 1551.

> Frightful laws have been published in France so that new ways of expressing hatred towards the pious ones are manifested. What has hitherto been granted to sourcerers, forgers and thieves, namely that they have a right of appeal to a sovereign court, is now taken away from Christians. Ordinary magistrates without any appeal may order them to be delivered to the flames forthwith. It is forbidden for relatives of those whose lives are at risk to venture to protest on pain of being treated as accessories. In order to keep the flames well fanned, one third of their goods is allotted to informers.
>
> The Lord Chancellor is to take care not to admit any person to a public office who may, at any time, have fallen under the slightest suspicion, with a result that no-one can become a Judge who is not hostile to Christ... The law now requires the sovereign Courts to be sure that any lawyers who are known to favour our teaching should clear themselves upon oath. They are all required to worship the bread-God by the usual genuflexions.

Source C

A letter from Calvin to Richard Lefevre, 19 January 1551.

Richard Lefevre was a goldsmith from Rouen who had visited Geneva in 1544. Calvin wrote the following letter which was smuggled to him while he was awaiting trial. It was reproduced by Crespin in his *Lives of the Martyrs*, 1554.

> All that you have felt and experienced until now of the abounding goodness of God ought to confirm you in the assured hope that He will not fail you in the future. Meanwhile, pray to Him that He will make you understand even better what a treasure there is in the beliefs for which you fight.

The reply from Richard Lefevre to Calvin from his prison, 3 May 1554:

> The present is to let you know that I hope to go and keep Whitsuntide in the kingdom of Heaven and be present at the marriage of the Son of God. If I am not sooner called away by this good Lord and Master whose voice I am now ready to obey.

1 What do these letters tell you about John Calvin as a leader? What do they tell you about his faith? And what do they tell you about his other skills?

2 What do these sources tell you about the reasons for the spread of Calvinism in France?

3 What light does source E throw on Calvin's leadership of the Calvinist church in France?

Source D

Calvin's letter to the five scholars of Lyon, December 1552.
Five French scholars from the Midi had studied theology at Lausanne and were on their way back to the south west when they were betrayed by a fellow traveller, imprisoned and burned at the stake in Lyon on 16 May 1553.

You know the courage that you must use in your fight. In this way all those who have relied on you will never be taken by surprise and still less be thrown into confusion. So, my brethren, be assured that you will be strengthened in your hour of need by the Spirit of our Lord Jesus Christ, not to give way under stress of temptation, however severe.

Source E

Calvin's letter to Bullinger, May 1561.

It is unbelievable to see how impetuously our brothers are rushing forward. Pastors are demanded from all parts of France. The title of Pastor is solicited with as much enthusiasm as the efforts made to obtain benefices in the Roman Church. My door is beseiged like that of a King. Vacant posts are fought over as if the reign of Christ had been peaceably established in France. But our resources are exhausted, we are reduced to searching everywhere, even in the artisans workshop, to find men with some smattering of doctrine and of piety as candidates for the Ministry in France.

Source F

Theodore Vaser's description of the founding of the Church in Paris, September 1555.

The founding of this Church came about through a nobleman from Maine, the Lord De la Farriere, who had come to Paris with his family to escape observation because of his religion. In particular, his wife was pregnant and he didn't want the child to be baptised with the usual superstitious ceremonial and ritual of the Roman Church. Sometime later a group of nobles met together in the house of this Lord at a time when the lady had had her baby. He asked the gathering not to allow the child to be deprived of baptism by which Christian children ought to be dedicated to God. So he asked them to choose a minister who could undertake the baptism. The company didn't want to agree but he argued that it was impossible for him to go to Geneve for baptism and if the child died without his service he would be extremely sorry. This event was the occasion for the first meetings of the Church in Paris. La Riviere was chosen by the congregation after prayer and fasting, as was appropriate, and taken even more carefully and seriously than usual since it was an innovation there. Then they set up a small establishment as far as their limited numbers would allow by forming a consistory of some of the Elders and Deacons to supervise the Church.

Source G

Calvin's letter to the Church in Paris, 16 September 1557.
This letter followed the incident in the Rue Saint Jacques in the Latin quarter of the city. At a night-time meeting of the Calvinist congregation, a group of students from a nearby college broke in. A religious riots resulted and many Protestants were arrested and badly treated in prison.

Beyond our prayers on your behalf we cannot do much, although other means of coming to your aid are not neglected by us. We do not know if they will help you, but do not doubt that God has you in mind and that your tears of lamentations will be listened to by Him. For if we do not trust to His providence, distress will swallow us all up.

Source H

A letter to the French churches, 19 April 1556.

For the rest I have heard that some are debating among themselves whether, if an atrocity is committed against them, they would resort to violence rather than allow themselves to be hunted down. I beseech you, beloved brethren, to abandon any such notions, for there will never God's blessing and will never succeed since He disapproves of such things.

Source I

Letter to Antoine Bourbon, King of Navarre, 14 December 1557.

Sire, the sighs and groans of so many true believers deserve your attention. You should be courageous and come to their aid procuring their relief so far as it is in your power to do so.

Source J

Geneva controlled the development of the French Evangelical Church.

R.M. Kingdon, *Geneva and the Coming of the French Wars of Religion*, 1956.

Source K

Calvin's influence over the French Evangelical Movement long pre-dates the 1550's.

H. Heller, *The Conquest of Poverty*, 1986.

In 1555 the Calvinist Church in Paris was founded, giving an internal focal point distinct from the international Calvinist capital in Geneva... The years from around 1555–1562 saw an explosion of Calvinist conversions. The foundation of the Paris church set the tone for a mood of defiance, almost of triumph, and the will to resist replaced the cult of martyrdom.

Menna Prestwich, *International Calvinism*, 1985.

Source L

Calvin penned elegant exhortations to Princes and noblemen. He appealed to Francis I on behalf of the Vaudois peasants and to Henry II on behalf of the prisoners taken after the raid upon the Rue Saint Jacques in 1557. Calvin was thus initiating a policy of international Calvinism, but totally ineffectively as far as the victims of persecution were concerned. By contrast he was successful in giving cohesion to the churches of France. From 1555 the Structure of the Consistory with Elders and Deacons was made obligatory and trustworthy ministers were made available on request by the company of Pastors in Geneva.

Menna Prestwich, *International Calvinism*, 1985.

4 What difficulties were faced by early Calvinists in France?
5 What organisation and policies did they set up to face their difficulties? How did Calvin help?

6 Use all the information provided in the text and the sources provided in this section. Write the following essay: How far did Calvin personally direct the growth of the Calvinist Church in France up to 1560? Was his leadership effective?

7.2 Francis I – Renaissance King and Patron of the Arts

Francis's pride in his palace at Fontainebleau is well attested by Sir John Wallop, the English Ambassador to France in 1540. The King told the Ambassador that he had heard that Henry VIII used much gilding in his houses whereas he himself used little or none. He preferred 'timber finely wrought with divers colours of wood natural as ebony, brazil and certain others' which he reckoned were richer than gilding and also more durable. Soon afterwards Wallop was able to see all this for himself at Fontainebleau. He found the royal bedchamber 'very singular, as well with antique borders as costly ceiling and a chimney right well made'.

R.J. Knecht, *Francis I*, 1982.

CELLINI'S SKETCH FOR HIS SCULPTURE *JUNO*.

Benvenuto Cellini

Benvenuto Cellini, a great goldsmith and sculptor from Florence visited France in 1537 and then for five years in 1540. He was housed in Paris on the left bank of the Seine, near the Louvre, and given a team of assistants.

Francis and Paintings

Francis's victory at Marignano in 1515 and his conquest of Milan gave him an opportunity to see a number of Italian masterpieces, including Leonardo da Vinci's *Last Supper*. As a result Leonardo, then aged 65, was invited to live near Amboise in 1516, and given an annual income. Francis also became the patron of other international artists. Perhaps best known is the Dutchman John Clouet, a portrait painter who painted not only Francis but also members of his family. By 1525 Francis's collection consisted of many Florentine and Roman paintings. Agents like Aretino in Venice were given large sums of money to send paintings back to France.

AN 18TH-CENTURY DEPICTION OF FRANCIS I CRADLING THE DYING LEONARDO DA VINCI IN HIS ARMS.

Francis's Library and Patronage of Literature

In 1522 Guillaume Bude became the Master of the King's Library. The library contained 1626 volumes at this time. 'These books are all of parchment', wrote one contemporary, 'handwritten in beautiful lettering and bound in silk of various colours with elaborate locks and clasps of silver gilt'. Bude supported his master's wish to add to the library and began a search for rare manuscripts, especially in Greek. Within a few years Francis had three libraries, a new one in his chateau at Fontainebleau, and a third one which accompanied him on his travels. He liked to read the books himself, or at least have them read aloud to him at mealtimes.

The most dramatic development in the King's library occurred in an Edict of 28 December 1537, which decreed that all printers and booksellers were to send a copy of every new book, in any language, by any author, to the keeper of the King's library. Unfortunately, it was difficult to enforce this Edict and only a hundred or so such books were sent. In May 1544, therefore, Francis ordered the centralization of all his libraries to Fontainebleau. There were thus one thousand, eight hundred and ninety-four volumes. Francis was genuinely interested in scholarship 'far from grudging to anyone the records of ancient writers' one contemporary wrote, 'he intends to put them at the disposal of, and service of, all men'.

GUILLAUME BUDE, MASTER OF THE KING'S LIBRARY.

GVILLAVME BVDE, PARISIEN.

Francis and Architecture

When the Emperor Charles V visited Paris in the winter of 1539–1540, the Louvre was given a hasty facelift, but the Great Hall of the Palace, headquarters of the Parlement, had to be used for a banquet. All this must have convinced Francis of the need to rebuild the Louvre, but this could not be achieved quickly. There were many physical difficulties in the way. Thus it was only in 1546, shortly before his death, that Pierre Lescot was given the task. Meanwhile the King had to make do with other chateau outside Paris where there was more room to build and also where he could more easily indulge his taste for hunting.

R.J. Knecht, *Francis I*, 1982.

REVIEW

The Origins of the French Religious Wars

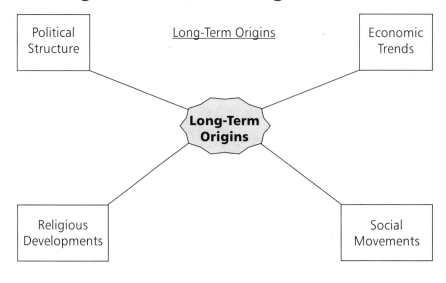

Long-Term Origins

- Political Structure
- Economic Trends
- **Long-Term Origins**
- Religious Developments
- Social Movements

Use the material in this chapter and that at the beginning of Chapter 11 to explain why French Religious Wars broke out in 1560.

It would be particularly challenging to write it as *one* of the following:

- A script for a radio documentary programme. You could tape it.
- A newspaper major article for a particular audience.
- A presentation to a group of French students.

Immediate Causes, 1547–59

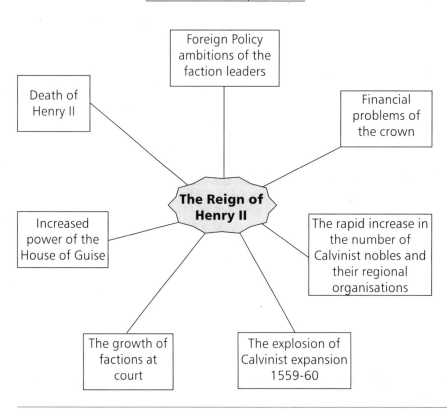

- Foreign Policy ambitions of the faction leaders
- Death of Henry II
- Financial problems of the crown
- **The Reign of Henry II**
- Increased power of the House of Guise
- The rapid increase in the number of Calvinist nobles and their regional organisations
- The growth of factions at court
- The explosion of Calvinist expansion 1559-60

8 The Empire of Charles V, 1519–55

TALKING POINT

Identify several historical figures – male and female – 'who must be called great'. What have they done to deserve the title?

PREVIEW

There are in History certain men whose productive energy is more than human. They create out of their own elemental strength, and lay down the laws of thought and action for centuries to come. The Emperor Charles V was not one of these. Rather did he belong to that other group who must be called Great, because ancient historic forces were concentrated in their single being, because they moulded inherited ideas of power, belief and behaviour into new forms... In this way he also was a builder.

With these words, Professor Karl Brandi began his monumental biography of the Emperor Charles V, first published in 1939.

The Emperor had reached the height of his power and the third stage of career was now [1547] completed. The first had centred on making peace in the Spanish dominion, identifying himself with the country that was to become the main source of his Imperial power. During that period he had also become emotionally attached to the land of his maternal predecessors. In the second stage he had concentrated on securing Italy and removing the Turkish threat from Central Europe as well as from the Western Mediterranean. In the third stage of his career he had endeavoured to end the Lutheran heresy and bring the Protestants back to the Catholic Church by concessions negotiated with Lutheran participation at the Council of Trent. Throughout the three stages of his career he had had to reckon with his fierce rival, the King of France.

What remained, the fourth and last stage of his career, was the consolidation of his work for the benefit of his heirs. By his great exertions and constant efforts he had managed to build up a large empire. Now he wishes to make sure that this impressive building, the work of his whole lifetime, should not collapse.

M.F. Alvarez, *Charles V,* 1975.

TALKING POINT

Manual Alvarez summarises Charles V's career in these words. Use this chapter to discuss the following questions:

- Can you attach dates to each of the four stages?
- Do you accept Alvarez's classification?
- Do you agree with his phrase 'this impressive building'?
- What success did Charles have in each of the four stages?

The Holy Roman Empire in the 16th Century

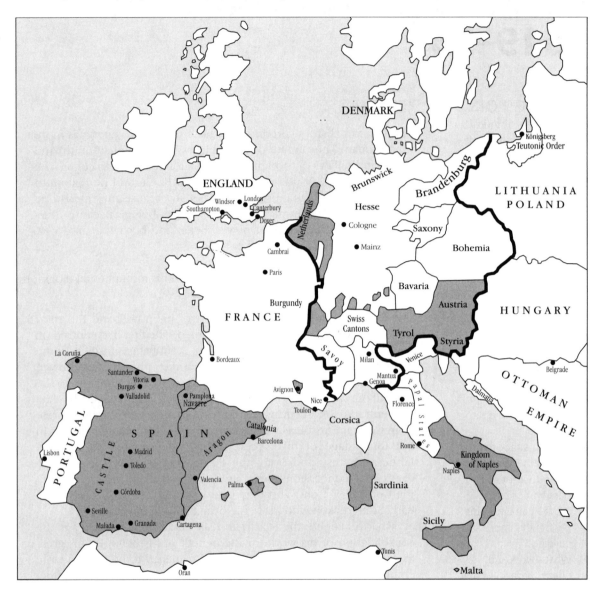

England
Windsor ● ●London
Southampton ● ●Canterbury
Dover ●

DENMARK

Brunswick

Brandenburg

● Königsberg
Teutonic Order

LITHUANIA
POLAND

Hesse
● Cologne

Saxony

Cambrai ●

Netherlands

● Mainz

Bohemia

Paris ●

Bavaria

Burgundy

Austria

HUNGARY

FRANCE

Swiss
Cantons

Tyrol

Styria

Savoy

Milan ●

Venice

● Bordeaux

Belgrade

Mantua
Genoa ●

OTTOMAN

La Coruña
Santander ●
Vitoria ●
Burgos ●
● Valladolid

Avignon ●

Nice ●
Toulon ●

Florence ●

Papal States

Dalmatia

EMPIRE

● Pamplona
Navarre

Corsica

Rome ●

SPAIN

Catalonia

Kingdom
of Naples

PORTUGAL

Madrid ●

Aragon

Barcelona

Naples ●

CASTILE

● Toledo

Valencia ●
Palma ●

Sardinia

Lisbon ●

● Córdoba

● Seville
Malada ● ● Granada

Cartagena

Sicily

Tunis ●

◆Malta

Oran ●

───── Boundary of Holy Roman Empire

▓▓▓ Habsburg Lands

The Inheritance of Charles V

Charles was born in the Netherlands in the year 1500. His father was Duke Philip the Handsome, son of the Holy Roman Emperor Maximilian I, and ruler of the Netherlands. His mother was Juana, the daughter of Ferdinand of Aragon and Isabella of Castile. Charles's younger brother Ferdinand was born in 1503.

In 1506 Philip the Handsome died and Juana retreated in isolation to the monastery of Tordesillias in Spain. The young prince thus inherited the Netherlands under the regency of his aunt Margaret, and the throne of Castile under the governorship of his grandfather Ferdinand of Aragon.

In 1515 Charles was declared of age and he succeeded to the Netherlands. The following year, on the death of Ferdinand of Aragon, he finally took control of Castile and Aragon, and with them Naples, Sicily and the Castilian empire in South America.

Finally, in 1519, the Emperor Maximilian I died, and, after a bitter dispute with King Francis I of France, Charles was elected Holy Roman Emperor. His vast territorial acquisition was complete.

> The dominions of Charles V may be called a world empire not only because they stretched over the Old and New Worlds, but because of their international and Christian character...
>
> Yet this empire was not imperial in any sense of conquest. It was based on the most peaceful of all foundations, on the rights of a family. It was a legacy of Maximilian, the inheritance of the House of Austria... In fact, the House of Austria and Spain was soon to engross every crown in Europe. Charles's aunt, Katherine, was Queen of England; his sisters were, or were to become, Queens of Denmark, Norway and Sweden, of Bohemia and Hungary, of Portugal and France...
>
> It was in accordance with his all-embracing theory of the dynasty that Charles undertook to divide his inheritance with his aunt Margaret and his brother Ferdinand... in the year 1521
>
> K. Brandi, Charles V, 1939.

Charles gave the Habsburg lands of Austria to his twenty-year-old brother Ferdinand, and in April of the same year Ferdinand married Anne, the heiress of Bohemia and Hungary, Ferdinand immediately reorganised his court and began to raise troops to help his brother-in-law, King Louis of Hungary, in his fight against the Turks. In July, this alliance was further cemented by the marriage of Charles and Ferdinand's sister, Mary, to the same King Louis. This alliance was to protect Christian Europe from the onslaught of Suleiman's Turkish troops in the following years.

In his frequent and prolonged absences from the Netherlands, Charles appointed as regent his able and loyal aunt Margaret, Archduchess of Austria. She ensured his peaceful control of the Low Countries for most of his reign.

The Family Tree of Charles V

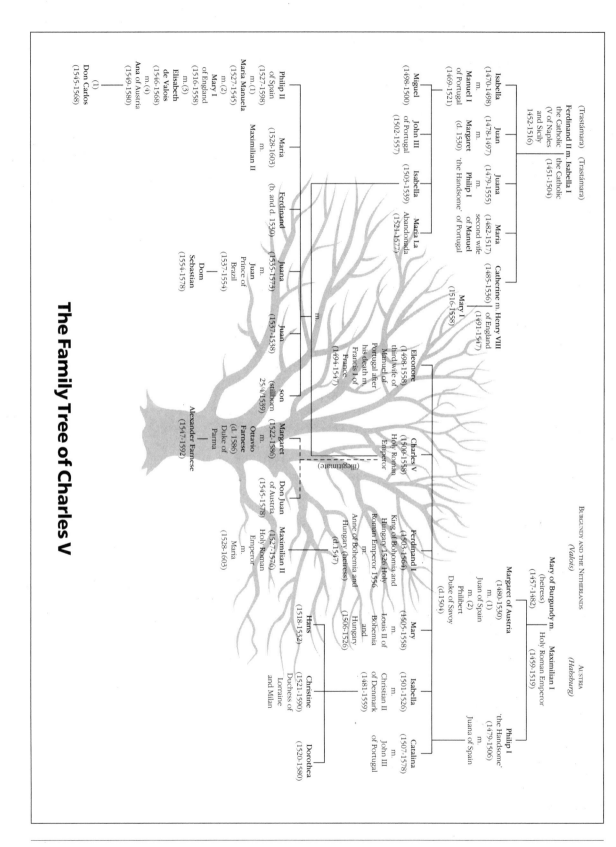

FOCUS

8.1 The History of the Holy Roman Empire

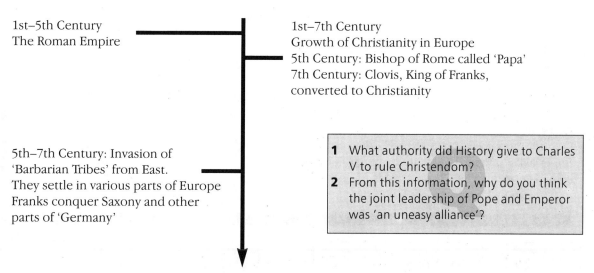

1st–5th Century
The Roman Empire

1st–7th Century
Growth of Christianity in Europe
5th Century: Bishop of Rome called 'Papa'
7th Century: Clovis, King of Franks,
converted to Christianity

5th–7th Century: Invasion of
'Barbarian Tribes' from East.
They settle in various parts of Europe
Franks conquer Saxony and other
parts of 'Germany'

1 What authority did History give to Charles
   V to rule Christendom?
2 From this information, why do you think
   the joint leadership of Pope and Emperor
   was 'an uneasy alliance'?

800 Christmas Day, Charles the Christian
King of Franks crowned Roman Emperor in Rome by Pope Leo
9th–11C: Successive German princes continued the title
11th C: Conflict between Pope and Emperor ('Investiture Contest')
over supremacy
Secular Sword v Spiritual Sword – who had power to do what?
Popes build up propaganda of Petrine Commission and Apostolic Succession

12th C: Frederick Barbarossa crowned 'Holy Roman Emperor'
Led crusade against the 'Infidel Turks'

12th–16th C: Successive German princes elected as
Holy Roman Emperor
Papal leadership embarrassed by Great Schism and Avignon Schism
and by several meetings of Church Councils
(Conciliar Movement) and by the growth of heresy

1519 Charles V elected Holy Roman Emperor

The Concepts of the 'Holy Roman Empire' of Charles V

The Holy Roman Empire was the fusion in the Middle Ages of two dynamic forces: the ancient Roman Empire and the growth of Christianity.

'God has set you on the path towards world monarchy'. Gattinara saw Charles's headship as divinely ordained: 'Ordained by God Himself and approved by the birth, life and death of our Redeemer Christ'.

Charles's duty was to wield the secular sword: In order to protect Christendom he must attack the 'Infidel' by land and sea and eradicate heresy and all threats to the religious, moral and political life of his people.

After his coronation in 1520 Charles moved on to the city of Worms in January 1521 for his first Imperial Diet. When confronted with Luther's determined and insistent stance Charles adopted his own. 'I am determined to set my kingdoms and dominions, my friends, my body, my blood, my life, my soul upon it'.

Different views of Charles's Empire

There were a number of different views of Charles's Empire and different views of the role he needed to play. These views sometimes overlapped but often contradicted each other.

- Gattinara's idea of a moral and political leadership of Christendom against the 'infidel'. This view centred on the history of the Holy Roman Empire and Charles's duty to protect the political and moral lives of his people. There was no notion of political infighting in Europe.
- The idea of Imperium Romanorum, the revival of the ancient Roman Empire with Rome as its capital. The emphasis here was on Italy rather than Germany.
- The idea of 'Moinarchia'. This was the idea of world empire in which Charles would add his conquests in the new world to his dynastic inherited empire in Europe.

What did Charles V mean by the term mean 'Holy Roman Empire'?

When he was elected in 1519, what did he think he was elected to? And what did his advisers, not least his Burgundian chancellor Gattinara, mean by the term?

Charles' Early Years

The young prince was an orphan virtually from the age of six, when his father died and his mother fled to the seclusion of a monastery in Spain. He and his three sisters were left in the Netherlands and looked after by their aunt, the Arch Duchess Margaret of Austria.

At the Burgundian court in Malines, Charles's tutor was Adrian of Utrecht, who was described by contemporaries as 'a remarkable teacher'. He grew up steeped in the genuine love of the Christian church and attending confession and mass regularly, and also endowed with a deep understanding of the traditions of chivalry. In his first year of life he had been made a member of the Order of the Golden Fleece, and he took his chivalric duties seriously. The ceremony of court life, with its banquets and pageantry, was always important to him, as were the qualities of honour, dignity and glory. He grew up alone – a shy and aloof young man.

One continuing problem throughout his reign was the problem of who to trust. This manifested itself as early as 1515, when the Estates General of the Netherlands applauded his grandfather Maximilian for declaring the young Charles of age and fit to rule the Netherlands. Charles was immediately caught in a power struggle between his aunt, the Arch Duchess Margaret of Austria, and the powerful Duke of Chievres. Chievres had always taken it upon himself to supervise the personal life of the young prince and Charles now decided in his favour. Fortunately the potential damage of his decision was short lived.

Charles I – King of Spain, 1517–55

> To this request I replied that I see the sense of it and I am in fact trying to learn Castilian. I realise that the request is being made on behalf of the Kingdom of Castile; therefore I have already started consulting with you, its deputies, and also with other subjects in these Kingdoms.

In this way Charles addressed the first meeting of the *Cortes* of Castile in his reign in 1518. He was replying to their request that he should learn to speak their language. They had also stressed to him that he remember the last will and testament of Queen Isabella, in which she expressly prohibited the giving of Castilian offices to foreigners. Charles had already made the mistake of giving the Presidency of the *Cortes* to his Burgundian Chancellor, and a battle of wills ensued. Charles promised to respect the laws and privileges of Castile and obtained a subsidy of 600,000 ducats. Later that year he moved to Aragon where the subsidy was 200,000 ducats. Finally, having married his sister to the King of Portugal and arranged for his brother Ferdinand to be sent to the Netherlands, Charles began to feel secure.

But Charles's success was short lived. On hearing of the death of his grandfather, the Emperor Maximilian, Charles decided to leave Spain to compete for the title. He broke his promise to the Castilian *Cortes* by leaving a non-Castilian, his old tutor, Adrian of Utrecht, as Regent. And he bullied the *Cortes* into another big subsidy. Led by Toledo, many of the cities of Castile broke out into open rebellion. By 1520 the situation had become grave. Juan Padilla from Toledo had built an army which put the city of Medina del Campo to flames. In September, the Comuneros seized Charles's mother, Joanna the Mad, and threatened to use her as a potential rival figurehead for the throne. Charles was forced to compromise. Two Castilians were made co-Regents, along with Adrian, and Charles was forced to appeal to the city of Burgos and to the Castilian aristocracy for their support. With support from Portugal, the new regents captured Tordesillias and released the Queen Mother. In the spring of 1521 they defeated Padilla's army at Villalar and the revolt was effectively over. Similarly, in Valencia, the revolt of the Germania was defeated by a combination of aristocratic loyalty and government troops.

In July 1522 Charles returned to Spain secure and powerful. He was to remain there for the next seven years, and in many ways these were the happiest years of his life. From this base, he travelled widely, securing the support of the constituent kingdoms. In 1526 he married Isabella of Portugal and thus confirmed his Castilian identity. He also ensured diplomatic relations between the two European kingdoms with the greatest overseas empires. Isabella's dowry of 900,000 ducats was also worth the wedding.

In fact, Charles's marriage to Isabella was not simply a matter of convenience and the birth of their first son, Philip, in 1527, was a cause of much rejoicing.

Charles I's Government of Spain

Following the defeat of the Comuneros revolt Charles accepted the recommendations of the Junta that corrupt officials be removed. To replace them he established a permanent bureaucracy of lawyers, chosen and trained by his secretary Los Cobos. Cobos used *Hidalgos* as officials and thus made the court more Spanish in both language and culture.

Charles continued Ferdinand and Isabella's policy of ruling through councils. Two major councils advised him on policy. In 1522, the Council of War was set up and in 1526 the Council of State. The Council of State became Charles's inner Cabinet and consisted of his closest advisers. In addition, new administrative councils were set up to support the work of the Council of Castile. In 1523 Charles created the Council of Finance, a small group of intimates, including Los Cobos, to run the revenues of the state and in the following year he established the Council of the Indies and the Council of Aragon. The system was extended further in 1555 when the Council of Italy was set up under his son Philip II. Deliberations of councils were presented to Charles as reports or *'consultas'*. Charles would authorise these reports and thus turn them into policy.

TALKING POINT

Around one quarter of Charles' days were spent in travelling. Suggest how this would affect his role as emperor.

Charles's use of the *Cortes* was also perceptive, because it allowed him to keep him in touch with the political elite. Indeed, Charles considered it essential to listen to the petitions of the *Cortes* and the *Cortes* of Castile met fifteen times, and that of Aragon ten times, during his reign. Charles allowed them to speak freely and in return they gave him subsidies. He also used the *Cortes* for various administrative duties, such as the assessment and collection of taxes.

Indeed it was in the area of taxation that Charles's main governmental developments occurred. He received large subsidies from Castile and Aragon, as well as from the church and from the Americas. Yet in order to balance his books he had to borrow. All loans were made on the security of the Castilian crown and thus it was that Castile came to bear the cost of the Holy Roman Empire. Five financiers, including those from Italy and south Germany, came to dominate the Spanish economy – in fact, the Spanish monarchy never shook off the legacy of debt bequeathed to it by the Emperor Charles V. In addition, Charles also raised cash by selling the *Asientos*, the licences for importing slaves to the Indies. He also sold public offices and certificates of nobility.

The Economy Under Charles V

Charles's reign in Castile saw a 50 per cent population rise between the years 1530 and 1580. The increased demand for food pushed prices up, forcing Spain to import wheat. There has been much debate about the causes of inflation in the 16th century; but in Charles's reign bullion imports and the pressures of an increasing population undoubtedly played their part. Many of his subjects were living on fixed incomes and higher prices hit them hard. Those who were adaptable were those who flourished and social change began to accelerate. There were other results too: the growth of the south-west – in particular its ports of Cadiz and Seville – and the decline of manufactures.

There was considerable social change in Charles' reign, with a rapid increase in the number of *Hidalgos* and nobles. Since they were exempt from taxes, such titles were worth acquiring. American wealth and trade also caused considerable social climbing as trade and titles in nobility were incompatible. This was now a society where money and trade were valued, yet manufacture was not valued since a manual or mechanical worker could not become a nobleman. If there was an increase in the aristocracy, there was also a corresponding increase in poverty, begging and seasonal work.

Economy and Society

The debate about the economy and society in the reign of Charles V is raised by Henry Kamen in his book *The Golden Age of Spain*: 'Despite the continuous participation of Spaniards in trade, industry and agriculture, many historians have argued that Spaniards were anti-capitalist in spirit and in fact'. Attempting to explain why Spanish traders were unable to benefit from the favourable conjuncture of the 16th century, Braudel proposed the notable thesis of a 'betrayal by the bourgeoisie' (*trahison de la bourgeoisie*), according to which those who were active in trade withdrew their money once they had made their fortunes and thus prejudiced the chance of further capitalist investment. The competence of Spaniards – not only Catalans and Basques but also Castilians – as capitalists during the early modern period has, however, been firmly stressed by several recent writers and most recently by Molas, by J.A. Maravall and by Kamen; and there is substantial evidence of Castilians in international trade in the 16th century. Two specific problems, those of investment and status, are worth noting here. The presence or absence of a strong native capitalist sector depended obviously on opportunities for investment: we might expect to find the sector in a protected wool market (Burgos) or an average regional port (Barcelona), but the sector might not be strong in a big international port with heavy competition (Seville). The evolution of a capitalist sector, then, was always related to available opportunity and not to any pre-existent 'capitalist spirit'. In the same way, one might invest in government bonds (*juros*) rather than in commerce or agriculture not because one was anti-capitalist but simply because the rate of return was higher: it is significant that at the end of the sixteenth century, when *juros* gave 7 per cent interest, money flowed into them; but by the late seventeenth, when the rate was down to 5 per cent, money was diverted back into land. The search for status, both then and now, was a normal aspiration for someone who had money but little rank to go with it; and though in some parts of the peninsula those with new status felt that they were required to 'live nobly' there is ample evidence that throughout the early modern period the nouveaux-riches managed to combine both rank and business, so that by the early 18th century the trade guilds in the great cities were powerful instruments of the merchant bourgeoisie.

This presentation contradicts the traditional picture, popularised by literary scholars who drew their evidence largely from the imaginative literature of the theatre (Lope de Vega) and the novel (the Lazarillo, the Quijote), according to which Spaniards were so obsessed by the notion of 'honour' that they were unable to progress economically, thereby dooming their nation to backwardness because of a psychological prejudice. Support has sometimes been given to this view by presenting Spaniards as a nation of (in the words of the contemporary Gonzalez de Cellorigo) 'bewitched beings, living outside the natural order of things'. Rhetoric apart, there seems to be no justification for thinking that Spaniards, alone of all peoples, lived outside a natural, normal, framework of problems; and the course of Spain's economic history shows few significant divergences from the experience of other nations in Europe.

Charles V and Italy, 1521–9

In 1515 the young newly-crowned King Francis I of France defeated the Spanish troops in the battle of Marignano near Milan. They then took control of the city of Milan, a vitally important point on the route linking Italy with the north. In the following year Francis made peace with the new Spanish king, Charles V, by which he maintained his control over Milan.

However, as soon as Charles had won over his enemies in Spain, he turned his attention to Italy. Italy was of course part of Gattinara's imperial dream and Rome was the centre of the Holy Roman Empire. In 1521 a combined Imperial Papal army defeated the French and recaptured the city of Milan. They restored the former Habsburg Duke, Francesco Sforza, and in the following year defeated the French army at the battle of Bicocca near Milan. Secure in his victory, Charles then captured many northern Italian cities. Furthermore, in 1525 the Imperial army decisively crushed the French at Pavia and Francis was himself captured. He was taken as a prisoner to Madrid and kept there for a year. Under the terms of the Treaty of Madrid in 1526, Francis was released but had to leave his two sons in Spain as hostages and had to promise to hand over Burgundy to Charles. Charles, a man of chivalry and honour, believed that Francis would keep his word. However, as soon as the French king landed on French soil he claimed that his promise had been made under duress and abandoned the terms of the treaty. In addition, the papacy, together with other Italian states like Venice and Florence, now feared the developing power of the Emperor. They formed themselves together in the League of Cognac in 1526 to oppose Habsburg control of Italy. When Charles's troops sacked Rome in 1527 and Pope Clement VII was captured, the result was the collapse of the League. Then, dramatically, Henry VIII, King of England, changed sides and supported the French with men and money in Italy, and it looked as though a French victory could be possible. However, when the Genoese admiral Andrea Doria also changed sides and joined the Emperor, Francis's opportunity was lost. Charles could break the French blockade of Naples and stalemate ensued with Charles continuing to control the land.

Peace was made in August 1529 at Cambrai and Charles gained breathing space to concentrate on affairs in Germany.

Charles V and the Netherlands

Throughout his reign, the Netherlands remained one of the most secure and supportive of Charles V's territories. After the Diet of Worms in 1521, Charles spent most of the next year in his former patrimony. He confirmed his aunt Margaret as Regent and gave her the power to rule the Netherlands on his behalf while he focused his attention elsewhere. His reign saw the consolidation of the geographical make-up of the Netherlands. In 1521 Tournai was added by force, and in 1523 the estates of Friesland formerly acknowledged Charles's overlordship. A similar acknowledgement came from the territories of Utrecht in 1527 and Overijssel in 1528. Then during the 1530s and 1540s Maastricht, Groningen and Gelderland were conquered.

Charles also consolidated his control over the church and central authority in the Netherlands. In 1530 Pope Clement VII confirmed his right to choose bishops and in the following year agreed that papal bulls would only have force in the Netherlandsy when confirmed by Charles's government. In addition, Charles reformed the central government of the Netherlands: in 1531 the authority of Brussels was enlarged over the provinces. Charles's bailiffs were given increased power and stadholders were forced to come to live in Brussels where Margaret could keep an eye on them. Yet Charles ruled with the support of his people. He always sought the support of Estates before levying taxation, and he continued to uphold provincial privileges and the chivalric rights of the aristocracy. These dominated the Council of State and even, on occasions, criticised the king.

Charles adopted a tough attitude towards religious heretics. Even before the Edict of Worms, the printing and reading of Luther's works was forbidden in the Netherlands. Any disputes over matters of faith could result in the death sentence and Margaret decreed the execution of over 2000 Dutch people. The Inquisition was started in 1522 and the first Index of proscribed books was set up in 1543. In spite of this, Lutheranism and Anabaptism grew slowly but steadily, the former near Antwerp, the latter in Ghent and one or two other cities. In addition, the government in the provinces made life difficult for Margaret. And by the 1550s their opposition to Margaret's rule was becoming dangerous.

As a secure base for Charles, the Netherlands provided him with a considerable source of finance for his wars and diplomacy. Prominent in fishing and trade, the Netherlands developed its wealth and contributed significantly to Charles's financial requests. Each year in the 1520s and 1530s they gave between 1 and 1.5 million livres to the Emperor's coffers. By 1544, the contribution was over 5 million livres, and by 1555, around 6.5 million. The additional money was found by increased taxation which made both Charles and the States General unpopular. Revolts and conspiracies began to grow, most significant of which was in Ghent in 1539. However, the threat of a major uprising was always avoided.

The Threat from the Ottoman Turks

The main military and political threat to Charles's empire came from the Ottoman Turks. They threatened Charles on two major fronts: the land army which marched up the River Danube and attacked the gates of Vienna in 1529; and the naval threat through the eastern Mediterranean and even to North Africa, the Eastern shores of Spain and the main ports of Italy and Sicily. In the latter area, the Turkish forces were supplemented by fleets of pirates or corsairs. From their north African bases pirate galleys attacked Spanish and Italian shipping all over the Mediterranean. This sapped the economic vitality of Spain and Italy and threatened Charles's lines of communication and supply. Grain supplies from Sicily to Spain were under constant threat.

Charles's concept of empire gave him a clear idea of a Holy War against the Turks. He upheld the tradition of crusading against the 'Infidel'. In addition, he inherited the *Reconquista* – the Spanish Christian policy of reoccupying the parts of the peninsula occupied by Muslims. Christendom depended on his leadership.

Early in Charles's reign, the Turks had enjoyed considerable success. They captured the island of Rhodes from the Christians in 1522 and in 1529 a Spanish fleet was defeated by Barbarossa, the pirate leader off the island of Ibiza. However, with the support of the Genoese admiral, Andrea Doria, Charles's fleet recovered several ports on the Greek mainland, and in 1534 spread the news throughout Europe that the Spanish fleet had captured the African stronghold of Tunis. Charles led the assault himself with a fleet of 400 ships and 60,000 men. Barbarossa's 80 galleons were captured and Barbarossa himself forced to flee. The victory reinforced Charles's reputation as a soldier and as a champion of Christendom against the 'Infidel'. However, Charles had neither the resources nor the time to press an attack on the main pirate stronghold at Algiers.

Meanwhile, the Turkish threat was reinforced on the Danube. In 1521 Suleiman's armies captured Belgrade and then advanced into Hungary. At the Battle of Mohacs, the Turks won a famous victory and advanced and captured the Hungarian capital of Buda. By 1529 they were at the gates of Vienna. Disease weakened the Turkish army and Vienna was stoutly defended.

Charles saw the need to compromise with the Lutheran princes in order to defeat the Turks. Throughout these campaigns, Charles's courage was undoubted.

> I am determined that if the Turk comes in person he will not do so unless he is at the head of a large army. Therefore I shall face him myself, and resist his attack with all the forces I can muster.

Fortunately for Charles, Suleiman was also pressed on his eastern border by war with the Persians, and in 1532 was forced to retreat from Vienna in order to concentrate on his Persian front. Charles arrived in Vienna in September 1532 to find the enemy gone. In 1547 Suleiman again captured Hungary and this time Charles was forced to recognise the loss of the kingdom. Similarly, at sea Charles was defeated at Prevesa in 1538 and at Algiers in 1541, and only the death of Barbarossa in 1546 prevented an overwhelming defeat. The ultimate humiliation was the loss of Tripoli in 1551.

The Ottoman threat was a constant drain on Charles's energy and resources. The alliance between Turks and Francis I of France and the connection between Turkish advance and the toleration of Lutheran princes was a powerful one. Charles's honour as the Emperor of Christendom forced him to make his Crusade against the Turkish attacks a major priority.

Examining the Evidence

The Sack of Rome, 1527

THE SACK OF ROME.

Source A

An eye-witness account of the sack, written by one of the leaders of the Imperial army.

On the sixth of May we took Rome by storm, killed 6,000 men, plundered the houses, carried off what we found in churches and elsewhere, and finally set fire to a good portion of the town. A strange life indeed! We tore up, destroyed the deeds of copyists, the records, letters, and documents of the Curia. The Pope fled to Castel Sant'Angelo with his bodyguard, the Cardinals, Bishops, Romans, and members of the Curia who had escaped the massacre. For three weeks we lay siege until, forced by hunger, he had to surrender the castle. Four Spanish commanders, one of whom was a nobleman, the Abbot of Najera, and an Imperial secretary, were delegated by the Prince of Orange to receive the castle. This was done. Inside, we found Pope Clement with twelve Cardinals in a storeroom. The Pope had to sign the surrender treaty that the secretary read to him. They all bemoaned themselves piteously and wept a lot. Here we are, all of us, rich.

Less than two months after we occupied Rome 5,000 of our men had died of the plague, for the corpses remained unburied. In July, half dead, we left the city for the Marches to find cleaner air...

In September, back in Rome, we pillaged the city more thoroughly and found great hidden treasures. We remained billeted there for another six months.

Source B

Two secondary sources outline the events of the Sack.

Throughout 1527 the French more than held their own in Italy; Charles's only success, if it deserves the name, sent a wave of horror throughout Christendom. In the Spring the Imperial troops mutineed; as usual, they had not been paid for a long time. Frundsberg suffered a stroke; Bourbon thought to do better by putting himself at the mutineers' head. They marched on Rome, home of that Pope who had betrayed their Prince, and in addition was anti-Christ to the many Lutherans among them. On 6 May, Bourbon dying in the first assault, the veterans stormed the city and sacked it.

G.R. Elton, *Reformation Europe*, 1963.

Charles was even more enraged to learn that the Pope should abandon him to ally with the French. He therefore ordered Bourbon to take Rome. This was done in 1527 but the troops got out of hand and the city was sacked.

D. Maland, *Europe in the 16th Century*, 1973.

Source C

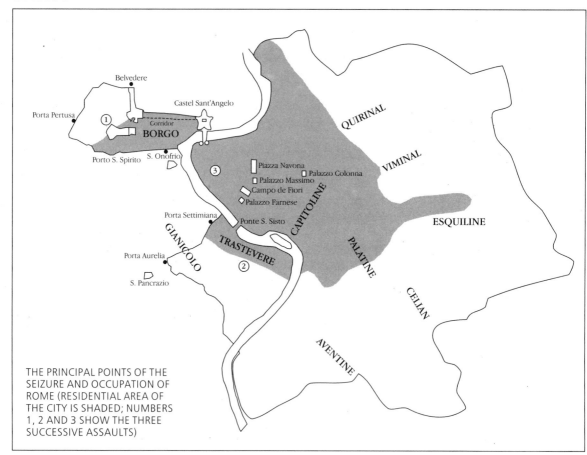

THE PRINCIPAL POINTS OF THE SEIZURE AND OCCUPATION OF ROME (RESIDENTIAL AREA OF THE CITY IS SHADED; NUMBERS 1, 2 AND 3 SHOW THE THREE SUCCESSIVE ASSAULTS)

MAP OF ROME IN 1527.

Source D

THE CASTEL SANT' ANGELO.

Source E

An eye-witness account of Roman markets, May 1527.

Everything that had been stolen during the sack was sold there: robes embroidered with gold thread, silks, velvets, bolts of wool and linen, rings, jewels, pearls, ... Then the pillaging began anew.

Source F

Charles V's political dilemmas, 1527.

The disaster at Mohacs caused a stir throughout Castile. It meant that Austria had now become the frontier against the Turk, with grave danger to Ferdinand; and Ferdinand was a Spanish prince, born and brought up in Castile. Furthermore, as long as Charles had no heir of his own body, Ferdinand was the heir to the Hispanic kingdoms. It was necessary, therefore, from the Castilian point of view, to go to the aid of the distant court of Vienna.

For Charles his war with France took priority. To assume that this was due only to the rivalry between Charles and Francis and that it could easily be settled – and thus leave the Catholic Monarch free to face the Turk – would be a complete misreading of the situation. Suleiman's offensive had, in fact, been solicited by the French king, and Charles was right in coping first with the military threat against his Spanish dominions by papal and French forces. He therefore ordered Ferdinand to recall troops from Germany to strengthen the Imperial forces in Italy, which were in the greatest danger towards the end of the year 1526.

The war against the Pope placed Charles in a most embarrassing situation. How was he to explain to his subjects that he, the Catholic Monarch, Emperor and Shield of the Church, felt it necessary to fight the soldiers of the Pope? At the meeting of the Cortes in Valladolid in 1527 there was a general outcry that the Infante Ferdinand must be saved from the grave danger which threatened Austria. The army which was fitted out, however, never arrived in Vienna; it was sent by Charles against Rome.

Charles' soldiers, led by Charles de Bourbon, after a tentative assault on Florence, sped by forced marches to Rome and took the Eternal City in a daring attack, in which it lost its commander. The victorious army – starving, unpaid and without a leader – proceeded to sack Rome. For a whole week the Soldiers looted and pillaged.

M.F. Alvarez, *Charles V,* 1975.

Source G

Opinion throughout Europe.

It was the scandal of Europe – and yet it also aroused reluctant admiration. Charles had hardly made his appearance on the European stage and his armies had already defeated the King of France and taken him prisoner, and now the Pope himself was defeated; who would dare stand in his way? His sailors, Magellan and Elcano, had circumnavigated the world and his conquistadores had established a firm foothold on the mainland of the Americas, gaining quick control of the Aztec empire. How fortunate he was to rule over such enterprising subjects! But Charles himself had to face up to his critics at home and try to find an excuse for his action against Rome. The style of his memoirs when he deals with these events seems to indicate a perplexed state of mind: The main responsibility lay not with him but rather with those who had forced him to defend himself and send so large an army which had proved difficult to control.

Charles' propaganda machine did all it could to formulate an acceptable version of the Sack of Rome.

M.F. Alvarez, *Charles V,* 1975.

The whole of Europe was filled with amazement. The prophecy of Luis Vives, another friend of Erasmus, had come to pass. From Bruges he wrote, 'This is the destiny of Charles; to defeat only enemies in great numbers so as to make his victory all the more spectacular.'

Public opinion in Spain was, however, much troubled. Some defended Charles as strongly as Valdes, but most Spaniards disapproved of the sacking of the Holy City. If Charles had dared attack Rome, they argued, why wonder at Francis' aligning himself with Suleiman?

Such hostile comments came also from outside Spain, and Charles realized that he must explain his attack on Rome, especially to his old ally Henry VIII of England. Valdes quotes the Latin letter Charles wrote to Henry in which he argued that God had exacted vengeance for the sins of the Pope: 'God, wishing to take revenge for the injuries inflicted upon us, had already decided what the future was to be, and although the action taken against Rome was His Will rather than a deliberate act of force, without intervention, consent or will on our part, nevertheless we have felt great pain and shame for the offence given to the Holy See, indeed we would have preferred not to win rather than to be left with such a victory.'

In the opinion of a modern Spanish historian the war for Italy, including the Sacking of Rome, was a war waged for 'justice and reason'.

M.F. Alvarez, *Charles V,* 1975.

Source H

The Dramatic Increase in the study of monstrosities, omens and prognostications (Chastel).

On the eve of the sack, Italy was rife with superstitions, calculations and obsessions... In an atmosphere of indefinable events and disquieting omens, one can measure the degree of anxiety and general confusion by the diversity of the many predictions... Two obsessions that recur constantly are the end of the world and the destruction of Rome and the Papacy. In J. Carion's *Prognosticatio* 1521 an explicit drawing shows the Sun (Emperor), Saturn (Peasant), Jupiter (The Pope) and Mars (The Knight) in such an alarming position that the Sack of Rome is already foretold.

Source I

Roman Political Theory under Pope Clement VII.

On 19 November 1523 the Florentine Cardinal Giulio de'Medici was elected Pope as Clement VII. He faced major diplomatic problems in Europe: Ambitious young Kings in France, Spain and England, and the challenge of Martin Luther among others in the Holy Roman Empire. In addition, the Roman families were now so powerful that the Colonnas could attack the Vatican itself in 1526. And within the Roman Catholic Church, many wanted reform and despised the concentration of Rome on artistic beauty.

Pope Clement's response to these difficulties was to rebuild the Hall of Constantine. This was the official reception hall for meetings of the College of Cadinals and for the reception of diplomats and visitors from all over the world. Around the walls of the Hall of Constantine, Giulio Romano was commissioned to produce a series of frescoes to tell the legendary story of the Donation of Constantine. In the 5th century the Roman Emperor Constantine was baptised a Christian, and, he presented the City of Rome to Pope Silvester. In the 14th century the legend had been criticised by Lorenzo Valla. Pope Clement VII clearly wanted to restate it.

Source J

"THE GREAT WHORE OF BABYLON" BY HANS HOLBEIN 1523

"THE JUDGEMENT OF BABYLON"

"THE DESTRUCTION OF BABYLON"

1 Use the sources to describe, in your own narrative, the main events in the Sack of Rome, May 1527.
2 List the factors that may be responsible for the Sack. Then place them in order of importance and give your reasons.
3 Did the Sack of Rome damage or benefit Charles V's reputation?
4 Is there enough evidence here to suggest that Chastel has indeed invaded 'the territory of historians using unconventional weapons'.

Source K

A German pamphlet written by one of Frundsberg's soldiers.

They looked for the Papal Bulls, letters and accounts in the monasteries and convents so as to burn them and destroy them. Their shreds replaced straw in the houses and stables for donkeys and horses.

In all the churches, chalices, chasubles, monstrances and ornaments were taken; not find the veronica, the looters took other relics.

Source L

Chastel on the motives of Lutherans.

The legitimacy of Papal authority expressed itself through sealed Papal Bulls; the amounts received in payment for indulgences were recorded in account books... The assault on the Pope's city was a kind of inverse pilgrimage for a large portion of the Imperial army... an act of calculated profanation.

'Historical narrative can, and should, be continuously improved'. Andre Chastel in his book *The Sack of Rome*, 1983, challenges previous interpretations of this dramatic and notorious event. 'This study was inspired by a challenge', he argues, 'to invade the territory of historians using unconventional weapons'.

Examining the Evidence

The Diet of Worms, January–May 1521

The Participants at the Diet

Charles V

After his coronation Charles's court moved to the western city of Worms to hold the first Imperial Diet of his reign. The Diet was a meeting of princes and representatives of cities to deal with important questions and business matters. The first Diet of any reign was an opportunity to look at the organisation of Imperial government, the payment of judges, and other such important issues. It was also an opportunity to tackle the new question of the 'heresy' of Martin Luther. The young Emperor was already in a difficult position. He had recently given offence to his Spanish subjects and could not afford a similar incident in the Empire. It was important that he adopted traditional legal processes and treated his German subjects fairly. He knew of Luther's increasing popularity and summoned him to appear before the Diet of Worms under a guaranteed of Imperial safe conduct.

Cardinal Jerome Aleander

Aleander was the Papal Nuncio or representative at the Diet. The Pope had already excommunicated Luther in 1519 in the Bull 'Exsurge, Domine'. Aleander believed that it was the Pope's job to deal with Luther as a heretic, and not for the Imperial Diet. 'Secular princes, including the Emperor, are not in a position to review this case. The only competent judge is the Pope.'

Frederick the Wise, Duke of Saxony

Frederick was one of the leaders among the German princes of the Diet. His position over Luther was ambiguous. He stood up for Luther's right to be given a hearing but his own religious beliefs remained unclear. 'It is sometimes difficult to know whether he was simply neutral or feigning neutrality to protect Luther. The latter seems to be nearer the truth in the total view' (J. Atkinson, *Martin Luther and the Birth of Protestantism,* 1968).

Martin Luther Himself

Luther was aware of his own increasing popularity in Germany. As he approached the Diet, Aleander said of him 'but now the whole of Germany is in full revolt; nine-tenths raise the war cry 'Luther' while the watch-word of the other tenth who are indifferent to Luther is 'death to the Roman curia'.

In spite of this, Luther was aware of the danger of going to the Diet. The fate of the earlier heretic, John Huss, who had been arrested under a guarantee of safe conduct and burnt at the stake, was very much in his mind. In spite of the danger, Luther was determined to proceed; he wrote this to Frederick the Wise 'you ask me what I shall do if I am called by the Emperor. I will go even if I am too sick to stand on my feet... This is no time to think of safety. I must take care that the Gospel is not brought into contempt by our fear to confess and seal our teaching with blood.'

Luther certainly benefited from anti-papal feeling in the city. Aleander himself commented 'I cannot go out on the streets but the Germans put their hands to their swords and gnash their teeth at me. I hope the Pope will give me a plenary indulgence and look after my brothers and sisters if anything happens to me.'

Three different views of the proceedings at Worms

The scene lends itself to dramatic portrayal. Here was Charles, heir of a long line of Catholic sovereigns, ruling over a vaster domain than any since Charlemagne, symbol of all the medieval unities, incarnation of a glorious if vanishing heritage. And here before him was a simple monk, a miner's son, with nothing to sustain him save his own faith in the word of God. Here the past and the future were met.

R.H. Bainton, *Here I Stand*, 1987.

After a wait of two hours, Luther was brought into that august assembly in the packed and suffocating hall. The members of the Diet were astounded at the appearance of a slender, emaciated, pale monk of some forty years of age. Luther had arrive in Worms only the day before, both tired and ill, and stood under very great strain.

J. Atkinson, *The Trial of Luther*, 1968.

What different views of Luther do these passages and the picture contain?

The Case Against Martin Luther

At Aleander's suggestion, Luther was invited only to respond to the case against him. He was not allowed to make a statement of his own views.

Luther was then shown a pile of his books, including religious works and more controversial writings, some of which were critical of the Pope. He was asked two simple questions: Had he written these books, and secondly, did he stand by the opinions expressed in them?

'Is it not the case that you want Holy Scripture to be understood by your whim and your ideas? Is it right to open to question and drag into dispute those matters which the Catholic church has judiciously settled, matters which have turned upon the usage, the rights and the observances which our Fathers held with absolute faith, for which there was no punishment, no torment they would not have undergone, indeed they would rather have endured a thousand deaths than of deviated from them a hair's breadth? Are you asking us to turn aside from the path which our Fathers faithfully trod? Do not, I entreat you, Martin, do not arrogate to yourself that you, I repeat that you are the one and only person who has knowledge of the scriptures, who alone grasps the true sense of Holy Scripture. Do not make your judgements superior to that of so many of the most brilliant men. Do not seem to be wiser than all others. Do not case doubt upon the most Holy orthodox faith, which Christ, the Perfect Law Giver, instituted'.

Luther's Response at the Diet of Worms

Luther had come to the Diet expecting to be able to state his case. He hadn't expected the two simple questions. He asked for a day to decide his response. Somewhat surprisingly, Charles V granted his request.

The Politics of Delay

By keeping the Riechstag waiting for an answer, Luther remained in control of the theatre of the situation, so perhaps it was not so much timidity as a deliberate delaying tactic that underlay Luther's strange behaviour at the initial hearing. The delay produced an added bonus for, in the adjourned session, Luther got the chance to speak to the Riechstag, not as on the 17 April to a section of it.

M. Mullet, *Martin Luther*, 1986.

The request for time for deliberation was a very clever move on Luther's part. Aleander had prepared the questions so as to prevent Luther from making any justifying statement and to rest from him a recantation. It is to Luther's lasting credit that, overwhelmed with the stifling heat, utterly ill and exhausted, overawed as a monk, countryman and scholar before the might and splendour of the Empire, he saw that the manoeuvres were meant to give the outward appearance of a constitutional hearing without providing any at all. The request for time for thought dumbfounded the court. Luther's short answers and humble request showed the Papal party what to expect, impress the Princes and laity with the integrity of the man, and gave Luther one quiet night to pray and think over what he was going to say.

J. Atkinson, *The Trial of Luther*, 1975.

Despite the nuncio, Charles gave him twenty-four hours – twenty-four hours which, it is not extravagant to say, were to cost him thirty-four years of trouble.

G.R. Elton, *Reformation Europe*, 1963.

The Events of 18 April 1521

On the following morning, before the assembled Diet, Luther accepted that the written works were his. He also argued that he was open to debate, and claimed that if he were proved wrong by the Bible he would be the first to destroy his work. However, he made a clear statement of his position. "It is impossible for me to recant unless I am proved to be in the wrong by the testimony of scripture or by evident reasoning; I cannot trust either the decisions of councils or of Popes, for it is plain that they have not only erred, but have contradicted each other. My conscience is bound to the Word of God and it is neither safe nor honest to act against one's conscience. God helped me. Amen.

Charles listened to Luther's eloquence but it did not affect his sense of duty as Defender of the Faith.

I am descended from a long line of Christian Emperors of this noble German nation, faithful to the death to the Church of Rome. I have resolved to follow in their steps. A single Friar who goes counter to all Christianity for a thousand years must be wrong. Therefore I am determined to set my kingdoms and dominions, my friends, my body, my blood, my life, my soul, upon it.

Compromise was out of the question. Luther was to be outlawed – it was not a matter of Church politics or Church order, it was fundamentally a difference in the interpretation of Christianity.

J. Atkinson, *Martin Luther and the Birth of Protestantism*, 1968.

Under the terms of safe conduct Luther was allowed to return to Wurttemberg. The Edict of Worms was then published.

We pronounce and declare that the said Martin Luther shall be held in detestation by us and each and all of you as a limb severed from the Church of God, the author of a pernicious schism, a manifest and obstinate heretic. When the time of the safe conduct is up, no one is to harbour him. His followers also are to be condemned. His books are to be eradicated from the memory of man.

What was the Significance of the Diet of Worms?

The Diet of Worms has always been regarded as a key turning point, not only for Luther but also for Charles V. But how important actually was it?

> Luther's appearance at Worms proved to be the true beginning of the Reformation, a blow to the many hopes placed in the Emperor, but also the certainty that the new theology had come to stay.
>
> G.R. Elton, *Reformation Europe*, 1963.

> The Edict of Worms, passed by a secular tribunal entrusted with the case of heresy at the insistence of Lutherans and against the opposition of papalists, was at once repudiated by the Lutherans as having been passed by only a rump, and was sponsored by the papalists because it was a confirmation of the Catholic faith. The Church of Rome which had so strenuously sought to prevent turning the Diet of Worms into an Ecclesiastical Council, became in the light of the outcome the great vindicator of the pronouncement of the secular tribunal on heresy.
>
> R.H. Bainton, *Here I Stand*, 1987.

> The Diet supported Charles and, in the Edict of Worms, declared Luther a heretic and an outlaw. Yet despite all these grand sounding statements the consequences of the Diet of Worms were slight. Many of the princes who had endorse the Edict were sympathetic to much of Luther's criticism of the Roman Church. Hence, while in some parts of Germany the Edict was implemented rigorously, in others it was largely ignored.
>
> S. McDonald, *Charles V,* 1987.

> Luther himself thought the Diet had been an anti climax, almost a waste of time. 'I expected', he wrote to the artist Cranach, that his majesty the Emperor could have collected fifty doctors of divinity to confute the monk in argument. But all they said was "are these books yours" "yes" "will you recant" "no!" then get out".'
>
> O. Chadwick, *The Reformation*, 1972.

Charles V and the Lutheran Question in Germany

Main Events

1521 - The Diet of Worms – Luther condemned by the Diet

1526 - The Diet of Speyer – Princes and Imperial Cities command the right to reform the religions of their States.

1529 - Second Diet of Speyer – Princes and cities 'protest' against Charles V's wish for Catholicsm.

1530 - Diet of Augsburg

1531 - Princes and cities form Schmalkaldenic League

1539 - The interim of Frankfurt – Charles makes concessions to the Protestants.

1541 - The Diet of Regensburg – Attempts to reconcile Protestants and Catholics fail.

1546 - Charles begins military campaign against Lutherans.

1547 - Battle of Muhlberg – Charles defeats Protestants.

1552 - Treaty of Chambord – Lutherans and French plan to attack Charles. Charles defeated.

1555 - Diet of Augsburg – Lutherans in the right to reform their own States.

The Growth of Lutheranism 1521–30

During the decade after the Diet of Worms, Charles was absent from Germany, concentrating on his affairs in Italy and Spain. Over this period, Lutheranism spread steadily amongst the peasantry, the towns and cities, and was adopted by an increasing number of important princes. Leaders such as Philip of Hesse, who reformed his territories in 1526, and Frederick the Wise of Saxony gave powerful support to a growing political movement. Charles delegated authority in Germany during these years to his brother Ferdinand, but he was often distracted by the threat of the Turks in the east.

From a distance, Charles tried during these years to bring the Lutherans back into the Catholic fold through diplomacy. At the Diet of Speyer in 1526, Ferdinand tried to bring the two sides together. He insisted that the Edict of Worms should be enforced throughout Germany. However, he promised the Lutherans that their grievances could be considered at a future meeting of a General Council of the Church. The Lutheran princes and cities were, however, determined to retain their reformed faith and Charles, pressed by the Turks and the French, could do little.

By 1529, however, Charles was in a stronger position. Ferdinand again called the sides together at the Second Diet of Speyer and tried to enforce the Edict of Worms. Six princes and 14 cities objected and signed a 'protest' against Charles's demands. This protest was the beginning of the word Protestant. Matters became even worse in the following year at the Diet of Augsburg. The Protestants produced their Augsburg Confession, a clear statement of Lutheran beliefs, while the Catholics in reply produced the Augsburg Recess, a similar statement of their position. A call to arms developed and the Lutherans formed the Schmalkaldic League.

The Consolidation of Lutheranism 1531–41

Charles was again absent from Germany during the second decade of Lutheranism and the Lutheran princes now took the lead. Saddled with problems with the French and the Turks, Charles could do nothing to prevent the restoration of the Protestant Duke of Wurttemberg to his important Duchy in 1534. The Schmalkaldic League was being strengthened. Even the pope was conspiring against the Emperor and in 1533 made an agreement with Francis I of France, who in turn was allied with Suleiman the Magnificent, the Ottoman Sultan.

In practice Charles could do nothing to prevent the growth of Lutheranism. In 1539, in return for their support against the threatening menace of the Turks, he agreed the Interim of Frankfurt: again Charles granted them temporary concessions in exchange for their support against the Turks.

The Diet of Regensburg 1541

In 1541 Charles made a further attempt to reconcile the opposing factions. He was able to attend the Diet of Regensburg in person and theologians were asked to search for a compromise between the Lutheran and Catholic positions, but by this time it was too late. Both Lutheran and Papal representatives refused to compromise. Charles had no alternative now but to resort to force to try and defeat the Lutheran threat. Unfortunately for him, he had given it twenty years in which the seeds could grow.

The Battle for the Empire 1541–7

Charles spent most of the rest of his reign in Germany, because the defeat of Lutheranism was now his greatest priority. Both sides prepared their forces and looked towards war. Moreover, the long-awaited Council of Trent held its first meeting in 1545, but Charles could see that it would not produce the desired reconciliation of the Protestants. By the middle of the 1540s Charles was resolved on war.

Charles had taken deliberate steps to strengthen his hand in preparation for the conflict. In 1543 he made an alliance with Henry VIII of England and in the following year the Peace of Krepy brought peace with France. By 1546, even the Pope was agreeable to supporting Charles in Germany. In addition, the Schmalkaldic League was divided, with Philip of Hesse's leadership having been called into question as a result of his bigamous marriages. Charles's army, including the powerful Duke Alva and his hardened Spanish Tercios, met the Lutheran troops at the Battle of Muhlberg in Saxony in 1547. The Imperial forces were easily victorious, the Elector, John Frederick of Saxony, was captured and imprisoned and Philip of Hesse also surrendered.

Charles's Failure to Win the Peace

Remarkably by 1552, only five years later, Charles's armies were in disarray and he himself was forced to flee from Germany for the last time.

There are many reasons which explain Charles's disastrous inability to follow up his victory at Muhlberg. International politics again pressurised him. By 1551, the Turks were again at his door. The French under their new King Henry II began again to intrigue with the Lutheran princes and made the Treaty of Chambord in 1552. In addition, the Papacy was very suspicious of Charles after the Battle of Muhlberg and feared the potential of a victorious German Emperor. But most important of all Charles underestimated the depth and strength of Lutheranism in the German princes and cities. He may have defeated them in battle but he failed to appreciate that their Lutheran beliefs and ties were still strong. In 1550 the princes were scheming again, this time with Henry II of France. Finally, the drain on Charles's finances of three decades of continuous war meant that his German army in 1552 were unpaid and dissatisfied. He could do nothing to counter the 1552 Lutheran Revolt. And he was now forced to accept the climax of the Diet of Augsburg in 1555. The statement 'Curus Regio, Eius Religio' has been enshrined in religious, political and diplomatic history ever since. It allowed the Protestants to freedom to develop their faith in their own states and territories and guaranteed the break-up of Charles's Imperial authority. His abdication was a foregone conclusion from this, the biggest blow to his Imperial greed.

REVIEW

'Chasing a Dream'? The Achievement of the Emperor Charles V

CHARLES V, THE HOLY ROMAN EMPEROR, AND POPE CLEMENT VII PARADE IN SPLENDOUR.

CLEMENS VII PONT MAX IMP CAES CAROLVS V P F AVG

Charles took failure hard. It was the strongest contributing factor to his abdication, and at Yuste the retired Monarch, the erstwhile advocate of reconciliation between Protestants and Catholics, became haunted by the prospect of heresy – with consequent social strife – in the hereditary dominions which he had handed over to Philip II. His advice to Philip and to the Regence, who traditionally governed where the hereditary ruler was not present, was: 'exterminate heresy, lest it take root and overturn the state and the social order'.

1 If these were some of Charles's successes, can you identify the others?
2 What, then, were Charles's failures?

Yet this advice of an old man, anxious to end his days in a Spain religiously united, should not overshadow what he had achieved in his period of office: containment of the Ottoman, both to the Empire and to the hereditary dominions; the sensible settlement of the Franco-Habsburg struggle with France giving up claims in Italy, and himself sacrificing his title to the French province of Burgundy; and the calling of the Council of Trent to remedy those abuses of the Catholic church of which the Protestants had, with justice, complained.

M.F. Alvarez, *Charles V*, 1975.

3 Make a list of the main concepts which are categorised in Rady's summary of Charles's reign.

4 Which of these concepts do you think epitomised Charles's reign?

5 How do you think Charles would wish to summarise his achievement on his own tombstone? And how would you, with the benefit of hindsight, summarise it?

It was Charles's misfortune to reign at a time when two ages overlapped. Behind him lay the period of the Crusades, of chivalry, of Catholic universalism and of its secular counterpart, universal empire. Before Charles stretched a divided Christendom and, if not quite yet the nation state, then at least the smaller unitary state. The common theme of both ages was dynasticism, although this concept was also undergoing metamorphosis – from a narrowly patrimonial idea to the quasi religious idea which would in time legitimise absolutism. Along with all his contemporaries, Charles was unaware of the transition from medieval to modern, and yet in his political philosophy he unconsciously absorbed the motives of both epochs. Thus he was the crusader, the shield of the Church universal, and world Monarch. Simultaneously he was the modern dynast during whose reign a centralised state structure and administration was developed in Spain and the Netherlands. Because Charles assumed such a wide variety of purposes, it was inevitable that his energy should have been dissipated and his reign seem ultimately purposeless. In a sense also, Charles's own verdict on himself passed at his abdication was likewise inescapable 'I have done what I could and I am sorry that I could not do better'.

M. Rady, *The Emperor, Charles V*, 1988.

9 War, Politics and Diplomacy, 1494–1559

SCOTLAND

Edinburgh

IRELAND

Dublin

DENMARK

Copenhagen

Köni

Lübeck

Hamburg

BRANDENBURG

Bremen

ENGLAND

London

NETHERLANDS

Antwerp

Cologne

THE
HOLY
ROMAN
EMPIRE

Prague

BOHEM

Rouen

Paris

Blois

Rheims

Nuremburg

Augsburg

2

1

3

TYROL

AUSTRIA

STYRIA

La Rochelle

FRANCE

4

5

VENICE

Venice

Bordeaux

Avignon

14

Milan

8

Genoa

9

Corunna

Burgos

NAVARRE

Toulouse

Marseilles

7

6

13

Florence

PAPAL STATES

10

11

DALM

Valladolid

Salamanca

12

Lisbon

PORTUGAL

CASTILE

Madrid

ARAGON

Barcelona

CORSICA

Rome

KINGDOM OF NAPLES

Toledo

Seville

Granada

BALEARIC IS.
(Aragon)

SARDINIA
(Aragon)

Naples

Palermo

SICILY
(Aragon)

Riga

MUSCOVY

Moscow

Smolensk

LITHUANIA

Kiev

CRIMEA

MOLDAVIA

WALLACHIA

BLACK SEA

OTTOMAN

Constantinople

nika

EMPIRE

Athens

	Boundary of the Holy Roman Empire
	Ottoman Empire
	Venetian Dominions
	Aragon

1. Swiss Confederation
2. Franche Comté
3. Grissons
4. Duchy of Savoy
5. Duchy of Milan
6. Republic of Genoa
7. Saluzzo
8. Marquisate of Mantua
9. Duchy of Ferrara
10. Republic of Lucca
11. Republic of Florence
12. Republic of Siena
13. Duchy of Modena
14. Montferrat

MAP OF EUROPE AROUND 1500.

PREVIEW

The State of Italy in 1494

Between 1494 and 1515 the states of Italy were invaded on a number of occasions by armies from France and Spain.

> That Italy failed to organise herself against invaders was due to the selfish policies of princes and the localism of outlook which marked Italians in general. Outside the kingdom of Naples, Italy remained essentially a land of city states and civic patriotisms, while in Naples a backward looking feudalism still obstructed the emergence of a 'modern' state. Everywhere, it is true, the word 'Italia' could move many hearts. Despite the cynical councils offered in *The Prince*, Machiavelli ended his book with an emotional plea for the unification of Italy. Even the more sardonic and detached historian Guicciardini could take patriotic pride in the individual prowess of Italians, as when at Barletta a group of Italian champions vanquished their French opponents in personal combat. On the other hand, it must be conceded that a feeling for Italy as a whole underlay singularly few political decisions.
>
> A.G. Dickens, *The Age of Humanism and Reformation*, 1977.

1 What does Dickens suggest about the state of Italy in 1494?
2 Why would this be an encouragement to invading armies?

As you can see from the map on p. 4, the Italian states in 1494 were extremely vulnerable. They were economically wealthy and artistically proud. They had much to reward an invader. In addition, their frontiers were insecure and their allies unreliable. It was no surprise, therefore, that in 1454 the important Italian states made peace in the Peace of Lodi. This peace established a balance of power between the leading Italian states: no one state could dominate the others, and no individual state would fall prey to an aggressor. The powerful leadership of Milan, Florence and Naples was crucial. When, for example, in 1482, Venice and its neighbour Ferrara went to war, the powerful trio ensured Ferrara's survival.

These years also saw the development of the new science of diplomacy, with permanent resident ambassadors being sent from state to state to help maintain the peace. It was cheaper and more effective to contain war through diplomacy and negotiation. Each ambassador at the court of another city-state eyed its rivals with suspicion.

The Florentine historian Guicciardini could thus describe Italy in the 1490s:

> Italy has never enjoyed such prosperity, or known so favourable a situation as that in which it found itself so securely at rest in the year of our Christian salvation 1490 and the years immediately before and after. The greatest peace and tranquillity reigned everywhere; the mountains and arid areas as well as the fertile plains were under cultivation; she was dominated by no other power than her own and not only did Italy abound in men, merchandise and riches, but she was also famous for the magnificence of many princes, the splendour of many noble and beautiful cities as being the centre of

1 How does Guicciardini's description differ from that of A.G. Dickens?

2 What similarities are there between Guicciardini's description and that of Dickens?

The Italian Wars

1494	King Charles VIII of France invaded Italy
1495	The Holy League was formed against France
1499	King Louis XII of France invaded Italy
1510–14	The War of the Holy League
1515	King Francis I of France invaded Italy

religion. She flourished with men adept at administering public affairs and had the high standards of knowledge in all the arts. According to all the standards of the day Italy was not lacking in military glory. Blessed with so many gifts she deservedly held a celebrated name and reputation among all nations.

Thus, the wealthy Italian states were unprepared for invasion in 1494. Perhaps most important of all, none of the Italian states had a strong military army. Instead they relied on mercenary commanders known as *condottieri*. These professional soldiers were uninterested in victory or defeat: either would spell financial disaster. Instead they preferred the continuation of war and were thus ill equipped to cope with the attack from France.

The Reasons for the Italian Wars

The Peace of Lodi was a fragile treaty, papering over the cracks of Italian politics. The major city-states were rivals and soon enough this rivalry was bound to erupt. The crisis which precipitated the wars occurred in the year 1492, after the death in Florence of Lorenzo de Medici, the principal agent of peace. In Milan, the young Giangaleazzo Sforza was under the

LUDOVICO SFORZA – 'THE MOOR'.

control of his uncle Ludovico, known as 'The Moor'. Giangaleazzo was married to Isabella, the grand-daughter of King Ferrante of Naples. Isabella was constantly complaining to her grandfather that she and her husband were allowed little freedom by Ludovico. Ferrante and his son, Alfonso, threatened to attack Milan in 1493. Ludovico, in desperation, looked round for allies and invited Charles VIII, the new king of France, to come to his aid. Perhaps to Ludovico's surprise Charles VIII accepted the invitation – the opportunity to conquer Naples and to control Milan was too great to be missed.

King Charles VIII had inherited the throne of France in a better position than that of most of his predecessors. The Hundred Years War had been ended earlier in the 15th century and the English had been forced to retreat across the Channel. In addition, the reign of Louis XI (1461–83) saw a greater unification of the kingdom and the defeat of the rival power of Burgundy. In addition, in 1491, the young Charles VIII married Anne of Brittany, adding the Duchy of Brittany was added to the French kingdom. The request from Ludovico therefore offered a perfect opportunity for Charles to engage in a foreign war and so unite French forces behind him.

Charles also had a legal claim to rule Naples. This territory had been ruled by the House of Anjou until they were driven out in 1442. Charles inherited this claim from Rene, Duke of Anjou, who died without a son in 1481. Charles was also advised by a number of leading Italians, permanently resident in his court. Among these, Cardinal Juliano della Vere had been defeated by Pope Alexander VI in the Papal Election of 1492. Thus supported, Charles made plans for invasion. By the Treaty of Etaples in 1492 he promised an annual pension to King Henry VII of England to prevent any attacks on his rear during this absence. Similarly, at Barcelona in 1493 he returned the provinces of Cerdagne and Roussillon to Spain in return for support from Ferdinand of Aragon. He even surrendered Artois and Franche-Comte to the Netherlands in order to gain, by the Treaty of Senlis, the support of Emperor Maximilian.

Indeed it could be said that Charles VIII, in order to gain the security to attack Italy, had wasted much of the work in confirming the French borders done by his predecessor Louis XI. However, Charles was ready for war in Italy.

CARLO VIII·RE DI FRANCIA

CHARLES VIII OF FRANCE.

1 What factors does Mattingly suggest encouraged Charles VIII to invade Italy?
2 Can you identify any features of Mattingly's written style which makes his argument convincing?

The Reasons for the French Invasion of Italy

Garrett Mattingly, in his outstanding book *Renaissance Diplomacy* (1989), tellingly describes the motivation for the French invasions:

> The regular revenues and powerful standing army which the French crown found at its disposal tempted it into foreign adventures; but once the English had been expelled and the Burgundian threat parried, France was driven by no such necessity to conquer or be crushed, eat or be eaten. In the 1490's France was in no more danger of being conquered by her neighbours than she was capable of conquering any of the larger of them. Probably for this very reason, because European political space was less organised and the pressures of European power politics less acute, the French monarchy lacked some of the nerves and sinews which made other states formidable.
>
> For one thing France had developed nothing comparable to the Milanese chancery and diplomatic service. In part the failure must be ascribed to the temperaments of rulers and to the less flexible structure of French administration. But in large part it was because the mere size of France dwarfed and obscured the significance of activities abroad and diminished from its rulers the importance of foreign relations... In the first generation of European power politics France remained as laggard in diplomacy as she was forward in war.
>
> Nor in the decade in which by invading Italy she began the age of modern European diplomacy had France any coherent foreign policy either. She went to war simply because it was always assumed that when Charles VIII came of age she would go to war. What else would a young healthy King with money in his treasury and men at arms to follow him be expected to do? War was the business of Kings.
>
> The reputable theory of the time recognised two main motives for it, honour and profit. Statesmanship consisted in finding an acceptable combination of both. Honour dictated war to avenge an injury or to make good a legal claim. Profits were reaped in booty, ransoms and indemnities and above all in taxable conquests. The commonest political arithmetic throughout the Renaissance consisted in balancing the cost of a campaign (so many thousand men for so many months at such and such a rate) against the value of a province in terms of its annual revenue. Optimists were usually able to demonstrate that the war the King wanted was a good investment.

TALKING POINT

Garrett Mattingly is described as an 'outstanding Historian'. What makes an outstanding Historian? By what criteria would you decide on the merits of a Historian?

The Events of the Italian Wars, 1494–1515

The Invasion of Charles VIII, 1494–5

In 1494 King Charles VIII crossed the Alps with his heavily armed cavalry and 8000 mercenary Swiss pikemen. He quickly took control of Milan and marched south towards Florence. His new artillery bombarded a number of Florentine cities and his treatment of the captured garrisons was swift and severe. Guicciardini commented that 'this was a thing unheard of and very frightening in Italy, which for a long time had been used to seeing wars staged with beautiful pomp and display rather than waged with bloodshed and danger'. A number of Florentine cities immediately surrendered and Charles was able to march into Florence and force Piero de Medici to flee. On the last day of the year he entered Rome and Pope Alexander VI retreated to the Castle of Sant Angelo.

Further south still, early in 1495 Charles used again the new short-barrelled guns designed by Jacques de Genouillac. His artillery quickly battered the walls of several border fortresses and garrisons were slaughtered. Alfonzo, King of Naples abdicated under pressure and Charles entered the city in triumph. In just a few months his army had marched the length of Italy and captured its four major cities.

The Formation of The Holy League, 1495

The speed and fury of Charles VIII's success alarmed the other powers of Europe. In March 1495 they formed a coalition to hold the French at bay. The coalition or Holy League consisted of a number of partners.

King Ferdinand of Aragon was anxious that the French occupation of Naples would now threaten Sicily. Pope Alexander VI in Rome and the people of Venice were keen to join such a coalition to protect their own interests. Even Lodovico Sforza, now the Duke of Milan, would join a coalition to remove the French. Lastly, the Emperor Maximilian I, at first pacified by the Treaty of Senlis, now feared Charles's influence in Italy.

In the spring of 1495 Charles decided to return home. He left a large garrison in Naples and marched north. The army of the League of Venice, or Holy League, confronted him at Fornovo. Charles's cavalry won a complete victory and Charles returned to France to sign the Peace of Vercelli with the League. However, the army he left in Naples faced considerable problems. The garrison was unpopular and the new King of Naples, Ferrantino, was joined by Spanish troops to defeat the French at Atella. Charles VIII died in 1498 with very little to show for his efforts.

Lodovico Sforza, according to one contemporary, was 'the man who turned a lion loose in his house to catch a mouse'. What do you think the author meant by this statement?

It will be challenging to see whether the prediction came true.

TALKING POINT
Is it possible to describe the 20th century as an age of war or an age of diplomacy?

The Motive for Spanish Intervention

The resources of Spain were no match for those of France. But the wars in Granada had trained a tough infantry and able commanders who might find ways of coping with the apparently irresistible masses of French heavy cavalry. And unlike their French rivals Ferdinand and Isabella had not neglected the other arm of the new state. Even before the beginning of the Italian wars Spain, under Ferdinand's leadership, had begun to develop an active diplomacy and an experienced body of diplomats.

In the team of the Catholic Kings, Ferdinand represented the Aragonese tradition, and a reliance on diplomacy had been practically forced on Aragon. It was a small kingdom, yet in the high politics of medieval Christendom it had played a major role. In Provence and Languedoc its Kings had once held wide domains. These they had lost, but in compensation they had conquered the Balearics, Sicily, Sardinia, Corsica, and finally Naples, though this last Alfonzo the Magnanimous had ruled away from the legitimate line to his bastard son. In all these gains and losses the enemy had always been French, and usually in superior force. In the long feud with France, diplomacy had succeeded for Aragon more often than war...

As long as the French did not cross the Alps, as long as the war in Granada lasted, Spanish diplomats in Italy had no mission except to support Ferrante, advance Spanish prestige when possible, and help maintain the uneasy balance of peninsular power. But the French danger was never far from Ferdinand's mind. Camping in the Sierra Nevadas, pounding at the Moorish strongholds with his new artillery, slowly clearing the passes that lead southward, Ferdinand kept looking back over his shoulders, towards the north...

The diplomatic pattern in the 1490's was clear. England, Spain and Austria were joined against France with dynastic marriages being worked out between Spain and the two northern allies, and the Spanish ambassadors, resident in fact if not in title, co-ordinating the alliance. Then suddenly the whole thing fell apart... Charles VIII had made reckless concessions for peace in the north because he was in a hurry to go to Italy, there the full scale power struggle was about to begin.

Even as he ratified the Treaty which released Charles VIII for his Italian adventure, Ferdinand must have been thinking about another coalition against France. He had already sent Fonseca and a colleague back to Flanders to re-open the Habsburg marriage negotiations. Presently he reinforced them by Francisco de Rojas, whose real mission seems to have been to stick close to Maximilian wherever that errant monarch might go and talk to him about Italy. Doctor de Puebla was warned to stand by for England. And Don Lorenzo Suarez was on his way to Venice with credentials as resident ambassador. At Rome there were two ambassadors, Medina and Carvajal already stood guard and another envoy was waiting to present his credentials to Lodovico Sforza in Milan.

Each Spanish ambassador was instructed to urge his hosts during the Holy League, of which the Pope was to be head and Spain the right arm, a League to restore the independence of Naples and exclude the French from Italy for ever.

G. Mattingly, *Renaissance Diplomacy*, 1989.

T ALKING POINT

What are the consequences of the long wars between France and Spain in this period?

Read again the chapters on Charles V and Francis I and attempt to gauge the effect of the wars on the internal history of the two states.

1 What were the motives of Ferdinand of Aragon in conducting his affairs against France? How did Ferdinand differ from Charles VIII?

2 What methods did Ferdinand use to gain his ends?

The Invasion by Louis XII of France, 1499

Louis XII succeeded to the French throne in 1498. He also succeeded to the Angevin claim to Naples. In addition, through his grandmother, he inherited the Visconti claim to Milan and this gave him a double justification for invading Italy. Louis was also encouraged to invade by other members of his court. George d'Amboise, the Archbishop of Rouen, believed that he should be a cardinal and perhaps, ultimately, pope. In addition, Louis was encouraged by Pope Alexander VI who wished to extend his Borgia control over central Italy. In return Louis XII would be allowed to divorce his barren wife and marry the widow of Charles VIII.

KING LOUIS XII OF FRANCE

In 1498 Cesare Borgia, the son of Alexander VI, arrived in France with the pope's permission for Louis to marry Anne of Brittany and also a cardinal's hat for the Archbishop of Rouen. While there, Cesare married a French princess and he later rode with the French army into Italy.

In 1499 Louis XII invaded Italy, captured Milan, and forced Lodovico Sforza to flee. In the following year, at the Battle of Novara, the French defeated Sforza's troops. Sforza himself was captured and spent the rest of his life in captivity in France.

In November, most unusually, Louis tried diplomacy rather than risking a military march to Naples. By the Treaty of Granada, he and Ferdinand divided the kingdom of Naples into two. It was a treaty which was destined to fail. Within two years, the two sides were quarrelling in Naples, and the French attacked the Spanish portion. At the famous Battle of Cerignola, probably the first to be fought with hand-held artillery, the Spanish captain Cordoba decisively defeated the French cavalry and their Swiss allies. He then captured the city of Naples and defeated the French again at Garigliano. By the Peace of Blois in 1505, Louis XII was forced to agree to surrender his claim to Naples and to admit Spanish control. From this time, the French concentrated on the strategically important city of Milan.

The War of the Holy League, 1510–14

In 1510 Pope Julius II revived the Holy League with support from Spain, Venice and King Henry VIII of England. In 1511 the new French commander Gaston de Foix, only 21 years of age, moved his army swiftly to gain control over the whole of northern Italy and then marched south to attack the city of Ravenna. In April 1512 the most bloody battle of the Italian wars took place. The Spanish lost 9000 troops from an army of 16,000 and the French, though victorious, lost their young commander.

POPE JULIUS II.

Louis XII now faced mounting problems. The Emperor Maximilian joined forces with the Holy League and the Swiss occupied Rouen, in order to protect their southern boundaries and secure supplies of corn and wine. In 1512, the Swiss defeated the French at Novara and installed the son of Lodovico Sforza as Duke of Milan. By 1515, when Louis XII died, it looked as though the French had again lost their control of northern Italy.

Francis I's Invasion of Italy, 1515

The new king lost no time in taking 30,000 troops to Italy. He paid the Swiss to leave Milan and fought a two-day battle at Marignano against those who remained. Francis became the new Duke of Milan, and signed a peace treaty with the Swiss at Fribourg in 1516 so that the Swiss would never fight again against the French in Milan. Francis I also conducted a treaty with Pope Leo X, known as the Concordat of Bologna. French control of northern Italy now seemed complete and the scene was set for a personal and dynastic rivalry between the new French king and the new Holy Roman Emperor, Charles V.

FOCUS

9.1 Changes in Warfare

The Medieval Background

Medieval warfare is characterised, or perhaps caricatured, by the picture of a great charge of chivalric knights. Every man would fight for himself, concerned about his own armour and the potential ransom for any enemy he managed to capture. While there were more organised tactics than this on some medieval battlefields, there was a general lack of discipline and too great a reliance on the social rank of the combatants.

J. Lotherington, *Years of Renewal*, 1988.

By the 15th century a man at arms with all his equipment and servitors was thus proving both inefficient on the battlefield and expensive to sustain. As their usefulness diminished, so their pretensions grew. Their armour became impossibly ornate, their tournaments were costly, their social status more jealously hedged around by a heraldic lure which concentrated the more on questions of status as it had less to do with military function.

Developments in Infantry

In the early stages the Italian wars had indicated the importance of heavy infantry. Although the famed Swiss infantry was crushed by the French at Marignano in 1515, infantry remained more important than cavalry. The heir to the Swiss column was the Spanish 'tercio' which lorded the battlefields of Europe from the date of its creation in 1534 to the day of Spanish defeat at Roicroi in 1643. Elevated by the Swiss column and the Spanish tercio the infantry lost its inferior status.

M.L. Bush, *Renaissance, Reformation and the Outer World*, 1967.

By the end of the 15th century battalions of pikemen were a necessary part of every serious armed force. And increasingly there were attached to them contingents of men armed with handguns, especially the hooked gun, Hackenbusche or Arquebus, which with its successor the musket was to be the infantry's fire arm for another two hundred years. Infantry had arrived.

M. Howard, *War in European History*, 1976.

1 Outline the main changes in military tactics during the Italian wars.
2 Estimate some consequences of these changes. Consider the effects of the wars on the following:
The speed of warfare.
The expense of warfare.
The professionalisation and specialisation of warfare.
The morale of troops, the nature of wounds, and the development of military medicine.
The size and nature of the support which armies needed.
The nature of armies: whether mercenary or national?
The consequences of all of this for taxation and the economy of the states of Europe.
3 Now read the following two extracts and test your own summary of developments against them.

Artillery and Firearms

What the Italian wars really demonstrated was the ascendancy of shot. The Battle of Novara in 1512 was won by artillery. In the closing stages of the wars small arms, like hand guns and the wheel lock pistol, made their decisive entrance.

M.L. Bush, *Renaissance, Reformation and the Outer World,* 1967.

In battle artillery could condition the timing of an action, to a lesser extent its tactics, but its outcome depended on numbers, experience, skill, command intelligence and above all, morale.

Military firearms, though handmade, were mass produced and this utilitarian characterlessness helped in the rapid growth of their use. When Louis XI, intent on employing pikes modelled on those which had given the Swiss their victories, rejected one batch after another of those submitted by French armourers as inadequate, an observer was moved to comment that the fuss would only be justified 'if he would also manufacture men capable of handling them'. In a sense the pike was a national weapon. Other countries borrowed it. But firearms could do appreciable damage with less training than was required for other arms and their spread had been so rapid and so universal that they had picked up no national overtones.

J.R. Hale, *War and Society in Renaissance Europe,* 1985.

BATTLE OF MARIGNANO. Designed from contemporary authorities.

THE BATTLE OF MARIGNANO, 1515.

In the thirty-one years of fighting between the Battle of Fornovo in 1494 and the Battle of Pavia in 1525, we can see fire power moving from a purely auxiliary role to one where it was central and decisive; where the arquebus was no longer a minor importance of the pike square, but where the pike square's principle function was to protect the shot. This the Spaniards recognised when they reorganised their infantry in 1534 into tercios of 3,000 men each. Instead of having one musketeer to every six pikeman, as had been habitual in the Italian wars, they had equal numbers of each, and the musketeers received specialist pay.

M. Howard, *War in European History,* 1976.

Fortifications and Siege Warfare

The result of improved artillery and the appearance of efficient small arms were developments in fortifications: city walls were made impregnable and sieges became more difficult and much longer. In the field temporary fortifications were introduced with the same slowing effect. By the 1520's the warfare waged by Charles VIII, was part of the past.

M.L. Bush, *Renaissance, Reformation and the Outer World*, 1967.

The solution for defenders was to build lower walls. The 'trace Italienne' was developed – low broad walls protected by extensive earth works with bastions jutting out, diamond shaped projections in masonry making it very difficult to approach the main wall. All this meant that sieges tended to be long and very expensive.

J.R. Lotherington, *Years of Renewal*, 1988.

By the end of the Italian wars the broad outlines of siege-craft had been established by such experts as Pedro Novarro and Properro Colona. To counter the fire of the defence the besieging force took to the spade. First they surrounded the fortress with a containing line of trenches just beyond range of the defending batteries. From this they drove forward trenches in zig-zag lines at angles broad enough to prevent their being enfiladed by the fire of the garrison, and established concealed batteries at intervals along these lines. Then sappers would drive mines under the fortifications and fill them with explosive charges; which the defender would counter with mines of their own. At the climax the besieger would unmask his batteries, concentrate their fire at the point which he had selected for a breach, spring his mines and launch his assault. This climax might come only after weeks of sapping and skirmishing in the trenches. This type of trench warfare, tedious, dangerous, murderously unhealthy, was to be the staple fare of the European soldier for over two hundred years.

M. Howard, *War in European History*, 1976.

---

4 Which do you think were the most significant military developments in this period and what were their consequences? In what ways were your original ideas challenged by these two sources?

5 Why is it unwise to make too great claims for a military 'revolution' in this period?

Battle Tactics and Formation

Always sensitive to the need for the most necessary reform of all, that of formation and tactics. The balance between horse and foot, the emergence within both of men performing increasingly specialized functions, the predominance of fire arms among the weaponry of both which led an English writer to comment that 'it is rarely seen in our day that men come often to handblows as in old times they did'. All called for a rethinking of how armies were brigaded for administrative purposes, formed up in battle array, and divided into tactical units upon whose inter-dependence and flexibility an army's capacity to adjust to the circumstances of combat depended.

J.R. Hale, *War and Society in Renaissance Europe,* 1985.

One of the bulletins Charles VIII sent back to be printed and circulated in France during his triumphant campaign of 1494-95 showed with what nonchalance he was able to knock out one unmodified fortified place after another on his route to Naples: 'Today (4 February 1495) I besieged one of the strongest places in this whole region, both for its defences and its situation. It's called Monte San Giovanni. My cousin Montpensier had arrived before me with my artillery and after firing for four hours my said artillery had made a breach wide enough for an assault. I ordered it to be made by men at arms and others and though the place was held by 500-600 good fighting men, as well as its inhabitants, they went in such a manner that, thanks to God, the town has been taken with little loss to me and to the defenders great loss.

Punishment and great example to those others who might think of so obstructing me.

J.R. Hale, *War and Society in Renaissance Europe,* 1985

A far more significant aspect of the period lies in the technical development of warfare, within which these decades advance more rapidly than during any similar period before the 20th Century. Armies of considerable size and complexity were often involved. For example, in 1494 Charles VIII of France invaded Italy with 60,000 men, including 1,600 lances of cavalry (each containing six horses), 8,000 Gascon infantry, 8,000 Swiss, and an impressive train of horsedrawn field artillery. On the other hand the narratives of the campaigns and major battles indicate that relatively little advance had been made in the communications required to integrate – either strategically or tactically – the action of these various elements. Of the effectual advances perhaps the most striking was the improvement of artillery in numbers, mobility and rate of fire. Guns contributed to the issues in several of the greater and more decisive battles: most notably at Ravenna, but also at Marignano and Pavia. Prevailing over the prejudices of a generation still nourished upon chivalric ideals, artillery engaged zealous study of eminent commanders and appealed to the pride of rulers. Alongside the field gun, a serviceable hand weapon emerged with the arquebus and by the later stages of the Italian wars this had replaced the crossbow. On the other hand it could hardly be said that gunpowder had fully achieved its modern significance yet. Most battles were still decided in the main by pike and sword, while small arms could only be employed under the protection of these weapons.

A.G. Dickens, *The Age of Humanism and Reformation,* 1977.

The Habsburg–Valois Rivalry, 1519–59

For the forty years following Charles V's successful election as Holy Roman Emperor, France and the Empire were locked in a constant battle. It is important to understand the factors which motivated both sides in this conflict. These can be summarised under the following headings. As you study the events of the next forty years, identify which of these factors is most important and say why you think so. Place them in order of priority. You may work in class groups and present a group report to the class.

- Tradition and history.
- Personal aims and ambitions.
- Personal rivalry.
- Territorial and dynastic ambitions.
- 'National' orientation.
- Power and prestige, including the balance of power.
- Safety and security.

The dynastic and personal ambitions of Charles V and Francis I were very evident in their early years. The French claimed Flanders and Artois, held by the Duke of Burgundy, while the Burgundians claimed Tournai, which was held by France. Charles's early life was spent as Duke of Burgundy in the Netherlands and he was keen to recover his ancestral lands. In Italy, the conflict was particularly severe as both had a personal claim to Naples. In addition, Milan 'was a dynastic as well as a strategic bone of contention' (Stewart MacDonald, *Charles V*).

Francis I's capture of the city in 1515 and the peace treaty he made with the young Charles in the following year at the Treaty of Noyon enabled the French to consider Milan as theirs. But in 1519 Charles became Holy Roman Emperor: Milan was an essential strategic centre, enabling communications between Spain, Netherlands, Austria and Naples. Milan was a vital gateway for Charles and he could no longer tolerate French control. Thus the scene was set for forty years of dynastic rivalry.

The Habsburg–Valois Wars, 1521–9

The early stage of the conflict centred around Northern Italy and Spain. By the Treaty of Noyon, Charles V had given both Milan and Spanish Navarre to France. However, Charles was reluctant to honour his promise and by 1520 the French were looking to conquer Navarre by force. The attack came in the following year at a time when Charles was embarrassed by the Comuneros revolt in Castile. Charles's response was swift: he defeated the Comuneros rebels and then encouraged them to join him in pushing the French from Navarre. Following this incident, the stage of war moved to Italy.

Counselled by his Burgundian chancellor Gattinara, Charles considered himself one of the joint heads of Christendom. As such Italy, and particularly the city of Rome and the city of Milan, were vital to his ideological and strategic responsibilities. In 1521, he made a treaty with Pope Leo X and together they drove the French out of Milan. The same year, he captured Tournai and incorporated it into the Netherlands. In the following year Charles defeated Francis at the Battle of Bicocca near Milan.

KING FRANCIS I OF FRANCE.

The Habsburg–Valois Rivalry, 1519–59

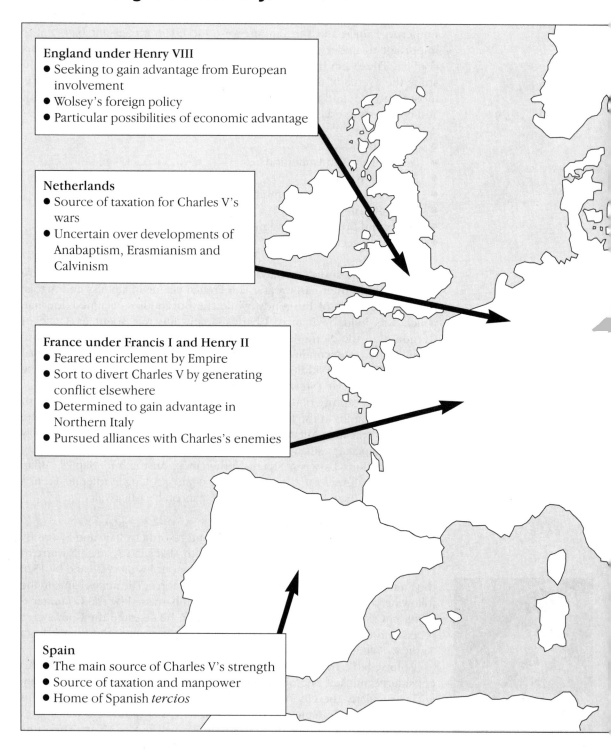

England under Henry VIII
- Seeking to gain advantage from European involvement
- Wolsey's foreign policy
- Particular possibilities of economic advantage

Netherlands
- Source of taxation for Charles V's wars
- Uncertain over developments of Anabaptism, Erasmianism and Calvinism

France under Francis I and Henry II
- Feared encirclement by Empire
- Sort to divert Charles V by generating conflict elsewhere
- Determined to gain advantage in Northern Italy
- Pursued alliances with Charles's enemies

Spain
- The main source of Charles V's strength
- Source of taxation and manpower
- Home of Spanish *tercios*

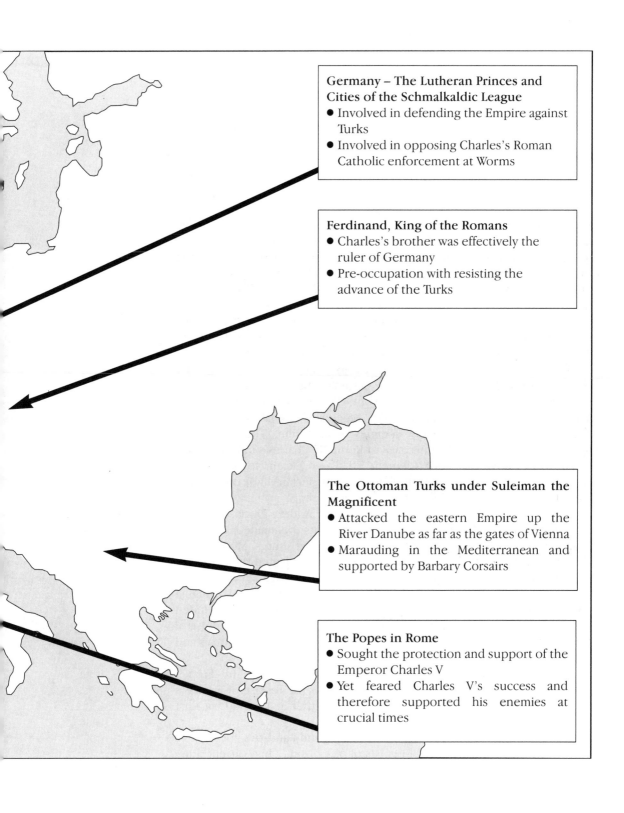

Germany – The Lutheran Princes and Cities of the Schmalkaldic League
- Involved in defending the Empire against Turks
- Involved in opposing Charles's Roman Catholic enforcement at Worms

Ferdinand, King of the Romans
- Charles's brother was effectively the ruler of Germany
- Pre-occupation with resisting the advance of the Turks

The Ottoman Turks under Suleiman the Magnificent
- Attacked the eastern Empire up the River Danube as far as the gates of Vienna
- Marauding in the Mediterranean and supported by Barbary Corsairs

The Popes in Rome
- Sought the protection and support of the Emperor Charles V
- Yet feared Charles V's success and therefore supported his enemies at crucial times

Charles was now seemingly in complete control. In 1523 he plotted an invasion of France with the help of Henry VIII who would attack from Calais, and the powerful Duke of Bourbon who would join the Habsburg attack from Italy.

However, the attacks went badly and Francis was able to counter. He made an agreement with the new pope, Clement VII, and also made alliances with Venice and Florence. Francis's armies again captured Milan.

It took a decisive Habsburg victory in the Battle of Pavia in 1525 to finally drive the French out of Northern Italy. Francis I himself was captured and taken to Madrid as a prisoner.

The problem now was what to do with the captured French king. Charles's brother Ferdinand urged harsh measures. 'Now is the time for the Emperor and myself to devise means of getting full satisfaction from France. Not an hour is to be lost'. Charles, however, had too much personal honour to be so involved. He negotiated with Francis, who agreed to renounce his claims to Flanders, Artois and Tournai. Charles also wanted the recovery of ancestral Burgundy, a major plank in his dynastic policy. The Treaty of Madrid in January 1526 resulted in Francis abandoning all these territories. Francis was also to be married to Charles's sister Eleanor and Francis's two sons were to be kept hostage in Madrid until the Treaty was implemented. However, Francis returned to Paris and declared the Treaty of Madrid void because it had been agreed under duress.

Other states were now anxious to join Francis in curbing the overmighty power of the Emperor. The Ottoman Turks agreed to attack up the Danube. Henry VIII of England, Pope Clement VII and other Italian states feared Hapsburg supremacy. The League of Cognac was signed in 1526 and Charles found many enemies against him. The war which followed included the notorious Sack of Rome by Charles's unpaid troops in May 1527. After that Pope Clement VII was reluctant to oppose the Emperor, but in 1528 England and France jointly declared war on him and Henry VIII sent money to the French campaign in Italy.

The Sack of Rome is discussed in Chapter 8.

A French fleet, led by the Genoese admiral Andrea Doria, was now attacking Naples. However, Charles's diplomats persuaded Doria to change sides and this resulted in victory for the Habsburgs. Moreover, in June 1529 at the Battle of Landriano, Charles again defeated the French in Northern Italy.

Peace was secured at the famous ladies' Peace of Cambrai in August 1529. Both sides were financially exhausted. The peace was concluded between Charles's aunt Margaret of Austria and Francis's mother, Louise of Savoy. The French surrendered their claims to Naples, Flanders, Artois and Tournai and they also renounced their claim to Milan.

Francis married Charles's sister Eleanor in 1530, and the French promised to pay Charles a vast sum of money for the release of Francis's two sons. The two sides also agreed to join together in a crusade against the Turk.

However, Francis was allowed to keep Burgundy and this for Charles was still a major blow. Yet in the interests of peace and of his concentrating his mind on events in Germany, the Peace of Cambrai served him very well.

The Habsburg–Valois Wars, 1529–44

It was immediately clear that the Peace of Cambrai was inadequate for Francis. He was particularly anxious to recover Milan and to disturb Charles V's route centre and particularly his transport of troops up the Spanish road. In addition, Francis recognised the need to distract Charles at every turn and to side with Charles's enemies. He made approaches to Henry VIII and to the emerging Protestant princes and cities in Germany. In addition, he married his son, the future King Henry II, to a niece of Pope Clement VII, Catherine de Medici. He also began to conspire with the Ottoman sultan Suleiman the Magnificent.

Charles himself aggravated the situation: in 1535, following the death of the last of the Sforza dukes, Charles took the Duchy of Milan for himself. In return the following year Francis took Turin and looked to be threatening Milan. Charles in turn invaded southern France and attacked the Port of Marseilles. The two monarchs tried to patch up their differences at the Treaty of Nice in 1538, but the problem of Milan was unresolved and conflict inevitably continued.

The situation was aggravated in 1540 when Charles made his son Philip the new Duke of Milan. Between 1542 and 1544, the two sides were at war again and in a series of minor battles stalemate was reached. In diplomacy Charles accused Francis of treachery and made much propaganda of Francis's alliance with the Turks. Even the Lutheran princes in Germany were prepared to join Charles in an offensive against the Turks. The two exhausted parties made peace once again at Crepy in 1544. It was a hesitant peace which allowed Charles to maintain his hold on Italy. In addition, Francis ended his alliance with the Turks and promised not to interfere in Charles's attempts to subdue the Lutherans in Germany.

The Habsburg–Valois Wars, 1544–59

The later years of the wars were indecisive for both parties. Charles defeated the German princes at Muhlberg in 1547, but the union of Protestant and Catholic princes ensured that Charles lost the subsequent peace. In 1551 he lost Tripoli to the Ottoman Turks and his peace with the Sultan collapsed. Moreover, in 1547 Francis I and Henry VIII both died and Henry II, the new King of France, had problems to deal with at home. In 1552 Henry signed the Treaty of Chambord with the Lutherans and, in return for his support, they returned three important bishoprics to France – Metz, Toul and Verdun. In 1555 Henry was also able to form an agreement with the new pope, Paul IV. On the other hand in 1554 Charles's son Philip was married to Mary Tudor, Queen of England. Charles abdicated in 1555 and Philip succeeded to Spain and the Netherlands, while Ferdinand took over the Empire. Both sides were increasingly hesitant and circumspect. Thus the Treaty of Cateau-Cambresis was signed in 1559. By its terms, the Habsburg–Valois conflict was ended. Artois, Flanders, Tournai and Navarre were returned to Spain, but France kept Burgundy, Metz, Toul and Verdun. The Habsburg possession of Milan and Naples was confirmed. Peace between Habsburg and Valois was at long last secured.

EXAMINING THE EVIDENCE

The Balance of Power

Source A

Historians have been able to discover one general principle in 16th century diplomacy related to the idea of national interest, the principle of the balance of power. There are indeed episodes in the period 1494–1559 when it looks as if that principle was really being applied, especially when it was a question of a combination of two or more strong states against a weak one. Here the principle requires such a partition of the victim's territories as not to change decisively the strength of any victor in relation to his partners. In the arrangements for cutting up the Milanese between France and Venice, or Naples between France and Spain, or the Venetian territories of all the allies of the League of Cambrai, the principle was more or less consciously observed. But since it really means little more than the biggest dog gets the meatiest bone, and others help themselves in order of size, its hard to be sure that the 16th century appreciated the full beauty of a balanced system. It is harder because none of the arrangements lasted, and because each was upset with the full sanction of the chief Italian power, the Papacy, which had presided over them in its role of special custodian of the idea of balance.

The League of Cognac of 1526 illustrates another aspect of what is taken for balance of power diplomacy, the combination of a group of powers against an apparent victor. In the 16th century however what the allies always hoped was not just to balance the strongest power, but to outweigh it. A real balance of power requires at least two groups, so evenly matched that neither can easily defeat the other, with the third holding the balance between them. This classic English conception is usually supposed to have been invented by Cardinal Wolsey somewhere in the reign of the first two Tudors. But though Wolsey may have had more in mind than he told his master, on the evidence, what Henry VIII wanted and what Wolsey persuaded each time he would get, was not just to preserve the status quo but to be on the winning sides so as to share the spoils. None of Henry VII's fellow sovereigns was any more altruistic than he.

Actually, except for a jealousy of success, nobody had worked out any idea of a European balance of power. All that existed was a rough idea of such a balance in Italy.

G. Mattingly, *Renaissance Diplomacy*, 1989.

TALKING POINT

Can we learn lessons from the 16th century to help us understand the events of the modern world?

1 What types of balance of power does Mattingly identify in this passage?
2 Can you identify examples of each of the types from your reading of this chapter?
3 Mattingly concludes that there was 'a rough idea of such a balance in Italy'. Can you find evidence of this? Do you agree with Mattingly's conclusion? Is there evidence of balance of power outside Italy?
4 Does the concept of balance of power help us to understand diplomacy today? Are there areas in the world where the concept of balance is helpful?

REVIEW

Essay

'Examine the consequences of the wars between France and Spain between 1492 and 1559.'

This is an open-ended and extremely wide-ranging question, which demands a thorough reading of Chapters 7, 8 and 9 in this book. You will also need to read widely from your school library.

It is a complex question that must be tackled in stages.

Stage 1: Audience and Information

Consider the demands of the question, who will be reading it, your purpose in producing it, and its length. For example, it could be a Personal Study or Dissertation which is part of your formal assessment; as such its length would be perhaps 5000 or even 10,000 words.

Certainly, you will wish to explore the following:
- The consequences of the wars for the internal history of France and Spain. Consider their government, economy, finances, structures and military and diplomatic organisation.
- The consequences of the wars for other areas of Europe like the Italian States, the Papacy and parts of the Holy Roman Empire.
- The military consequences and the methods of warfare.
- The consequences for diplomacy.

Stage 2: Planning

Create a draft paragraph or section plan to identify which of the above aspects you will examine and in which order.

What does the word 'examine' require you to do? You will certainly need to review the impact of the wars on each aspect.

Now construct a timeplan for each of Stages 3–6.

Stage 3: Research

Read as widely as you can and incorporate references from important sources into your paragraph plan.

Consider important facts, opinions and even judgements. Record quotations where these may be helpful to you.

Stage 4: Draft

Write out, preferably using a word processor, the first draft of your answer. You may choose to do this section by section and discuss each part with your teacher, particularly if you are tackling an examination piece.

Stage 5: Review
Re-read your draft and any further sources you can find. Improve and amend the text where necessary.

Challenge yourself:
- Have I covered all aspects of the topic? Is there a proper balance between the consequences on France, Spain and those on other areas?
- Have I 'examined' the impact of the wars?
- Is my paragraph structure clear?
- Are the first sentences of each paragraph helpful as signposts to the development of my points?

Stage 6
Now add an Introductory and Concluding paragraph.
What purpose do these two paragraphs serve?
What interesting alternative ways can I lead into this essay?
How can I end it really effectively?

Stage 7: Process Review
Have I used my time effectively? Did I allocate enough time for planning, research, drafting and reviews?

10 The Catholic and Counter Reformations

PREVIEW

The Catholic Church and the People in 1500

The idea of marriage as a social alliance was embedded in the rites of the Church. In most regions of Christendom it took place at the Church door. Standing upon his threshold, the priest was not enacting or administering a sacrament but verifying the proper conduct of a social operation... Of this social operation, at once secular and sacred, the priest was an important but not a necessary part. It could be properly accomplished without him, and if completed by sexual relations created, in the theory of the canonists and in widely observed practice, a lawful and sacramental marriage... Yet the priest's participation in the business of getting married was becoming more central in the last two centuries of the middle ages.

The first reason for this was that an increasing fear of diabolic intervention inspired a mounting pressure for his services in the blessing of the ring, the couple and the marriage bed. The principal form taken by this intervention involved the knotting by a malevolent participant at the appropriate point in the marriage rite of a sort of shoelace; by the power of the devil to which the sexual organs were especially vulnerable, this anti-ring would ensure the failure of intercourse between the spouses and divert the process of social amity into recrimination, hostility and adultery. Fear of this and similar acts encouraged a resort to the blessing, a rite of blessing over the couple on their first entrance into the marriage bed, of the bed itself and the bridal chamber which had been available in most western liturgies since the 11th century.

In the 15th century it became established in Germany and it flourished in particularly elaborate form in Scandinavia, though not apparently in England. ... The ring, now blessed immediately before being placed on the bride's finger, became a talisman of fidelity and perhaps of fertility, as well as a symbol of social alliance: an object whose mystic endowments inspired the godly in 16th century England to seek, with little success, to ban it from the marriage rite. Spousals unblessed began to appear as risky a prospect as a child unexorcised.

J. Bossy, *Christianity in the West,* 1985.

You will also say that we frankly confess that God permits this persecution to afflict His Church because of the sins of men, especially of the priests and prelates of the church... We know that for many years many abominable things have occurred in this Holy See, abuses in spiritual matters, transgressions of the Commandments, and finally in everything a change for the worse. No wonder that the onus has spread from the head to the members, from the supreme pontiffs to the prelates below them. All of us, that is priests and clergy, each one of us, have strayed from our paths; not for a long time has anyone done good; no, not even one.

Speech of the reforming Pope Adrian VI in 1522. Adrian died the following year after being pope for just eighteen months.

The Roman Catholic church in the year 1500 consisted of the pope, cardinals, archbishops and bishops, as well as local parish priests and the members of their congregations.

In the 16th century, there was an intense renewal of this church and it affected all these groups. The renewal flowed in three main streams:

- an indigenous Catholic renewal. Its origins lay in earlier centuries and its consequences developed far into the future.
- a counter reformation which aimed to halt the expansion of Protestantism and fight back for the Catholic church.
- a parallel development in the beliefs and behaviours of the ordinary people indicated in the link between religion and popular culture.

By the end of the 16th century all three streams were merging into a powerful flood to continue the growth of the Roman Catholic church into modern times.

As you study this chapter, consider the terms 'Catholic Reformation' and 'Counter Reformation'. What do they mean? Is their definition important?

The Origins of the Reformations

The Catholic and Counter Reformations owe their origins to the renewal of Christian piety in the two centuries before 1500. This was a period when disease and disaster were common. The Black Death in the middle of the 14th century killed perhaps a third of the people of Europe. Bad harvests caused regular price fluctuations and many years saw a total crop failure in many parts of Europe. The situation was also aggravated by the ravages of war. Whole villages were often de-populated and settled social orders needed to be rearranged. A new disease, syphilis, also caused the need for renewal. Through all of this it was not surprising that men developed an obsessive preoccupation with death and salvation. It was this renewal of piety and a focus on the Cross of Christ that heralded the Catholic and Counter Reformations.

Die Jacobs Brüder.

Wir Jacobs brüder mit grossem hauffen
Jm land sind hin vnd her gelauffen/
Von Sanct Jacob/Ach vnd gen Rom
Singen vnd bettlen one schom/
Gleich anderen presthafften armen/
Offt thut vns der Bettel Stab erwarmen
In Händen/alsdenn wir es treibn
Vnser lebtag faul Bettler bleibn.
C ij   Der

People looked to the church to provide order among the chaos. Prayer, meditation, the regular use of the Sacraments, pious readings, and regular penances, including pilgrimages, were the order of the day. A pilgrimage was a daunting penance: 'Catholics could still be found in the year 1700 at holy wells and springs, nearly up to their necks in icy water to say their penitential prayers. The hazards of the long-range pilgrimages to St. James at Compostella and Our Lady at Rocamadour, from sea sickness upwards, were such as to make them a satisfaction acceptable to the victims of violence.' In addition, the Carnival became increasingly popular through Europe. For either three or six days before Shrove Tuesday, people enjoyed a public feasting. The purpose was to bring all their sins to light so that they could get rid of them in time for Lent. The feast was dominated by a carnival figure who was carried in procession, tried, condemned and usually burned, at the end of the carnival. The Seven Deadly Sins were represented by gluttony – a sin very much absent during the following 40 days.

Other members of the church followed St Augustine's teaching that salvation could not be gained by good works, but rather by faith. Cardinal Contarini, a Venetian aristocrat, had a clear belief in justification by faith 'suppose I underwent every imaginable penance and more besides, that would still be insufficient to make me a great Saint'. Contarini argued that penance 'would not compensate for my past misdeeds'. Indeed, Contarini was one of the main negotiators with the Lutherans at the Council of Regensburg in 1541 where an attempt to heal the breach between Protestants and Catholics finally and narrowly failed.

Other people looked for order in religious associations, especially those for laymen and woman in the everyday world. The Brethren of the Common Life founded in 14th century Holland by Gerard Groote produced the 'devotio moderna'. The publication of the devotional work, the *Imitation of Christ*, by Thomas A Kempis around the year 1400, encouraged people to pursue lives of meditation and piety. Churchmen, led by Renaissance popes who saw themselves largely as Italian politicians, could not satisfy the needs of the people at this time. Some, like Cardinal Cisneros in Spain, did try. Cisneros was a Franciscan who became the confessor to Queen Isabella and the chancellor of Castile. He founded the university at Alcala and sponsored the printing of the Bible.

PAVLVS · IV · PAPA · NEAPOLITANVS ·

In Italy, new monastic orders were set up: the Capuchins were formed as an Order in 1528 and had over 2500 members by the mid-16th century. They aimed to return to the poverty and self-denial of the New Testament and also to dedicate themselves to work for the poor. The Oratory of Divine Love, which met in Rome between 1517 and 1527, was a body formed by aristocrats committed to a life of contemplation, worship, study and charitable work.

Interestingly, they devoted their lives to their own families as well as to their religious purposes. The Ursuline Order was set up in 1535 as groups of unmarried women to visit the sick and provide the religious instruction for women in their own homes. Most members were lay people. The Theatines, on the contrary, consisted entirely of priests. They were also aristocratic.

They were led by important members of the Catholic church like Cardinal Carafa who later became a very determined reforming pope as Paul IV. Perhaps the most formative single event in the early development of the Catholic and Counter Reformations was the Sack of Rome in 1527 by the army of Charles V. Rome had been the centre of the Renaissance popes. Its Sack had dramatic consequences. A number of Roman churchmen, seeing the Sack as a manifestation of the wrath of God, immediately pledged themselves to reform. One such was the Bishop of Verona, Gian Matteo Ghiberti. In 1528 he left Rome to return to his diocese – where he remained until his death. He set a personal example of dedication and reform – checking every parish, inspecting his priests, establishing schools and seminaries, and encouraging preaching and the regular administration of Mass. Ghiberti's personal religious renewal had great consequences for his own see and for others throughout Europe. Many copied his example.

The Sack of Rome and its consequences is considered in some detail in Chapter 8.

In 1537, Pope Paul III commissioned an enquiry into the condition of the Roman Catholic church. The report attacked superstition, the excesses of indulgences, prostitution in Rome, papal abuses and wealth, and pluralistic cardinals and bishops. The nine cardinals who produced it fired a warning shot across the bows of the church.

TALKING POINT

Can an established church ever be broad enough to accommodate all forms of personal spirituality?

10. 1 'The Spiritual Exercises': Release of Spiritual Energy or Brainwashing Cult?

IGNATIUS LOYOLA –
A 19TH-CENTURY
ENGRAVING.

Ignatius Loyola

Ignatius Loyola is one of the most dramatic and important characters in 16th century history. He was born in 1491 to a noble family in Castile in Spain. He was trained as a soldier and fought for King Ferdinand and later Charles V against the invading armies of France.

In May 1521, while he was defending the city of Pamplona a French cannon ball smashed his right leg. Ironically a French doctor tried to set it but it had to be broken and reset twice. He was lame for life. He then underwent a mystical religious conversion and began to fight, instead, for the Mother of Christ and the salvation of souls. He set out on pilgrimage, gave away his rich garments to the poor and put on a cloak of sackcloth. At the small town of Manresa near Barcelona he remained for a year wrestling with spiritual questions. It was here that he drafted his 'Spiritual Exercises' which were finally written up in 1541.

Talking Point

Having considered the evidence in this focus, did the Spiritual Exercises release spiritual energy or were the Jesuits a type of brainwashed cult?

What were the consequences of the exercises for the members of the Society of Jesus? And for other Catholics?

'The Spiritual Exercises'

The Four 'Weeks'

Week 1
To purge away the rotten elements in one's spiritual life, to put one's life in order. 'I shall turn to myself and I shall enquire that I have so far done for Jesus Christ, what I am now doing for Jesus Christ, and what I ought to do for Jesus Christ. After meditation on the solemn themes of hell, judgement and death, the soul comes through to the door of hope, Jesus Christ'.

Weeks 2 and 3
Meditation and contemplation on every aspect of Christ's earthly life in all its suffering and glory. The penitent is taught to pray and to sacrifice his needs to the needs of Christ.

Week 4
The purpose is to complete an unselfish love for Christ and a joy in His glory and a total trust in Him.

Appendix Rules for thinking with the church.
This identifies Ignatius's view of the Roman Catholic church and the need to ensure that one's thinking conforms to the teaching of the church.

The Aim of the 'Exercises'

The central aim and purpose of the spiritual exercises is to bring the mind and heart of the person who makes a retreat into every closer conformity with the mind and heart of Christ, so that out of love of Christ and a desire to be more like Him, he may learn to prefer and embrace poverty with Jesus Christ rather than riches: shame and insults with Jesus Christ rather than honours; the reputation of a fool with Jesus Christ rather than a great name for wisdom among men. It is a terrifying programme to flesh and blood but no more than an application in an inexorably logical unfolding of our Lord's own words 'if any man will come after me and be my disciple let him deny himself and take up his cross daily and follow me'.

J. Brodrick, *The Origin of the Jesuits,* 1986.

Man is created to praise, reverence and serve God our Lord and by this means to save his soul. The other things on the face of the earth are created for man to help him in attaining the end for which he is created. Hence, man is to make use of them in as far as they help him in the attainment of his end.

If we wish to proceed securely in all things, we must hold fast to the following principle: what seems to be white, I would believe black if the Church defines.

Appendix to 'The Spiritual Exercises'.

In the fourth week, 'instead of giving myself up to penitence I shall aim at preserving temperance and keeping a middle course in all things... The soul ought to establish itself firmly and wisely in a middle position'. In choosing a way of life, 'one should examine the question in all its various aspects and consider which way common sense suggests'. 'We must enter into the exercises with great bravery and great generosity towards our Creator and Lord, offering up to Him our whole will and our whole freedom, for love should consist in works far more than in words'.

Extracts from 'The Spiritual Exercises'.

The Effects of 'The Spiritual Exercises'

The Spiritual Exercises have yet set so many loving hearts on fire and filled the history of the church with heroes.

J. Brodrick, *The Origin of The Jesuits*, 1986.

The exercises aimed to develop willpower to produce active apostles as opposed to quiet contemplatives. By a paradox comparable with that in Calvanism this systematic subordination of the individual personality ended by producing no more dehumanised agents, but instead, men of initiative and originality.

A.G. Dickens, *The Age of Humanism & Reformation*, 1977.

In practice Jesuits evidenced special concern for the conscience of each member of the Society.

L.W. Spitz, *The Protestant Reformation*, 1969.

For most people the effect of following the spiritual exercises was to release a flood of spiritual energy and to engender a feeling of inner well-being. One of the strengths of the exercises was their infinite flexibility. There was no standard formula. Although the published edition achieved widespread circulation in Europe, it was in no sense a self instruction manual. Without careful guidance the publication was largely meaningless. What made the spiritual exercises so influential so the ready availability of well-trained guides to accompany clients through their spiritual journeys. Part of the skill of the guide was in assessing the spiritual needs and abilities of each client and in tailoring the exercises accordingly. Some clients were not, and never would be ready to undertake the full programme.

K. Randell, *The Catholic and Counter Reformations*, 1990.

The Jesuit Contribution to the Reformations

THE FOUNDATION OF THE JESUITS.

From his life as a hermit in the cave near Manresa, Ignatius Loyola set out on a pilgrimage to the Holy Land. From there he went for seven years, 1528–35, to study in the cosmopolitan atmosphere of Paris. Both these experiences gave him an awareness of his world mission. In August 1534, he and five companions climbed to the Chapel of St Denis in Montmartre, where they made their vows of poverty and chastity and determined to undertake a missionary crusade. They also took a vow of absolute obedience to the pope's orders. The six soon became nine and although the Spiritual Exercises were not yet in print, they were very much at the heart of their work.

In 1535 the group left Paris for Italy and they spent the appalling winter of 1538–9 in Rome. Here they tended the sick and looked after the poor and were able to present their Charter of Foundation to Pope Paul III. A Papal Bull of 1540 formally established the Society of Jesus:

> He who desires to fight for God under the banner of the Cross in our society, and to serve God alone and the Roman Pontiff, his Vicar on earth, after a solemn vow of perpetual chastity, shall set this thought before his mind, that he is a part of a society founded for the special purpose of providing for the advancement of souls in Christian life and doctrine and for the propagation of the faith through public preaching and the ministry of the word of God, spiritual exercises and deeds of charity, and particularly through the training of the young and ignorant in Christianity and through the spiritual consolation of the faithful in Christ in hearing confessions; and he shall take care to keep first God and next the purpose of this organisation always before his eyes.

The Society of Jesus grew quickly and in 1541 Ignatius Loyola was elected as General. In Italy houses were established in many cities, including Florence, Venice and Padua. Jesuit preachers found their sermons attended by vast crowds and aristocratic support was quick in coming.

Jesuit training colleges and seminaries were founded in Bologna in 1546, Messina 1548, and Palermo in 1549. In 1550 Ignatius Loyola founded the famous Collegium Romanum in Rome, and two years later the Collegium Germanicum, which was to train priests for missionary work in the Protestant areas of Germany. Similarly in Spain many colleges were established in the 1540s and 1550s such as Valencia in 1544, Barcelona in 1545 and Alcala in 1546, and in Germany too with the help of the Duke of Bavaria, a college at Ingolstadt was founded in 1555 and Munich in 1559. The outstanding leadership of Peter Canisius in Germany was of major importance in the strength of their establishment there. Canisius was, amongst many other things, a phenomenal preacher: it is said that he preached well over 200 sermons in a year in Augsburg itself. Gradually these colleges began to teach not only Jesuit priests but also non-Jesuit pupils.

Ignatius Loyola and his followers always remembered their original aim of missionary work throughout the world. Partly because of their influence with the king of Portugal, Jesuits played the leading role in missionary work in Brazil and Paraguay. They were also the main agents in the Christian missions to Asia, where their great leader was St Francis Xavier, one of the initial group of Loyola's followers in Paris. Xavier followed Loyola to Italy, worked in a hospital for incurable people in Venice and was then made a priest. He led the Portuguese mission to the East Indies, sailing to Southern India in 1542 and preaching for the following three years all along the Indian coast. Following this, he sailed to the Portuguese colonies of Malacca and Ceylon and finally, in 1549, reached Japan where he stayed for another successful year. He finally died of a fever at the age of 46, while preparing to begin a mission to China, but that mission was continued by Matthew Ricci who was received in Peking and honoured for his learning and piety.

The importance of the Jesuits in the Catholic and Counter Reformations cannot be over emphasised. They were the educators of the aristocracy and the confessors of princes. Their missionary work stretched throughout Europe. And their loyalty to the Papacy placed their support firmly behind the reforming Papal leadership of the Council of Trent. 'To a striking degree', says A.G. Dickens, 'the heroic achievements of the Counter Reformation, those which modified the religious map of Europe, were accomplished by the Society of Jesus, which not only checked the further spread of Protestantism but greatly weakened its hold upon southern and central Europe and Poland, the areas where it stood least securely established'. Most important, however, was the Jesuit world mission which contributed so much to the development of Christianity throughout subsequent centuries.

EXAMINING THE EVIDENCE

The Council of Trent

Section 1: Information

The Conciliar Movement of the 15th Century

During the Middle Ages, at times when there were several competing popes, a Council of the Bishops of the Church became the possible controlling body. For example, in 1414 a Council met in the Swiss city of Constance. It deposed the existing competing Popes and argued that their election was not valid. It chose a new pope and established the principle that a General Council of the Church had supreme authority. And it urged that Councils should meet regularly in the future.

Pope Paul III 1534–49

In spite of the fact that popes had control over the church when Councils did not meet, Pope Paul III realised that a Council was necessary. Following the report of his Papal commission in 1537 he understood that to get the whole church together to fight against the Protestants it would be necessary to call a Council. In spite of delays caused by the quarrel between Charles V and Francis I, the first session of the Council of Trent was held in 1545. The Pope preferred a meeting in Italy where he would have more control. Charles V preferred a meeting in Germany. The final compromise was a small, staunchly Catholic town, technically within the Empire, but close to Italy. The Town of Trent is of course today part of the country of Italy.

The Sessions of the Council of Trent				
Meeting	Pope	No. of Sessions	Achievements	No. of Voting Members
1545–9	Paul III	8	Definitions of Church Teaching	72
1551–2	Julius III	3	Definitions of Faith made it impossible to heal rift with Lutherans	59
1562–3	Pius IV	11	Confirmed earlier definitions Reformed Church Discipline	235

Section 2: Achievements of the Council of Trent

Primary Sources

Read the following primary and secondary sources. In spite of the difficulties and defects of the evidence about the Council of Trent, assess its overall achievement.

Source A

Canons of the Council on Authority, 1546.

> The truth and way of living are contained in written books and in unwritten traditions which were received by the Apostles from the mouth of Christ himself or were received by the same Apostles at the dictation of the Holy Spirit and passed on from mouth to mouth until they came down to us, so... this Council receives and venerates, with equal affection and reverence, all the books of the New and Old Testaments since one God is author of both, together with the said traditions, as having been given either from the lips of Christ or by the dictation of the Holy Spirit, and preserved by unbroken succession in the Catholic Church.

Source B

Canons of The Council on Justification by Faith 1546.

> *Canon 12*   If anyone should say that justifying faith is nothing other than trust in the Divine Mercy which remits sins for Christ's sake, or that we are justified by such trust alone, let him be anathema.
>
> *Canon 26*   If anyone should say that for their good works, performed in godly wise, the just ought not to expect and hope for an eternal reward from God, through his mercy in the merits of Jesus Christ... let him be anathema.
>
> *Canon 32*   If anyone should say that the good works of a justified man are so exclusively the gifts of God that they are not also the good merits of the man himself... let him be anathema.

Canon 30   If anyone should say that, for every penitent sinner who receives the grace of justification, of the wiping out the guilt and the debt of eternal punishment means that there remains no debt of temporal punishment to be paid in this world or the next, before he can enter the kingdom of Heaven... let him be anathema.

Source C
Canons of the Council on Transubstantiation.

Since Christ our Redeemer said that which He offered under the appearance of Bread was truly His Body, it has therefore always been held in the Church of God and this Holy Council now declares anew that through consecration of the Bread and Wine there comes about a conversion of the whole substance of the Bread into the substance of the Body of Christ our Lord and the whole substance of the Wine into the substance of His Blood, and this conversion is by the Holy Catholic Church conveniently and properly transubstantiation.

Source D
The Council's Decree on Preaching, 1547.

Bishops, Archbishops, Metropolitans and others responsible for the Churches will be bound and obliged to preach the Holy Gospel of Jesus Christ themselves. Should they be legitimately prevented from doing so they should delegate persons capable of fulfilling this duty. If anyone neglects his obligations in this regard, he should be liable to severe penalties... priests too, parish priests, and all those in whatever manner have been placed in charge of parish churches will see the spiritual nourishment of their people, at least on Sundays and major feast days, either in person or through other capable persons.

Source E
Decree of the Council on Pluralism, 1547.

No one, of whatever dignity, position or pre-eminence, should be so presumptuous as to receive or conserve simultaneously more than one Episcopal Church... for it is quite as much as he can do if a Bishop rule a single Church well for the benefit and salvation of the souls in his care.

Source F
The Decree of the Council on the Establishment of Seminaries to train Priests, 1562.

Canon 18   If they are not well educated, young people are all too easily led astray by the pleasures of the world, thus unless they are formed in piety and religion at the tenderest age, before vicious habits have entirely taken hold of them, it is impossible for them to persevere perfectly in ecclesiastical discipline without the special and powerful protection of Almighty God.

1   Identify what each of the decrees actually said.
2   What difficulties would the church experience in putting the decrees into effect?
3   Which of the decrees quoted here would be most important?

Secondary Sources

Source G

The significance of the Council of Trent extended far beyond its ostensible reforms. Its direct contribution lay chiefly in its attack upon the old problem of clerical education, especially in its provision of a seminary in each Diocese. Yet even more important was its indirect role as the Council to end Councils, as the Council which lay the unquiet ghost of conciliarism and delivered the Church to a long era of Papal monarchy.

A.G. Dickens, *Reformation and Society in 16th Century Europe*, 1966.

Source H

On 5th December 1563, 255 Bishops, representing all the areas that remained Catholic, signed doctrinal and disciplinary decisions that had been taken some times fifteen or seventeen years previously by other Fathers. They therefore took over the work of the entire Council period. They did so with all the more conviction because between 1545–9 and 1562–3 the Fathers present had changed because Pope Paul III and Julius III and Paul IV had done all they could to choose better Bishops.

The greatness of Trent lies in the fact that it met the religious needs of its time... At the time of the pre-reformation western Christianity was living through a profound change. It opened itself to personal piety. It hungered for God... Christian people needed a limpid and reassuring teaching of structured theology which could be imparted only by an invigorated, instructed disciplined clergy, attentive to its pastoral duties. It goes without saying that Trent had no intention of meeting Protestantism half way. Its chief concern was to counter the Protestant challenge and it retained to the end the mentality of a beleaguered citadel. Having established the fact of a rupture it gave those who remained faithful to Rome two things which all western Christians aspired to at the threshold of the modern age: a Catechism and Pastors.

J. Delumeau, *Catholicism Between Luther and Voltaire*, 1977.

Source I

The Catholic Renaissance then found its way obstructed by a variety of factors. The regular rhythm of provincial synods (every three years) and diocesan synods (every year) laid down by the Council and the regular visitations of parishes (each to be inspected every two years) were disregarded... Finally, if the lower clergy were for a long time reluctant to educate themselves, wear clerical dress and teach the Catechism, the higher clergy frequently forgot the first chapter of the reform decree: Cardinals and Prelates will live a simple and frugal life. Wealth remained the great weakness in the higher echelons of the Roman Church.

However, one of Trent's most important reform decisions was undoubtedly that which led to the institution of Seminaries, which immediately proliferated in Italy and Spain. In Italy some twenty Seminaries were inaugurated between 1564 and 1584. In Spain twenty-six other establishments for the formation of the parish clergy were opened between 1565 and 1616. In the low countries eight Seminaries there were before 1620.

J. Delumeau, *Catholicism Between Luther and Voltaire*, 1977.

Source J

Patterns of Attendance.

The statistics reveal a clear pattern. A total of 270 Bishops attended the Council at one time or another. 187 of these were from Italy, 31 were from Spain, 26 were from France (almost all in the third period), and only two were from Germany. The overwhelming Italian attendance at the Council might be interpreted as more evidence of Papal domination. However, it would be a mistake to assume that Papal control was absolute.

K Randell, *The Catholic and Counter Reformations*, 1990.

Section 3: The Case of Cardinal Reginald Pole in 1545

The other perspective on the Council of Trent concludes with the collapse of the eventful but neglected movement in the Catholic Church to avert the Counter Reformation. The object of this movement was to establish reunion with the Protestants in northern Europe...

Pole emerges as the figurehead of that movement, culminating in his experience of defeat at Trent as resulting in recriminations from Italian Protestants and Catholics. The realisation that reunion was intrinsically unattainable marked the moment of deliverance for the Counter Reformation.

Use all the evidence on the Council of Trent above and the material provided in the following section to write a brief history of the Council of Trent as it may have been written from the standpoint of Cardinal Pole.

In May 1545, as the first session of the Council of Trent was due to meet, Pope Paul III clearly believed that the clarification of doctrine was the key priority. On the other hand the Emperor, Charles V, believed that the priority was discipline. He wished to delay the clarification of doctrine until he could get the German Protestants around the table.

The pope had appointed three Presidents for the Council – Cardinals Del Monte and Cervini were to work alongside an Englishman, Cardinal Reginald Pole. In April 1545, the first two were despatched to prepare for the meeting but Cardinal Pole was delayed by the pope in Rome for a further month in order to write a clear paper on the broad aims and procedures of the Council. Cardinal Pole dedicated his treatise, called *De Consilio*, to Cervini and Del Monte. In it Pole saw his main aim as reunification of the church and the broad peace of the Church. In order to achieve this he was perfectly happy to accept Luther's view of justification by faith alone: 'faith justifies', wrote Pole, 'and henceforth love directs men to good works'.

Upon his final arrival at Trent, Pole said and did very little. He was described by another churchman 'as a man who refrained from uttering his mind unless commanded or impelled by necessity to speak'. He was an idealist not a political activist and remote from the greater political cunning of Cervini and Del Monte. When the others decided to start the debate with original sin and justification by faith alone, Pole urgently wished to summon the Lutherans to the Council. He sent to Regensburg to Charles V for advice, but none came. Pole's idealism was defeated and the Canons of the Council record that by 1547 reunion with the Lutherans was impossible.

TALKING POINT

Cardinal Reginald Pole was amongst the many major figures in History who have been defeated.

Is his contribution devalued by his failure? Or is it enriched?

1 Write Pole's last speech at Trent in your own words to capture the drama of his position.
2 Form your own judgement on Cardinal Pole. Did the Catholic church lose when his attempts at compromise with the Lutherans failed?

Cardinal Reginald Pole – An Appeal to the Council of Trent 1546

Each of us should, above all things, keep before his eyes the things that are expected of this Holy Council. Each one will easily see therein what is the duty resting upon him. To put it briefly, these duties are what are contained in the Bull summoning the Council, i.e. the uprooting of heresies, the reformation of ecclesiastical discipline and or morals, and lastly the external peace of the whole church. These are the things we must see to, or rather for which we must untiringly pray in order that by God's mercy they may be done...

Before the tribunal of God's mercy, we, the shepherds, should make ourselves responsible for all the evils now burdening the flock of Christ. The sins of all we should take upon ourselves, not in generosity, but in justice.

The Catholic and Counter Reformations and the People

The Catholic and Counter Reformations affected the behaviour of the laity, the ordinary people of Europe. By the 17th century marriage, baptism and death were all essential processes controlled and administered by the Church. Marriage in the later Middle Ages was a vague and developing social process. Church law allowed two people to agree a private contract, and if it was followed by a sexual relationship, it constituted a Christian marriage. Alternatively, there was a significant variety of customary rites and arrangements which had no power in Church law. Clandestine marriages, like that of Romeo and Juliet, were carried out without parental consent, but with the witness of a priest. Luther had denied that marriage was a sacrament at all: he argued that the clergy should not meddle with the law of marriage and yet that parental consent should be obligatory. In 1563 the matter was debated at the Council of Trent. The chairman, Cardinal Morone, proposed an important solution. In future all marriages should be contracted in the face of the church before the parish priest and witnesses, after the publication of three banns. The marriage would then be entered in a register. All other marriages were to be null and void. Couples were encouraged, but it was not essential, to postpone sexual relations until the marriage had been blessed. As J. Bossy has written in his book *Christianity in the West*, 'it is unclear how far Council was aware that it was enacting a revolution in Christianity... It transformed marriage from a social process which the Church guaranteed to an ecclesiastical process which it administered'.

Baptism was another feature of life through which people in the 14th and 15th centuries sought order amidst chaos. There had long been a tradition of taking the new born child to be exorcised by the priest at the church door. Gradually, by the 14th century, it became customary for the child to be given a name at the baptism which followed this exorcism. This of course became his Christian name and it was common for two godparents to be asked to give the child the name. A century later,

Catholic priests were increasingly insisting that the name be that of one of the Saints and they opposed severely the suggestion of an alternative name – even when this was a way of continuing a powerful family tradition. This led to the development of surnames to enable family traditions to be maintained. Catholic priests also introduced baptismal registers in order to prevent the marriage of closely related kin.

Death too remained part of the church. When a villager died the bell was tolled and the neighbourhood was encouraged to drop what it was doing and follow the priest to the bedside. The priest might spend time alone before death, but afterwards the whole village would take part in the funeral procession to the church. Many traditional rites also continued: the laying out of the body, the procession to the church, and so on. Once inside the church, the saying of a Mass for the soul of the dead was obligatory for all ranks of society. It is no surprise that one of the major holy days throughout this period was the day of All Souls, where prayers were said for the souls of all those dead people who no longer had friends to pray for them. On this day, all over Europe church bells rang throughout the night, candles were lit, cakes were laid on graves, bonfires were lit in the churchyard. Briefly, during this feast, souls would be released from their torments and seek warmth and kindness with their friends. Hot metal ovens would be covered up so that souls, naked, could not burn themselves. All these rites and practises continued through the 16th century. Wisely, the church continued to provide order in death.

Of course, many traditional rites of the ordinary people were now considered by the educated classes to be 'ignorance and superstition, a lack of basic doctrinal knowledge, or some movement towards magical belief and practice'. The reform movement within the Catholic church sought, through the Inquisition, to control such practises. The Roman Inquisition after the Council of Trent witnessed an intensive period of heresy trials from 1540 to 1570, but after this date most offences concerned magic and superstition. The major categories of error which the Inquisition pursued were magical healing, love magic and divination, and the largest number of cases were directives against healers, such healers were often deposed by their clients, perhaps because their healing was unsuccessful.

In addition, censorship began to develop the process of thought control which made many parts of Europe into 'closed societies' by the second half of the 16th century. This was particularly true in Spain. A Dominican judge, defending the Spanish Inquisition in Rome, declared

> it is as impossible to err by being too active in prohibiting works by these moderns full of a thousand innovations, as it is easy to make a mistake by acting timidly and late. Ever since they began to practise this perverse excess of printing books, the Church has been greatly damaged and every day it is confronted by greater and more obvious perils, as men exchange the ancient and secure doctrine of the virtuous doctors for the sophisticated and adulterated of the moderns.

A FRENCH ENGRAVING CRITICAL OF THE WORK OF THE SPANISH INQUISITION.

TALKING POINT

We live in a society where certain materials – books and films – have been subject to censorship, or banned outright. What are the usual effects of such censorship. Is censorship ever wise?

TALKING POINT

Is it fair to suggest that Counter Reformation Historians have concentrated on Italy and Spain and neglected achievements elsewhere?

Consequently, the Spanish Inquisition placed commissioners in all of the sea ports and along the frontiers with France. They were responsible for examining the merchandise carried aboard, ships and carts, in order to prevent banned books from entering the country. Moreover, in 1558 bookshops were placed under supervision. Regular inspections were carried out each time a new index was established, and by 1605 Spanish booksellers were forced to maintain a list of all the books they had sold.

A fundamental theme which ran throughout the Catholic and Counter Reformations was the need of laymen to perceive order in a chaotic, distressing, and uncomfortable world. The renewal of the Roman Catholic Church in the 16th Century could provide that order. Before the Catholic and Counter Reformations, in the words of L.W. Spitz, 'a religious chasm was developing between the growth in religious intensity on the popular level and the inability of institutional church to satisfy those powerful religious impulses stirring throughout society... The failure of the Church of the Renaissance Popes to respond created a revolutionary situation'. This revolutionary situation produced the Catholic Reformation and the Catholic Reformation affected the lives and behaviour of the people of Europe.

The Reforming Popes of the Catholic and Counter Reformations

Pope Paul III 1534–49

- Appointed many new cardinals, like John Fisher, Contarini, Carafa and Pole.
- Set up the Commission of enquiry into the state of the church in 1537.
- Finally summoned the Church Council to Trent in 1545.
- Fostered the Ursulites, the Barnabites and others.
- Approved the constitution of the Jesuits.
- Supported overseas missions.
- Enriched the Vatican library.
- Appointed Michelangelo as the chief architect of St Peter's in Rome.
- In 1540 he discovered 80 absentee bishops in Rome and ordered them to return to their sees.

Pope Paul IV 1555–9

- He was formerly the Inquisitor Cardinal Carafa.
- Presided over harsh punishment of heretics, absentee bishops and prostitutes.
- Sent wandering monks to the galleys.
- The *Index* of Proscribed Books (1559) included all of Erasmus' works and all translations of the Bible into the vernacular.
- He expanded the Roman Inquisition – burning many heretics.
- When he died, the Roman people burnt the records of the Inquisition.

TALKING POINT

Did Pope Paul IV establish 'thought control' in Rome? Did a 'closed society' exist elsewhere in Europe at this time?

Pope Pius IV 1559–65

- Brought the Council of Trent to a successful confession, with emphasis on a Papal monarch – popes to implement decrees.
- Encouraged Charles Borroneo in his work with the sick and poor of Milan.
- Continued the work of the Inquisition.

Pope Pius V 1565–72

- Supported Roman Inquisition.
- Removed traces of Protestantism of Italy.
- Persecuted sorcerers and homosexuals.
- Abolished annates, indulgences and preaching.
- Reduced Papal Curia from 1000 to 500 members.
- Enforced clerical discipline and episcopal residence in Italy, Portugal and Netherlands.
- Great financial support to Spanish victory at Lepanto.
- Congratulated Alva on Council of Blood in Netherlands.
- Deposed Elizabeth I in 1570.
- Encouraged Charles IX of France to kill Huguenots.

Pope Gregory XIII 1572–85

- Encouraged missions against heretics in Northern Europe.
- Re-endowed all Jesuit colleges in Rome.
- Encouraged Guise in battles against Protestants in France.
- Sent emissary to Ireland to plot against Elizabeth I.
- Encouraged Edmund Campion in his mission to England.

Pope Sixtus V 1585–90

- Supported Sigismund III with Catholics in Poland.
- Urged the Duke of Savoy to attack Geneva.
- Began discussions which led to Henry IV of France to convert to Catholicism.
- In 1587 he set up congregations in Rome – these ministries or departments created important functions: food supply, roads and bridges, criminal justice. Others led the religious efforts of Rome in the Inquisition, the enforcement of decrees of the Council of Trent.

REVIEW

The Achievement of the Catholic and Counter Reformations

Now that you have read all the evidence in this chapter, assess the contribution of each of the following to the Catholic and Counter Reformations. Rank them in order of their contribution, with no equals. Explain why you place each in the order they come.

- The Spiritual Exercises.
- Bishop Ghiberti of Verona.
- The Educational Work of the Jesuits.
- The Papal Commission of 1536–7.
- Pope Sixtus V.
- The Roman Inquisition.
- The Sessions of the Council of Trent.
- The Developments in Popular Culture which resulted from the renewal of the Church.

Essay

'How far is it possible to argue that the main purpose of the Catholic and Counter Reformations was the defeat of Lutheranism?'

Use the six stages to plan and write this essay. In Stage 2, draft your outline plan around the following questions.

- In what ways was its purpose to defeat Lutheranism?
- What limitations are there in this?
- What other purposes lay behind these Reformations?

11 The Religious Wars in France, 1559–89

PREVIEW

The Nature of the Religious Wars

What then can we learn of the goals of popular religious violence? What were the crowds intending to do and why did they think they must do it? Their behaviour suggests, first of all, a goal akin to preaching: the defence of true doctrine and the refutation of false doctrine through dramatic challenges and tests... 'Look' cries a weaver in Tournai as he seizes the elevated host from the priest, 'deceived people, do you believe this is the King, Jesus Christ the true God? Look' and he crumbles the wafer and escapes...

Catholic crowds in Angers answer this kind of claim to truth by taking a French Bible – well bounded and gilded, seized in the home of a rich merchant – and parading it through the streets on the end of a halberd. 'There's the truth hung, there's the truth of the Huguenots the truth of all the devils'. Then, throwing it into the river, 'there's the truth of all the devils drowned' and if the Huguenots' doctrine was true why didn't the Lord come and save them from their killers? So a crowd of Orlean Catholics taunted its victim in 1572: 'Where is your God, where are your prayers and psalms? Let Him save you if He can'.

N.Z. Davis, 'The Rites of Violence', from *Society and Culture in Early Modern France*, 1975.

The death of Francis II obliged the Guises to step down from their position of authority in the State, for his brother, Charles IX who succeeded him, was only 10 years old so that a Regent had to be appointed. By custom the Regency should have belonged to the first Prince of the Blood, Antoine of Navarre, but he had forfeited his position by his recent intrigues. Thus it was the Queen Mother, Catherine de Medici, who assumed the Regency. She was forty-one years old and free of any compromise in commitment to either the Bourbon or the Guise. Her main wish was to preserve the independence of the throne and in order to achieve this she strove to maintain a fine, if uneasy, balance between the two families, favouring each in turn.

R.J. Knecht, *The French Wars of Religion*, 1989.

It was about 8.00 a.m. when the King, sitting naked on his stool, except for a dressing gown over his shoulders, was informed that a monk from Paris wished to speak to him. Hearing that his guards were barring the monk's way, he angrily ordered the monk to be admitted, saying that otherwise he would be accused in Paris of chasing monks away. The Jacobean monk, with knife hidden up his sleeve, entered and introduced himself to the King, who, having just risen, had not yet fastened his breaches. After making a deep bow the monk handed to the King a letter from the Count of Brien, who was then a prisoner in Paris, and said that he had also been charged to convey an important secret message to him. The King, believing he was in no danger from such a weedy little monk, ordered his attendants to withdraw. He opened the letter and began reading it whereupon the monk seeing the King thus engrossed, pulled out his knife and plunged it deeply into the King's stomach just above the navel. With a great effort the King pulled it out and struck the monk's left eyebrow with its point, at the same time he shouted 'Ah, the wicked monk has killed me! Kill him!' The King's guards and others hearing his shouts rushed into the room and those nearest the Jacobean felled him to the ground at the King's feet.

Pierre de L'Estoile, *Journal of the Reign of Henry III*, written in Paris in 1593.

The French Wars of Religion lasted from 1559 until 1593. Their origins stretch back into earlier decades and their consequences reach out into the succeeding centuries. They were amongst the most bloody and dramatic of civil wars.

The French Religious Wars 1559–92: An Overview

1559–62 – The Crisis of the Monarchy

Death of King Henry II. His wife, Catherine de Medici acts as Regent for young Francis II and Charles IX. Guise influence threatens Huguenots. Much religious violence.

1562–70 – First Three Civil Wars

Taking up arms, desultory skirmishes and small battles, religious violence. Unsatisfactory peace treaties that satisfied neither Catholics nor Protestants. Each side seeking allies abroad.

First Civil War 1562–3
Death of Antoine of Navarre and Assassination of Duke of Guise.
Peace of Amboise 1563.
Second Civil War 1567–8
Battle of St Denis.
Peace of Longjumeau 1568.
Third Civil War 1568–70
Battles of Jarnac and Montcontour.
Peace of St Germain 1570.

CATHERINE DE MEDICI.

1572 – Massacres of St Bartholomew's Eve and Assassination of Coligny

1572–7 – Fourth, Fifth and Sixth Civil Wars

Regional civil wars between Guise and Catholic League and Huguenot opponents. Firmer peace treaties than earlier.

Fourth and Fifth Civil Wars 1572–6
Indecisive. Charles IX replaced by Henry III.
Peace of Monsieur (1576) gave Huguenots much religious freedom.
Sixth Civil War 1576–7
Catholic League fought back. Peace of Bergerac 1577. Limited Huguenot worship, except in Huguenot areas. Peace lasted for seven years.

1585–9 – War of the Three Henrys

International war between Henry of Guise, the Catholic League, the city of Paris and Spain against Henry of Navarre, Henry III, the Netherlands and England. Death of Henry III in 1589 resulted in ascension of Huguenot Henry IV.

1589–93 – Henry IV Victories over Catholic League and Spain

Kings of France in the 16th Century

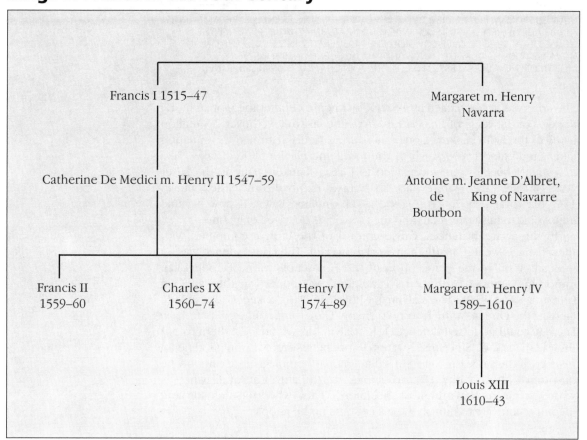

The Crisis of the Monarchy 1559–62

ON 30 JUNE 1559, KING HENRY II PLAYED A PERSONAL ROLE IN A BRILLIANT
TOURNAMENT HELD IN PARIS. THE TOURNAMENT WAS IN CELEBRATION OF THE
DOUBLE MARRIAGE OF HIS SISTER AND HIS DAUGHTER AND OF PEACE WITH SPAIN.
DURING THE EVENT HE WAS STRUCK VIOLENTLY IN THE FACE BY A LANCE, SUFFERING
INJURIES FROM WHICH HE DIED TWO DAYS LATER. HIS SON, FRANCIS II, BECAME KING
AT THE AGE OF FIFTEEN, BUT SUCH WAS HIS IMMATURITY THAT IN PRACTICE THE
HOUSE OF GUISE TOOK OVER CONTROL. THE HUGUENOTS, INCLUDING THE KING OF
NAVARRE AND THE DUKE OF CONDE AND THE HUGUENOT NEPHEWS OF
MONTMORENCY, THE CELEBRATED COLIGNY AND CHATILLON, WERE SIDELINED.

The crisis was accompanied by a period of intense debt for the monarchy. By
the end of the reign of Francis I in 1547, the crown owed over 2.5 million
livres to the Lyon bankers alone, and during Henry II's reign the situation
had deteriorated badly. Much of the *taille* and all the indirect taxes, like
aides and *gabelle*, were mortgaged to foreign bankers. During the latter
years of Henry II's reign, extraordinary taxes had had to be raised, but in
1559 the royal debt to Lyon stood at 11.7 million livres. It now became
impossible to raise new loans and the crown was deprived of income.

In these circumstances, Guise control of the crown, combined with
their family's wealth, made them very powerful. The consequence was an
intensification of the persecution of the Huguenots. Anne Dubourg, an
important member of the Paris Parlement, was burned at the stake on
Christmas Eve 1559. The Calvinist Church in Paris asked Catherine de
Medici, the Queen Mother, to help them. They were confused as to how
far they could go in self defence. John Calvin himself advised them to put
their faith in God. 'Since magistrates cannot be resisted without God being
resisted at the same time, it seems that an unarmed magistrate can only be
despised with impunity... We are subject to the authority of all who, by
whatever means, have control of affairs... They who rule unjustly and
incompetently are to punish the wickedness of the people'.

THE THREE GUISE BROTHERS.

Since the support of leading Huguenots was to no avail the younger nobility, led by the Duke de la Renaudi, a petty nobleman, took their own action in the autumn of 1559. They conspired to defeat the Guise in the so-called 'Tumult of Amboise'. Their conspiracy aimed to remove the Guise and place the Duke of Conde in power. The plot came to nothing and in 1560 Catherine de Medici published the Edict of Amboise, granting a pardon and release for all religious prisoners.

The dramatic death of Francis II in December 1560 released pent-up passions. His successor Charles IX was just ten years old and Catherine de Medici now assumed the Regency and overturned the power of the Guise. 'Her main wish', as R. J. Knecht has said, 'was to preserve the independence of the throne, and in order to achieve this she strove to maintain a fine, if uneasy, balance between the two families, favouring each in turn'. The Huguenots were now given an opportunity at court and in the country. Conde and Coligny became members of the King's Council and Antoine of Navarre was appointed Lieutenant General of the kingdom in place of the Duke of Guise. The Guise replied with force. They set up the Triumvirate with other leading nobles, and religious riots and disturbances took place all over the country. Catherine and her chancellor wanted peace. 'Let us', the Chancellor said, 'banish those devilish names Luther and Huguenot and Papist which breed only faction and sedition; let us retain only one name, Christian'.

The situation was now tense and Catherine summoned all important factions to the Colloquy of Poissy in September 1561, with the aim of bringing together both Catholics and Calvinists. But she was not successful. The failure of the Colloquy of Poissy set France on the final road to the religious wars.

The First Three Civil Wars, 1562–70

THE MASSACRE AT VASSY.

In March 1562, the Duke of Guise returned from a meeting with the Duke of Wurttemberg in Germany. In the village of Vassy, he encountered hundreds of Huguenots worshipping in a barn. The Catholics claimed they were pelted with stones and that the duke was hit in the face. The Huguenots denied the claim. The Catholic soldiers certainly fired on the worshippers and caused significant casualties. The barn was set on fire and many died. The consequences were significant: the Guise and Montmorency returned to Paris in triumph and the Huguenots, in desperation, resorted to arms.

During the first war, Conde, the Huguenot leader, established his headquarters in the mid-Loire valley and immediately captured Orleans, Lyon and several other important cities. Religious passions were now raised, with both sides resorting to violence in many local communities. In December, the Huguenots pushed north into Normandy reinforced by 7000 German mercenaries, and attempted to link up with an army from England. The Catholics, led by Montmorency, barred their way at Dreux. In the battle Montmorency and Conde were taken prisoner.

KING CHARLES IX OF FRANCE.

In February 1563, the Duke of Guise was assassinated and Coligny was accused of the crime. Although he consistently denied his involvement, a family feud immediately developed between the Guise and Chatillon houses. In March 1563 both sides agreed to the Peace of Amboise. This allowed freedom of conscience for Huguenots, but limited their rights of worship. Nobles were granted complete freedom of worship, but the lower classes could only worship within their own houses.

In 1564 Charles IX came of age and he and his mother went on a two-year progress throughout France, during which they met the Duke of Alva, the representative of King Philip of Spain, at Bayonne. This fuelled the worst Huguenot fears and a further war seemed inevitable. At the Battle of Saint Denis in November, the Huguenots were defeated and the Peace of Longjumeau was signed in March 1568, renewing the terms of Amboise. Yet even this was viewed as only a temporary cessation. Conde and Coligny, fearing a Catholic plot, fled with their followers to La Rochelle, making the western port their new headquarters. At the Battle of Jarnac, they were defeated by the Royalists and Conde was killed. Coligny now took over the leadership of the Huguenot cause and tried to convince Charles IX that the civil war in France was a Spanish plot to draw French attention away from the Netherlands. He encouraged King

GASPARD DE COLIGNY.

Charles to provide religious freedom for Huguenots and to move his attention towards the Netherlands and the war with Spain. From this time, the French wars were inexplicably tied to the Spanish wars in the Netherlands.

In 1570 the Peace of St Germain ended the first main phase of the wars. Huguenots were granted four security towns for two years, and were allowed freedom of conscience throughout the realm and freedom of worship in a number of other cities. They were also given access to universities and schools and all confiscated property was to be returned to them. The peace treaty made possible a reconciliation between the crown and the Protestants.

FOCUS

11.1 The Issue of Violence in the Religious Wars

Throughout the religious wars in France, crowd violence was endemic. It was particularly severe in the years 1561–2 and in 1572. We need to understand what lay behind such violence In these early years of the wars.

How is it possible for people to engage in large-scale killing? How is it possible for whole communities to plan blood-thirsty murders? How is it possible to forget that your victims are human beings? These questions are particularly important in a civil war when the victims were fellow members of local and national communities and they are still important today.

Natalie Zemon Davis, in her article 'The Rites of Violence', has addressed these questions, suggesting that only after 'a process of dehumanisation' can people perpetrate such violence. This dehumanisation can result from the rites and rituals of religion. It is not a fellow human being you are mutilating, but rather an agent of the devil.

'The Calvinists have polluted their hands with every kind of sacrilege men can think of' writes a Doctor of Theology in 1562. Not long after, a man seizes the elevated host with his 'polluted hands' and crushes it under foot. The worshippers beat him up and deliver him to the agents of the Parlement. The extent to which Protestants could be viewed as vessels of pollution is suggested by a popular belief about the origin of the nickname Huguenots. In the city of Tours, Huguet was the generic name for ghosts, who, instead of spending their time in purgatory, came back to rattle doors and haunt and harm people at night. Protestants went out at night to their lascivious conventicles, and so the priests and people began to call them Huguenots in Tours, and then elsewhere. Protestants were thus as sinister as the spirits of the dead.

N.Z. Davis, 'The Rites of Violence'.

The Protestant sense of Catholic pollution also stemmed to some extent from their sexual uncleanness, here specifically of the clergy. Protestant polemic never tired of pointing to the lewdness of the clergy with their concubines. It was rumoured that the church in Lyon had an organisation of hundreds of women at the disposition of priests and canons, and an observer pointed out with disgust, how, after the first religious wars, the mass and the brothel re-entered Rouen together. But more serious than the sexual abominations of the clergy was the diabolic magic of the mass. The mass is 'vile filth', 'no people pollute the House of the Lord in every way more than the clergy'. Protestant converts talked of their own past lives as a time of befoulment and dreaded contamination from catholic churches and rites.

N.Z. Davis, 'The Rites of Violence'.

1 Why did certain individuals in 16th century France commit acts of violence?

2 Why do crowds go further than individuals may do?

3 What religious factors underpinned the violence? What other factors did so?

Many crowds involved in violence also believed that they were following the official line of the government. Often, clerics and political officers were active members of the crowd. In Lyon in 1562, the Calvinist Pastor John Ruffy took part in the sack of the cathedral with a sword in his hand. In Rouen in 1560, the priests walked alongside their parishioners in a Corpus Christi parade, and then broke into the houses of Protestants who refused to honour the procession. Priests and pastors encouraged violence against the other side in their sermons. A Huguenot preacher at Sens was said to have told his congregation 'to exterminate Papal vermin would be a great sacrifice to God'. In Bordeaux in 1572 the Jesuit Priest, Emond Auger, preached that the Angel of the Lord had already executed God's judgement in Paris and other cities and must now do so in Bordeaux. Three days after his sermon massacres started in the city.

The experience of singing the psalms together in French in a large armed group intent on challenging the religious practices of the world around it, the very experience of being part of a Corpus Christi day procession at a time when danger threatened the sanctity of the host – these processional experiences in themselves would feed a popular certitude that the group did indeed have the right on occasion to move into the realm of violence for the sake of religion.

Almost every type of public religious event has a disturbance associated with it. The sight of a statue of the Virgin at a crossroads provokes a Protestant group to mockery of those who reverence Her. The fight ensues. Catholics hide in a house to entrap Huguenots who refuse to doff their hats to a Virgin nearby and then rush out and beat up the heretics.

Baptism: In Manur a Protestant family has its baby baptised on All Souls Day, according to the new Reformed rite. With the help of an aunt, a group of Catholics steals it away for re-baptism. A drunkard sees the father and the godfather and other Protestants discussing the event in the streets. 'Here are the Huguenots who have come to massacre us'. A crowd assembles, the tocsin is rung and a three hour battle takes place.

Funeral: In Toulouse, at Easter time, a Protestant carpenter tried to bury his Catholic wife by the new Reformed rite. A Catholic crowd seizes the corpse and buries it. The Protestants dig it up and re-bury it. The bells are rung and with great noise, a Catholic crowd assembles with staves and sticks. Fighting ensues.

Even in the extreme cases of religious violence, crowds do not act in a mindless way. They have a sense that what they are doing is legitimate.

EXAMINING THE EVIDENCE

The Massacres of St Bartholomew's Eve 1572: A Study in Recent Historiography

Source A

Catherine's new policy employed a suspension of internal disagreement and a war against Spain in alliance with the heretics of England and the Netherlands. This would have been a daring, and yet in a way a traditional plan. Catherine however withdrew her support almost before it was under way. The reason was as follows.

Coligny had come to court in 1571 and Charles IX had fallen completely under his influence and had allowed him to organise a Huguenot expedition against the Spanish. The troops met disaster at Mons... Coligny must be removed.

Catherine moved swiftly. In August 1572 all the nobility were in Paris for the wedding of her daughter Margaret and the Huguenot, Henry of Navarre. There can be very little doubt that she organised the Guise family to carry out their blood feud and assassinate Coligny. Unfortunately for Catherine, Coligny, shot from a window by an arquebusier, was only wounded and the King supported the demand for a full inquiry. It seemed to the Queen Mother that the only way to maintain her influence was to conceal the lesser crime by a greater. Charles was persuaded of the existence of a Huguenot plot against him. On the morning of August 14th a general slaughter of Huguenots in Paris took place, arranged by the Duke of Guise, with Royal approval. The news spread to the provinces where many towns followed suit. Coligny died and so did about four thousand Huguenots in Paris, and perhaps as many more in the rest of France.

P.J. Helm, *History of Europe*, 1961.

Source B

As the weeks of peace passed, the Queen Mother came to view with alarm Coligny's growing influence at Court, the more so in the light of her obsessive fear of Spanish arms. She also resented the personal arrogance of the Huguenot leader, who was reported as advising the King to liberate himself from her tutelage. Though Catherine had so often been compelled to work with the Guise, her attitude had hitherto deserved respect because she had sincerely aimed at the restoration of national unity and order under the crown. Yet in August 1572 she determined to take a short cut and plotted with Anjou and Henry of Guise to assassinate Coligny amid the festivities surrounding the marriage of her daughter Margaret with the young Henry of Navarre. In the event, Coligny was merely wounded, and the conspirators decided, probably on the spur of the moment, to cover their traces by organising a greater crime and committing the nation to a new war against the Protestants. Inventing the Huguenot plot, they prevailed upon the hysterical King to authorise a general attack upon the Huguenot leaders assembled for the wedding. On the fatal day, August

24th, Henry of Guise personally supervised the killing of Coligny while the Paris mob, completely out of hand, butchered a thousand or more victims. Henry of Navarre escaped only by pretending to abjure Protestantism. In other places the action depended on local circumstances. At Orleans a massacre was perpetrated by command of the City Council, while at Lyon the Governor sought to protect the Huguenots, yet was thrust aside by popular revolt. At Montpellier, Bayonne and Nimes, the authorities preserved order and no killing occurred. The total number of victims throughout France cannot be closely computed, but it is generally thought to have exceeded ten thousand.

A.G. Dickens, *The Age of Humanism and Reformation*,1977.

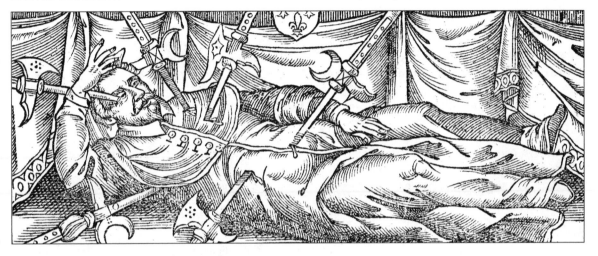

ENGRAVING SHOWING THE ASSASSINATION OF GASPARD DE COLIGNY.

1 What different murders may have taken place in August 1572?
2 Who seems to have been responsible for these murders? What were their motives?
3 What literary techniques does Dickens use to make his a dramatic account?

Source C

The burning question, therefore, which came to dominate all others, was that of war with Spain. To Coligny the King was irretrievably committed and war was in any case inevitable. There were, however, compelling reasons why Charles was unable or unwilling to declare publicly in favour of war. Not only was the powerful Catholic faction against the war, but also Catherine, the marshalls, and the entire Council with the sole exception of Coligny. Charles was therefore committed to a policy that he refused to avow and was unable to execute... The precipitation of the war in the Netherlands, before anything in France was ready for the enterprise, produced a series of crises through the summer which ended in the massacre of St Bartholomew.

In order to ratify the English Treaty, the Court reassembled in Paris at the beginning of June 1572. Coligny, flanked by three hundred horsemen, arrived on the 6th June. In facing the extreme danger of Paris, Coligny had two purposes. One was to persuade the King, in view of what had happened, to allow him to go to the Netherlands. He believed that if he did not go Alva would have extinguished all resistance within a couple of months. It was then to be feared that he would turn on France... Coligny's second reason for braving the City of Paris was to see the English Ambassadors who arrived on the 8th June... Before the English departed on the 22nd June the Council began a long debate on the problem of war with Spain. All in the Council strongly opposed war. Coligny continued to press the King for an open declaration, but in vain. It was then that he determined, if necessary, to go alone to the Netherlands... If Coligny did not leave in time and with adequate forces, Orange would be overthrown. In that case, not only would Charles have been unable to protect the Huguenots, but all France as well as England would have been in grave danger. The forces of Catholicism might then have won the desperate struggle of the 16th century in which power and ideology were inseparably joined.

4 How does Sutherland explain the massacre of St Bartholomew's Eve?

The situation was now explosive. Coligny's planned departure on the 25th August might – just – have been in time. He had to await the Royal Wedding on the 23rd August.

The massacre of St Bartholomew comprised three distinctive events. The first was an abortive attack on Coligny on Friday morning 22nd August. The second was the murder of Coligny, together with his principal followers, during the night of Saturday 23rd/24th August. This was followed or accompanied by the massacre in the popular sense.

On 26th August, Charles made a statement in the Parlement to the effect that everything had been done on his instructions. Thus, although Charles was probably innocent of Huguenot blood, in any direct sense, the Crown was disastrously implicated in the massacre, for which it incurred the responsibility.

N.M. Sutherland, *The Huguenot Struggle for Recognition*, 1980.

Source D

Coligny was an enemy of Spain, also of international Catholicism as a politico-religious movement, which, in 1571–72 at least, was more actively promoted from Rome than from Madrid. The reason why Coligny had to die just then, having contrived to evade or otherwise survive all previous attempts to despatch him, was because he had command of an impending invasion of the Netherlands. Indeed, he actually had Royal permission to depart in the week beginning 25th August... One way therefore of describing the second and fortuitous stage of the massacre would be as the elimination of those who were about to invade the Netherlands, and therefore, about to make war on Spain.

N.M. Sutherland, *Princes, Politics and Liberty*, 1984.

Source E

Early in June the Council reassembled... The majority of the Council were opposed to war with Spain. Among the papers presented, was that prepared by John De Morvillier, which carried the greatest weight. He reasoned boldly that if the Crown lacked authority to keep the peace at home, it was in no position to wage foreign war. He spoke of the disruption of trade, the impoverishment of the nobility, the oppression of the peasantry, and the uncertainty of English intentions.

The Bourbon marriage was celebrated on 18th August. Four days later an assassin shot down the Admiral, but failed to wound him mortally. The implication of the Guise seems probable, but the extent to which Catherine was also involved remains a matter of conjecture. The

Huguenot nobility, who had gathered in Paris for the wedding, clamoured for justice against the perpetrators and the King promised them satisfaction. His Mother seems to have played a major role in the sudden transformation that then occurred. If her resentment at Coligny's ascendancy over the King and her fear of war with Spain had decided her to support the assassination attempt, its failure placed her in a perilous situation. On 23rd August she deliberated with Anjou, Tavannes, Nevers, Retz and Birague, the new Keeper of the Seals. Somehow, as a result of these discussions, Charles IX was persuaded that the Huguenots were not merely threatening indignantly to take the punishment of the Guise into their own hands but intended to overthrow the ruling dynasty itself. He therefore sanctioned the summary execution of the Protestant leaders... The massacre was not of course limited to the high Huguenot nobles. Its extension was the consequence of summoning the city militia to take part in the killings, for the Protestant presence in the capital was too formidable for the Guisards and the Royal Guards to accomplish the work on their own. Thus, what had been intended as a purge of the Huguenot leadership, became, with the unleashing of fanatical popular passions, a blood bath in which all Protestants, and some who were not Protestant at all, served as victims.

J.H.M. Salmon, *Society in Crisis*, 1975.

A 16TH-CENTURY GERMAN WOODCUT DEPICTING THE ST BARTHOLOMEW'S DAY MASSACRE.

Source F

Historians are now generally agreed that the series of massacres that took place throughout France in August and September were not the product of a pre-meditated royal scheme to exterminate the Huguenots. Even when Charles IX succumbed to his mother's brow-beating on the night of August 23rd and ordered the murder of the leading Protestant noblemen gathered at court for the marriage, he neither expected nor desired the general massacre which subsequently ensued. The King's orders for a selective strike were distorted into a call for a general massacre by ultra-Catholic elements at court and in Parisian municipal government. What developed in Paris and then spread to a dozen provincial cities were mass religious riots essentially similar in motivation to the numerous disorders which had already punctured the country's tranquility, albeit of far greater proportions.

Correspondence between Charles IX and Rouen's municipal officials corroborates that the King did not wish the violence to spread beyond a limited strike against the few Huguenot leaders. On August 24th, shortly after the mass bloodbath began in Paris, Charles wrote to the Lieutenant General in Rouen. 'I pray you, as soon as you receive this present letter, to have announced in every area under your charge that everybody is to remain in peace and security in his house, not taking up arms or giving offence to one another on pain of death'. The Lieutenant General immediately reported the contents of this letter to the local Council and to the authorities of other cities. Several days later, in response to another letter from the King, local Protestants were rounded up and imprisoned for their own protection. Many went willingly, thinking themselves more secure, others chose to leave immediately for the safety of England. Thus the city authorities managed to maintain order within Rouen for almost four weeks following the massacre in Paris.

What finally broke this calm and touched off the local massacre on September 17th? Here is where the sources are mute. In many provincial cities the violence was sparked by the arrival of couriers bearing reports that the King wished the Protestants exterminated... Perhaps the arrival of such reports precipitated Rouen's massacre. Perhaps a group of hardened Catholics simply decided, after waiting in vain for four weeks for such a royal command, that they had better strike in any case on 17th September. All that is known for sure is that on that day Catholic zealots gained control of the city, locked the gates to prevent Calvinists from escaping, broke into the jail where they were being detained, and systematically butchered them... The mob then gave itself over to its organised campaign of looting and violence which lasted for four days. Estimates of the number of those killed ranged from three to four hundred to around five hundred.

P. Benedict, *Rouen During the Wars of Religion*, 1981.

5 According to Philip Benedict (source F), what explains the massacre in Rouen?

6 What links are suggested here between religious wars and popular riots? Does any evidence support the notion of class war?

Source G

These encounters are as nothing compared to the disturbances that cluster around processional life. Corpus Christi Day, with its crowds, coloured banners and great crosses, was the chance for Protestants not to put rugs in front of their doors, for Protestant women to sit ostentatiously in their windows spinning, for heroic individuals to throw themselves on the 'God of paste' so as to 'destroy Him in every parish in the world'. Corpus Christi Day was the chance for a procession to turn into an assault on, and slaughter of, those who had so offended the Catholic faith, its participants shouting as in Lyon in 1561 'for the Flesh of God we must kill all the Huguenots'. A Protestant procession was a parade of armed men and women in their dark clothes going off to services at their temple or outside the city gates singing psalms and spiritual songs, that to Catholic ears sounded like insults against the Church and her sacraments. It was an occasion for children to throw stones, for an exchange of scandalous words, and then finally for fighting. Sometimes the two processions encountered each other as in Sens in 1562. The Calvinists would not give way and insisted upon passing through the centre of the Catholic procession. The groups confronted each other again after the services and the Catholics, aided by processions from peasant villages, prevailed in a bloody battle.

N.Z. Davis, 'The Rites of Violence', in *Culture and Society in Early Modern France*, 1975.

Source H

Social-occupational of Male Victims in Contemporary Listings of 1572 Massacres						
City	Nobles	Lawyers	Merchants	Teachers	Artisans	Unskilled	Unknown
Bourges	–	7	6	–	8	–	2
Meaux	–	5	13	–	10	1	–
Troyes	–	1	11	–	22	2	–
Orleaus	2	15	50	2	47	11	15
Rouen	3	9	18	3	119	3	31
Lyon	–	6	34	3	88	5	5
Paris	36	14	13	5	40	2	11

Is Janine Estèbe right in suggesting that the 1572 massacres were also an expression of class hatred?

Quoted in N.Z. Davis, 'The Rites of Violence', in *Culture and Society in Early Modern France*, 1975.

Source I

Almost every religious movement finds it useful and perhaps necessary to protect and treasure the memory of martyrs. Martyrs are men and women honoured for facing savage persecution, even death, solely for their ideas and affiliations. Detailed and highly dramatic records of their sufferings are carefully preserved by their followers... In our own day we can observe creations of scores of martyrs. Perhaps the most striking example is provided by the International Jewish Community, which has devoted energy and resources to preparing careful records of the horrifying holocaust of European Jews, perpetrated by the Government of Nazi Germany. Modern Jewish spokesmen use these records for two purposes: to make sure that no-one of any background ever forgets this appalling example of the depth to which the persecution of innocent beings can descend, and to strengthen, amongst Jews, a sense of identity and worth, particularly as those sentiments can be used to build and support the State of Israel.

The various factions into which the Christian community of Europe split as a consequence of the Protestant Reformation, felt a similar need to protect and validate their identities, by developing cults of their martyrs... Jean Crespin, a French Calvinist publisher, provided a more traditional form of martyrology that emphasised gory descriptions of how Protestants were put to death by 16th century Catholic governments...

The record of the St Bartholomew's massacre was primarily the creation of Calvinist refugees from Catholic France. It was entrusted to the relatively new medium of print in a number of loosely connected publishing centres, the most important of which was Calvinist Geneva. Co-ordination of this drive to develop a full record of the massacres came primarily from Geneva, which in this, as in so many other areas, was the most effective single source of leadership for the International Reform Movement. The most complete single source of our knowledge of the reactions to the St Bartholomew's massacres, is a collection assembled by Pastor Simon Goulart of Geneva. Goulart was a clergyman who spent most of a long career in the service of the Calvinist City State. At the time of the massacres he was on leave from his recently assumed position, attending to family business in his native France. Only with difficulty was he able to escape from his ancestral land and return to his new residence. This experience no doubt helps explain the personal sense of outrage that pervades his memoirs.

R.M. Kingdon, *Myths about the St Bartholomew's Day Massacre*, 1988.

The Religious Wars Continued, 1572–7

The Massacre of St Bartholomew's Eve Began in Paris

Initially it was in the area around the Louvre, but then it spread. Throughout the commercial quarter of the right bank of the city, the university district, and the Faubourg St German. It lasted for three vicious days, while the city gates remained closed. Those killed included jewellers, goldsmiths, bankers, booksellers, bookbinders, printers and royal office-

TALKING POINT

Why are martyrs often important to reform or revolutionary movements?

7 Make a list of the points we can say for certain about the St Bartholomew's Day massacres.

8 Using the evidence in this section, and the information provided in the focus section, write an essay to explain the causes of the St Bartholomew's Day Massacre:
'How far was the massacre of St Bartholomew's Eve caused by short-term political activity in the city of Paris in 1572?'

holders. In addition, the massacre spread to other cities: quite quickly to Orleans, Bruges, Lyon and others, and to Rouen and Bordeaux within a month or six weeks. On 24 August the king wrote to all provincial governors, urging them to keep the peace – but to no avail. It is difficult to calculate the number of Huguenots who were butchered, but their only crime seems to have been the disruption of the Catholic faith. Many Huguenots sought protection in prison, though in some cases it did them no good.

In the south and south-west of France, the Huguenots were quick to respond. Led by the Duke of Conde and Henry of Navarre, the surviving local gentry swore a solemn oath of union. They fortified important towns like La Rochelle against royalist siege. They met in assemblies in many of the main cities and formed the United Provinces of the Midi, setting up a Huguenot republic in the south-west with its own Estates General, taxation system, and administration.

The fourth civil war in May 1573 was a brief affair. The Duke of Anjou besieged La Rochelle but was then elected King of Poland and left France to take up his new position. The Peace Treaty was unsatisfactory to the Huguenots and could not last.

A year later, Charles IX died and Catherine de Medici became Regent to await the return from Poland of the Duke of Anjou, now King Henry III.

The new king was subject to much contemporary criticism. He encouraged many young men, his 'mignons', to his court and their unprincipled and licentious behaviour caused much adverse comment. The wealth and extravagance of the court, its silly fashions and lavish entertainment, repaid the heavy taxation on the people very poorly. In these circumstances the king's young brother, the Duke of Alencon, set up an army. In addition, the Huguenots under Conde invaded the east and Henry of Navarre escaped from Paris. Faced by an alliance of Alencon, Navarre and Conde, Henry III accepted the Peace of Monsieur in May 1576. For the first time Huguenots were allowed free public and general exercise of their religion. They could build churches, they could hold synods and they were to occupy eight towns. It was a dramatic turnaround.

The following years saw relative calm in France but much international activity. The Duke of Alencon negotiated with England and the Netherlands, until his sudden death in 1584. His successor was the Huguenot, Henry of Navarre, which showed how the balance of power within the state had changed – alarming many Catholic nobles. In September 1584, Henry of Guise and his brothers forged an alliance with Philip II of Spain to keep Navarre from the throne. They also determined to remove Protestantism from France and the Netherlands.

Going to war immediately, they recovered much of northern and central France. The fear of a Catholic succession combined with the personal unpopularity of Henry III and a series of bad harvests which increased the price of bread to give the Guise a clear advantage. In addition, they quickly gained the support of Paris, which became almost an independent city, under the control of *Les Seize* (the Sixteen).

Henry of Navarre (afterwards Henry IV. of France.) From an old Engraving of that period.

In the War of the Three Henrys, the king was defeated by Navarre, although the Guise kept up their position with a defeat of the king's German mercenary allies. King Henry III was the only party whose star was on the wane. On 13 May 1588 Henry was faced down by the Duke of Guise in Paris and was forced to flee the city. The Duke of Guise now assumed control of the capital and Henry was playing for time. In a desperate act in October 1588, Henry lured the Duke of Guise to the Royal Chamber at Blois, where the king's bodyguard brutally murdered the Duke. The next day, other prominent members of the Catholic League were thrown into prison.

IN 1590, THE CATHOLIC LEAGUE'S SUPPORTERS IN PARIS PARADED BEFORE A PAPAL LEGATE TO SHOW THEIR RESOLVE TO FIGHT THE HUGUENOTS.

With the death of Catherine de Medici in January 1589, Henry was now completely alone. His assassination by the slight Jacobean friar was the last and possibly fitting act in the drama.

FOCUS

11.2 The City of Rouen and the Religious Wars: A Local Study

In Rouen news of the massacre of Vassy and of the actions of the Duke of Guise provoked an alarmed reaction from the Protestants. Their fears were aroused by letters circulating in Huguenot circles warning of future Vassys and instructing all churches to be ready... with arms if necessary. Rouen's Huguenots immediately began to mount an armed guard around their assemblies. When two armed captains entered the city early in April bearing a commission from the now captive King, to levy troops, the Huguenots, fearful that the troops were intended for use against them, attacked these recruiters and drove them from the town.

Philip Benedict, in his book *Rouen in the Wars of Religion*, is in no doubt as to the importance of local history.

Contemporaries tended to analyse politics as if Les Grandes were the only men who mattered... but the Wars of Religion were not episodes in normal politics. The religious divisions cut deep into society provoking bitter conflict in provincial cities such as Rouen. The religious parties had an existence at the local level that were substantially independent of the actions of the Court Elites. Their fate was determined as much or more by the play of local forces as it was by events in Paris.

In the light of this, is it fair to say that local history should be studied for its own sake or can it be a valid reflection of the national scene?

It was in the period after 1559 that Calvinism became a true mass movement in France. The rare Protestant baptismal registers, stretching back to the years before the outbreak of the Civil Wars, indicate the speed of the new faith's growth. In a Reformed Church of San Lo, founded in 1555, only sixteen baptisms were celebrated in 1557. The number has risen to eighty-eight by 1560 and reached one hundred and thirty in the following year. At the other end of France, in Montpellier, the growth in these later years was even more rapid: the number of baptisms per month tripled over the course of twelve months following September 1560, then doubled again in the succeeding five months.

A Calvinist minister visited a Norman fair in 1561 near Rouen. He was surprised to find that placards against the mass were being carried openly by Huguenots among the stalls of the fair 'the abolition of the mass! the ruin of the stinking mass! see how the merchants who peddle us their fine wares are about to be done away with! cried the Huguenot hawkers'. When several priests tried to silence the vendors they were quickly surrounded by a menacing crowd shouting at them 'go out and glean, it's good weather, learn how to work you fine merchants, you've eaten too long without doing

How far can the Historian of national events benefit from local studies? This is a particularly important question to ask in the context of the French Religious Wars.

any work'... The Calvinist preacher then began to preach daily at the fair. His audience grew regularly and he estimated the Sunday crowd at between five and six thousand people. That night the stallholders began to sing psalms in front of their stalls.

Clearly, any local example of the St Bartholomew's Massacre would be of considerable value to the national historian. Benedict presents a dramatic local viewpoint.

Historians have long recognised the St Bartholomew's Day Massacre as an important turning point for both French Protestantism and the Wars of Religion. This has been so for two reasons. First, most of the faith's noble leaders were either killed or imprisoned in the course of the event, so the Protestant movement, of necessity, took on a more radical, democratically organised and urban based character in subsequent years... Second, because Charles IX was generally thought at the time to have given the order for the general massacre, more forthright theories of the right of resistance to a tyrant King were enunciated and came to be accepted within the movement. During the first Civil Wars the Protestants had always maintained they were loyal to the Monarch: they merely were trying to save him from his evil counsellors. Now they began to claim that a higher loyalty to the true religion could permit the lesser magistrates to disobey their sovereign when he transgressed against fundamental principles of law and religion. In Rouen the event was also a turning point for a third and quite different reason: it radically transformed the Huguenot community. The preceding decade had been hard for the Calvinists in those regions where they were physically outnumbered and politically vulnerable. The effect of the massacre was to crystallize their growing sense of disillusionment, precipitate a wave of defections, and alter the attitudes of those who remained faithful to the cause. By the end of 1572 the large and still militant minority of the mid 1560s would give way to a far smaller and more docile group that would never again pose a serious threat to local Catholic dominance.

TABLE OF BAPTISMS IN CITIES
Average Number of Baptisms Per Year in Terms For Which Baptismal Registers Are Well Maintained

Caen		Rouen		Montauban		La Rochelle		Montpellier	
1564–8	430	1563–5	111	1565–71	571	1564–9	539	1563–8	413
1570–2	270	1570–2	65	1573–7	600	1573–7	935	1570–2	211
1578–84	152	1578–85	60	1578–84	648	1578–84	674	1575–84	253
1591–4	187	1591–4	57	1585–94	606	1585–94	728	1585–94	320

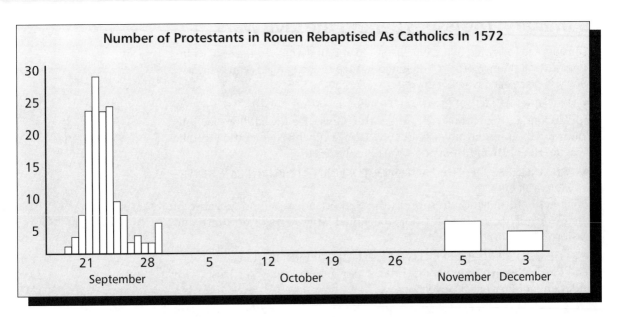

Number of Protestants in Rouen Rebaptised As Catholics In 1572

By the aftermath of St Bartholomew's Day the Protestants had been reduced to a far smaller and more politically docile group in Rouen than had been the case in the mid 50's. In most regions this was so. Just the opposite evolution occurred in a few regions. In communities such as La Rochelle and Montauban, generally located far from Paris in terrain that was easy for the Huguenots to defend, the Huguenot party was able to seize control and withstand Royal efforts to force them back into the fold. The popular violence of the massacres only bred a determined policy of resistance in these areas. The Catholics who remained were cowed into submission. There were thus two contrasting patterns of development in France, but in either case, whether it was the Protestants or the Catholics who had cemented their domination by 1573, the religious struggle was essentially settled on the local level.

1 Describe the events in Rouen in your own words.
2 What local factors contributed to the massacre in the city? What national factors did?
3 What can we learn from a study of Rouen about national politics in 1572?

REVIEW

Summary: The Issues Behind the Civil Wars

Consider the following issues which caused and underpinned the conflict in France. Rank them in order of their importance to the conflict, and explain why you place each where it is.

- FEUDING BETWEEN RIVAL FACTIONS

For example, the conflict between the Guise and Chatillon factions following the murder of Guise in 1563. The conflict between the Catholic League, Henry III and Henry of Navarre in the 1580s.

- WILLINGNESS OF THE FACTIONS TO TURN TO EUROPEAN STATES FOR SUPPORT

Coligny's determination to support the Netherlands was a prime cause of the events of 1572. Spanish troops occupied large parts of northern and eastern France in the 1580s.

- THE COLLAPSE OF EFFECTIVE CENTRAL GOVERNMENT

The 'crown' gave conflicting orders: so power came to rest with independent Provincial Governors,

For example, Toulouse 'League for the Defence of the Catholic Religion' with own administration, taxes and army.

Protestant 'United Provinces for the Midi' in Languedoc after 1573.

The Sixteen ('seize') who governed Paris in the late 1580s.

- THE REPLACEMENT OF EFFECTIVE CENTRAL GOVERNMENT BY REPRESENTATIVE INSTITUTIONS

Henry of Navarre used Estates General in his provinces.

Estates in Normandy opposed royal demands for taxation.

- THE IMPOVERISHMENT OF THE CROWN

1560 Royal debts totalled 43 million livres

1583 Royal debts totalled 114 million livres

1576 Crown revenue 13 million livres per year

1583 Crown revenue 23 1/2 million livres per year

Aggravated by a war which cost money and devastated many areas of France.

- ECONOMIC DAMAGE TO THE KINGDOM

Rural population growth stopped after 1570s.

In many regions payments of tithes, feudal dues and rents ceased.

Textile manufacture collapsed in many cities.

In Lyon, 3/4 of banking houses closed and silk industry declined.

- RELIGIOUS ISSUES AND CONFLICT

- WEAKENING BONDS OF FRENCH SOCIETY

Nobles – duels allowed them to slaughter each other.

Peasants opposed taxation and class structure in a wave of riots in 1580s.

Carnival of Romans.

Croquants united peasant rebels in western provinces after 1593.

Opposed taxes, Lords and invading armies.

- IDEOLOGICAL CONFLICTS AND DEBATES

Conde Manifesto 1567: 'A Monarch limited by the authority of the nobility and the communities of the Provinces and the great towns of the kingdom'.

Hotman's 'Franco Gallia', 1573: Monarch elective, Estates General important.

Du Plessis-Mornay, 'Vindiciae Contra Tyrannos', 1579: Inferior magistrates had a duty to resist tyrannical kings. People born to liberty – Kings can only rule with their consent. Magistrates and kings have a duty to uphold the law, both to God and to the people.

12 King Henry IV of France, 1589–1610

PREVIEW

The Assassination of the Man for all Seasons

The King had cultivated his image by careful propaganda... The manner of his death transfigured him into an active legend... Henry IV proved, in his legend, as in his life, a man for all seasons.

> M. Greengrass, *France in the Age of Henry IV*, 1984.

Henry may not have been a model husband or a man of great constancy, but he was an extraordinary personality, and when he died things could never again be the same.

> D. Buissaret, *Henry IV*, 1984.

The picture illustrates the manner of Henry IV's death in 1610 at the hands of the fanatic Ravaillac. Henry had insisted that he should go in a coach to supervise the arrangements for the arrival of his Queen, Marie de Medici, into Paris. When pressed to take a bodyguard, he was disdainful. He would go alone in a coach with a few of his nobles. On the Rue De La Ferronnerie, the coach was confronted with a mass of people. One of the footmen walked ahead in an attempt to remove the traffic jam. Meanwhile

King Henry moved back the curtain of the coach in order to see out. Suddenly, a tall, red-haired man leapt onto the wheel of the coach and stabbed the king twice in the chest. The Duke of Epernon acted quickly and the man was arrested by guards. Blood was pouring from the king's mouth and Epernon threw a cloak over him, told all the bystanders that the king was not seriously hurt, and drove him straight back to the Louvre, where King Henry IV was dead on arrival. The news of his death stunned Parisian nobles, the members of the Parlement who were in session, the members of the King's Council who were also meeting, Queen Marie de Medici and her family, and all the people of Paris.

The hatred and agitation against Ravaillac was immediate and intense. As he was led away, the crowd vented its spleen violently upon him. He was tortured and pressed to reveal his accomplices, but throughout he stressed that he had acted alone.

Under further torture, Ravaillac revealed some of his motives. He was a religious fanatic, a member of the Catholic Fuillant Group, and possibly had links with the Jesuits. For him, the Edict of Nantes was an evil measure; it was the king's duty to convert Protestants and he had failed to do it. Ravaillac may also have believed that Protestants wished to slaughter Catholics in retaliation for the Massacre of St Bartholomew's Eve. Finally, he

A GRAPHIC ENGRAVING DEPICTING THE EXECUTION OF RAVAILLAC.

said, according to one eye-witness, 'the common soldiers make no secret of their willingness to support the King and die in battle if he wished to make war on the Pope. Such talk made Ravaillac even more determined to kill the King, because fighting against the Pope was fighting against God.'

Ravaillac's death was horrific. To cries of 'traitor' and 'murderer', he was taken to Notre Dame. He mounted the scaffold and was forced to make public confession of his sins.

> The arm which had committed the murder was plunged into burning sulphur... The flesh on his chest, arms, thighs and legs was torn by red hot pincers, then molten lead, boiling oil, boiling resin, a mixture of molten wax and sulphur were poured into the wounds. The victim re-doubled his cries and his prayers. He was then allowed a breathing space so that we would know the severity of his pain... The second stage involved tying Ravaillac's arms and legs to four horses which then pulled in different directions. Still the mob yelled its hatred. Some began tugging at the ropes to help the horses... After a hour and a half of this torture Ravaillac finally died.
>
> R. Mousnier, *The Assassination of King Henry IV*, 1973.

> The assassination of Henry IV was an event and nothing more... The election of Hitler as Chancellor, the French campaign of June 1940, the assassination at Sarajevo on 28th June 1914 which led to the outbreak of the First World War, were all mere events, and yet no-one would deny that they affected tens of millions of human lives. A sure means for an historian to discover whether or not he should concern himself with a particular event, is to see what facts it brings to light and what its apparent consequences were.
>
> Some events are of the utmost importance because they are the symptoms of deep and continuous processses. They reflect the clash of opposing ideas, changing modes of thought, social conflict, shifting social patterns, and economic strife. They are important because their effects are widespread... In my view the assassination of Henry IV is one of those events.
>
> R. Mousnier, *The Assassination of Henry IV*, 1973.

TALKING POINT

Was it necessary to impose so brutal a punishment on Ravaillac? What does it tell us about the nature of contemporary Paris? What may it tell us about the reputation of King Henry IV? What are the dangers of using such punishments?

TALKING POINT

You will have come across a number of political assassinations in your study of the 16th century. Which were the most important and what were there consequences? What does Mousnier mean by 'the symptoms of deep and continuous processes'?

In the 20th century there have been a number of major political assassinations, including that of US President John Kennedy in 1963. What were the consequences of his death? Is it too early yet to assess any 'symptoms of deep and continuous processes'? Why has his death aroused so much suspicion and so much questioning?

12.1 Henry's Youth: What Could He Have Learned from His Early Experiences?

Some snapshots from his early life

In February 1557, the young Henry and his mother, Jeanne D'Albret, made a journey northwards to the Court of King Henry II. They were welcomed by the King, who playfully asked the little Prince if 'he would like to be his son'. In reply Henry turned to his father Antoine (Duke of Navarre) and replied 'here is my father'. The King, amused by this composed answer, then suggested that, if he could not be his son he might like to be his son in law, to which Henry replied 'Oh yes'.

D. Buissaret, *Henry IV*, 1984.

In 1560, when the prince was nearly seven, his mother took him back to the French Court. Her husband Antoine had never been faithful to her and he now began to act with spectacular infidelity. He was extremely 'ondoyant', incapable for long of sustaining a fixed course or policy... He also quarrelled with Jeanne over religious matters... The quarrels between the couple became more and more scandalous until in March 1562 Antoine ordered Jeanne to return to Guienne. At the age of eight Henry was thus separated from his mother and left to fend for himself at Court.

D. Buissaret, *Henry IV*, 1984.

In March 1569 the Duke of Conde died and Henry became the formal head of the Protestant army in the French Religious Wars. He spent the next sixteen months on campaign.

In June 1572 Henry's mother Jeanne died. His grief was sincere and intense, different from the mourning for his father several years earlier. He was now on his way to Paris to celebrate his marriage to Margaret, the daughter of Catherine de Medici. It was here, during the festivities that surrounded the marriage, that Coligny was assassinated and the Massacre of St Bartholomew's Eve was instigated. During the massacre, Henry was held under royal guard in the King's chamber. Many of his supporters, including his tutor, were killed. Henry was given a simple choice: either he endure conversion to the Roman Catholic church or he would die.

Henry immediately acquiesced. On 3 October he wrote to the pope begging forgiveness and on 16 October he agreed to return Guienne to Catholicism. He became amicable with the Duke of Guise and he even joined the king's army, which was sent to beseige the Huguenot stronghold of La Rochelle. It was not until 1576 that he was able to escape from the Court and re-establish his position.

In 1576 Henry returned to Guienne. Now he tried to gain the support of local people by an appeal to their patriotism and to their toler-ance, rather than to their religious loyalty. He wrote to one of the Catholic captains, 'those who unswervingly follow their conscience are of my religion as I am of all those who are brave and virtuous...'.

In this new role he was constantly travelling the countryside getting to know his people. He talked and listened and was always keen to understand the views of his people about their state.

In 1584, during the War of the Three Henrys, King Henry III sent an emissary to Guienne to try to per-suade Henry, now Duke of Navarre, to reconvert to Catholicism. This offer presented Henry with a real challenge: if he reconverted it would certainly improve his relations with the King and the Court and possibly enhance his future expectations. On the other hand, he would risk losing his strength with the Huguenots in the south west. In addition, in spite of his actions in Paris in 1572, he also seemed to have genuine religious concerns about conversion. He wrote to the Archbishop of Rouen 'tell those who advocate my conversion that religion, if they had ever known what it is, is not something you discard like a shirt for it dwells in the heart'. He therefore declined the offer but confirmed his loyalty to the King and even offered to join in a religious Council to debate the religion of France.

In the following year, when Henry III made an alliance with Henry of Guise at the Treaty of Nemours, Henry of Navarre condemned it with the following published statement.

> A peace made with foreigners at the expense of the Princes of the blood; with the House of Lorraine at the expense of the House of France; with rebels at the expense of obedient subjects; with agitators at the expense of those who have brought peace by every means with-in their power. I intend to oppose it with all my heart and to this end rally round me all true Frenchmen without regard to religion, since this time it is a question of the defence of the State against the usurpation of foreigners.

In the following year, the king sent an army under the Duke of Joyeuse to drive into the heartland of Henry's support. Henry met Joyeuse's army at the Battle of Coutras in 1587. Henry's victory over Joyeuse was decisive, the result of his magnificently led cavalry charge.

1 Some principles of effective leadership or political statesmanship are listed below. Which of these had the young Henry of Navarre learned something about before he became king in 1589?
- The effective use of public relations.
- The importance of retaining your own power base.
- The ability to win people to your side.
- The essential skills of military leadership.
- The importance of effective personal communication.
- The value of securing the political centre
- The need to balance principle with pragmatism.
2 In what ways did the young Henry reveal political inexperience? It would be interesting to see if, in his later career, he learned from this inexperience.

Securing the Realm, 1589–1602

Early Victories over the Guise and Spain, 1589–93

In 1589, on the death of Henry III without an heir, Henry, Duke of Navarre became King Henry IV.

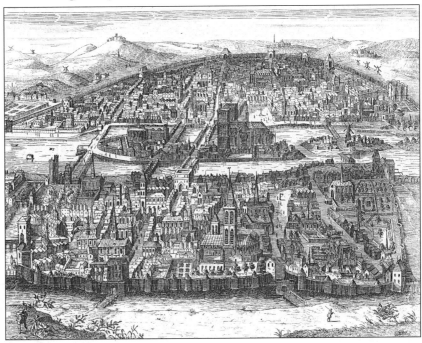

PARIS IN THE LATE 16TH CENTURY.

The young king now needed to secure his realm and bring peace. The Guise forces, augmented by those of Spain, were still a threat and in 1589 Mayenne followed him into Normandy. In spite of Mayenne's superior forces, 24,000 troops against Henry's 5000, Henry defeated him at the Battle of Arques. After a lightning but unsuccessful raid on Paris, Henry again returned to Normandy and rapidly conquered a number of major cities. In March 1590 he smashed the forces of Mayenne, supplemented by those of Philip II of Spain, at the Battle of Ivry in which his leadership of the cavalry charge again proved decisive. Again he camped his armies around Paris. King Philip II, fearing the fall of the city, ordered the Duke of Parma to leave the southern Netherlands and cross into France. Parma joined Mayenne and the League forces and their combined troops numbered about 24,000, put to the aid of Paris. Henry was forced to withdraw yet again.

Henry retreated in order to focus his attention on the capture of the League stronghold in Normandy, the city of Rouen, which he attacked in November 1591. One contemporary was close to him in the action 'I go nearly every day with the King to the trench and to the batteries, and wherever I may learn and observe something. The King takes me to the very front line where bullets whizz past all the time, for this lord never stays still, sees to everything himself, goes everywhere, wants to know about everthing, and exposes himself to every danger. His activity is admirable, and those who wish to obtain his favour have to do as he does, without sparing themselves.'

In spite of this Parma's army relieved Rouen and forced Henry back. As the Estates General met in Paris in 1593, Henry had won two major battles against the League, but he had failed to capture either Paris or Rouen.

1593: Henry's Conversion to Catholicism and the Capture of Paris

When the Catholic Estates General failed to find a suitable candidate for the monarchy a ten-day truce was agreed with the king. Dramatically, on 17 May the Archbishop of Bourges announced that Henry would again become a Catholic: this was the occasion of Henry's famous observation that 'Paris is worth a Mass'. In July, the king went to St Denis to receive instruction from a group of bishops. The subsequent ceremony was typical of Henry's skill in public relations. On Sunday 25 July he abjured his Protestant faith. 'The streets were hung with tapestries and strewn with flowers from Pisare. In front of the king marched a large number of Princes and Nobles, followed by the Swiss Guard with their drums beating, the Scots and other guards, and finally twelve trumpeters. The king himself was magnificently dressed in white satin with a black cloak and hat, and as he slowly paced through the streets found a great crown constantly shouting "long live the King"'. A circular letter to all French provinces and to many European rulers announced the change. Early in 1594, the king was crowned at Chartres. He took the usual Coronation Oath, including the promise 'to expel from all lands under my jurisdiction all heretics denounced by the Church'. Two months later, Henry's armies were converging on Paris from three directions. The gates were opened from within. Henry's troops entered the city at 6 o'clock in the morning and he made his way to Notre Dame where he attended Mass. He allegedly watched from a window as the Spanish garrison left. His action won the support of most of the Catholic nobles and cities of the north, as well as many of the Huguenot leaders, although the more extreme supporters in each party still refused to join him. Town Governors sold their loyalty to the king – Henry decided it was more economical to buy their support than to win it in battle.

Henry's success was completed with the blessing from the pope in 1595 and the final victory over Spanish troops with the reconquest of Amiens in 1597 and the Peace of Vervins in 1598.

The treaty ended Spanish involvement in northern France and confirmed the terms of the Peace of Cateau-Cambresis of 1559. With his usual eye for public relations, the King celebrated in a magnificent ceremony in Notre Dame and publicly burned the instruments of war – drums, trumpets, lances and swords – in front of the Hotel D'Ville.

The Religious Peace: The Edict of Nantes, 1598

Henry's purpose in signing the Edict of Nantes was to 'establish the good and lasting peace'. The Edict certainly gave the Huguenots every opportunity to practise their own religion. They were allowed to worship on the estates of noblemen, at two places in each baillage to be decided by royal commissioners, and also wherever they could prove that their faith

TALKING POINT

Is it hypocrisy to change one's religious faith for political advantage?

had been openly practised in 1596 and 1597. They were allowed to hold any office of state and enter any profession or occupation and they were granted access to schools, universities and hospitals. Legal cases were to be judged by courts comprising both Catholics and Protestants. And public funds were to provide both for Protestant Pastors and for the protection of Huguenot fortified towns.

Thereafter, Henry's relations with Catholics and Protestants was guided by the Edict. Once registered by the Parlements, the Edict of Nantes was the basis at least for keeping the peace in France and ending the religious wars of the 16th century.

Social and Political Revolts

During these early years of his reign Henry's security was threatened by three significant revolts.

In 1594, a number of groups of peasants in central and south western France began to group together under the name of the *Croquants*. Their aim was to resist excessive taxation and the depredations of local nobles. Henry wrote to Provincial Governors, urging that 'disorder should be ended by gentle means if possible'. The peasants were given assurances and eventually laid down their arms.

The following year Henry survived an assassination attempt. The Jesuit John Chastel had tried to stab the king in the throat. The blow had been deflected, but one of the king's teeth had been damaged. Jesuit complicity in the plot was never proved but the king was subsequently always on guard against would-be assassins.

A major plot emerged in the year 1602. The Duke of Biron had conspired with Spain, the Duke of Savoy and other gentlemen of France, against the king. The plot was betrayed by a former friend, who was rewarded handsomely by the king. Biron was tried by the Parlement and executed in the Bastille. It was a celebrated case and again confirmed Henry's authority.

Further, in 1606, George Carew, the English Ambassador, reported to London that 'I learned of late of the gunpowder treason, intended against this King, to have been executed by laying powder under a gallery that passes through the Louvre to the lodging of the Contesse D'Morre, his last mistress'. Shades of England the year before.

Rebuilding the Realm, 1599–1610

Economic Reconstruction

Henry's avowed aim had been to bring peace to France. He now began the programme of reconstruction, using the Duke of Sully as his main agent. Symbolic of his reconstruction was rebuilding. As one contemporary put it 'as soon as he was master of Paris you saw masons at work everywhere'. 'This town is growing much fairer than you have seen it', said an English agent. He rebuilt the North embankment of the Seine and added the Quai de Louvre. He then developed the extension to the Louvre which ran alongside the river. And the Madrid Palace was at the heart of his plans. He completed the Petite Gallery and by 1606 he had nearly completed the Grand Gallery. He also did much developmental work on the royal gardens at Fontainebleau, St Germaine and Etuillery. 'In sixteen years', said David Buissaret, 'the King had left an indelible mark on the outward appearance of Paris...'

Henry also adopted a programme of industrial development, presented to him by Bartolemi d'Laffemas in 1597. In 1602 he set up a Council of Commerce to decide which industrial schemes to support. They fostered the silk industry in Lyon, Orleans, Paris, Poitiers and Tour, though not all were successful. He also set up factories for tapestry production at Amiens, Calais and Tour and the Gobbelins factory in Paris acquired an international reputation. Progress was also made in the production of morocco leather, paper, fine glass and a variety of metallurgical industries. This kind of venture was obviously new for a developing mercantilist state like France.

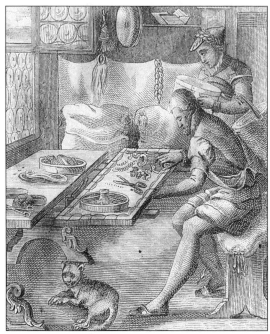

SILK WORKERS IN THE 16TH CENTURY.

The new stability of Henry's reign also started an agricultural revival. With the coming of peace, grain prices fell and harvests from 1604 to 1609 were good. New cash crops were produced in this climate – maize, vegetables, vines and oil. It is interesting that Olivier De Serres wrote the first textbook of French farming, *The Theatre of Agriculture*, in 1600 and it was widely read and used. De Serres advised farmers on the administration of their farms, the cultivation of crops, the development of vineyards or meadows, and the production of new crops. He also commented on various agricultural techniques.

The Duke of Sully also fostered the infrastructure of economic revival by developing bridges and canals and improving roads. Dutch drainage engineers were employed on the construction of land reclamation schemes. Much of this work was facilitated by Sully as the Grande Voyer with a large capital investment. Sully insisted on strict costing and a tight supervision of contracts. He inspected all the work done through a team of inspectors and treasurers. In all this work, Henry and Sully were beginning to see France as an economic whole, with fewer provincial provisions and easy communication from one part to another.

Henry IV and the Provinces: Governors, Provincial Estates, Parlements, and Private Agents

Henry exercised power through his twelve Provincial Governors and had little choice in them, since most were already in post. However, it was important for Henry to retain control of them and several were moved to unfamiliar territory – the young Duke of Guise was sent to Provence and the young Duke of Conde to Guienne. In addition, they were given Lieutenant Governors who would keep an eye on them and Henry used his own agents often to help them, but often to watch them. Henry also had a number of close advisors, like Raymond d'Vicose, who were often to be found negotiating on his behalf with important people away from Paris.

Governors were, of course, military commanders, but they did much more besides. They attended the opening of the estates in the province, relaying a message from the king. They ensured the effective expenditure of taxation, they worked on roads, bridges and fords, and they tried to exercise control over the nobility and other local political groups. Many local nobles were prepared to take Spanish gold in return for opposition to the king and Henry had constantly to be on the watch.

The local Parlements were also extremely active. The king appointed their presidents and tried to influence their work. But often they objected to his Edicts, in both religion and taxation. Similarly, the local estates, meeting once a year for a fortnight, saw it as their duty to present their thoughts to the Provincial Governor on behalf of the king. For example, in 1604, the Estates of Languedoc complained that 'the replies which Monsier d'Rosny and other Lords of the Council had put forward on the cahiers sent to them did not in any way meet the wishes of the Province'.

Henry worked constantly to maintain his hold over all these groups, and in this work his local agents were very important. Even so, there were frequent local revolts, the murder of a royal official here, urban rioting and sedition there, and the hand of the king of Spain was often behind such intrigues.

TALKING POINT

Henry IV was a masterly delegator; when a king delegates responsibility, what does it tell you about him?

Is there a difference between delegating responsibility and delegating power?

MARIE DE MEDICI.

The King and his Family

Henry's marriage to Marie de Medici was a financial and political expedient. She must have been extremely surprised to find that she shared the Court with the King's several mistresses. 'Very soon after her arrival Henry had presented the Marquis de Vernay to her, thus causing a famous scene in which, judging that Vernay's curtsey was insufficiently low, he had personally forced her into a lower obeisance. After that though the King did kindly entertain her, and since all three have dined on Sunday together in public, he had provided a house for her hard by the Louvre and will follow the track of Henry II who did keep his mistress in Court in presence of the Queen Mother.'

The king, however, seemed to care for his wife.

Henry arrived at Fontainebleau mid September and it was at midnight on 26th September that he had to send for the midwife, since the Queen was feeling uneasy. Soon it was clear that the labour pains had begun. Henry was constantly at her bedside holding Marie and comforting. The labour was very long and lasting nearly a whole day, but eventually Marie gave birth to a fine son.

D. Buissaret, *Henry IV*, 1984.

Over the ensuing years the king became immensely fond of the dauphin and would often go to play with him, butter his bread at breakfast, or to take him to see the fish in the pond. By 1606 all nine of his children were brought up together at court: his three by marriage to Marie de Medici and six others by three different mistresses. Clearly, King Henry IV was 'ondiante' with his personal relationships as well as in his kingship.

TALKING POINT
What does the organisation of Henry's personal life tell us about his professional life?

EXAMINING THE EVIDENCE

The Registration of the Edict of Nantes: The King's Political Skill

Source A

Speech made by Henry IV to the Parlements of Paris requesting them to register the Edict of Nantes, 7th January 1599. Recorded by Pierre de l'Estoile in his contemporary memoirs.

On Thursday 7th of this month the King summoned his Parlements to the Louvre to confirm the Edict relating to the Huguenots. He addressed them as a King and in well chosen terms:

Before coming to my reasons for calling you together, I should like to tell you a story. Immediately after St Bartholomew's Day, four of us who were playing at dice, saw some drops of blood appear on the table. We wiped them away twice but they reappeared a third time. After this I refused to go on playing and saying it was an augury threatening those who had shed blood. Monsieur De Guise was one of the company.

Now you see me here in my study, where I have come to speak to you. I am not in royal attire like my predecessors, nor am I dressed with cloak and sword, nor as a Prince who has come to speak with foreign ambassadors, but I am dressed like the father of the family, in a doublet, to speak freely to his children.

What I have to say to you is a request to verify the Edict I have granted to the Huguenots. What I have done is in the cause of peace. I have secured peace abroad and now I desire peace at home. You are obliged to obey me, if for no other reason than the duty all my subjects have towards me, particularly all of you, members of my Parlement. To some of you I have restored the homes from which you were banished; to others I have given back your faith you have lost. If obedience was due to my predecessors, surely it should be even more due to me, now that I have re-established the State.

I am aware that there have been intrigues in the Parlement, and preachers urge you to talk sedition, but I shall take care of them without expecting any help from you. Sedition led straight to the barricades and then by degrees to the late King's assassination. I shall avoid all that kind of thing: I shall nip in the bud all factions and all attempts at seditious preaching; and I shall behead all those who encourage it. I have leapt onto the walls of towns; surely I can leap over barricades.

Do not use as an argument your defence of the Catholic faith. I love it as much as you do and I am a better Catholic than you. I am the eldest son of the church. I enjoy the Pope's favour more than you do.

Those of you who wish to block the passage of my Edict want war; I may well declare a war on the Huguenots, but I will never wage it, whereas you really would go to war, in your legal robes, just looking like the procession of Capuchins bearing muskets over their habits. What a sight you would make! If you refuse to pass my Edict I shall have to come into the Parlement. It would show me great ingratitude to cause me this trouble.

I can easily cause as witnesses those members of my Council who approved of this Edict and thought it necessary in the present state of affairs: the constable, the chancellor, De Bellierre, Sansey, and Sillery. I acted on their advice and on the advice of Dukes and Peers. There is not one of them who would dare to style himself a protector of the Catholic religion or who would dare deny giving me this advice. But I am the only preserver of the faith, I shall dispel the rumours that are spread.

There has been a complaint in Paris that I was about to call out the Swiss guard as some other body of troops. If I did so you would have to approve, and it would be to some effect as is evident from my past exploits. I am King now and I speak as King and expect to be obeyed! Even if you will not verify the Edict I shall still pass it.

The king then publicly mentioned the name of Monsier De Sillery. He told him that his brother had been preaching against the king and against the Edict of Nantes. The family had tried to argue that he was a young man who had got carried away. The king publicly declared this was unacceptable.

He then returned to speak openly to the Parlement:

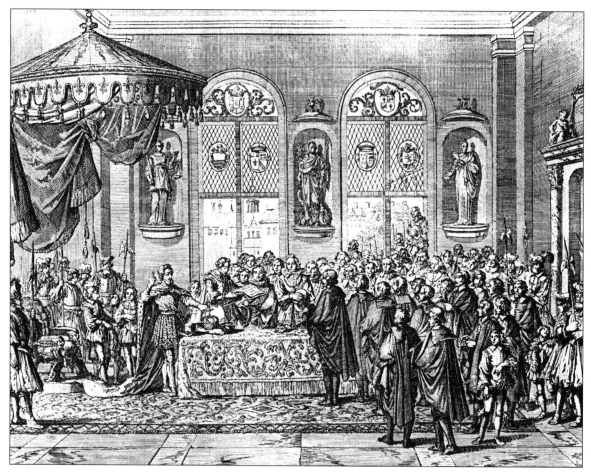

THE SIGNING OF THE EDICT OF NANTES IN 1598.

there is not a single one of you who does not find me well disposed towards you when you have business with me. Despite my great goodness to you you treat me badly. It was only late yesterday that I decided to summon you here. You must realise that the Edict for which I am asking your approval is the late King's Edict, but it is also mine too, for it was made with my help.

My last word to you is to urge you to follow Monsieur De Mayenne's example. He was pressed to protest against my wishes. He replied that he was under too great an obligation to me, as were all my subjects, because I have set France on her feet again, in spite of those bent on ruining her. He says he will always be prepared to risk his life to please me whereas formally he tried his utmost to ruin the State. And if the leader of the League utters these sentiments, how much more should you do so in return.

I shall utter no threats to you. Simply do as I command you, or rather what I beg you. You will do it not only for me but also for yourselves and for the fair cause of peace.

1 Identify the passages in Henry's speech which indicate his political skill. What particular skills does each passage indicate?
2 What effect would his speech have on his audience?
3 In his book *France and the Age of Henry IV*, Mark Greengrass has called the speech 'an harangue of great force and finesse'. Is this a fair conclusion?

The Edict of Nantes was written by the king and his advisers in 1598. It took nearly a year to persuade the Parlement of Paris to register it. Much of this time was spent in political lobbying, although the threat of force was also used. Finally, the Parlement of Paris registered it on 25 February 1599, and within the following year most of the other Parlements followed suit. However, the Parlement of Rouen held out until 1609. Even then, one or two aspects of the Edict were changed.

Finally, to ensure that the Edict was accepted in each local area, commissioners were sent round the provinces. For the most part, they set up various sites for Huguenot worship in each province, but in some areas like Picardy they encountered great opposition. In Burgundy where the Catholic League was strong, they also found it extremely difficult to persuade local people to accept the Edict. But as long as the Huguenots were under King Henry's favour, and as long as his political view of religion remained a grey area, most people would accept his will.

Source B

The Edict of Nantes was a civil measure, an act of state imposed upon a country in which two competing religions had reached momentary deadlock. If the King had been stronger it would not have been necessary; if he had been weaker, it would not have survived.

J.H. Elliott, *Europe Divided*, 1968.

Source C

The Edict was not regarded as satisfactory at all, not either by the protestants, by the King or the Parlements. Nevertheless it was a sane and reasonable compromise... Henry did not ask his Catholic courts to enforce a principle of toleration – nowhere does the Edict so much as hint at such a thing – for Henry was not concerned with toleration, he was concerned with peace. He could not legislate for the one, but he could provide for the other.

N.M. Sutherland, *The Huguenot Struggle for Recognition*, 1980.

4 What different opinions about the Edict are reflected in sources B, C and D?
5 In the light of the evidence in this chapter, what did Henry achieve with the Edict of Nantes?

Source D

To the Pope and to good Catholics everywhere 'the Edict of Nantes cast doubts on the sincerity of the King's conversion. Nor did the enforcement of the Edict make matters any better. In several Catholic provinces the sudden public observance of protestant worship appears an incredible outrageous innovation. The Royal Commissioners encountered wild outbreaks of hostility and every kind of obstruction was put in the way of the Protestant worship, particularly in Burgundy, Normandy and Maine. The fierce hatreds that had lain dormant since the League were now revived. The populace defaced gravestones in Protestant cemeteries and hurled abuse at their funeral processions, even though they took place after sunset. Inevitably clashes occurred which inflamed passions still further.'

...Henry's conduct would have seemed more acceptable to the Catholics had he been satisfied with the enforcement of the Edict. But he went far beyond the terms of the Edict and heaped favours on the Protestants. He allowed them, for example, to sell Protestant publications in Paris. The Edict expressly forbade Protestants to establish places of worship within twelve miles of Paris, but they opened one at Grigny, then another at Ablon'.

R. Mousnier, *The Assassination of Henry IV*, 1973.

The Duke of Sully: Financial and Economic Reconstruction

The system for collecting taxes at the beginning of Henry's reign was open to corruption; it was also unwieldy and unproductive. The capital debt of 138 million livres was compounded by a deficit of 12 million livres on the previous year's income. The Crown owed money to Queen Elizabeth I, many German princes and Swiss Cantons, and the Grand Duke of Tuscany. In addition, the king was in debt by nearly two million livres to the bankers of Lyon and additional sums to Italian financiers. Corruption was also rife. In 1589, the floorboards of the Treasurer, Pierre Molan, were dug up in Paris and a huge hoard of coins was found.

King Henry IV thus inherited major debts. The burden of debt was a major problem in the first ten years of his reign. Wars proved difficult to win when mercenary captains could not be paid. The major victory at Ivry in 1590 over the League could not be exploited because Swiss troops could not be paid. Later that year, Henry IV could not proceed with the siege of Paris because there were no funds for his army. Many provinces found it increasingly difficult to pay the tithe as the financial crisis of the 1590's developed, and taxes had to be cancelled. Pensions had to be paid to League nobles and a further declaration of war against Spain in 1595 proved a financially disastrous step. In 1596, when Henry IV summoned an assembly of notables to try to find a way of making him solvent, they failed to come up with a solution. Henry was very aware that his authority was weakened by financial instability.

The year 1598 brought peace. This presented an opportunity for a reconstruction of the king's finances, and this was increasingly entrusted to the Duke of Sully (1560–1641).

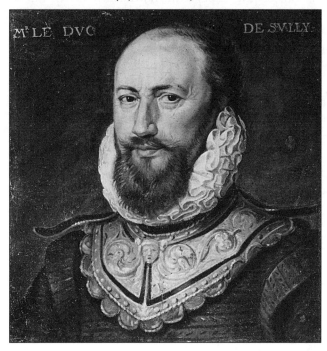

SULLY WAS A COMMITTED HUGUENOT WHO HAD BARELY ESCAPED FROM PARIS IN 1572 AFTER THE MASSACRE OF ST BARTHOLOMEW'S EVE. HE THREW IN HIS LOT WITH THE YOUNG HENRY OF NAVARRE AND SUPPORTED HIM THROUGH A NUMBER OF MILITARY ENGAGEMENTS AND ADMINISTRATIVE REFORMS.

When Henry entered Paris as king in 1593, Sully was with him and in 1596 he became a member of the Council of Finance. The same year, he was commissioned to tour the provinces in search of money and to discover means of improving Henry's dismal financial situation.

Sully's support for Henry was total, and his determination to rescue funds, which were going elsewhere, was his strongest recommendation to the king. Sully was tough – not the cautious diplomat, but rather the assured and determined administrator. Mark Greengrass has emphasised the conceit which appears in Sully's memoirs; his achievements are often exaggerated. Yet his enormous achievements, in reducing royal debt and redistributing and increasing royal income from 1596 to 1610, deserve high praise.

Sully's Reconstruction of Royal Finances

The storage of bullion in the Royal Treasury
By 1605 the Treasury in the Bastille contained a magnificent total of 1520 sacks of coins. A further 42 barrels also contained over 2000 sacks. The treasury totalled about 3.4 million livres. Two years later, this amount had doubled, and by 1610 over 11 million livres were contained in Provincial Treasuries. Sully also developed the contents of the Royal Arsenal, so that Sir George Carew, the English Ambassador, could observe King Henry walking in the corridor between the Bastille and the Arsenal: 'none other have such an alley to walk in, having at the one end thereof armour for forty thousand men ready prepared; and at the other end, money to pay them, even to the end of a long war'.

The reduction of debts to foreign states
Sully shrewdly renegotiated the debts with individual Swiss Cantons and many settled privately for token repayments. By 1607, the debt to the Swiss was halved. In addition, the political marriage to Marie de Medici, had a financial purpose. France wrote off the debt of three and a half million livres, and in addition received a dowry of nearly two million livres.

Assignations on Revenues for past debts
Treasurers were instructed not to pass any of these into existing budgets.

The 'Rentes'
Creditors were members of the Parlement, especially the Parlement of Paris, and were therefore politically powerful. A special commission in 1604 recommended that certain Rentes should be discontinued and that interest rates should be reduced on others. Francois Miron, the City Provost to Paris, was forced to reflect 'Kings cannot be constrained – only in so much as it pleases them – to pay debts to their subjects'.

Reducing direct and increasing indirect taxes

This brought great benefits in that the income to the Treasury was not affected by a lower purchasing power of money. Increases in the Gabelle redistributed wealth because salt was bought by all members of society. And when prices were falling, an increase in the Gabelle kept prices up. Finally, reduced direct taxes meant less strain on the financial machinery of the State.

Introduction of the *Paulette*, 1604

This tax on heredity was the idea of Charles Paulet, a nobleman from Languedoc. The government invited a cash payment each year of one-sixtieth of the assessed price of an office. In return, the officeholder was granted the inheritance of the office. The tax appealed to all parties, but particularly to the king. It was easy to collect and a regular, and undeniable, source of income.

L'Estoile despised the new tax and called it 'the miserable conception of the century, the vain and scandalous ambition of men of the age, which makes the prices of offices rise so high... Councillors of the Court go for forty-six thousand francs, that is forty-six thousand follies'.

The Effective Work of Provincial Treasurers

Sully inspired them to efficiency. An Edict of 1601 defined their duties. He often checked up on defaulters.

Sully's tight supervision of expenditure

As superintendent of buildings, artillery, roads and bridges, he could reduce expenditure when times were hard. In addition, he could control expenditure on the King's Court. He also supervised judicial enquiries against tax farmers and financiers.

The attempted reform of provincial financial administration

Sully wished to extend the concept of elections to various parts of the Pays D'Etat. He was not wholly successful in this, and in Languedoc and Deauphine it proved impossible. In Guinne, Sully was cautiously able to introduce the Central Office of Elus, although it only became realistic after 1609.

The growth of central control of the Privy Council

Gradually, during the early years of the 17th century, the Privy Council and the Masters of Requests, who prepared its briefs and carried out its decisions, prospered. It became the source of future Intendants to supervise financial administration in the provinces.

12.2 Pierre de L'Estoile – Parliamentarian and Diarist of Paris

Pierre de L'Estoile was an eye-witness of events in Paris from 1574 until 1611. His diary is full of shrewd and moral observations of events both humble and great. It is of inestimable value to the Historian.

Pierre came from a long line of senior royal officials in Paris. His grandfather had been a Professor of Law, and, interestingly, a teacher of Calvin. His father was a senior royal official in the city. Pierre was thus a member of the Parlement of Paris, a parliamentarian whose main loyalty was to the crown within the fundamental laws of the realm and aided by the courts.

It is interesting that from his diaries we learn almost nothing of his family life, of his two marriages, of the seventeen children, ten of whom lived to maturity. For Pierre, these things were not of public importance. What he records are the sensational rebellions, murders, sieges, and other episodes in the city of Paris during the Religious Wars and the reign of Henry IV. Yet as an aside his diary also reveals so much of the social and economic life of the ordinary people of the city. In truth this diary is a record of the life of the city of Paris.

Read the following extract from de L'Estoile's diary for January to April 1596.

- What, in detail, does the extract tell you about the author of the diary?
- What does it tell you about King Henry IV?
- What does it tell you about the life of the city of Paris?
- Do you think that the evidence of the diary is reliable?

1596: Capitulation of Mayenne

January

Wednesday, the 24th, the little prince [Conde], who was at St. Germain-en-Laye at the express command of His Majesty, changed his religion, and was instructed by M. Pierre de Gondi, Cardinal-Bishop of Paris, who catechised him as much as his age would permit. He changed his religion and went to Mass.

Wednesday, the last day of this month, the Duke of Mayenne, accompanied by only six gentlemen, went to the King at Mousseaux to yield to him. Madama la Marquise [Gabrielle] did the honours of the house. She met him at the door of the Chateau, where, after receiving him with as much graciousness and as many caresses as possible, [she] conducted him by the hand to the King, herself. His Majesty awaited the Duke seated on a dais.

The Duke of Mayenne, entering the room, bowed deeply three times. At the third, as he knelt to kiss His Majesty's hand, the King, smiling, raised him and kissed him, saying, 'My cousin, is it you? or am I having a dream?' To this the Duke replied with great submission and reverence. The King said a few words which nobody else could hear, then took him by the arm, and, after a few turns around the room, led him to his study where they spent some time together. Afterward they dined, the King with the Marquise at his side, the Duke at a table adjoining, with Madamoiselle Diane d'Estrees, sister of the Marquise. The two sisters did the honours, and the King drank to the Duke...

[Meanwhile] processions of the poor took place in Paris, in such numbers as were never seen; they cried for hunger while in their mansions the rich gorged themselves with banquets and luxuries, an abominable affront to God, whatever excuse if given...

February

The King, in this month, was constrained by need of money to re-establish the Intendants of Finances whom he had abolished the month before, and he said to one of them... that neither he nor any of his fellows had a tooth in his head that hadn't cost [the King] ten thousand crowns.

March

Friday, the first day of March, a woman was burned in Paris, in front of St. Nicholas-des-Champs, for having killed two of her children with her own hands. She said that she had done it because she had nothing to give them to eat.

Saturday, the 2nd, a Te Deum was sung in Paris for the reduction of the city of Marseilles to the King's obedience, by the valor of the Duke of Guise. The said Duke did a signal service to the King in this, because if His Majesty had lost the city, the Spaniards could have made themselves masters of Provence and Languedoc.

Friday, the 8th, there was hanged in the Place de Greve one La Ramee, a young man of twenty-three or twenty-four who claimed to be the natural son of King Charles IX, and demanded to be crowned King... in another time he would be locked up in some monastery, which would seem about right for such a poor fool. Thus one saw, this day, a 'son of France' in the Place de Greve.

Saturday, the 16th, the number of poor in Paris rose by two-thirds, six or seven thousand having arrived in recent days.

April

Monday, the 21st, came to Paris the sad news of the taking of Calais by the Cardinal of Austria... by the same stratagem that the [former] Duke of Guise used to take it from the English... Two days later came a false rumour that it had been retaken... The people, who by themselves are an animal volatile, inconstant, and stupid, began to speak ill of the King... making an excuse that he spent too much time with Madame la Marquise...

The Managers of the Hotel-Dieu report that more than six hundred persons died in the hospital in this month.

Diary entries are taken from
W. L. Roelker (ed.), *The Diaries of Pierre De L'Estoile*, Harvard University Press, 1958.

REVIEW

Henry IV – The Myth and the Man

King Henry IV of France became a legend even in his own lifetime. His own machinery ensured effective public relations. In addition, so many of the sources for his reign, such as the memoirs of Sully, exaggerate the importance of individual characters. The problem was further complicated by the need in the 17th century to hark back to the golden age of Henry IV.

'Galant' and 'Ondoyant' are two adjectives attributed to Henry IV. Can we see beneath the evidence and gain a true picture of his political genius? What was the achievement of King Henry IV of France?

Verbatim account of the last audience given by the late King Henry the Great to the Spanish Ambassador

The Ambassador

Sire, I am here on behalf of the King of Spain, my master, to ask your Majesty why you are fitting out such a powerful army, and whether it is directed against him.

The King

Had I behaved as badly towards him as he has towards me, he might well have cause for complaint.

The Ambassador

I beg your Majesty, Sire, to specify in what way the King my master has ever treated you badly.

The King

He has attacked my cities, corrupted Marshal de Biron and the Count of Auvergne, and now he has taken the Prince of Conde away from me.

The Ambassador

Sire, he could hardly turn away a prince who threw himself on his mercy, any more than your Majesty would if a foreign prince came and asked a similar favour.

The King

If such a thing happened I should try to make peace between him and his King and send him back to his own country. In addition, your master has never seen fit to lend the Emperor any money until now, when he has assited him to the tune of four hundred thousand crowns to wage war against my friends and allies.

The Ambassador

Sire, you accepted openly, for all to see, both men and money from the Netherlands, and you recalled Antonio Perez to France. I wish to know whether it is against the King my master that you are massing such a powerful army.

The King

I arm my head and shoulders to avoid getting hurt, and I shall grasp my sword and strike those who anger me.

The Ambassador

But what am I to tell the King my master?

The King

You may tell him anything you please.

Reality could never have matched the legend. Henry IV could not eliminate the forces of instability in France. What he could do was establish a political consensus.

Mark Greengrass, *France in the Age of Henry IV*, 1984.

France in the Person of Henry IV, Absolutist, Gallican, Patriotic, Nationalistic France.

R. Mousnier, *The Assassination of Henry IV*, 1973.

13 Spain Under Philip II, 1556–98

PREVIEW

The Accession of King Philip II, 1556

MAP OF SPAIN c.1550

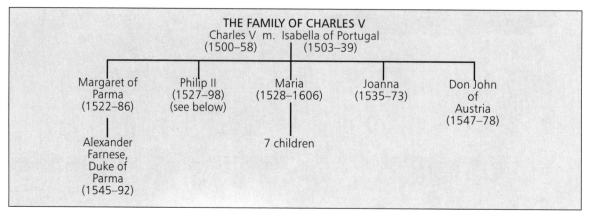

THE FAMILY OF CHARLES V

Charles V m. Isabella of Portugal
(1500–58)   (1503–39)

| Margaret of Parma (1522–86) | Philip II (1527–98) (see below) | Maria (1528–1606) | Joanna (1535–73) | Don John of Austria (1547–78) |

Alexander Farnese, Duke of Parma (1545–92)

7 children

```
PHILIP II's FAMILY
(1527–98)
```

Married	Children
1. Maria of Portugal	- Don Carlos (1545–68)
2. Mary Tudor	
3. Elizabeth de Valois	- Isabella
	- Catalina
4. Anne of Austria	- Ferdinand (1571–8)
	- Carlos Lorenzo (1573–5)
	- Diego (1575–82)
	- Philip III (1578–1621)
	- Maria (1580–3)

Main Events in the Reign of Philip II

1555–6	Charles V abdicated from the Netherlands and Spain.
1557	First Royal bankruptcy.
1559	Peace of Cateau-Cambresis with France.
1559	Philip II arrived from the Netherlands and subsequently never left Spain.
1561	The Mediterranean War against the Turks.
1566	Beginning of the revolt in the Netherlands.
1568	Death of Don Carlos.
1568–9	*Moriscos* revolt in Granada.
1571	Battle of Lepanto in the Mediterranean.
1575–6	Second major bankruptcy.
1579	Arrest of Antonio Perez.
1580	Annexation of Portugal.
1588	Launching of the Armada.
1590	The *Millones* Tax.
1591	The revolt in Aragon.
1592	Parma's invasion.
1596	Final Royal bankruptcy.
1598	Peace Treaty of Vervins with France.

How Should We View the Reign of Philip II?

How should we view Philip II after his reign of nearly 43 years? Was he the heroic and prudent king as seen by his Catholic Spanish contemporaries? Was he a ruler with boundless power? Or was he a weak man, a person of moderate intelligence who always felt he lived in the shadow of his father?

Was he the protector of Catholicism and the supporter of the Counter Reformation against the growing threat of Protestantism? Or was he on the other hand the cruel bigot who developed the Spanish Inquisition and took personal delight in the *auto-da-fe*?

Did Philip usher in the Golden Century of Spain? Or did his reign sow the seeds of the dramatic decline that occurred in the 17th century?

On 25 August 1559, nearly a year after the death of his father, King Philip set sail from Flushing in the Netherlands to take up his rightful inheritance of Spain. As Fernand Braudel has noted 'it was in a euphoric atmosphere that Philip left the Netherlands. Representatives from all over Italy flocked round him, offering money and presenting petitions, Cosimo de'Medici asking to keep Siena, the Grand Master of Malta asking for the orders necessary for an expedition against Tripoli, the Republic of Genoa seeking detailed rulings on the recovery of Corsica, the Farnese seeking to drive out the Duchess of Lorraine and to ensure that the Government of the Netherlands was safely in the hands of Margaret of Parma. Amid the reception and the Te Deums, Philip II distributed his final favours to the Lords of Flanders and defined the powers of the new Governor.'

'The situation in Spain in 1559 was serious indeed. Although the country had been spared the direct experience of war, it had provided Charles V with an endless supply of men, ships and money, especially money. Socially, economically and politically, the country was plunged into chaos, racked by deep discontent aggravated even further by a religious crisis which was taken very seriously.'

In 1558 the Inquisition uncovered the presence of several Protestant cells, in Seville, Valladolid and other cities. The cells contained the ideas of Erasmus and Luther, and an *auto-da-fe* was held in Valladolid and Seville within a month of Philip's arrival.

In addition, the years 1556–9 seemed to have witnessed significant political unrest. Royal authority was opposed by the wealthy clergy, the independent aristocracy, and by the *Moriscos*. The *Fueros*, the local

TALKING POINT

In 1559, the Venetian Ambassador said that Philip's aim was 'not to wage war to add to his kingdoms, but to wage peace in order to keep that that he has'.

Can it ever be anything more than propaganda to allege that you were waging war to maintain the peace?

privileges of towns and nobles, were always being maintained. Furthermore, the crown officially declared itself bankrupt on 1 January 1557: Government debts to the bankers would be paid back in *Juros* or life annuities, with an interest of 5 per cent. The first repayment was on 1 January 1557. The bankers accepted the arrangement. Spain was now paying the price for Charles V's empire and the continual state of war.

At the same time a run of bad harvests damaged local agriculture. Food became scarce and the cost of bread rose to famine prices. Taxation remained high and the standard of living deteriorated.

On the other hand, however, not all news was bad news. The Peace of Cateau-Cambresis, signed with France, was a great victory for Spain. One Spanish commentator wrote at the time 'truly these peace talks have been directed by God Himself, because, although we have settled things so much to our own advantage, the French are delighted with it.' For the next 40 years, France was to be enveloped in religious and civil wars, whilst Spain, with the benefit of the Madrid–Vienna axis, was at least free to concentrate on foreign policy issues in both the Mediterranean and the north Atlantic.

Philip's sister Maria had married the son of the Holy Roman Emperor Ferdinand, thus cementing the links with Vienna. And Philip himself later married one of Ferdinand's daughters Ann. Support could be relied upon from Genoa and Savoy and the bankers of Genoa were a great advantage at a time of financial uncertainty.

ANN OF AUSTRIA, WIFE OF PHILIP II.

Focus

13.1 Philip II – The Man

In this focus, three aspects of Philip's life will be considered. You will be offered information, evidence and facts about each aspect and then you will be asked either to form an opinion or to make a judgement about Philip.

It is very curious that Philip refused to have a biography written. He allowed no official memoirs and he kept no personal journal or diary. Most of our evidence for his reign is therefore circumstantial or anecdotal. How will this affect your view of him? How does it affect Historians' views of him?

It is important to understand that the problem of understanding Philip is partly offset by the fact that his role as administrator/king meant that he spent much of his time in writing. The official records of his administration tell us much about Philip the man.

Making a Judgement

Judgements should always be:
- **Fair**
  Taking alternative views into consideration.
- **Objective**
  Based on facts where possible, i.e. historical evidence.
- **Prepared to acknowledge opinions**
- **The result of rational processes of thought**

It is important to understand that judgements may not be sound even though they are based on facts. For example: who supplied the facts in the first place and how reliable are they?

Forming an Opinion

Opinions may be:
- **Biased**
- **Subjective**
- **Speculative** – what does this mean?
- **Arrived at without sufficient reference to evidence and facts**
- **Without sufficient acknowledgment** – will not acknowledge other views or judgements.
- **Affected by a person's background feelings and beliefs**

It is important to emphasise that opinions may well be valid, but judgements are more objective and more properly thought through.

Philip's Childhood and Upbringing

How did Philip's childhood and upbringing affect his adult life?

From the evidence below try to form an opinion, or a judgement, on this question. It is important to understand which of the two you are making.

- Philip was brought up in a huge household of 191 people; he was rarely alone.
- His mother, Isabella of Portugal, brought him up strictly until her death when he was only twelve years old. His father, the Emperor Charles V, was often away.
- His first tutor, Zuniga, was very strict with the young Philip, who wrote to his father to complain. His father's reply was clear: 'if he gave in to your every caprice he would be like the rest of mankind and you would have no-one to tell you the truth'.
- He was taught self-discipline and self-restraint and became skilful at concealing his feelings and emotions.
- He loved nature from an early age, kept cage birds and wanted to be out of doors. He especially loved hunting. He went on retreat in Holy Week and this became a lifelong practice. It was interesting that as a young boy he took hunting equipment with him for the return journey. His health was always poor and sickly. In 1535, he was very ill indeed with some sort of severe gastric problem. Bowel trouble dogged him all his life.
- He had a wide and rigorous education with a Spanish emphasis: the Castilian grammar book, Latin, Greek, Mathematics, Architecture, Geography, History. Interestingly, he learned no contemporary foreign languages.
- On his grand tour as a young man in 1548 his father wanted to counter the critics of his son's narrow experience. When he was freed from the confines of home for the first time aged twenty-one, his tutor complained about his lazy and careless behaviour to Charles, who called his son to the Netherlands and gave him a telling off. Nevertheless, this time in the Netherlands gave him his life-long love of gardens, paintings and fine buildings.
- The essential advice he received from his father just before his accession was 'transact business with many and do not bind yourself to or become dependent upon any individual, because although it may save time it does no good'.

Philip as a Husband and Father

The traditional view of Philip was as a cold and calculating administrator. Does the evidence about his role as husband and father suggest a different character: a man of warmth and care and sympathy?

Form an opinion or judgement in the light of the evidence below.

- On Philip's first marriage at the age of fifteen, his father gave him the following advice: to keep away from his wife as much as possible once the marriage had been consummated. Charles believed that excessive sexual activity would damage the still developing boy and prevent him from fathering heirs to the throne. He told his tutor to make sure Philip followed this advice 'keep her (his wife) away from the Prince except for the times which his life and health can stand'.
- His father also advised him not to indulge in physical relationships outside marriage: 'apart from the discomfort and ills that may ensue... it will destroy the effects of your keeping away from her'.
- Philip married four times and three of his wives were young and died relatively young in childbirth:
    Maria of Portugal, 1543–5, died giving birth to Don Carlos.
    Mary Tudor of England, 1554–8.
    Elizabeth of Valois, 1560–8, had five pregnancies. Two daughters survived – Isabella and Catalina. Elizabeth died with the fifth and stillborn child.
    Ann of Austria, 1570–80, after seven pregnancies she died in the last. Philip III, the heir to the throne, was her fifth child.
- Philip was often thought to be a caring father. He bought dolls as presents for his daughters and soldiers for the boys, encouraging them all to keep birds and taking them into the country with him.
- When Philip was in Portugal from 1580 to 1583 he wrote 34 letters to his teenage daughters. Catalina also kept a further 93. Philip destroyed their letters to him.

Philip's Personal Interests and Court Activities

In spite of Philip's huge political commitments, he still had a wide range of personal interests. In the light of the evidence below, form an opinion or a judgement about Philip the Man.

- Philip attended Mass every day and humbly joined Monks bareheaded at Christmas or on the Feast of Corpus Christi in freezing cold or blazing heat. He expressed an interest in a wide range of activities when he had the time: painting – he enthusiastically developed a collection of Flemish art and enjoyed both painting and the music of choirs, organs and minstrels.
- He wanted gardens like those in the Netherlands and sent architects and gardeners to tour Northern Europe to create a Flemish garden in Spain. He also imported the gardeners as Spaniards knew little about trees and shrubs.

- The size of his gardens was legendary. For example, the lake at Cassa del Campo was big enough to stage a mock galley battle.
- He created two small zoos at Aranjuez and Cassa del Campo. Security was not always adequate and a lioness once escaped and mauled a courtier to death in front of the royal party.
- He loved books and read widely. He followed other pastimes, including tapestry, needlework and games. He was interested in herbalism and alchemy.
- Amongst the books he read were Aesop's fables, classical authors like Ovid and Josephus, and many others. By his bed, he kept forty-two books – all but one was religious.

Government and Administration

Philip II was king of Spain from his father's abdication in January 1556 until his death in 1598. It is interesting to observe the changes he made in government and administration during that time.

Philip inherited a clear system from his father and was much influenced by his father's advice. Charles's advice centred on 'the defence of the Empire, the propagating of the Holy Faith of Jesus Christ, and the preserving of our peoples in peace and security'.

From the beginning of his reign Philip recognised what J.H. Elliott has called his 'double trusteeship'. Philip's mission to rule came from God, but in addition he had a clear responsibility for his subjects 'for the people were not made for the sake of the Prince, but the Prince was instituted at the instance of the people'. This comment from Philip II to his Viceroy in Naples makes clear the king's belief in his responsibilities. As Elliott has said, 'it was his task to protect them from foreign enemies and to dispense justice among them, for the essence of good government was that it should be just government in which the king rewarded the good, punished the wicked, and saw that all men, irrespective of rank, remained in undisturbed possession of their rights and property'.

In practice, government administration was slow. Philip ruled by sitting at his desk and reading and signing papers. He read the *consultas*, the statements of advice from all his many councils. He read petitions from nobles and townsmen and other people. He annotated these in the margins and issued his own comments through his secretaries. Thus decision-making was slow: in May 1571, 1252 separate pieces of paper were dealt with by the king. In 1560 one of his secretaries grumbled that 'decisions are taken so slowly that even a cripple could keep up with them'.

From 1573 Philip's personal secretary and confidant' was Mateo Vazquez. Vazquez's role was crucial and described by another secretary as follows:

> Papers were dealt with in this way. His Majesty used to sit down at his table and the secretary came up to it with his papers. Sitting on a stool, Vazquez would make a report to his Majesty on what those secret letters and memorials on serious matters contained. When his Majesty had listened, he decided what he wished to be done in each case... The secretary at once took a note of his Majesty's resolutions and subsequently turned these into memorandums for the ministers concerned in his Majesty's name... If the matter was serious the memorandum were written by Vazquez, but initialled by the King... When his Majesty dealt with *consultas* secretary Vazquez would read out the substance of them with the Council's recommendation, and his Majesty having heard their contents, took the decision which seemed best in each case in the presence of the secretary. The latter noted down a decision on a sheet of paper and afterward, using the most clear and concise reasons, he put the decision in the margin of the *consulta* in his handwriting, which the King subsequently initialled.

Taken from G. Parker, *Philip II*, 1978.

Philip took all final decisions personally. His government was not in any way similar to a modern cabinet or ministerial government. All decisions were made and signed by him, often in response to *consultas* from the various councils. The system was inevitably cumbersome. In 1565 Gonzalo Perez, the secretary of the Council of State, complained 'his Majesty makes mistakes and will continue to do so in many matters because he discusses them with different people, sometimes with one, at other times with another, concealing something from one minister and revealing it to another. It is therefore small wonder that different and even contradictory decisions are issued'.

A.W. Lovett in his book *Early Habsburg Spain*, 1986, is very doubtful about Philip's understanding.

> Yet just how much Philip understood of what passed across his table, or what was said to him in his private office, is an open question. For the most part he read the dispatches of the day and his advisers' comments without taking a clear position. Perhaps he hoped that application and annotation would do service for insight and resolution, the two qualities he most obviously lacked. Only in matters of administrative minutiae did Philip show confidence in his own judgement; otherwise he dithered... The bonding, under intense pressure, of moral calling and limited intelligence, had the inevitable result. The King was high minded, weak and devious.

The mainstay of the central system was the existence of Central Councils. The chart indicates the hierarchy of these. As business increased, so the Central Councils had to meet more often. From 1571, the Council of the Indies met three afternoons a week, as well as every morning, in order to get through its agenda. The quantity of paperwork increased enormously. For example, the Council of War which produced two or three bundles of working papers a year in 1560, was turning out over 30 bundles by the 1590s.

It was not surprising, therefore, that Philip began to seek more intimate advice through the setting up of an informal Junta. In 1571, for example, he met regularly with three senior advisers to plan the naval campaign in the Mediterranean and the Battle of Lepanto. In 1585, such was the burden of paperwork, that the King called five advisers to him before his evening meal. This was nicknamed the `Junta Noche'. Moreover, in 1589 Philip extended the idea and established the *Junta Grande*, a regular meeting of eight to ten Councillors, to plan the new *Millones* tax and the suppression of the revolt in Aragon. The *Junta Grande* continued to meet throughout the 1590s.

Much of the discussions in the Juntas was secret. Yet Philip saw the need for the systematic ordering of official documents – the state archives at Simancas were established in 1566 and a separate archive for the Indies was established at Seville. From 1575, a census of population was produced for Castile, and an attempt was made to conduct a similar survey of the Americas.

In all these councils, the factions of the court were an important influence on the king. Two major factions emerged: the families of Toledo under the Duke of Alva were thought by some to represent a closed Castilian policy, and a warlike approach in the Netherlands. On the other hand, the Mendosa faction, led by the Prince of Eboli and the Perez family, were considered to stand for a more open federal policy and a more peaceful approach to the Netherlands.

PORTRAIT OF PHILIP II (MOUNTED ON A COW), THE DUKE OF ALENCON, THE DUKE OF ALVA AND WILLIAM OF ORANGE.

With the establishment of a permanent capital city at Madrid in 1561, the court remained fairly static and Philip was seen by few of his subjects. In addition, the Escorial Royal Palace was built between 1563 and 1584 and occupied by Philip from 1570.

Thereafter Philip's movements from one royal palace to another were limited to a small geographical area.

In the government of Castile, the position of the *Cortes* continued to be important. Philip summoned it on twelve occasions, a reflection of his need for finance in a contained period of overseas war. He made it clear that the *Cortes* had no legislative responsibility. Its role was to agree and approve his financial requests. However, there was always much political debate and the influence of members of the *Cortes* continued to be significant.

Similarly local government throughout Castile continued through the use of royal officials known as *Corregidores*. And Philip's rule over local provinces was always an informal alliance between himself and the local nobility. In Salamanca province, for example, the crown controlled only one third of the population. The rest were ruled by the local nobility. Philip continued to delegate local power to nobles and towns in these areas. It is clear that Philip, because of the need for money to fight wars, was forced to have a strong central government for taxation and recruitment. Yet Philip depended crucially on the local nobles and towns and he contracted out for supplies and gave more authority to the regions because they alone could, in practice, provide him with his needs.

Other parts of the Iberian peninsula were not so easily ruled as Castile. The Basque provinces in the north were, in practice, self-governing republics, and the *Cortes* in Aragon and Navarre followed clear procedures for the presentation of their grievances before they would grant any taxes. Indeed, Philip visited Aragon only three times during his reign and summoned the *Cortes* only twice – in 1563 and in 1585. In all of these areas the power of the great lords was very important. In Valencia one local official described the 73 towns controlled by the king and over 300 controlled by the nobles and the church. The head of the Mendosa family, one of the major court factions, controlled nearly 800 towns and villages and nominated over 500 public officials. These Lordships were 'senorios'. Here the Lord was granted by the king the right to administer justice, collect taxes, nominate officials, and enlist men for the king's army. The Lord may or may not have owned all the land.

Philip, always desperate for money, developed a policy of selling more towns and church land to local lords. Between 1516 and 1575, 80 towns in new Castile, 43 per cent of the total, were sold to the jurisdiction of senorios. It is clear from this that Philip was not an absolute King throughout the whole of Spain. He relied very heavily on local Lords, towns and churchmen to ensure good Government.

Overseas Trade with the Americas

Throughout the first half of the 16th century, Spanish trade with the Americas was growing. It reached a peak between 1544 and 1550. In 1545 prospectors discovered the silver mines of Potosi in upper Peru, the greatest source of silver in the world. As a result of this discovery the volume of trade and the demand for ships to carry it increased dramatically.

This was felt most clearly during the reign of Philip II. Over this period, the number of ships on the Indies route increased by 176 per cent and the volume of tonnage by 238 per cent. And, as J. Lynch has shown, 'there were other signs of prosperity – new exports, such as timber for American shipyards, more manufactured goods in proportion to agricultural products, new types of ships, more foreign ships, and more foreign merchants at Seville. And the whole trade now enjoyed more efficient protection for the convoy system was finally perfected in 1564'.

From about 1560, silver mines became even more productive. German methods of mining by amalgamating silver with mercury were transported to the New World. Production increased dramatically. The increasing wealth of the Americas in turn demanded more European manufactured goods, and Spanish shipyards in the Bay of Biscay also experienced a boom. In spite of the raids of Hawkins and Drake – and Drake's raid on Panama in 1572 was a sensational event – the wealth of the Americas continued to pour into Seville. The period between 1584 and 1586 was one of particular prosperity, not least because of the addition of the Portuguese base in the Azores and the greater security now possible for communications and protection. Even the defeat of the Spanish Armada and the consequent loss of Spanish shipping could not cripple the Atlantic trade. New ships were quickly built in Spanish shipyards and older ones kept going. Within two years of the Armada armed escorts returned to the annual treasure fleets. Spain continued to benefit from her richest possession.

It is clear therefore that the government and administration of the Americas was an important priority for Philip II. The Council for the Indies had been set up by his father in 1524 with a president and eight councillors. It was the Supreme Law Court and it enabled the crown to impose its authority on territory which was originally conquered by private individuals. The council worked through two *Audiencias*. These bodies were both administrative and judicial and by 1550 there were ten of them. The crown also worked through their personal representatives, the Viceroys, who were appointed in Mexico in 1535 and Peru in 1542. Most senior officials were also appointed by the crown, and the Seville monopoly enabled the control of shipping and trade. Of course, in practice, there was much delegation of authority. Local officials, and particularly the councils who controlled the towns, were given much independence. The six-week minimum time-scale for travelling between Madrid and the Americas demanded that this should be so.

The Spanish Economy

The wealth of Spain in the reign of Philip II was great, but superficial. Its own natural resources were limited and undeveloped. Its social structure continued to give precedence to members of the nobility and the *hidalgo* class, who contributed little to the economy. Its wealth from the New World flattered to deceive and it failed to fully exploit the potential of New World markets.

Philip II was able to gain credit in order to fight his foreign wars and retain his supremacy in Europe. But his wealth was an illusion and in the following century Spain was to suffer dramatically.

The Wealth of Spain

Regional growth 1530–91, as a percentage of the total population				
	1530	%	1591	%
Castile	4,485,389	78.39	6,617,251	81.48
Aragon	289,776	5.06	348,533	4.29
Catalonia	312,227	5.45	373,490	4.59
Valencia	(300,000)	5.24	409,979	5.04
Guipuzcoa	(67,000)	1.17	(75,000)	0.92
Biscay	(65,000)	1.13	(72,500)	0.89
Alava	50,093	0.87	65,604	0.80
Navarre	151,885	2.65	157,980	1.94

Note: Figures in parentheses are estimated.
(Source: Felipe Ruiz Martin, 'La Poblacion espanola al comienzo de los tiempos modernos' (Cuadernos de Historia 1, Madrid, 1967, 199))

Population figures for individual towns (in vecinos)

	Caceres	Murcia	Valladolid	Cordoba
c.1500				5,500–6,000
1530		2,595	6,750	6,222
1557	1,401			
1561	1,471	2,956	6,644	8,889–9,333
1570		5,258		
1571				11,111–12,000
1584	1,540*			
1586	1,547	2,996		
1587			6,941	10,000–10,667
1591		3,370	8,112	9,556–10,000
1595	1,674			
1608	1,571			
1618				6,889–7,556
1626–33				6,889–8,000
1646	1,370			

* Variant: 1,463

(Sources: Caceres: Angel Rodriguez Sanchez, *Caceres... en el Siglo XVI*; Murcia: Francisco Chacon Jimenez, *Murcia en la centuria del quinientos*; Valladolid: Bartolome Bennassar, *Valladolid au siecle d'or*; Cordoba: J.I. Fortea Perez, *Cordoba en el Siglo XVI*, part 1)

Population Growth

The charts above demonstrate the significant increase in the population of the Iberian peninsula during Philip's reign. The reasons for this growth cannot be precisely known. But some factors certainly contributed: the development of political stability by Ferdinand and Isabella, Charles V and Philip; the prosperity of the *Mesta*-dominated woollen industry; the woollen trade based on the *Consulado* of Burgos; and the consequent increased employment from this industrial development. In addition, agricultural developments, like the extension of land under cultivation, were significant. In the province of Murcia between 1480 and 1621, the area of land under cultivation increased by 25 per cent. In addition, drainage and irrigation were also improved.

The consequences of this population rise were significant.

> Castile's demographic vigour had implications both for domestic and international politics. It guaranteed the standing of Castile as the principal support of the Habsburg dynasty... And it may also explain the success of the Habsburgs during the 16th century in dealing with France.

A.W. Lovett, *Early Habsburg Spain*, 1986.

Checks on Farming and Agriculture

During Philip's reign, however, the demographic and agricultural development was not uniform. In 1557 and in 1565 major epidemics accompanied poor harvests. In 1580, the year of the annexation of Portugal, plague killed 35,000 in Lisbon alone.

Industrial Development

During the first half of Philip II's reign the woollen industry also continued to grow. Segovia was the main centre with 600 looms by 1580, and a production of 13,000 pieces of cloth a year. In Granada, hundreds of Morisco families exported their silk to Italy. And the *Consulado* at Burgos continued to export Castilian wool to Flanders, Italy and England.

But from the year 1557 the woollen industry began to be checked. Communal lands on which sheep grazed were sold off increasingly to make money for the crown. The sale of communal land, usually to cities, denied pasture to the herds of smaller flock masters and the overall numbering of sheep was reduced. Common lands were also increasingly enclosed.

Trade

The export of woollen manufacture to Flanders, Italy and England was a central plank in the wealth of Philip II's Spain. Indeed, exports to Italy continued to grow right into the 17th century. However, the largest market, Flanders, which took about 60 per cent of Spain's wool, collapsed towards the end of the century. Interestingly, the Netherlands also supplied Spain with wheat and other essentials. 'The volume of mutual trade', according to Henry Kamen, 'was a cogent reason for Spain to keep hold of the rebellious provinces'. The fact that Philip II failed to see this as a priority is a significant indicator of his own limitations as a monarch. Moreover, Spain's dependence upon the merchants of Antwerp and Genoa, not least for mercantile insurance, was a major indicator of vulnerability. 'From the late 1560's these developments changed Spain from a country that might have become rich through its own imperial connections, into a nation whose economic fate was dictated by international capitalism' (Henry Kamen).

Inflation

The traditional view that Spanish bullion imports brought increasing inflation to Spain has now been discredited. Indeed it is clear that inflation in Spain was higher before 1562 than after it. Prices rose more quickly before the arrival of American bullion. However, the consequences of inflation were severe: the people of Spain could no longer afford to pay higher prices for food; consequently they could not afford to buy manufactured goods or pay increased taxes. Both these factors had damaging long-term effects.

Government Finances

The Costs of War

From the 1560s, Spain was fighting major world wars as both a Mediterranean and a northern European power. Consequently, the size of the Spanish army consequently increased dramatically. Between 1567 and 1574, nearly 43,000 Spaniards fought in Italy and the Low Countries – at a time when they were very much needed at home. In 1580, 46,000 men made up the army in the Netherlands while another 37,000 captured Portugal.

The costs of this army were enormous and wages of soldiers were often unpaid.

Taxes and Income

The income with which to pay the costs of war came largely from traditional sources:

- all states of the empire contributed, particularly when wars were fought on their own territories. For example, the Italian states contributed 400,000 ducats for the Battle of Lepanto.
- all the territories in Spain also contributed.
- the church increased its contribution: the *subsidio* became a regular tax after 1561 and the *excruzado* and the *cruzada* were increased. Their total yield by the 1590s was approximately 1.5 million ducats.
- other ordinary taxes in Spain like customs duties and the *encabeza-miento* were tripled between 1559 and 1577. The *Cortes* of Castile met 12 times during the reign and was always being asked for more and more money.
- in 1590 a new tax on four basic foodstuffs – meat, wine, oil and vinegar – was known as the *millones* and struck right at the heart of the subsistence of every Spaniard.
- the silver mines in America, fortunately for Philip, were now beginning to bring huge sums regularly to Spain. It has been estimated that America provided 64 million ducats in government income during Philip's reign.

The consequence of taxation on the ordinary Castilian was savage. It has been calculated that the burden of tax increased by 430 per cent during Philip's reign at a time when wages rose by only 80 per cent.

Bankruptcies

Because Philip did not have enough money to fight his wars, he had to declare himself bankrupt on no less than four occasions – 1557, 1560, 1576 and 1596. Equally damaging was the fact that he was constantly mortgaging future income to pay off his debts. The issue of *Juros* (government bonds) in exchange for cash mortgaged the government for generations to come.

Conclusion

The economic crash of the 1590s was totally predictable. Spain was living an economic illusion. In spite of Fernand Braudel's insistence that long-term economic and social trends would maintain Spain's wealth beyond 1650, the government was now facing a dramatic financial crisis.

By the early 17th century, population decline and economic confidence were both on the turn. Taxation was punishing and there was no appropriate industrial base to respond. In addition, the so-called 'Atlantic Plague', first reported in 1598, spread dramatically throughout the peninsula and in 1599 entered Seville. As one contemporary noted 'it deprived all Castile, the heartland of the monarchy, of its last trump, its richness in men. Segovia, the centre of the woollen industry, may have lost over 10% of its population in three years. The consequences were dramatic. The decline of Spain was under way'.

Religion and Society

Philip II and the Catholic Church

As mentioned above, Philip's arrival in Spain in 1559 coincided with the discovery of 'Lutheran' groups in Valladolid and Seville. Dramatic *auto-da-fe* were held in both cities and the leading perpetrators of heresy were executed. Philip himself was present on several of these occasions. In Seville alone, over 30 victims perished at the stake.

PHILIP II DECLARING HIS FAITH.

It was in this context that Philip II encouraged the final meeting of the Council of Trent from 1562 to 1563. Spanish support was a major factor in its success – there were 130 Spaniards at the final meeting. In addition, 11 of the 14 Papal theologians at the Council were also Spaniards.

Yet Philip was undecided on whether to publish the decrees of the Council of Trent in Spain. Finally, in 1564 he published them, provided they did not encroach on the rights and privileges of the Spanish crown, especially in the appointment of bishops. In spite of this delay, the Council of Trent did help the reform of the Spanish church. Indeed Kamen argues that 'Trent revolutionised Spanish Catholicism'. The introduction of the Roman Missal and Breviary imposed a unified form of service and phased out curious local customs. And if the implementation of this reform was gradual it was nonetheless real. In addition, local bishops now had the power to reform their local parish clergy. Cardinal Quiroga in Toledo arranged provincial synods and organised his bishopric into clear parishes, each with its own clergy. In this context education continued to improve. From 1563, an additional 20 seminaries were established in Spain for the training of priests, and in most parishes the priest was now preaching a regular Sunday sermon. Sunday Schools for the children of the parish were obligatory.

The consequences for the Spanish church were real. Kamen talks of 'a revolutionary sense of the sacred' and many innovations reflected this. Priests were to wear distinctive robes; they were no longer to attend wedding parties; carnivals, plays and dances were banned from church buildings; unseemly images were destroyed in churches. A famous painter, Francisco Pacheco, was commissioned by the Inquisition to study the acceptability of images in churches. Special plays were written to be performed on the Feast of Corpus Christi called 'Autos Sacramentales'. The dramatist Lope De Vega used these as a vehicle for his work. The ultimate consequence was a period of high spiritual creativity in Spain. St John of the Cross and St Teresa of Avila were celebrated spiritual mystics, and a more personal Christianity was emphasised in the writings of Luis de Granada, whose *Book of Prayer* in 1544 went through 23 editions in its first five years. In spite of all this, Philip's relations with the Papacy were invariably poor. Indeed, Philip resented the lack of help given by the Papacy in his struggle to maintain Catholicism in the Netherlands. In 1581 Philip wrote to his confidante, Cardinal Granville, 'I assure you that the Pope is wearing me out and has me on the point of losing my patience. It is clear to me that if the Netherlands were ruled by somebody else, the Pope would have performed miracles to prevent them being lost to the church, but because they are my states, I believe he is prepared to see them lost because they will thus be lost to me'. The pope was also hostile on other occasions: Gregory XIII tried to prevent the capture of Portugal in 1580 and Sixtus V would not support the invasion of England by the Armada. Philip's work with the Catholic church in Spain was separate from any movements for Papal reform.

The Spanish Inquisition

19th century Protestant Historians, inspired by the martyrology of the 16th century, and influenced by the libertarian and anti-Spanish feeling in America, saw the Spanish Inquisition as the 'Black Legend', a cruel and fanatical and violent preservation of Catholic absolutism. Led by the American historian J.L. Motley, they described the Inquisition in the darkest terms.

> The executioner, enveloped in a black robe from head to foot, with his eyes glaring at his victim through holes cut in the hood which muffled his face, practised successively all the forms of torture which the devilish ingenuity of the monks had invented. The imagination sickens when striving to keep pace with these dreadful realities.
>
> It taught the savages of India and America to shudder at the name of Christianity... It was court owning allegiance to no temporal authority, superior to all other tribunals. It was a bench of monks without appeal, having its familiars in every house, diving into the secrets of every fireside, judging and executing its horrible decrees without responsibility.

TALKING POINT
Philip wrote to his ambassador in Rome: 'I would prefer to lose all my dominions and a hundred lives if I had them, because I do not wish to be lord over heretics.'
Is it ever wise to believe what people say about their own motivations?

Recent research, particularly the work of Henry Kamen, has shown the prejudice and deliberate misrepresentation in much of this work. In his books, *The Spanish Inquisition* and *The Inquisition and Society in Spain*, Kamen has demonstrated that there was a never a serious threat to Catholic supremacy in Spain.

> The only religious problem confronting the Inquisition came from the Moriscos who produced most of the accused in the tribunals and who, over Spain as a whole, counted for about twenty-nine per cent of the cases tried between 1540 and 1614... Nearly two-thirds of all those arrested by the Holy Office were orderly Catholic Spaniards, unconnected with heresy... In Spain the clergy and the Inquisition were devoting their energies to the re-conversion of their own people to the faith. The relatively mild impact of the Holy Office in this allegedly ferocious period is indicated by the fact that its executions totalled no more than 1% per year of those arrested or some two to three annual executions in the whole of the Spanish realms, including America. The Inquisition centred on three main targets: enforcing respect for the sacred, issues of sexual morality, and the persecution of the Moriscos.
>
> H. Kamen, *The Inquisition and Society in Spain*, 1985.

The activity of the Inquisition in Granada between 1520 and 1570 illustrates the point.

Activity of the Inquisition of Granada, 1520–70				
Years	Number of Auto de Fe	Total No. Condemned	No. of Moriscos	Moriscos as % of Total Condemned
1520–9	1	89	3	3
1550–9	4	377	271	72
1563–9	4	420	368	88

In the Inquisition in Toledo between 1540 and 1614, half those arrested were for blasphemy, sacrilege or disrespect. Approximately one-third were for sexual offences, particularly sex outside marriage. Bigamy was also a significant offence. In addition, the Inquisition encouraged ordinary Spanish people to learn the Creed and the essential tenets of Catholicism. As Kamen has indicated 'after the initial period of terror against conversos... The Inquisition evolved from an instrument of repression into one or persuasion'. Indeed, given its limited personnel – perhaps only 45 inquisitors throughout Spain – and limited income, it could not be an oppressive institution. It had no secret police, torture was rarely used and the death penalty was statistically insignificant.

The Papal Index was another mechanism for enforcing Catholic authority. In 1558 a Royal Decree confirmed the censorship of Ferdinand and Isabella. The importation of books without a royal licence was made a crime punishable by death and confiscation of property. The Spanish Inquisition published its own Index in 1551, and this was periodically revised and extended. By 1583, all heretical works were included and also the works of many loyal Catholics like Thomas More. Even Luis de Granada's *Book of Prayer* and *Guide for Sinners* were prescribed.

Typical of the prosecutions of the Inquisition was the case of Cardinal de Carranza. He was arrested in 1559 because his writings, published in the Netherlands, were said to be heretical. He was kept in prison by the Inquisition for seven years. Eventually he was summoned to Rome, where he died in 1576. Most Roman Catholic theologians considered his work perfectly acceptable. He seems to have been no more than the victim of personal hostility amongst leading Spanish inquisitors.

The Persecution of *Moriscos*

During the reign of Philip II, the problem of overlapping civilisations was most severe in Granada. Here the *Moriscos* – the descendants of Spanish Moslems –constituted 54 per cent of the population. The tension between land-hungry Christians and free *Moriscos* became a major problem.

There were many Christian petty persecutions and discriminations against *Moriscos*. Indeed, in 1565 a synod of clergy in Granada petitioned the king to pursue a policy of repression. They argued that *Moriscos* in future should not be allowed to use their own language, dress, literature or dances, and that their houses should be regularly inspected. In 1567 the King published a Royal Decree agreeing to these proposals. The anger of the *Moriscos* exploded into rebellion between 1568 and 1570. Within a year the rebel army numbered 30,000 people, and Philip II's government was under genuine threat. Fortunately for Philip, the *Moriscos* received no help from the Turks of north Africa and the revolt collapsed.

Philip's solution to the problems of 'overlapping civilisations' was sharp and decisive. In 1570 he published a decree, and within a month over 50,000 *Moriscos* were expelled from their homeland and re-settled en masse in other parts of Spain. Between 1569 and 1573, indeed, it is possible that as many as 80,000 *Moriscos* were driven out of their homeland in Granada, with perhaps 50,000 Christians from Andalucia being re-settled on *Morisco* land in Granada. However, because they lacked the agricultural technology of the *Moriscos* they were unable to farm it effectively and Granada as a province was decimated.

In the Inquisitions of Saragosa and Valencia, the majority of those persecuted were *Moriscos*. In Toledo, one *Morisco* was arrested and accused of 'playing music at night, dancing the zambra, and eating cus-cus'. These national customs were now seen as clear evidence of heresy.

It was not until the 16th century, however, that it was clear that the *Morisco* population was growing more quickly than the Christian population. This increased the racialist threat to the Christians and extreme solutions were now suggested. One proposal was to remove all *Morisco* children from their parents and to forbid *Moriscos* from marriage. One bishop even suggested the castration of all *Moriscos*. In 1582, the Council of State concluded that only a general expulsion of *Moriscos* from Spain would do. Various factors delayed the implementation of their decree, but early in the 17th century the *Morisco* problem was finally solved by a wholesale expulsion.

FOCUS

13.2 Total History: The Only Perspective on Philip II's Spain?

This book represents an attempt to write a new kind of history, 'total history', written in three different registers on three different levels, perhaps best described as three different conceptions of time, the writer's aim being to bring to together in their multiplicity the different measures of timed past, to acquaint the reader with their co-existence, their conflicts and contradictions, and the richness of the experience they hold.

My favourite vision of history is as a song for many voices – but it has the obvious advantage that some will drown others: reality will not always adapt conveniently into a harmonised setting for solo and chorus... Only the sum of all the voices, brought together by the human sciences, can give us that total history whose image it is so difficult to reconstitute in its rich entirety.

F. Braudel, *The Mediterranean and the Mediterranean World of Philip II*, 1992.

Abbreviated Table of Contents

Geography

The Mediterranean as a unit, with its creative space, the amazing freedom of its sea routes, its cities born of movement, its complementary populations, its congenial enmities, is the unceasing work of human hands; but those hands have had to build with unpromising material, a natural environment far from fertile and often cruel, one that has imposed its own long lasting limitations and obstacles... I have therefore sought out within the framework of a geographical study, those local, permanent, unchanging and much repeated features which are the constance of Mediterranean history.

Economy and Society

The second undertaking of this book is to discover the collective destiny of the Mediterranean in the 16th Century, its social history in the fullest sense of the word... This brings us face to face continuously with economic decline. With the decline, one after the other, of Turkey, Islam, Italy, and the Iberian supremacy. An economic upswing beginning about 1470 reached a peak, or slowed down for a while, during the years of record high prices 1590–1600, then continued after a fashion until 1650... This long upward movement is confirmed essentially by variations in grain prices which give us a clear series of figures... It seems clear then that, during the long 16th Century, a slow but powerful upsurge favoured the advance of the material economy and of everything dependent upon it. It was the secret of the fundamental healthiness of the economy. Still waters run deep and we should not be misled by surface flurries. At all events, neither the reversal of the secular trend of the 1590's, nor the sharp shock of the brief crisis of 1619–21, mark the end of Mediterranean splendour.

Individuals and Events

Alongside such problems the role of the individual and the event necessarily dwindles. Are we right to take so Olympian a view? If we view history from such a distance, what becomes of man, his role in history, his freedom of action? The Italian historian Benedetto Croce has argued, not without reason, that any single event – let us say the assassination of Henry IV in 1610 – contains in embryo the entire history of mankind. To put it another way, history is the keyboard on which these individual notes are sounded. We must consider the importance of events and of individual freedom... What was Spain's freedom in 1571 in the sense of the courses open to her? What degree of freedom was possessed by Philip II or by Don John of Austria as he rode at anchor among his ships, allies and his troops? Each of these so called freedoms seems to me to resemble a tiny island almost a prison. By stating a narrowness of the limits of action, is one denying the role of the individual in history? I think not. One may only have the choice between striking two or three blows: the question still arises: will one be able to strike them at all? To do so in the knowledge that only this range of choices is open to one? I would conclude with the paradox that the true man of action is he who can measure most nearly the constraints upon him, who chooses to remain within them and even to take advantage of the weight of the inevitable, exerting his pressure in the same direction. All efforts against the prevailing tide of history – which is not always obvious – are doomed to failure.

Conclusion

So when I think of the individual, I am always inclined to see him imprisoned within a destiny in which he himself has little hand, fixed in a landscape in which the infinite perspectives of the long term stretch into the distance, both behind him and before. In historical analysis as I see it, rightly or wrongly, the long run always wins in the end.

---

1 What, in your view, is 'total history'?
2 What do you consider its merits to be?
3 What difficulties does the Historian have in pursuing it?
4 Would it be possible to create a total history of Europe in the 16th Century which saw Spain as much more a part of northern Europe and Atlantic Europe?
5 How does Braudel's notion of total history challenge your understanding of Philip II of Spain?

Examining the Evidence

The Cases of Don Carlos and Antonio Perez: Political Necessity or Personal Weakness?

In using historical sources, Historians must always consider:
- the context of the source; the influences on the writer;
- the purposes for which the source was written;
- the opinions of the author;
- any judgement reached by the author.

DON CARLOS, SON OF PHILIP II.

In the cases of the death of Don Carlos in 1568, and the trial and exile of the king's adviser Antonio Perez in 1590, it is difficult, and perhaps even impossible, to unravel the true story. Was Philip II exhibiting the weaknesses in his own character, as some historians have argued? Or was he simply acting out of political necessity in order to preserve his realm and do his duty?

Source A

Philip's instructions to his son, the young Philip III, 1598.

> Strive my son to love God with all your heart for no-one can be saved who does not love Him...

> If in your mind you contemplate doing something of importance, consult your Confessor, or some wise man with high moral principles, in order to determine the most suitable course to follow. Let those who become your friends and confidants be good, virtuous and respected men, whether they be laymen or clerics...

> You should take pride in according your subjects' peace and justice... Do not wage war especially against Christians without great thought and just cause; and if it is necessary to do so let it be without harm to churches and innocent persons. If you are at war with another, whenever it is within your power, strive for peace; and if you are not directly involved, mediate between those at war in order that discords cease.

> See to it that ministers of justice, councilmen, magistrates and judges be virtuous and wise, and secretly inform yourself as to the administration of their office.
>
> Quoted in J.C. Rule and J.J. Te Paske, *The Character of Philip II*, 1963.

Source B

The *Apologia* of 1580 of William of Orange.
William of Orange, the leader of the rebels in the Netherlands, was writing to respond to a series of personal accusations by King Philip II. The *Apologia* is a political statement designed as a work of propaganda against the King of Spain.

> My accuser seems not to have remembered the common maxim, that whoever ventures to accuse another, ought to be well assured that he

himself is innocent. And yet, is not this King who has endeavoured to stigmatise my lawful marriage with infamy, the husband of his own niece? It will be said by his partisans that he previously obtained a dispensation from the Pope. But does not the voice of nature cry aloud against such an incestuous conjunction? And in order to make room for this marriage is it not true that he put to death his former wife, the mother of his children, the daughter and sister of the Kings of France?... His son too, his only son, was sacrificed in order to furnish the Pope with the pretext for so unusual a dispensation; which was granted in order to prevent the Spanish monarchy from being left without a male heir. This was the true cause of the death of Don Carlos, against whom some misdemeanours were alleged. But not a single crime sufficient to justify his condemnation, much less to vindicate a father for imbrueing his hands in the blood of his son...

And now he addresses himself more particularly to criminals and malefactors, as those who are most likely to comply with his request 'and in order that his [William's] destruction may be the more effectually and speedily accomplished, we, desirous of punishing vice and rewarding virtue, promise on the word of the King, that if any person shall be found possessed of courage and public spirit, sufficient to free us from the aforesaid pest of society, we shall order to be delivered to him, the sum of twenty-five thousand crowns. And if he shall have committed any crime, however enormous, we promise to grant him our Royal Pardon'. Is not this in plain terms calling on every desperate wretch, every outcast from society, to assist him in the execution of his design? No crime, however enormous but shall be pardoned; no criminal, however detestable, but shall be crowned with honour. Does this King deserve the title which he assumes, a minister of God?

From J. C. Rule and J. J. Te Paske, *The Character of Philip II*, 1963.

ANTONIO PEREZ, SECRETARY TO PHILIP II.

Source C
Antonio Perez's Testimony Concerning the Murder of Escobedo.
In March 1578 Juan d'Escobedo, the personal secretary of Don John of Austria, was attacked by hired assassins and murdered in a side street in Madrid. He had been sent to Spain the previous year to argue on behalf of Don John at the court of the King. However, Escobedo had been allowed little direct access to Philip; instead he was obliged to proceed through an intermediary, Philip's chief secretary, Antonio Perez.

Rumours in Madrid suggested that Perez had arranged for the assassination of Escobedo. Philip initially discounted the rumours, but in the following year he received Don John 's official papers from the Netherlands, after his brother's untimely death. These pointed to the involvement of Perez, not only in the murder of Escobedo, but also in the blocking of communication between Don John and the King. There were also suggestions of an affair between Antonio Perez and the Princess of Eboli, a fact discovered by Escobedo. In July 1579 Perez was arrested. However, because the King was implicated in the plot, Perez was released. Only in January 1585 was he rearrested but even then the trial could not proceed. It was not until 1590 that Perez was finally tried for the murder of Escobedo. After torture, however, he escaped and fled to Aragon where he inspired the revolt of 1591. Subsequently, he fled further to France and published various documents in his own defence.

- A letter from the king to the judge in the Perez trial 1590:

  Antonio Perez knows very well the information I possess of his having Escobedo killed and the reasons he told me which existed for it.

- Perez's statement under torture, after outlining that he had already told the King of Escobedo's plotting with Don John:

  It then seemed that if they arrested Escobedo, which his majesty very nearly did, my Lord Don John would be uneasy. If Escobedo was allowed to return to the Netherlands, he would upset everything. A means was needed which would overcome both these drawbacks. It seemed best to the Marquis of Los Velas [a nobleman who had died the year before the torture] to give him a titbit of poison and end the whole thing.

- Perez's defence memorial written in Aragon in 1591:

  There were drawbacks in the way of arresting Escobedo legally. Thus, what was fitting was that the embarrassing situation should be solved by some titbit or other means.

- Entries on the book of Antonio Perez after his flight: Perez outlines the occasion when Philip II summoned him to the Escorial and in a private conversation in an inner room spoke to him as follows.

  Antonio Perez, many a time, watching and waking, I have considered my brother's affairs, or rather those of Escobedo, and what a path they are come to with their schemings. I find it very needful to make a decision quickly or we shall be too late. I find no fitter remedy for anybody than to be rid of Juan d'Escobedo. And thus I am determined upon it and I will entrust this deed to no other than you, since I have had good proofs of your fidelity and of your diligence.

  Sources quoted in G. Maranon, *Antonio Perez*, 1954.

Source D

J.L. Motley, *The Rise of the Dutch Republic,* 1856.
Motley was an American Protestant who saw many similarities between the freedom of 19th-century America and the freedom of the Dutch in the 16th Century.

> As for the royal criminal called Philip II, his life is his arraignment... Homicide such as was hardly ever compassed before by one human being was committed by Philip when in the famous Edict of 1568 he sentenced every man, woman and child in the Netherlands to death. But the whole of this population, three millions or more, were not positively destroyed because no human energy could suffice to execute the diabolical decree... It is superfluous to refer to such isolated misdeeds as his repeated attempts to procure the assination of the Prince of Orange... Or to poison the Queen of England.
>
> In J.C. Rule and J.J. Te Paske, *The Character of Philip II*, 1963.

Source E

Leopold Von Ranke, *The Ottoman and Spanish Empires*, 1827.
Von Ranke was the first historian of Spain to use hitherto unpublished reports from Venetian ambassadors. He was therefore in a position to appraise existing judgements of Philip II.

> There are in this dismal life some spots of surpassing gloom. Why was his son Don Carlos disposed to rebel against him? It is now but too certain that he wished to do so. Assuredly the Prince presented a decided contrast to his father; the latter particularly at first all calm and pacific; the former on the contrary fired with an enthusiastic love of arms, ardently attached to the soldiery, and of an impetuosity of character that disdained to conceal ambition, cruelty or any other passion. The more restrictions there were imposed upon him the more passionate became his inclinations. He was still very young when he began to be agitated of entrusting him with some lieutenancy. But this was not done. He had reason to expect a greater degree of independence from his marriage which he negotiated.
>
> As often as war broke out he longed to join in it, but he was always forced to remain at home. At last he made it the sole object of his wishes that the pacification of the Netherlands should be committed to him: Alva was preferred to him. Thus this impetuous spirit shut out on all sides from active exertion and driven back upon itself was thwarted and irritated to madness...
>
> Did his father then leave him to pine away and die in prison? Or is the story really true that the coffin in which Carlos lay was opened and his head was found severed from his body? Be it enough to say that Philip lived on such deplorable terms with his son that he must either fear everything at his hand or doom him to death without pity.
>
> In J.C. Rule and J. J. Te Paske, *The Character of Philip II*, 1963.

TALKING POINT
In 1598, Philip advised his son: 'Never condemn a man to death except unhappily or unwillingly when forced by the demands of justice and a necessity for law and order.' How does this relate to the death of Don Carlos, the trial of Antonio Perez and the murder of Escobedo?

Source F

In 1567 in the lull which followed the defence of Malta, Philip considered carefully the possibility of his return to the Netherlands and the difficulties this might present... The principal obstacle to any schemes was the question of who should rule Castile while the King was gone. A retarded heir with a record of violence could not be left and not to be nominated ruler of the low countries. By late 1567 the prince began to make a number of inept attempts to escape to Italy, relying foolishly on the assistance of his uncle, Don John of Austria.

Action needed to be taken, and quickly.

A.W. Lovett, *Early Habsburg Spain*, 1986.

Source G

It is certain... That it was not the King nor the Marquis of Los Velas who proposed killing Escobedo, but Antonio Perez himself. In several of his writings, when explaining the causes of the death, he vividly depicts Escobedo as the inspirer of Don John, and Don John's behaviour as a danger to the country. Without realising he is doing so, he reveals to us the argument he pestered his master with day and night. That master was prone to let himself be deceived and convinced of the need for the execution. Reading all this we feel once more convinced that Perez did not invent anything fundamental. What he did – and he was a past master at it – was to interpret the truth falsely in favour of his machinations...

Perez, before he was tortured, was asked to declare `the reasons there had been for his Majesty giving his consent for the death of secretary Escobedo'. The excuses for the King thus became obvious. He was weakwilled, not excessively far-sighted and fascinated by his secretary's brilliant mind, and thus he let himself be hood-winked and dragged into a tragic decision.

G. Maranon, *Antonio Perez*, 1954.

Source H

Philip's failure to overcome the problems facing him... was very much a personal one. The explanation lies largely in his own psychology... Although several more sophisticated justifications were advanced to explain Philip's aversion to compromise, underneath them all there lay a sort of idealism, Philip II was not a 'weak man with supreme power'; he was a man of rigid principle with supreme power. It was only when the course dictated by his principles seemed impossible, or when his principles broke down [as in the case of Escobedo and Perez] that the King showed real weakness. Without them he was simply at a loss...

However, his adherence to principle was not only reinforced by religion, there was also a deep-seated fear of appearing weak. The King seems to have been deeply afraid of changing his mind in public... The King's handling of the Perez affair displayed... the same reluctance to change course until the very last moment.

...We can no longer penetrate the obscurity that surrounds the whole affair, and for two reasons: first, much of the crucial evidence was never written down. As Philip wrote, tantalisingly, to Perez on one occasion:

1 How far does the evidence in Sources B and C contradict that in Source A? Is it conceivable, as suggested in Source B, that a king could plot to kill another political leader? What does this accusation tell us about the nature of diplomacy at the time?

2 Does any of the evidence in Source C *prove* the king's complicity in the death of Escobedo?

3 On what points do Sources F, G and H agree about the character of Philip II? Do they invalidate the judgements in Sources B and C?

4 Considering Parker's conclusions, what further evidence would the Historian need in order to formulate a clear judgement about the motivation behind the death of Don Carlos and the trial of Antonio Perez?
Are clear personal judgements possible in history?

'I am afraid of what Escobedo may do in this matter, but let us talk about it, for it is something to speak about rather than write about.' Second, many of the secrets consigned to paper were subsequently destroyed. In 1576, and again in 1579, Perez deliberately burned a large number of letters to and from Don John... All that survives are the copies made by Perez in a special book... He may have invented whole documents... it would have been easy [Escobedo and Don John both died in 1578]... and it would have been advantageous...

As Fernand Braudel has written, 'In this mysterious matter, no one will have the last word.'

G. Parker, *Philip II*, 1978.

REVIEW

The Policies of Philip II

If we attempt to analyse the policies of a king like Philip II who reigns for over 40 years with a huge world empire, it is essential that we break the subject down.

- Can we say that Philip's policies were the same throughout his lengthy reign?
- When we use the term 'policies', what do we mean?

The policies of a particular ruler or government can be broken up into the following categories:

- Beliefs and values.
- Broad aims.
- Important principles that underpin the broad aims.
- Specific targets, objectives or intended outcomes of any particular strategy.
- The purposes and potential consequences of any particular course of action.

In order to assess the policies of Philip II, produce a patterned note to enable you to consider and develop the above points. Now read through this chapter again, and fill out your patterned note in more detail. Given the length of Philip's reign you may wish to produce a patterned note for each of the main areas of his work:

- Government and Administration.
- The Economy.
- Religion.
- His Personal Life.

Alternatively, you may wish to break up his reign into a chronological framework. Geoffrey Parker in his biography uses the following chronology:

- The Delicate Years 1559–67.
- The Crusading Years 1568–72.
- The Years of Failure 1572–9.
- The Years of Triumph 1579–88.
- The Approach of Death 1589–98.

Finally, consider the following broad statements of policy from four of the major historians of Philip's reign:

> But above all who could fail to see that the centre of gravity of Philip II's empire was being shifted from the north to the south by force of circumstances? The Peace of Cateau-Cambresis, by confirming the Spanish presence in Italy, helped to make Southern Europe the focus of the foreign policy of the Catholic King at the expense of other more urgent and possibly more fruitful endeavours. Philip II's return visit to Spain in 1559 put the finishing touches to this process. From now on Philip was to remain in the peninsula, a prisoner so to speak in Spain.
>
> F. Braudel, *The Mediterranean and the Mediterranean World in the Age of Philip II*, 1992.

> During the 16th century Castile found itself in the forefront of European warfare and diplomacy. This prominence rested on two factors. The first was the relative freedom with which the early Habsburgs could tax the non-privileged orders of the kingdom. Until 1575 royal demands did not impose an undue strain: after that date, and as a consequence of the widening commitments in northern Europe, the crown became much harsher with its subjects.
>
> A.W. Lovett, *Early Habsburg Spain*. 1986.

> During his 55 years in power, over 40 of them as supreme ruler, responsible for the largest empire the world had ever seen, he was involved in many tragedies and many crises.
>
> Because he preferred to write down his thoughts at such moments he often appears uncertain, hesitant and indecisive...
>
> It has been noted, with some surprise, that the prudent king had no 'blueprint', no set of fixed objectives for his foreign policy; this was surely because, given the extreme uncertainties of politics in the later 16th century, no blueprint could conceivably have worked...
>
> Yet Philip II seems to have achieved less of what he wanted than most. By the side of the 'Taming of America' and the Conquest of Portugal and the Philippines, which were outstanding successes, one must set the Revolt in the Netherlands, the Exhaustion of Spain, the loss of almost all north Africa to Islam, the defeat of the Spanish Armada, and the triumph of Henry IV in France. All these failures came about in much the same way: an ambitious and intransigent policy was adopted, became increasingly impracticable, and yet was not altered until the cause was already lost.
>
> G. Parker, *Philip II*, 1978.

> He is, by any standards, one of the most remarkable men ever to sit on a throne in Europe.
>
> J.H. Plumb, 'Preface' to G. Parker, *Philip II*, 1978.

TALKING POINT

When people look back they often find that certain years have been critical in determining their success or failure of their life's work. Which year or years would Philip have said were critical in his life's work? Which year or years would you as a Historian feel were critical?

1 Identify each author's judgement on Philip II.
2 Is there much agreement between them?
3 **Essay**
'How far is it true to say that Philip II was successful before 1572 and a failure thereafter?'

14 The Revolt in the Netherlands

PREVIEW

The Various Revolts in the Netherlands, 1561–1609

There were many different revolts in the Netherlands in the second half of the 16th century. The major enemy was invariably Spain, but there were many different leaders and a variety of purposes behind each revolt.

Each of the following statements describes one of the revolts. They are not in chronological order. Use the information provided in this chapter to rearrange the statements into chronological order. In addition, give each a date, identify the origins and leadership of the revolt and assess its aims and purposes. You could do this by making a chart with four columns using the headings: Description of the revolt; Date; Origins; Aims and Purposes.

- Hundreds of churches in the Netherlands were damaged and Margaret of Parma told Philip that he had over 200,000 rebellious subjects.
- The States General refused to agree to a proposed permanent 10 per cent tax on all sales.
- Unpaid Spanish troops plundered cities in the Southern Provinces.
- Philip II proposed setting up 14 new bishoprics and many feared that he would introduce the Spanish Inquisition.
- Don John brought Spanish troops back to the Netherlands and William of Orange was welcomed in Antwerp as Governor of Brabant.
- The armies of the Estates General met the Duke of Parma at Gembloux.
- The Northern Provinces of Groningen and Overijssel joined the Union of Utrecht to make the seven United Provinces. The Netherlanders bitterly resented the tribunal set up to investigate heresy cases. They were also angered by the execution of Egmont and Horne.
- A 'motley mixture of pirates, exiled noblemen, and Calvinist seafarers' (M. Rady) captured towns in the Northern Provinces.
- William of Orange invaded Flanders and Brabant, but failed to get the support of French Huguenots because of the Massacre of St Bartholomew's Eve.
- Five Northern Provinces set up a union and called themselves the 'United Provinces'.

When you have completed your research and filled in the above chart, write your own narrative account of the story of the revolts in the Netherlands. Is it fair to speak of revolts, or do these events describe one coherent set of objectives?

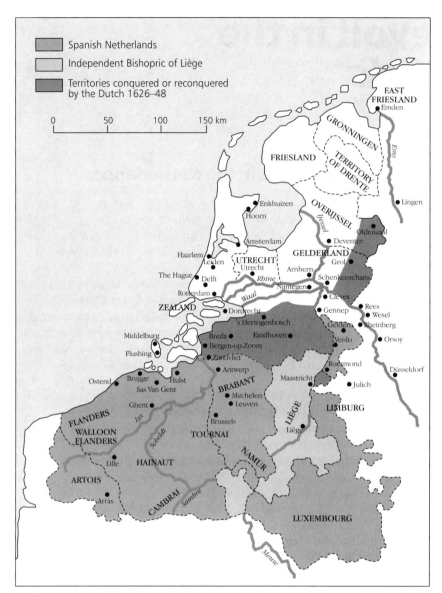

Map legend:
- Spanish Netherlands
- Independent Bishopric of Liège
- Territories conquered or reconquered by the Dutch 1626–48

0   50   100   150 km

EAST FRIESLAND
Emden
GRONNINGEN
Ems
FRIESLAND
TERRITORY OF DRENTE
Lingen
Enkhuizen
Hoorn
OVERIJSSEL
Oldenzaal
Amsterdam
Deventer
IJssel
Haarlem
Leiden
UTRECHT
GELDERLAND
Grol
Utrecht
Arnhem
Schenkenschans
The Hague
Delft
Rhine
Nijmegen
Rotterdam
Waal
Cleves
ZEALAND
Dordrecht
Gennep
Rees
Wesel
's Hertogenbosch
Geldern
Rheinberg
Middelburg
Breda
Eindhoven
Venlo
Orsoy
Bergen-op-Zoom
Flushing
Zandvliet
Roermond
Düsseldorf
Antwerp
Maastricht
Ostend
Brugge
Hulst
Julich
Sas Van Gent
Ghent
Mechelen
LIMBURG
Leuven
FLANDERS
Lys
BRABANT
WALLOON FLANDERS
Scheldt
Brussels
LIÈGE
Liège
Lille
HAINAUT
TOURNAI
NAMUR
ARTOIS
Arras
CAMBRAI
Sambre
LUXEMBOURG
Meuse

The Causes of the Disturbances in the Netherlands

The origins of the crisis in the Netherlands lay in the reign of Charles V. However, his son, Philip II, made a number of early mistakes which aggravated the situation considerably. When he sailed from the Netherlands in 1559, he left his half-sister Margaret, Duchess of Parma, as his Governor General in the Netherlands. He also appointed three important Dutch aristocrats to important Provincial Governorships: William of Nassau, the Prince of Orange, Count Egmont, and Count Horne. These moves were very promising and appropriate. However, Philip was determined to keep control over the Netherlands himself and he told his half-sister that the person she should really consult was a Burgundian civil servant Cardinal Granvelle, the son of Charles V's chancellor. These moves opened the door to conflict between Granvelle and the local aristocrats.

Spanish Regents in the Netherlands, 1559–92	
1559–67	Margaret of Parma
1567–73	The Duke of Alva
1573–6	Don Luis d' Requesens
1577–8	Don John of Austria
1578–92	The Duke of Parma

This struggle was further aggravated by Philip's plans to reorganise the Roman Catholic church in the Netherlands in 1561. He planned to create 14 new bishoprics and Granvelle was to become the Archbishop of Malines and Senior Archbishop in the Netherlands. This would give Granvelle considerable power and wealth at the expense of the local aristocracy. William of Orange led the revolt against Granvelle, supported by the widely held belief that the new bishoprics would mean the introduction of the Spanish Inquisition. As in France, the great aristocratic families sided either with Orange or with Granvelle.

Philip II himself was in no position to travel to the Netherlands. He could not afford to leave Spain at a time when the Turks were threatening to overrun the Mediterranean. He therefore tried to rule from afar. In order to appease the aristocracy he dismissed Granvelle in 1564, but refused to allow a meeting of the States General to discuss religious matters. The removal of Granvelle further weakened his central control.

At the same time, Calvinist preachers were beginning to spread their influence in the Southern States. Their sermons included references to armed resistance and seizing towns. The disturbance was compounded by bad harvests in 1565 and the price of wheat rose astronomically during the following winter. In 1566 rioting became endemic: in Antwerp, Ghent, and other cities, churches were looted and images broken. Margaret wrote to Philip asking for assistance and she was able to build an army to disperse the rioters. The situation was clearly so tense that something major had to be done.

The Duke of Alva and the Netherlands

In August 1566 Margaret of Parma told Philip II that the situation in the Netherlands was out of control. The 'iconoclast fury' was an indication that 200,000 of her subjects were in mutiny. Philip's reaction was one of force and repression. At the same time, he wrote a letter to Pope Pius V: 'Before suffering the slightest damage to religion and the service of God, I would rather lose all my States, and a hundred lives if I had them, because I do not propose to be the ruler of heretics. If it can be, I will try to settle the matter of religion without taking up arms, because I fear that to do so would lead to total ruin. But if I cannot settle matters as I wish without force, neither the danger nor the destruction of all I possess can deter me from this end.'

An army was prepared and in June 1567 the Duke of Alva led his troops along the Spanish Road and into the Netherlands.

The Duke of Alva in the Netherlands

- The Duke of Alva was a sixty-year old military veteran. He had formerly led Philip's armies in Italy, Germany and France.
- Alva's early life had been in a Grandee family in Spain. He had learned military drill from his grandfather, one of the closest advisers of Ferdinand of Aragon.

The lessons taught by his grandfather were not pretty. If the child learns self discipline, he also learned a spartan indifference that could be called bloody-minded. If he absorbed grand strategy, he also grew increasingly expert at the devious tactics of small war and discovered the manifold uses of cruelty...

TALKING POINT

'As for my journey to the Low Countries, I certainly have a great desire to be there before this winter. But there are several difficulties and it is already so late in the year that I do not see how I can do it. I expect to be with you at the latest next spring.'(Philip II to Margaret of Parma in a letter of July 1566)
What were the consequences of Philip's permanent residence in the Escorial?

TALKING POINT

Philip Marnix published a propaganda account of the riots of 1566. 'It is still uncertain who the persons were who did it and still more uncertain who advised them to do it.'
What are the benefits of an able propagandist in a revolutionary cause? What are the problems?

THE DUKE OF ALVA.

GᴿVAN EGMONT EN HOORN ONTHALST

THE EXECUTION OF COUNTS EGMONT AND HORNE.

He was a child of the Camps as much as of the Court, and he learned early that military life is far more than battles and heroics. Before he was well into his teens he had learned to manage estates, armies, and above all himself, for he had discovered what it meant to be always in the public eye and to be loved by grisled veterans and raw recruits alike, who first saw him as a mascot and then learned to trust him with their lives.

W.S. Maltby, *Alva*, 1983.

- Alva's first act in the Netherlands was to bypass Margaret and arrest and execute Egmont and Horne. Margaret's resignation was followed by Philip's appointment of Alva as Governor General.
- Alva's instructions from Philip were to bring peace to the Netherlands and to remove the threat of heresy. To do this, he established the Council of Troubles, sometimes called the 'Council of Blood'. This council was a judicial body set up to identify and punish heretics. It had local councils reporting to it, and by 1579 the main council, consisting largely of local people, was supplemented by about 170 Provincial Councillors. As Maltby has said, they were 'engaged in ferreting out sedition with the aid of malicious neighbours, jilted lovers, and disgruntled business competitors'.

TALKING POINT

'Priveleges granted by sovereigns are not contracts but gifts and so may be withdrawn if subjects misbehave.'
This was Alva's view of Philip's justification for the Council of Troubles. How might it be rephrased by Alva's opponents?

THE COUNCIL OF TROUBLES IS REFLECTED IN BREUGHEL'S PICTURE, *THE MASSACRE OF THE INNOCENTS*. IT AROUSED SUCH FEAR THAT NO ONE SUPPORTED WILLIAM OF ORANGE WHEN HE INVADED FROM GERMANY IN 1568.

- The Council of Troubles established a reign of terror in the Netherlands though undoubtedly its effects have been exaggerated by later Protestant propagandists. Between 1567 and 1576, nearly 9000 individuals were condemned. Many sought exile and 1083 were executed and another twenty banished. Most cases were settled within a four-year period and most of the executions occurred in 1568–9. Most of the executed were either artisans or relatively humble people.
- Alva also completed the reform of bishoprics which had been a contentious issue at the beginning of Philip's reign.
- In 1570 he issued the Ordinance of the Penal Law to standardise criminal law procedure and ensure protection for the innocent.
- In order to pay his large Spanish army, in March 1569 Alva required additional taxes. He asked the States General to approve a tax known as 'The Tenth Penny', a 10 per cent tax on all sales. This was a permanent tax and the States General considered it ruinous to trade. They did, however, agree a two-year tax and in 1572 Alva sought to renew the Tenth Penny. It was one of the most unpopular pieces of legislation, and its effects were felt very strongly in the revolt of 1572.

Don **FREDRICKS MOORT TOT NAERDEN**

PROPAGANDA CRITICAL OF THE
DUKE OF ALVA'S REPRESSIVE
RULE IN THE LOW COUNTRIES.
WHAT WOULD BE THE LIKELY
EFFECTS OF SUCH IMAGES?

FELLE STRAFFE TOT HAERLEM

Historians have been keen to damn the Duke of Alva's work in the Netherlands. For many, largely Dutch and/or Calvinist, he has been seen as an agent of the devil. It is, however, difficult to form judgements in the midst of such religious passion and prejudice. In his recent biography of Alva, W.S. Maltby has made the following comments:

> Alva was his (Philip's) best hope of restoring law and authority in the Netherlands and obedience to the Church as well. Moreover, had the initial plan been followed, it might very well have worked. As we have also seen, it was the King's failure to relieve Alva after he had completed his bloody work that started him on the short road to disaster.
>
> Yet it is impossible to deny that after defeating Orange in 1568 Alva made things much worse than they needed to have been.
>
> The key to his lapse is found in the personal crisis that befell him in the winter of 1568–69. Sick, depressed and furious at what he saw as betrayal, he fell into a pattern of behaviour that led to evermore disastrous mistakes... His instincts had always tended towards rigidity, dogmatism and xenophobia, but during most of his career they had been subordinated to a tactical flexibility born of intellect. After 1568 this check was gone.
>
> The most immediate consequence was that Alva failed to take the Netherlandish loyalists into his confidence and use them to develop an effective administration. An exclusive reliance on Spaniards and Italians is understandable in the midst of a purge. By 1568, however, the Netherlanders had proved themselves trustworthy, if not lovable, and by refusing to use them, Alva denied himself their full support and perpetuated a Government that was both alien and wilfully inefficient...
>
> A similar rigidity and distrust are evident in his mishandling of the Tenth Penny.

Alva the Symbol and Moral Judgements

In 1619, Don Antonio, Alva's grandson decided to move his body to a new resting place. During the move the coffin was opened. 'To everyone's astonishment Don Antonio immediately fell to his knees in a gesture of humility and respect. The Duke of Alva was still as he had been in his life. "The composure of his countenance, the gravity of his white hairs, the authority of a superior person, had not been lost"' (story quoted in W.S. Maltby, *Alva*).

Alva's Achievements

- Alva was the greatest soldier of his generation. A man of military victory. A practical man of intelligence, courage and a mastery of war. He led his troops well and was a popular general.
- He was a successful strategic analyst. One rival at court called him the 'Dead Shot'.
- Perhaps his only failure was in the Netherlands. Here critics say that he brought civil war to a peaceful country and spent 12 million ducats in failing to stop it.
- Alva is remembered not because he was a great soldier and statesman, but because he was a symbol. To one of the two Spains, he was the epitome of virtue: devout, spartan, courageous, prudent and above all loyal, not only to his church and king, but to the hard values of that land of Saints and stones which gave birth to the Golden Age. To much of the rest of the world he is therefore the epitome of intolerance, cruelty and harsh fanaticism, truly Breughel's Herod in the flesh.

  ... Alva was human, sometimes excessively so, but he wanted to be the symbol he became and he pursued his virtue with savage determination.

  Only in the Netherlands did he fail... Of course it is quite possible from Alva's point of view that he did not really fail at all. He died believing in the righteousness of his cause and the fundamental soundness of his policies, and perhaps he was right. It is for this reason that he would, from the grave, deny our judgements. Symbols are janus-faced, and each of their visages reflects the character of its beholder. Alva must be taken as he was. If there are paradoxes here it is we who must live with them.
- In writing his biography, W.S. Maltby declares his hopes in his preface: 'To display the interaction of personality with events.' At the same time he hopes 'to avoid the murkier depths of psycho history, for if the sources on Alva are sometimes revealing, they are not so intimate as to permit a clinical diagnosis. No attempt has been made to provide moral judgements. Readers who object to this omission are invited to supply their own.'

1 What did Alva accomplish in the Netherlands? And what were the motives behind his policies?
2 'Why are the persecutions of Alva remembered when others are long forgotten? First, Alva's side lost. Those he condemned became the founding martyrs of a new nation and history is notoriously written by the victors' (Maltby). In view of this: 'is it fair to see Alva as a symbol? Is there value in the creation of symbols in history? Or are they damaging?'
3 What are moral judgements? Should Historians provide them on characters like Alva? What are the dangers in making moral judgements?

Revolt and Invasion, 1572–6

In April 1572 the Sea Beggars, a group of licensed pirates, captured the fishing village of Brill on the coast of Holland. This has always been regarded by Historians as an event of major importance. During the following months, the Beggars moved inland and captured most of the towns of Zeeland and Holland. The support of William of Orange, the fear of Alva's repressive regime, and the distance of the towns from Brussels and Antwerp, were the main factors in the Sea Beggars' success. Many local town councils were now taken over by Calvinist minorities and in July the estates of Holland invited William of Orange to return as their governor.

Orange now clearly took over the leadership of the revolt. He detested Alva's repressive regime and all political and religious persecution.

Alva now found himself in a very vulnerable position. He had failed to halt the march of the Sea Beggars and only the Massacre of St Bartholomew's Eve in France had prevented another Calvinist invasion from the South. In 1573, he was ordered to return to Spain and Don Luis d'Requesens arrived in the Netherlands as his successor. Requesens, however, had little success either. Because the Tenth Penny tax was never collected he relied increasingly on Spain to finance the Royal armies. When he died in 1576 his unpaid army mutinied. This immediately spelt serious danger for Philip's position. He had declared himself bankrupt in September 1575 and now his unpaid troops plundered the Southern Provinces of the Netherlands to get rewards for their work. In the so-called 'Spanish Fury' of November 1576, Antwerp was sacked by the Catholic army.

The Pacification of Ghent 1576 and the Arrival of Don John of Austria 1576–9

On the death of Requesens and the mutiny of the Spanish forces, the only legitimate authority in the Netherlands was that of William of Orange. His armies helped to defend the Southern cities against the mutineers and he held discussions with the Estates General and the leaders of the Sea Beggars. Together, they formulated the Pacification of Ghent in November 1576.

By the terms of this peace treaty, the people of the Netherlands swore their loyalty to King Philip II. In exchange, however, all discussions of the Netherlands' future would be held by the Estates General. Philip had to accept the demands of the rebels and he sent his young half-brother Don John of Austria as the new Governor General to agree a reconciliation.

Don John's arrival in the following year was welcomed by the States General. He promptly removed all Spanish troops in the Netherlands, but insisted that the Catholic religion be re-established as the official religion of all Provinces. The Northerners of Holland and Zeeland would not accept this compromise.

DON JOHN OF AUSTRIA.

Civil War returned to the Northern Provinces. Even in the south, Calvinists urged on rebellion against the Spanish Lordship. The Estates General invited the French Duke of Anjou to come to their aid. In cities like Antwerp, Brussels and Ghent, Calvinists set up popular War Councils.

FOCUS

14.1 Why did the City of Gouda Join the Revolt, 1572–6?

In April 1572, the Sea Beggars captured the port of Brill. During the following year many of the major cities in the Provinces of Holland and Zeeland were also captured and went over to the rebels.

In a number of cities the decision to join the rebels was made by a small elite of City Councillors, Urban Oligarchies. It is important for historians to understand who these men were. What were their social, religious, and economic backgrounds? How did they view the war in 1572? Why did they pledge their support for Orange's cause? What ultimately did they hope to gain from their involvement in the war?

One way of understanding these issues is to look at one major city during these years.

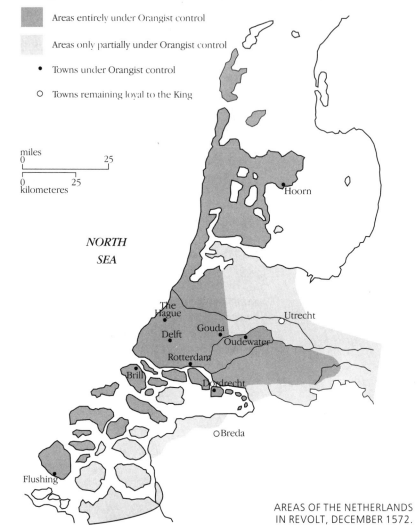

Areas entirely under Orangist control

Areas only partially under Orangist control

● Towns under Orangist control

○ Towns remaining loyal to the King

miles
0   25

0   25
kilometeres

NORTH SEA

Hoorn

The Hague

Delft   Gouda

Utrecht

Oudewater

Rotterdam

Brill

Dordrecht

○ Breda

Flushing

AREAS OF THE NETHERLANDS IN REVOLT, DECEMBER 1572.

- Gouda was the sixth of the chief towns of the Province of Holland.
- Its geographical position was extremely favourable.
- It was situated on the Binnenvaart, the inland canal system linking the north and south of Holland.
- Gouda's wealth was based on the brewing industry and the export of beer to the south. It also had a large community of boatmen and a significant part in the grain trade. The 16th century saw major economic and political decline: the brewing industry declined significantly, from 370,000 vats of beer in 1480 to 47,000 vats in 1571. As a consequence, Gouda's markets in the southern Netherlands were lost. In addition, other Holland towns, notably Rotterdam, attempted to trade without using the Binnenvaart.
- The City Council of Gouda, or Vroedchap, tried to enlist the support of the Central Government in defending Gouda's rights to control the Binnenvaart.

Gouda joined the revolt in June 1572.

> Gouda was the first of the chief towns of Holland to declare for the revolt on 21 June 1572, albeit with little enthusiasm and little sense of conviction. The town had muddled into rebellion; 'revolutionary fervour' was conspicuous by its absence, in both a political and religious sense. Yet neither Gouda, nor any of the chief towns which declared for Orange in the summer of 1572, defected from the revolt thereafter.
>
> C. Hibbert, *Gouda in Revolt*, 1983.

Some Factors Which Enabled the Sea Beggars to Take Control in Holland

- The Sea Beggars controlled the canals and waterways.
- Alva took native troops from Holland and Zeeland to join his army against William of Orange. It left the towns relatively defenceless.
- Sympathisers in many cities supported the Sea Beggars and opened their gates.
- Holland and Zeeland had no will to resist the sea beggars after Alva's work between 1567 and 1572.
- Calvinists made no progress at all in Gouda in the 1560s.
- There are only three recorded prosecutions for heresy in Gouda between 1530 and 1560 and none of the heretics were natives of the city.
- In 1566, the Vroedchap closed the gates of the city and refused to allow any potential heretics to come in.
- In 1567, the Vroedchap supported the Estates of Holland in asking the Regent to suspend the Inquisition.

- Gouda's revolt was stimulated by Alva's religious and financial policies.
- The Vroedchap of Gouda preferred that Calvinist heretics should be dealt with peacefully.
- The Catholic Pastor over the town, Judocus Bourgoi, however wanted a tougher line against heresy. He wanted to root out all indications of Calvinism in Gouda.
- In 1568 Alva's Council of Troubles prosecuted five or six local men. All fled the city and their property was seized. In 1570, Bourgoi also prosecuted several Anabaptists. One refused to flee and was executed in the city. This aroused very considerable local opposition.
- Alva's 'Tenth Penny Tax' had 'a devastating effect on the morale and prestige of the Vroedchap of Gouda' (Hibbert). The Vroedchap protested to Alva that the Tenth Penny 'will lead to the complete and utter ruin of the country'.

1 'The town had muddled into rebellion'. Does the evidence support this view of Gouda in 1572? How does it challenge previous judgements of the success of the Sea Beggars?

2 'There was at times a considerable diversity of aims and opinions within the rebel movement in Holland in the late 1570's and 1580's'. How is this reflected in Gouda?

3 What do the following terms mean and are they interchangeable: Orangist, Beggar, Revolutionary, Calvinist, Progressive?

4 Koenigsberger, Mosse and Bowler in their book *Europe in the 16th Century* describe the Sea Beggars as 'A highly organised and skilfully led military force'.

What value does a local study of Gouda provide for national historians of the Dutch Revolt? What broad patterns does it confirm? What does it challenge?

The Events from April to June 1572

There was much unrest in the city: the fear of government troops and the fear of the enforcement of the Tenth Penny damaged morale. The economic depression and the material hardship of the ordinary people was a threat to the city's stability.

In 1571 and 1572 Alva insisted that the Vroedchap should improve the defences of the city against future rebellion. The Vroedchap con-tinued to be nervous about their inability to resist the Sea Beggars. On 8 April, they wrote to Alva requesting reinforcements but there was none forthcoming. In May they put restrictions on the number of people who could enter the city. On 5 June a parade of some members of the city announced their open support for Orange and denounced Alva as a murderer.

The Events Leading up to Fall of the City in June 1572

The Sea Beggars were led by a nobleman called Van Swieten. With a small army of ill-disciplined troops, he had taken Oudewater on 19 June. He also began to negotiate with supporters within the city of Gouda. They agreed that they would open one of the cities gates to let him in. Undoubtedly, Van Swieten found support amongst the lower classes of Gouda, the unemployed and those affected by the economic depression.

- Van Swieten's conquering band was probably no more than 50–70 men. They may have been supported by some sympathisers in the city. They were all badly armed.
- Gouda could easily have offered resistance if it had wanted to, but the town was internally divided and demoralised by Alva's policies.
- 'For the Vroedchap at least 1572 did not represent the dawn of a new era. It was an unmitigated disaster' (Hibbert).

What were the Policies of the Gouda Vroedchap, 1572–3?

- After the June capture by the Sea Beggars, the composition of the Vroedchap was changed. But in the membership of the new Vroedchap there was no significant Orangist or Calvinist majority. There was still much continuity of policy and personnel from the previous body. The traditional policies of the Vroedchap of Gouda were for peace and their own particular concerns. They had often been conservative in religion and government, and had often opposed the more radical directions of the States of Holland.
- The Vroedchap often placed emphasis on local considerations and 'there was a notable lack of enthusiasm for the cause of reformed Protestantism'. After June 1572 the Vroedchap espoused freedom of conscience but it was as much a desire to protect Roman Catholic freedom as to allow the freedom of Calvinists. 'Religious passions had never risen very high in Gouda... The Reformed Church Order was seen by many as "A New Popery"'.
- The Vroedchap espoused a policy of peace because they feared that if war continued the rebels would be defeated. This policy was also dictated by economic considerations. War brought no material advantages and Gouda was being over-taken by Rotterdam. War also damaged the traditional support which Gouda got from Central Government in protecting her control of the inland waterways.

The Unions of Arras and Utrecht, 1579

The battle lines were now being clearly drawn. In January 1579, the three Southern Provinces of Flanders, Artois and Cambrai formed the League of Arras. They made a treaty with Philip II which enabled them to keep their traditional provincial privileges. In return, they promised loyalty to the king and accepted the Roman Catholic religion.

At the same time, five Northern Provinces formed the Union of Utrecht, a Calvinist Union governed by William of Orange and the Estates General. In 1581 the Union of Utrecht renounced its allegiance to Philip II.

TALKING POINT

In both armies, there were mercenaries. There was rarely enough money to pay the troops. There was also the problem of having troops unemployed at certain times of the year. What problems were created by these issues, and why was it particularly difficult for Philip?

ALEXANDER FARNESE, DUKE OF PARMA.

Philip's Governor General Don John was replaced with the Duke of Parma. As a shrewd military and political leader, he began the reconquest of Brabant and moved his armies north of the river into Groningen. In desperation, William of Orange asked the Estates General to swear allegiance to the brother of King Henry III of France. The Duke of Anjou proved, however, to be of little advantage. Parma's newly imported Spanish troops were singularly successful during the mid 1580s and with the death of the Duke of Anjou and the dramatic assassination of William of Orange, Parma looked on the brink of victory.

However, the martyrdom of Orange, and the support of an army of 5,000 Englishmen under the Earl of Leicester, enabled the northerners to survive. In 1594, under the leadership of Maurice of Nassau, Groningen and Overijssel were added to the Union of Utrecht to form the 'United Provinces'. The States General declared itself 'The Sovereign Institution of the Country' and the United Provinces became the Dutch Republic. In the 1590s, Parma's armies were more and more diverted by the need to concentrate on the civil war in Northern France and the new Northern Republic was relieved of his military presence. Philip's death in 1598 gave them even greater respite and the Peace of Antwerp in 1609 provided a 12-year truce between Spain and the United Provinces, which effectively resulted in international recognition for the new republic. The Dutch Republic, one of the most powerful forces in 17th-century world history, was born.

TALKING POINT
William of Orange's background led him to expect to assume responsibility. Are successful leaders born and not made?

EXAMINING THE EVIDENCE

The Character and Geography of the Netherlands

Source A

The Netherlands are a general sea land, the Great Bog of Europe. There is not such another marsh in the world that is flat. They are a universal quagmire: epitomised as a green cheese in pickle... The people live lower than the fishes in the very lap of the floods, and encircled in their watery arms. The waters wall them in and if they set open their sluices shall drown up their enemies.

Owen Feltham, *A Brief Character of the Low Countries*, 1648.

Source B

It was almost as hard for the Spanish army to operate in North Holland because of the great lakes, rivers and dykes which covered the country, much of which was below sea level. In 1573 at the Siege of Alkmaar and in 1574 at the Siege of Leiden, dykes were broken in order to flood the fields around the town and thus prevent the formidable Spanish infantry from launching an attack on the walls.

E.H. Kossmann, *Spain and the Netherlands*.

Source C

The States of Brabant complain to the States of Holland for not fighting to the last ditch.

Everyone knows that excellent resources which God has put in our hands to safeguard our liberty, to protect us one and all against the attack of our enemies. How many admirable oaths, alliances and unions have we formed and sworn to! If they have not born fruit, the reason is clearly that each Province, preferring its own particular interest, has scarcely bothered about the fate of its neighbours and allies, thinking it enough to make fine promises on paper without following them up or giving them any effect.

P. Limm, *Dutch Revolt*, 1989.

Source D

For the Sea Beggars, the Calvinists and the other exiles who returned to Holland and Zeeland in 1572, there would be no surrender: they, like the Prince of Orange, had decided to make Holland and Zeeland their tomb, either in victory or defeat.

E.H. Kossmann, *Spain and the Netherlands.*

Source E

It is unnecessary to subject to a set criticism the view that the split was determined by some inherent divergence within the Netherlands' people. A Protestant north (not without numerous Catholics however) and a Catholic south were not pre-determined by the natures of the populations. Those two great cultural currents of Catholicism and Protestantism originally mingled their courses in both north and south. It was only the outcome of strife, of war with a foreign ruler, which brought about that fatal re-distribution of forces which was to estrange the two regions for so long. That outcome was not determined by any greater courage by the north or even by Holland and Zeeland alone (for the conventional view conveniently overlooks the fact that the eastern provinces had to be re-conquered for the Republic by force!) That outcome was determined by the great rivers. Brabant and Flanders lay open for the enemy, and soon therefore their Protestants went to strengthen those in the impregnable river area. Gelderland, Overijssel and Groningen, although much less affected by Protestantism than Flanders and Brabant, could not be held for the Catholic church because the swords of Parma and Spinola lost their striking force when stretched precariously beyond the rivers.

P. Geyl, *The Revolt in the Netherlands*, 1932.

1 From the evidence, identify a number of factors which contributed to the success of the rebels in the 1570s and 1580s. Peter Geyl talks in source E about an 'inherent divergence' between the people of the Netherlands. What differences in language, culture and attitude can be identified?

2 In what ways did geography contribute in the 1570s and 1580s to the success of the revolt? In what ways did geography hinder the rebels?

Source F

The terrain of the Netherlands hampered the Spanish programme of re-conquest. The many bogs and fortified towns, all of which required lengthy sieges, prevented the Spaniards from taking full advantage of their numerical superiority. However, the view proposed over half a century ago by Peter Geyl that the great rivers – The Waal, Maas, Lek, provided an impregnable barrier behind which the rebels could shelter, has been exposed as untenable. The rivers could be crossed by the Spanish armies with relative ease as happened in 1605, and Maurice constructed his line of fortifications on the assumption that the river line might be breached. In any case most of the fighting took place south of the great rivers and the eventual boundary between the United Provinces and the Spanish Provinces did not follow any obvious geographical feature.

M. Rady, *From Revolt to Independence*, 1990.

Source G

These natural strengths were reinforced by others. Holland and Zeeland were difficult to attack from the south by land by reason of the four great rivers which reached the sea at the same delta. In early modern times it was not possible to cross them comfortably west of the

Lake of Biesbos. The Dutch added to this natural advantage by capturing the towns of Gorcum and others – the towns which commanded the most westerly crossings of the rivers Maas and Waal. Without these towns it was necessary for government forces to march far inland, sometimes as far as Nijmegen, in order to cross the river delta and enter Holland.

G. Parker, *The Dutch Revolt*, 1990.

Source H

Because the revolt was made up of a variety of overlapping movements, it possessed an endurance and capacity to withstand setbacks which a more narrowly based rebellion could not have enjoyed. The King of Spain was not just challenged by Grandees, Nobles, Patricians, Townsfolk, Calvinists and Religious Moderates operating in isolation, but by all of these joined together by a common concern for the restoration of liberties. For this reason the defection or defeat of one group could not bring the revolt to an end – as the desertion of the Catholic south in 1579 amply demonstrates.

M. Rady, *From Revolt to Independence*, 1990.

Examining the evidence

The Contribution of William of Orange, 'The Silent', 1559–84

The Years of Growing Mistrust, 1559–67

- William of Orange first met Prince Philip of Spain in 1549. William seemed easy to talk to, open, physically self-sufficient. By contrast, Philip seemed shy and diffident, impractical and suspicious. Philip demanded a nine-year subsidy from the Council of State. William supported the subsidy but only on condition that Spanish troops be removed from the Netherlands and the ancient rights of the Netherlands be preserved.
- William's marriage to the niece of the Elector of Saxony in 1561 ensured future support from some German princes.
- In 1561 William orchestrated a campaign against Cardinal Granvelle. Granvelle was supporting Philip's plan to create 14 new bishoprics in the Netherlands. William wrote cleverly to Philip suggesting that the king would enjoy the support of all the Netherlands' nobles once Granvelle had left.
- William's speech to the Council of State in 1564 advocated a radical change in religious policy. He argued that no prince should be able to rule the consciences of his subject. He played on a widespread fear of the Inquisition and of the effect of religious persecution on trade with Protestant neighbours.

Read the following information about William of Orange's contribution to the revolt in the Netherlands and decide which of the following statements most strongly applies to him.

A great patriotic leader.

An enthusiast for toleration.

A representative of his own social class.

A great military captain.

- William's religious policy, asking for freedom of conscience but not yet the right to public worship, aroused much support in the Netherlands and Germany. However, it antagonised the growing number of Calvinists and Sea Beggars, those lesser nobles who now secretly formed themselves into 'the compromise' to oppose Philip's religious policy. The Iconoclastic Riots in 1566 damaged William's cause in that Philip hardened his resolve to support Catholicism and the nobles of the Netherlands refused to associate with the rioters.
- The Calvinist rioters plotted open rebellion and asked William to lead them. He, however, declined and fled to security in Germany.

WILLIAM THE SILENT, PRINCE OF ORANGE AND NASSAU.

William's Difficult Decision, 1566–7

- There has been much debate about William's religious affiliations. In 1566 he wrote to the Elector of Saxony 'in my heart I am a true Protestant'. At the same time, however, he wrote to Philip of Spain 'I care for nothing more than our true Catholic Church'. However, he was probably closer to his own truth when in the same year he claimed 'all Christians subscribe to the same belief expressed in different ways'. His consistent line was to argue for freedom of conscience.
- In 1566–7, William seemed politically isolated. He refused to lead the Calvinist rebels because no other nobles supported the position. At this stage, William wanted reconciliation with Philip by constitutional means and he preferred to profess loyalty to the government. In addition, he had no German support because the Calvinists in the Netherlands refused to accept the Lutheran Creed of Saxony. In March 1567 William's last loyal contribution to Margaret, Duchess of Parma was to save Antwerp from the Calvinist rebels. He spent the following five years in exile.

William's Years in Exile, 1567–72

- In exile in Germany, William was summoned to appear before the Council of Troubles. He failed to appear but his property was confiscated, his son left behind in the Netherlands, was seized, and William himself developed a deep sense of personal wrong.
- He now focused on how to defeat Alva's dictatorship. His own personal strength and determination were strong: 'exert yourself to the utmost, however hopeless the situation, and persevere when all attempts have been unsuccessful'. He also sought allies amongst those who opposed Alva. These included the Sea Beggars, Calvinist pirates also exiles from the Netherlands, the burghers and middle-class people, and support from France and Saxony. Alva's own policies won him no friends: the proposed 'Tenth Penny' and deprivation of ancient privileges and rights were a severe blow to the people of the Netherlands.
- William now formed his plans and in 1572 they were put into effect. His own army attacked from Germany, the Sea Beggars captured Brill in April 1572 and Louis of Nassau, William's brother, took Mons at the end of May. The Huguenots were urged to join from France, although the Massacre of St Bartholomew's Eve prevented this.
- By the autumn of 1572, only the Sea Beggars were having success. William decided to take refuge in Holland and Zeeland and join their work. This was a major turning point for him. The Northern Provinces were increasingly Calvinist. William stated his own religious view 'there is to be no alteration in religion lest the common cause perish'. Calvinism was to be 'its servant not its master'.

William's Defence of Holland and Zeeland, 1572–6

- William's defence of Holland and Zeeland was essentially political. But there were also military victories. In 1573 Haarlem was captured. When threatened by the Spanish the citizens of Alkmaar and Leiden agreed to flood the cities.
- Politically, William promoted the view that once Spain's detested army had gone all the Provinces would live together in peace. He gained limited diplomatic and military support from England, the Huguenots, Scotland and the Palatinate. Philip Marnix proved an excellent propagandist and undermined Spanish support even in the South. As a result of William's work, the Union of Delft was signed in 1576 uniting the Provinces of Holland and Zeeland.
- There were many factors which enabled William's success. The location of Holland and Zeeland at the mouths of important rivers enabled trade and fishing to continue. Alva's ruthlessness aroused bitter opposition. His successor, Equesens, died in 1576 with no one to succeed him. Spanish troops were not regularly paid because of the cash crisis in Spain and their mutiny, called 'The Spanish Fury' in November 1576 resulted in the sack of the beautiful city of Antwerp. Yet William's political leadership in the North was also a vital factor.

William's Finest Hour? 1577–8

- The Pacification of Ghent in November 1576 was a major contribution to William's leadership of the Netherlands. He was recognised as Stadt Holder of Holland and Zeeland and Amsterdam and Utrecht joined the Northern Provinces. The arrival of Don John of Austria as the new Governor General also brought a conciliatory note, especially when Don John agreed to the withdrawal of Spanish troops and the recognition of the Pacification of Ghent.
- However, when Don John returned to a military policy and seized Namur in July 1577 William was recalled to Brussels and made Governor of Brabant.
- By the end of 1577, Spanish power had almost collapsed in the Netherlands. An English gentleman wrote of William 'the Prince is a rare man of great authority, beloved, very wise, resolute in all things and not dismayed with any loss or adversity'.

The Difficulties of Success, 1578–9

- William now held real power in the Netherlands. With the Archduke Matthias, the younger brother of the Holy Roman Emperor, the figurehead Governor General. Major problems now ensued. The Southern Provinces were more enthusiastic to fight each other than work for the common good. The new government was weak and inexperienced. The States General was not a national body, but an amalgamation of individual Provinces. Unity was difficult when there was no war against Spain. In addition, the religious peace failed. Radicals in the south established Catholic dictatorships in cities like Ghent and iconoclasm broke out again. Many influential Catholics left William's cause. Money was always a major problem, and as the Duke of Parma's troops advanced towards Antwerp in February 1579 William was forced to use English and French auxiliaries to resist.
- The Union of Utrecht in January 1579 failed to unite the Provinces and, along with the rival Union of Arras, indicated that divisions between the north and south were strong.
- Even in these darkest days William was always optimistic. A Huguenot friend said, 'you are too ready to think well, even of those who have done you most harm'.

William's Last Years, 1580–4

By June 1580, William and Philip were again directly opposed. Parma's armies had captured the Southern Provinces and William had lost the support of the Southern nobility. On Granvelle's advice, Philip put a price of 25,000 ducats and a free pardon on William's head. And William was proclaimed as an outlaw. He was described as 'the sole leader, author and promoter of the troubles in our State of the Netherlands... The chief disturber of the whole State of Christendom'.

- In December 1580, William published the apology as a presentation to the Estates General. He maintained his vision for the Netherlands as a united country in which conscience enabled people to worship as they wished. He outlined his own personal losses and indignities over the years and pledged himself to the leadership of his people.
- William's final years were spent in an apparently fruitless struggle. He was the victim of several assassination attempts. In July 1584 he was killed by an assassin's knife and his final words were 'may God have pity on my soul and this poor people'.

The Growth of Calvinism as a Revolutionary Force

There has been much debate on the influence of Calvinism on the revolts. In the early 1560s, most religious rebels in the southern cities were Anabaptists. There were no missionaries sent from Geneva and the village preachers who so influenced the artisans of the south were not formally Calvinists. It was only when Alva introduced widespread persecution that the formal power of Calvinism became real. 'Here was the greatest crisis that the monarchies of Western Europe had yet to face: revolutionary movements with organisations that came to match those of the monarchies and with patterns of loyalty which, at times, were not only more powerful than those the monarchies could call on, but which stretched across national boundaries'.

Koenigsberger, Mosse and Bowler go on to explain how Calvinism became powerful.

> Here was a creed which remained socially respectable, appealing to great senors and rich bankers, as much as to unemployed artisans. In an age when most men thought of economic and political problems in religious and moral terms, social discontent proved a fertile soil for revolutionary religious propaganda. Rising prices and taxes, lagging wages and periodic unemployment, burnt harvests and lost livestock brought misery to townsmen and country people. After two generations of Royal wars thousands of young men, both nobles and commoners, had no training but for warfare. Peace left them unemployed, unemployable and bored. Many were converted. Many more flocked happily to the standards of the leaders of religious movements, often without caring too much whether it was on the Catholic or the Calvinist side.
>
> Koengisberger, Mosse and Bowler, *Europe in the 16th Century*, 1989.

In October 1571, Calvinists in the Netherlands met in the city of Emden. Here they held a national synod to decide on the organisation and discipline of the Calvinist church in the Netherlands. As a result, it produced a well-organised church similar to that in Geneva and France.

The appeal of Calvinism spread quickly in the early 1570s: the theology of pre-destination appealed to those who wished to be numbered among the 'elect' and the detailed organisation created a force which the armies of Spain had to resist. At no time did Calvinists number more than 10 per cent of the native population, yet their influence was growing. The Sea Beggars' capture of Brill in April 1572 was followed by the further spread of Calvinist forces throughout many northern towns and cities.

However, it was not so much the strength of Calvinism that was the problem. Rather was it the determination of Philip II to wipe out all heresy in the Netherlands. In 1574 one English agent noted 'the pride of the Spanish government and the cause of religion are the chief hindrance to a good accord'.

People in the Netherlands opposed Philip's determined repression. It was their belief in freedom from persecution that was more important than the spread of Calvinism. Even in the northern provinces in the 1580s the Calvinist leadership was moderate and did not attempt to restrict the freedom of conscience of the people.

TALKING POINT
Can a sovereign hold power in office only by the consent of his or her subjects?

Did Philip II's Foreign Policy Cost Him the Netherlands?

In using this book, you will have discovered one of the particular challenges which historians face. It is that of examining sometimes contradictory evidence from primary and secondary sources in order to determine our interpretation of a series of historical events.

From the evidence presented in this chapter, draw up your own essay to assess how far it was the actions and policies of the king of Spain that contributed to Spain losing the Netherlands.

Factors To Consider

1. What were the crucial occasions when the Dutch revolts were furthered and what were the crucial occasions where Philip was able to slow them down?

   Consider Philip's actions in the crucial years of 1566, 1572, 1576, 1577–8, 1579, 1589–92.

2. Factors within the Netherlands which encouraged a successful rebellion.

   These are summarised in the Review section at the end of this chapter.

3. Factors in Philip II's foreign policy which contributed to his losing the Netherlands.
   - His concentration on the Mediterranean.
   - His financial problems.
   - His Catholicism.
   - His involvement with other European powers, notably France, England and Portugal.

Why Were the Northern Provinces Successful in Breaking Away from Spain?

THIS SATIRE SHOWS THE DUKE OF ALVA DANCING WITH THE PAPACY. THE PAPACY IS LABELLED AS BABYLON, ECHOING EARLIER CRITICISMS OF THE CATHOLIC CHURCH.

'SPANISH TYRANNY IN THE NETHERLANDS' WATCHED OVER BY MARGARET OF PARMA, PHILIP II AND CARDINAL GRANVELLE.

Read through this chapter again and consider the following factors in enabling the success of the Northern Provinces. Rank them in order of importance and give reasons for your ranking.

- Calvinist fervour and organisation.
- The leadership of William of Orange.
- Geography and the waterways of the Netherlands.
- The career of Cardinal Granvelle.
- The governorship of the Duke of Alva.
- 'The Spirit of Nationalism'.
- Charles V's policies towards the Netherlands.
- The work of the Sea Beggars.
- The execution of Egmont and Horne.

Anachronism in History

There are dangers in studying History from a modern viewpoint. In the 19th century the Dutch Historian Mottley interpreted the Dutch revolt as the conflict of good against evil. Of course, all history is rewritten by each new generation and the hopes and fears of each new generation are encapsulated in reinterpretations of the past.

However, it is always important to try to understand historical events from the perspective of the people who took part in them. Even in 1572, what did the main characters expect to gain from the revolt? What did the Sea Beggars expect to gain? William of Orange? The citizens of Gouda? What were the hopes of William of Orange at the highest point of his achievement in 1577? There is even the danger of translating William's hopes in 1577 or in 1580 when he published the *Apologia*, to his position in 1567 or 1572.

From whose perspective, therefore, is History best studied?

Postscript

> ## "Think 16th Century"

In using this book you should have discovered that it is possible to:

- Think yourself into the 16th century.
- Think yourself across the length and breadth of Europe.
- Think in the way that Historians think.

As a postscript to your work take any two dates from the 16th century, perhaps one from the first half and one from the second. Let us suggest 1521 and 1572. For each of these dates identify what was going on in Europe. Outline what was happening in England, Spain, France, Germany and the Holy Roman Empire, Italy, the Netherlands, as well as in developments with the Roman Catholic church and the Counter Reformation, and other religious changes.

If you refer back to the introduction of this book you will see a list of major things that happened during the course of the 16th century. Which of these can you identify in 1521 and which of these can you identify in 1572?

Now imagine that you are a citizen of Hesse in the city of Worms in 1521. Look outward from the city. What major developments in Europe are you aware of and how do they impact upon you?

Similarly, take the same position in Paris in 1572. Again look outward to Spain, to Rome, to the Netherlands, and to England. What other events have an effect upon you?

Perhaps this is the real challenge for the Historian.

Index

Note: page numbers in **bold** denote major section or chapter devoted to subject